THE ROUGH GUIDE TO
OMAN

WITHDRAWN

This second edition updated by
Anthon Jackson and Daniel Stables

Contents

Introduction to
Oman

Amid the ever-changing states of the Arabian Gulf, Oman offers a refreshing reminder of a seemingly bygone age. The country's breakneck development has yet to blight its most spectacular landscapes, while many of its cultural traditions remain on proud display, making the sultanate one of the best places in the Gulf to experience traditional Arabia. Quiet stretches of coast are shaded with nodding palm trees and dotted with fishing boats. Mudbrick villages nestle amid sprawling date plantations or cling to the sides of remote valleys. Craggy chains of towering mountains are scored with precipitous canyons and rocky wadis, while the wind-blown dunes and gravel plains of the great inland deserts stretch away into the distance.

Of course, it's not all savagely beautiful, sparsely populated landscapes. Oman has embraced the modern world, and in parts of the country the contemporary is very much in evidence, particularly in the low-key glitter and bustle of the capital, Muscat, and in the burgeoning cities of Salalah and Sohar. Despite the trappings of modernity, however, much of the rest of the country retains a powerful sense of place and past. Busy souks continue to resound with the clamour of shoppers bargaining over frankincense, jewellery and food. Venerable forts and crumbling watchtowers still stand sentinel over towns they once protected, goats wander past huddles of ochre-coloured houses, and the white-robed Omanis themselves saunter quietly amid the palms.

Where to go

Most visitors begin in **Muscat**, the nation's sprawling modern capital. Engaging reminders of times past persist in the lively commercial district of **Muttrah** and the historic quarter of Old Muscat, site of the sultan's palace and a pair of hoary old Portuguese forts. The city also boasts an alluring selection of upmarket hotels – including some of the Gulf's most memorably opulent Arabian-style establishments

– with fabulously ornate decor, marvellous beaches, and a selection of the country's finest restaurants and bars.

Inland from Muscat rise the spectacular mountains of the **Western Hajar**, centred on the beguiling regional capital of **Nizwa**, Oman's most historic and personable town. Nizwa also provides a convenient base from which to explore the myriad attractions of the surrounding mountains, including the mighty Jebel Shams (the highest peak in Oman), the spectacular traditional villages of the Saiq Plateau and the exhilarating off-road drive down the vertiginous **Wadi Bani Auf**. Other highlights include the lovely traditional mudbrick town of **Al Hamra** and the even more picture-perfect village of **Misfat al Abryeen**. Nearby lie two of the country's most absorbing forts: monumental **Bahla**, the largest in Oman, and the more intimate **Jabrin**, whose perfectly preserved interiors offer a fascinating insight into life in old Oman.

North of Muscat in the shadow of the Western Hajar lies the coastal region of **Al Batinah**, fringed with a long swathe of sleepy, palm-fringed beaches. A series of low-key towns dots the coast, including lively Seeb, sleepier Barka (home to a couple more interesting forts) and sprawling Sohar, one of the country's oldest cities, although few physical reminders of its long and illustrious past survive. The main attraction in Al Batinah is the day-long drive around the so-called **Rustaq Loop**, which winds inland in the shadow of the mountains via the majestic forts of Nakhal, Rustaq and Al Hazm, and provides access to some of Oman's most beautiful wadis – including Wadi Abyad, Wadi Bani Kharous and Wadi Bani Auf – en route.

At the far northern end of Oman (and separated from the rest of the country by a wide swathe of UAE territory) lies the **Musandam Peninsula**. This is where you'll find some of the sultanate's most dramatic landscapes, with the Hajar mountains tumbling down into the ultramarine waters of the Arabian Gulf, creating a spectacular sequence of steep-sided *khors* (fjords), best seen during a leisurely dhow cruise. Most visitors base themselves in the modest regional capital of **Khasab**, which also provides a good base for forays up into the magnificent interior, centred on the craggy heights of the Jebel Harim.

South of Muscat lies the region of **Sharqiya**, providing a beguiling microcosm of Oman, with historic forts, dramatic mountain canyons and rolling dunes. The still

FACT FILE

• The oldest independent state in the Arabian peninsula, Oman has been a sovereign entity since the expulsion of the Persians in 1747.

• The population is fast approaching 5 million, including more than two million expats, most of whom are from Bangladesh, India and Pakistan.

• Virtually all native Omanis are Muslim. About two thirds follow the Ibadhi creed (see page 232); the remainder are largely Sunni.

• Oman is an absolute monarchy, with the ruling Sultan Qaboos exercising ultimate power over all major decisions of state.

• Oil is the country's most important export, although dwindling reserves have forced the government into a wide-ranging programme of industrial diversification and tourism development.

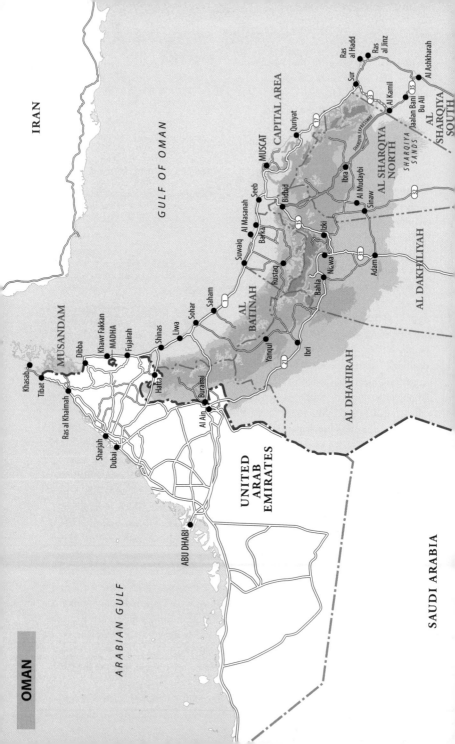

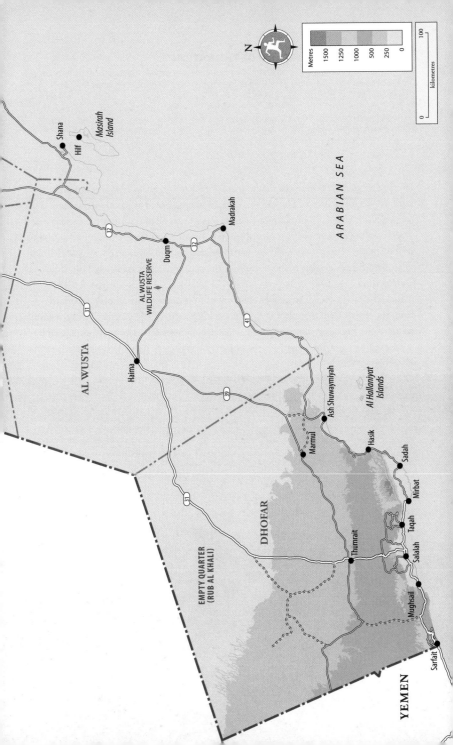

SULTAN QABOOS: FATHER OF THE NATION

You'll not go far in Oman without seeing a picture of the country's supreme ruler, **Sultan Qaboos**, whether framed in miniature above the counters of shops, cafés and hotels or emblazoned on supersized billboards towering above major highways. Coming to the throne in 1970 following the ousting of his father in a British-backed coup, the sultan has overseen the transformation of the backward and impoverished country he inherited into a prosperous modern state (see page 244). To this day he is widely held in almost religious reverence – even the tumultuous events of the Arab Spring in early 2011 (and their modest repercussions in Oman itself) failed to shake his universal popularity.

largely unspoiled coastline is a major draw, thanks to its generous swathes of pristine sand, the historic town of **Sur** and the turtle-watching beach at **Ras al Jinz**. Inland, the rugged Eastern Hajar mountains are cut through by some of the country's most scenic wadis. On the far side of the mountains, most visitors head for the magnificent dunes of the **Sharqiya Sands**, while it's also worth visiting the old-fashioned towns of Ibra and Jalan Bani Bu Ali nearby, home to some of the country's finest traditional mudbrick architecture.

Tucked away in the far southwestern corner of the country lies **Dhofar**, separated from the rest of Oman by almost a thousand kilometres of stony desert. At the region's centre is the engaging subtropical city of Salalah, famous for its annual inundation by

JEBEL AKHDAR MOUNTAIN RANGE

Author picks

Our authors have visited every corner of Oman – from the lively souks of Muscat to the Empty Quarter, via the craggy peaks of the Western Hajar and the rolling dunes of Sharqiya – while researching this book. Here are some of their favourite things to see and do in Oman.

Exhilarating off-roading Beyond its smooth highways, Oman is an off-roading paradise, with dozens of routes such as the hair-raising traverse of Wadi Bani Auf (see page 101) and the dizzying drive to Jaylah (see page 176).

Lively souks Some of Oman's traditional markets still attract a steady stream of colourfully attired local Bedu to trade in dates, *halwa*, aromatics, elaborately embroidered fabrics, and camels. The most absorbing are in Nizwa (see page 88), Ibra (see page 184) and Sinaw (see page 188).

Villages in the clouds Many of Oman's mountain villages are miniature marvels of traditional landscape design. Among the most impressive are the villages of the Saiq Plateau (see page 95), Musandam (see page 146), Misfat al Abryeen (see page 103), Bilad Sayt (see page 101) and Wekan (see page 123).

CAMPING AT JEBEL SHAMS
RAS AL JINZ BEACH

Sleeping under the stars You can set up your tent almost anywhere in Oman (on public land, that is). Top wild camping spots include Jebel Shams (see page 104), Masirah island (see page 195) and the coast south of Duqm (see page 198).

Wadis, canyons and khors Oman is a geological treasurebox, home to a series of dramatic landscapes, from the gaping abyss of Wadi Nakhr (see page 104) and the sepulchral Al Hoota Cave (see page 101) to the sinkholes of Tawi Attair and Taiq (see page 218) and the *khors* (fjords) of Musandam (see page 146).

Best beaches Oman's two-thousand-kilometre coastline packs an abundance of pristine stretches of sand, from the beaches that border Muscat and Sohar in the north to the vast stretches facing the Arabian Sea, the best of which are at Ras al Hadd (see page 182), Ras Madrakah (see page 199) and Mughsail (see page 224).

> Our author recommendations don't end here. We've flagged up our favourite places – a perfectly sited hotel, an atmospheric café, a special restaurant – throughout the Guide, highlighted with the ★ symbol.

AVERAGE TEMPERATURES AND RAINFALL

	Jan	Feb	Mar	Apr	May	Jun	Jul	Aug	Sep	Oct	Nov	Dec
MUSCAT												
Max/min (ºC)	25/17	26/18	29/20	34/24	40/29	40/30	38/30	36/28	36/27	35/24	30/21	27/18
Max/min (ºF)	77/62	79/64	85/69	94/76	103/84	103/86	100/85	96/83	96/80	94/76	86/69	80/64
Rainfall (mm)	10	5	17	11	0	33	0	3	0	0	4	3
SALALAH												
Max/min (ºC)	28/19	28/20	30/22	32/24	33/27	32/27	28/25	27/24	29/24	31/23	31/22	29/20
Max/min (ºF)	82/66	83/67	86/71	89/76	91/80	89/81	83/77	81/75	85/76	88/73	88/71	84/68
Rainfall (mm)	0	1	1	0	3	3	8	11	2	4	5	0
KHASAB												
Max/min (ºC)	24/17	27/19	30/22	35/26	40/31	41/32	41/34	41/33	39/31	36/27	31/23	26/18
Max/min (ºF)	76/62	80/65	87/71	95/78	104/87	105/90	106/93	105/92	102/88	97/81	87/73	79/65
Rainfall (mm)	40	13	15	5	0	0	0	2	0	1	10	14
SUR												
Max/min (ºC)	26/18	28/19	32/22	36/25	41/30	41/30	40/29	39/28	38/27	36/25	31/21	28/19
Max/min (ºF)	80/64	83/66	89/71	97/78	106/85	106/86	104/84	101/82	101/80	97/77	88/70	82/66
Rainfall (mm)	5	13	13	15	13	36	3	0	0	3	10	8

the monsoon rains of the *khareef*, during which the surrounding hills turn a lush green and cascades of water flow down the mountains, creating impromptu rivers, rock pools and waterfalls – one of Arabia's most memorably improbable spectacles. The city also makes a convenient base for forays along the rugged coast, through the majestic Dhofar Mountains and into the interminable sands of the Empty Quarter (Rub al Khali) – Oman's final frontier, stretching across northern Dhofar and on into Saudi Arabia.

When to go

Oman's climate is typical of the Arabian peninsula, with blisteringly hot summers and pleasantly mild, Mediterranean winters. During the **summer** months (March/April to September/October) almost the entire country is scorchingly hot; from May to July the thermometer tends to nudge up above 40°C. Visiting during this period is best avoided, with the exception of Salalah, where temperatures remain bearable thanks to the annual *khareef* which descends from June to August or early September. It's a memorable time to visit the area, although accommodation gets booked solid and prices go through the roof. The **winter** months (October/November to February/March) are pleasantly temperate by contrast, with an almost Mediterranean climate and daytime temperatures rarely climbing much above 30°C. Evenings and nights at this time of year can be breezy and even occasionally slightly chilly, especially up on the cool heights of the Saiq Plateau and other elevated spots in the mountains. Excepting Salalah during the *khareef*, the entire country is extremely arid, and **rainfall** is rare – although don't be surprised if you experience a modest shower or two, most likely from December through to March.

THE FRIDAY MOSQUE, NIZWA

20

things not to miss

It's not possible to see everything that Oman has to offer in a single trip – and we don't suggest you try. What follows, in no particular order, is a selection of the country's highlights, from traditional forts, souks and villages through to the spectacular landscapes of Oman's mountains, deserts and coast. Each entry has a page reference to take you straight into the Guide, where you can find out more. Coloured numbers refer to chapters in the Guide section.

1

1 SULTAN QABOOS GRAND MOSQUE
See page 60
A splendid example of modern Islamic architecture – and one of the few mosques in the country open to non-Muslims.

2 JEBEL HARIM
See page 160
The spectacular mountains of inland Musandam hold cave dwellings, bizarre rock formations and petroglyphs.

3 TURTLE-WATCHING AT RAS AL JINZ
See page 182
Hundreds of green turtles haul themselves up out of the ocean to lay their eggs on this remote beach.

4 JABRIN FORT
See page 107
The country's most absorbing fort is a maze of a place showcasing some of Oman's most memorable architecture and interiors.

5 MUTTRAH SOUK
See page 47
A labyrinth of tiny alleyways stacked with an array of exotic merchandise.

6 NIZWA
See page 85

Oman's most historic town, with a huddle of charming souks and sand-coloured buildings clustered around a mighty fort.

7 AL AYN
See page 143

Magical cluster of Bronze Age beehive tombs atop a ridge at the edge of the Western Hajar.

8 A NIGHT IN THE DESERT
See page 190

Sleep out amid the vast dunes of the Sharqiya Sands or the Empty Quarter under a sky full of stars.

9 MISFAT AL ABRYEEN
See page 103

Traditional Oman at its most magical, with a time-warped cluster of mudbrick houses in a lofty mountain setting.

10 THE COASTAL ROAD TO DHOFAR
See page 223

The newly completed coastal route is one of Oman's most rewarding journeys.

11 DIVING
See page 32
Explore the jaw-dropping topography, colourful corals and magnificent marine life of the Daymaniyat Islands, one of Oman's premier dive sites.

12 KHOR ASH SHAM
See page 155
Take a dhow cruise through Musandam's most spectacular *khor* (fjord), keeping an eye out for dolphins.

13 NAKHL FORT
See page 122
The most picturesque of Oman's countless forts, against a rugged mountain backdrop.

14 JEBEL SHAMS AND WADI NAKHR
See page 104
The country's highest peak, tumbling dramatically into the depths of Wadi Nakhr.

15 FRANKINCENSE
See page 208
Aromatic wafts of frankincense smoke pervade every corner of the country, from traditional souks to modern hotels.

11

12

Itineraries

Oman covers an impressive amount of territory, but its excellent roads allow you to see significant swathes of the country in a relatively short time. There's plenty to absorb you in the capital for a few days, while with a week to spare you could just about complete either of the first two itineraries below; with a month you could stitch the three itineraries together – and there's plenty more to be discovered beyond these suggested routes.

WEST OF MUSCAT

To the west of Muscat extend some of the country's most well-trodden trails, for good reason. Oman's highest mountains, the Western Hajar, offer breathtaking scenery and thrilling drives, while scattered here and across the Batinah plain below are some of the country's most historic towns, forts and souks.

❶ **Jebel Akhdar** Wind up to the Saiq Plateau from Birkat al Mauz to wander the clifftop villages high above Wadi al Ayn. See page 93

❷ **Nizwa** Wrapped in historic charm, Nizwa is home to an imposing fort and a laidback souk that hosts a lively Friday goat market. See page 85

❸ **Ibri** With a fine fort and souk, Ibri makes a good base for visiting the ruins of Al Suleif and the "beehive" tombs of Bat and Al Ayn. See page 140

❹ **Jebel Shams** Peer down into Oman's "Grand Canyon" from the country's highest peak. See page 104

❺ **Wadi Bani Auf** Tackle Oman's classic off-road drive through the chasm of Wadi Bani Auf, passing en route the fairy-tale village of Bilad Sayt. See page 101

❻ **Rustaq Loop** Rising from the date plantations of Al Batinah are three of the country's most picturesque forts: Rustaq, Al Hazm and Nakhal. See page 120

❼ **Musandam** Check out Khasab's fine fort and take in the wondrous scenery on a cruise through the *khors* or a drive to the top of Jebel Harim. See page 146

A SHARQIYA LOOP

Making the most of Sharqiya's smooth coastal and inland highways, this route takes in Oman at its most traditional and scenically diverse, featuring some of the country's most photographed landscapes, from palm-fringed canyons to undulating dunes.

❶ **Coastal highway from Quriyat to Sur** Dotted with natural beauty spots, from the Bimmah Sinkhole and the Salma Plateau to Oman's most spectacular pair of wadis. See page 173

❷ **Sur** This enchanting fishing town makes an excellent base, with a trio of forts, a picturesque harbour and a historic dhow-building yard. See page 178

❸ **Ras al Jinz** For millennia, turtles have found their way to this beach at the end of the Arabian peninsula to lay eggs in the sand: perhaps the country's most memorable natural spectacle. See page 182

❹ **Jalan Bani Bu Ali, Jalan Bani Bu Hassan and Al Kamil** Between the coast and the Sharqiya Expressway is a trio of interesting and staunchly conservative villages with historic forts and a surprising museum. See page 194

❺ Sharqiya Sands Desert camps are hidden deep within Oman's most accessible sea of sand, making ideal bases for camel riding or simply taking in the magical sunsets. See page 190

❻ Ibra This dusty town boasts one of the country's most vibrant and traditional souks, along with a pair of splendid old mudbrick villages. See page 184

SOUTHERN OMAN

Check your mileage allowance if headed down the long road to Dhofar, taking in the utter emptiness of the inland route or – preferably – the striking beauty of the new coastal road. The *khareef* (monsoon) paints Salalah and its surrounds a lush green from June to August.

❶ Salalah One of Oman's most dynamic cities and the obvious base for exploring Dhofar, with an enchanting souk, ancient ruins, miles of beaches and tropical flair. See page 205

❷ Mughsail Beach A spectacular stretch of coastline, with sheer cliffs towering over pristine beaches. See page 224

❸ The Empty Quarter You'll barely scratch the surface of this legendary stretch of sand. Stop off en route at Shisr – thought to be the ruins of ancient Ubar. See page 227

❹ Jebel Samhan There are freshwater springs, sinkholes and incredible views along the slopes of Jebel Samhan, towering over the coast to the east of Salalah. See page 218

❺ Coastal road from Hasik to Shuwaymiyah Some of Oman's most jaw-dropping scenery; look out for the pretty lagoon of Wadi Sanaq and the broad canyon of Wadi Shuwaymiyah. See page 223

❻ Al Wusta Wildlife Reserve The remote outpost of Duqm is a good base for visiting the herd of oryx at the Al Wusta Wildlife Reserve. See page 197

❼ Masirah island Continue up the gorgeously desolate coastline to Shana, from where you can access Oman's ultimate desert island, ringed with secluded beaches and turtle-nesting sites. See page 195

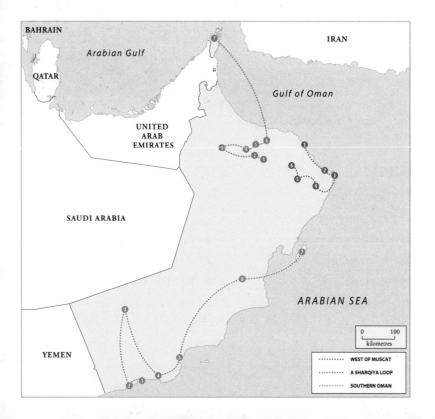

SPICES ON SALE AT THE SOUK

Basics

Getting there

Oman is well plugged into international air networks, either through the national carrier Oman Air or through other Gulf airlines such as Emirates, Qatar Airways and Etihad, meaning that it's now possible to reach Muscat from most major air-hubs in Europe, North America and Australasia with, at most, a single change of plane.

Overland routes into the country are more limited. Oman shares land borders with the UAE, Saudi Arabia and Yemen, though at the time of writing it was only feasible to enter the country via UAE border posts (see page 24). There are no regular international **ferry** routes into Oman, although the country is an increasingly popular stop on many cruise itineraries.

Flights from the UK and Ireland

Oman Air (Ⓦomanair.com) and British Airways (Ⓦbritishairways.com) offer direct flights from **London Heathrow** to Muscat, with Oman Air also flying direct from Manchester. There are numerous one-stop options with other carriers including Lufthansa (via Frankfurt; Ⓦlufthansa.com), Turkish Airlines (via Istanbul; Ⓦturkishairlines.com), Qatar Airways (via Doha; Ⓦqatarairways.com), Etihad (via Abu Dhabi; Ⓦetihad.com), Gulf Air (via Manama; Ⓦgulfair.com) and Emirates (via Dubai; Ⓦemirates.com). Fares start at around £300; flying time is around 7hr 30min outbound, 8hr on the way back. Travelling from **Ireland**, the easiest option is to get yourself to Heathrow and pick up a flight from there. British Airways (Ⓦbritishairways.com) and Aer Lingus (Ⓦaerlingus.com) operate codeshare flights from both Dublin and Belfast via Heathrow. From Dublin it's also possible to skip changing at Heathrow with various carriers, such as Emirates (via Dubai; Ⓦemirates.com), Turkish Airlines (via Istanbul; Ⓦturkishairlines.com), and Etihad (via Abu Dhabi; Ⓦetihad.com).

Flights from the US and Canada

The flight from North America to Oman is a long journey with myriad different route options. It's possible to get to Muscat with just one change of plane travelling from New York, with Turkish Airlines (via Istanbul; Ⓦturkishairlines.com), Etihad (via Abu Dhabi; Ⓦetihad.com), and Qatar Airways (via Doha; Ⓦqatarairways.com).

From Toronto, options include British Airways (via Heathrow; Ⓦbritishairways.com), Emirates (via Dubai; Ⓦemirates.com), and Lufthansa (via Frankfurt; Ⓦlufthansa.com). The same group of airlines offer routes from Washington, Chicago, Los Angeles and San Francisco.

From other destinations in Canada, including Montreal and Vancouver, you can fly to London with either British Airways (Ⓦbritishairways.com) or Air Canada (Ⓦaircanada.com), and then pick up a direct flight to Muscat with BA or Oman Air (Ⓦomanair.com), or go via Abu Dhabi with BA. Flying times from the east coast to Muscat can be as little as sixteen to seventeen hours depending on connections, although other flights can take anything up to 24 hours. From the west coast you're looking at a minimum flight time of 18 to twenty hours, possibly quite a bit longer. Fares from the east coast can start from as little as $700; from the west, from around double that.

Flights from Australia, New Zealand and South Africa

There are various one-stop routes from **Australia** to Oman. One option is to aim for a major Asian air-hub and pick up a direct flight with Oman Air (who currently operate nonstop flights to Muscat from Singapore, Kuala Lumpur, Bangkok, Hong Kong, Colombo, Mumbai and Delhi, among quite a few other places in Asia; Ⓦomanair.com). Other one-stop routes include travelling via Dubai with Emirates from Sydney, Melbourne, Brisbane and Perth (Ⓦemirates.com), or via Abu Dhabi with Etihad from Melbourne, Sydney and Brisbane (Ⓦetihad.com). Fares start at around A$1400, with flying times coming in at anywhere from 17 to thirty hours.

From **New Zealand**, it's easiest to travel to either Bangkok (with Thai Airways; Ⓦthaiairways.com), Singapore (with Singapore Airlines; Ⓦsingaporeair.com) or Kuala Lumpur (with Malaysia Airlines; Ⓦmalaysiaairlines.com) and pick up an Oman Air flight to Muscat from there – or alternatively to follow one of the routes via Australia described above. Fares start at around NZ$1900, with flying times from around twenty hours.

From **South Africa**, the simplest way of getting to Oman is to catch a direct South African Airways flight from Johannesburg, Cape Town or Durban to Doha or Dubai, and pick up a connection there (Ⓦflysaa.com). Fares start from around R12500. Another romantic, if slightly more time-consuming, option is to fly to Dar es Salaam and then make your way over to **Zanzibar**, from where direct Oman Air (Ⓦomanair.com) and Etihad flights (Ⓦetihad.com) leave for Muscat, allowing you to combine a visit

> ### A BETTER KIND OF TRAVEL
> At Rough Guides we are passionately committed to travel. We believe it helps us understand the world we live in and the people we share it with – and of course tourism is vital to many developing economies. But the scale of modern tourism has also damaged some places irreparably, and climate change is accelerated by most forms of transport, especially flying. All Rough Guides' flights are carbon-offset, and every year we donate money to a variety of environmental charities.

to Oman and its most important former colony in a single visit.

By land

Oman shares land borders with the UAE, Yemen and Saudi Arabia, although at present it's only possible to enter the country overland from the **UAE**, either via Mezyad or Khatm al Shikla near Buraimi/Al Ain (see page 137), Khatmat Milahah (see page 135) or Hatta (see page 135) – although at the time of writing, some travellers were being redirected to other border posts when trying to cross at Hatta. There's also a border between the UAE and the Musandam peninsula at Tibat (see page 152). Border formalities at all four posts are straightforward, and citizens of most European, North American and Australasian countries can buy a **visa** on the spot (see page 25). The whole process shouldn't usually take more than fifteen to thirty minutes, although you might have to wait considerably longer during weekends and local holidays.

AGENTS AND OPERATORS

For discounted flight-plus-hotel packages, British Airways (W britishairways.com), Qatar Airways (W qatarairwaysholidays.com) and, in particular, Oman Air (W holidays.omanair.com) all have a decent selection of offers.

OUTSIDE OMAN

Abercrombie & Kent UK ☎ 01242 386 500, W abercrombiekent.co.uk; US ☎ 800 554 7016, W abercrombiekent.com. Upmarket, tailor-made tours focusing on Jebel Akhdar, Muscat, Musandam, Nizwa, Salalah, Sur and the Wahiba Sands.

Kuoni ☎ 0800 140 4771, W kuoni.co.uk. Range of tours taking in Muscat, Nizwa, Wahiba Sands and Musandam. Also multi-centre trips taking in Dubai and Abu Dhabi.

North South Travel UK ☎ 01245 608291, W northsouthtravel.co.uk. Friendly, competitive travel agency, offering discounted fares worldwide. Profits are used to support projects in the developing world, especially the promotion of sustainable tourism.

Responsible Travel ☎ 01273 823 700, W responsibletravel.com. Refreshingly different – and socially responsible – tour operator offering an excellent selection of unusual and ethical tours across Oman. These range from mainstream country tours through to camping, hiking, camel

trekking and Empty Quarter safaris, as well as the chance to work on local conservation projects.

STA Travel UK ☎ 0333 321 0099, US ☎ 800 781 4040, Australia ☎ 134 782, New Zealand ☎ 0800 474 400, South Africa ☎ 0861 781 781; W statravel.co.uk. Worldwide specialists in independent travel; also student IDs, travel insurance, car rental, rail passes and more. Good discounts for students and under-26s.

Trailfinders UK ☎ 020 7368 1200, Ireland ☎ 01 677 7888; W trailfinders.com. One of the best-informed and most efficient agents for independent travellers.

Travel CUTS Canada ☎ 1800 667 2887, W travelcuts.com. Canadian youth and student travel firm.

The Ultimate Travel Company ☎ 020 3131 5588, W theultimatetravelcompany.co.uk. Numerous countrywide tours (1–2 weeks) spanning the whole of Oman, plus tailor-made tours, including trips into the Empty Quarter.

USIT Ireland ☎ 01 602 1906, Australia ☎ 1800 092 499, US ☎ 1866 647 3697; W usit.ie. Ireland's main student and youth travel specialists, with offices in Perth and New York.

Voyages Jules Verne ☎ 020 3811 5784, W vjv.com. Reliable group tours: "Frankincense & Fortresses" (7 days), takes in Muscat, the Hajar Mountains and Nizwa before heading down south to finish up in Salalah.

IN OMAN

Arabesque Travel ☎ 9530 2291, W arabesque.travel. Long-established local company under mixed Omani–British ownership offering a range of day and overnight trips from Muscat and Salalah, including wadi, fort, wildlife and Empty Quarter tours.

Gulf Leisure ☎ +44 7725 982550, W gulfleisure.com. Good range of adventure tours. On land there are desert safaris, mountain biking, climbing, trekking and canyoning, while water-based activities include game fishing, diving and glass-bottom boat tours.

Mark Tours ☎ 2478 2727, W marktoursoman.com. One of the largest local travel agents offering an excellent selection of one-day and overnight tours (including trips to places like Wadi Abyad, Wadi Shatan, Bat and As Suleif, which aren't covered by other operators), as well as customized camping trips. They can also arrange car hire, or 4WDs with guide-driver.

Muscat Diving & Adventure Centre ☎ 2454 3002, W holiday-in-oman.com. Oman's leading adventure specialists, with a big range of energetic outdoor activities on land and sea, including canyoning, caving, mountain biking, climbing, trekking and diving, along with more mainstream cultural tours and self-drive itineraries.

Zahara Tours ☎ 2440 0844, W zaharatours.com. Reputable local travel agents offering a wide range of one-day tours from Muscat, plus a few longer trips (2–10 days). They can also arrange car hire.

Visas and entry requirements

Citizens of most countries, including the UK, US, Ireland, Australia, New Zealand and South Africa, require a **visa** to enter Oman.

Under new rules announced in 2018, visas can no longer be purchased on arrival at the airport in Oman. Instead, an **e-visa** must be applied for online prior to your visit. At the time of writing, the changes had just been announced, and visitors arriving at Muscat Airport were being allowed to apply online once they arrived at the airport, before proceeding to immigration with their completed application. However, it was unclear at the time of writing whether this system would be permanent or not. In order to ensure smooth entry into Oman, you should apply for a visa in advance through the Royal Oman Police portal, at ⓦ evisa.rop.gov. om. You complete the process online and receive an electronic receipt, which you should print and present, along with your passport, upon arrival in Oman.

A **single-entry**, one-month e-visa costs 20 OR (£37/US$52). A **multiple-entry** visa, valid for a year for stays of up to one month at a time, costs 50 OR (£93/US$130). If you're driving from the main part of Oman up to the Musandam peninsula through the UAE, it's best to make sure you have a multiple-entry visa, so that you don't have to apply for an e-visa multiple times to get through the several border posts.

Note that embassy websites aren't well maintained, and the visa information and prices found on them may well be out of date; if in doubt, phone to check. The confusion surrounding the sudden changes to the visa rules will probably take some time to settle down, particularly at borders away from Muscat Airport. It's best to check ⓦ evisa. rop.gov.om regularly in advance of your trip.

Having an **Israeli stamp** in your passport is not a problem when entering Oman.

OMANI EMBASSIES AND CONSULATES ABROAD

Australia Level 4, Suite 2, 493 St Kilda Road, Melbourne 3004 ☏ 03 9820 4096, ⓦ oman.org.au.
Canada c/o US embassy (see below).
Ireland 4 Kenilworth Square, Dublin ☏ 01 491 2411.
New Zealand c/o Australian embassy (see above).
South Africa 11 Anderson St, Brooklyn, Pretoria ☏ 012 362 8301.
UK 167 Queen's Gate, London SW7 5HE, ☏ 020 7225 0001.
US 2535 Belmont Rd, Washington DC, 20008 ☏ 202 387 1980, ⓦ omani.info.

Getting around

There's very little public transport in Oman. Bus services are steadily improving and will get you between the main cities and, at a pinch, big towns, but to really see anything of the country you'll need your own transport, either by signing up for a tour, hiring a guide-driver, or getting behind the wheel yourself.

By car

Driving yourself is far and away the easiest way of getting around the country (for details of tour agencies providing cars with driver, see page 24). An extensive and ever-expanding network of modern roads now reaches most parts of the country and driving is largely straightforward, although not without a few challenges.

Standards of driving leave a certain amount to be desired, and the country's level of road-traffic accidents and fatalities is depressingly high (albeit not quite as bad as in the neighbouring UAE). Drive defensively at all times, expect the unexpected and be prepared for some lunatic in a landcruiser to come charging down on you at 150km/h.

Vehicles drive on the right in Oman. The usual **speed limits** are 120km/h on dual carriageways, 100km/h on single carriageways, and either 60km/h or 80km/h in built-up areas. Cars are fitted with a speed alarm which will beep at you when you reach 120km/h. A few of the main highways are monitored by speed cameras.

Common **road hazards** include vehicles driving after dark with no lights on; vehicles cutting suddenly in front of you without indicating; and livestock wandering onto roads, particularly goats and (in Salalah especially) camels. Rain often leads to **flash floods** which can cut off roads within a matter of minutes. Driving around you'll see endless signs saying "Stop when water is at red!" whenever you pass through even a slight depression in the landscape, meaning stop if the water level reaches the red paint on the poles on either side of the road. Keep a lookout too for **speed bumps**. These are found in towns and villages all over the country, but in many places the paint has peeled off them and there are no warning signs – a nasty (and potentially expensive) surprise if you hit one at 80km/h.

Penalties for **traffic infringements** are often stringent. Jumping a red light, for instance, leads to a mandatory two-day jail term. Wearing a seat belt is also obligatory, with an on-the-spot fine of 10

OFF-ROAD DRIVING IN OMAN

Going off-road in Oman, either as a passenger or driver, is one of the country's essential experiences. Driving off-road **in the mountains** is mainly a matter of common sense, and knowing the limits of your vehicle – something that you only really acquire with experience. Going out with an experienced off-road driver is, of course, the best training. Whatever you do, always err strongly on the side of caution, and always take a phone and lots of water.

Tearing across the desert in a 4WD – so-called **"dune-bashing"** – is another matter. It's a popular activity in Oman and neighbouring Dubai, but it is highly damaging to the delicate desert ecosystem, and there is a growing movement to have the practice banned. It's also, needless to say, not the best way to experience the magnificent stillness of the desert.

If you do find yourself driving in the desert, it's important to be aware that it's a specialized skill. The key to avoid getting bogged down is to stick to low gears and keep your revs up – but without revving so hard that you end up spinning the wheels and digging yourself in. Anticipating the terrain ahead, selecting the best route, working out which gear you need to be in and finding the correct gear-plus-revs combination is something of an acquired skill – particularly so when driving over large dunes.

Wherever you're going, take plenty of water and, ideally, travel with another vehicle (this is particularly important in the desert, where you're most at risk of getting stuck in dunes and needing to be towed out). And finally, check, if hiring a 4WD, that the insurance provided by the rental company actually covers off-road driving (not always the case).

The useful *Oman Off-Road*, published by Explorer, covers 26 of the finest off-road routes around the country in microscopic detail. Useful general points to remember include:

In the mountains, be very aware of the hazards of **rain**: it can take just minutes for flash floods to inundate wadis – if there's any possibility of rain in rough or remote areas, turn back or get out of the wadi as quickly as you can. If you get stuck in a flash flood, head for the highest ground in the vicinity. If the waters look like enveloping your vehicle, get out of it while you still can – floodwaters can rise with frightening speed.

If you find yourself having to cross a **flooded wadi**, it's a good idea to wade in first to test the depth of the water and strength of the current. If you decide it's safe to cross, use a low gear and maintain a steady 5–10km/h and keep your revs up to avoid stalling (using the differential-lock or low-range settings available on 4WDs can be useful if you're going to be driving through water for some time).

If you get **stuck on rocks**, jack the vehicle up and fill in the gaps under the wheels with stones, creating a ramp to clear the obstruction.

Always follow **existing tracks** (where they can be found) to avoid causing additional damage to the environment. These will also most likely follow the best route.

If you do get completely stuck and can't move your vehicle, it's usually better (especially in the desert) to stay with your car rather than wandering off on foot in search of help, unless you know exactly where you're going. A vehicle provides shade and is much easier to spot than a lone walker.

OR if you're caught without one on. Oman is also famous for its law requiring drivers to keep their vehicles clean; driving a dirty car can technically land you with a fine, although in practice the police will probably just direct you to the nearest car wash.

Road signs are usually (although not always) written in English as well as Arabic, although the transliteration is often inconsistent, which can lead to confusion. Even in Muscat, for example, one sign could be rendered "Muttrah", the next as "Matrah" and the next as "Mutrah", with no ostensible rhyme or reason.

If you have an **accident** you'll need to inform the police (emergency number ☎9999). It's best, if possible, to leave your vehicle exactly where it

is until the police have arrived and had a look at it. Moving it before they reach the scene can be construed as an admission of guilt.

Car rental

Car rental is reasonably inexpensive. The international car-rental agencies can provide cars from around 13–15 OR per day, rising to around 32–35 OR for a 4WD. Local firms may be able to provide a vehicle for as little as 10 OR, although, obviously, such vehicles may not be in such good condition as those hired from a more reputable company. Collision-damage waiver costs around 2 OR per day – you may consider it money well spent for the extra peace of mind it gives you. Your national **driving licence** should be sufficient documentation, although if in doubt check in advance with the car rental firm you intend renting from. Strictly speaking you should carry both parts of your driving licence with you (card and paper). It's well worth getting an International Driving Permit from the post office – it costs £5.50 and, while car rental agencies may not ask for it, it can make proceedings go more smoothly in the unlikely event you have to deal with the police. Note that most car-rental firms won't hire vehicles to those aged under 21, and most firms will charge heavy premiums for anyone up to the age of 25. Before you drive off, always check that the vehicle has a copy of the **registration card** – usually a photocopy in the glove compartment – and that it is in date, as this is sometimes checked at police checkpoints. **Petrol** is extremely cheap by European standards, at roughly 40p per litre.

By bus and micro

All the major towns in the country are connected by **bus**. These will do – just about – to get you between the country's major towns and cities, but no more. Buses are mainly operated by the government-run Mwasalat (Ⓦ mwasalat.om), along with a few private operators on the Muscat–Salalah route (see page 211).

Buses are reasonably fast and comfortable, although there are only two or three departures daily, and getting information about exactly where they depart from and when can be difficult (although if you use buses much you'll learn to recognize the distinctive Mwasalat concrete bus-stops-cum-shelters). **Fares** are extremely modest – no more than 3–4 OR for most inter-city journeys, rising to 7.5 OR for the long journey to Salalah.

Within larger towns (Muscat especially) local transport is provided by taxis (see below) and **micros** (also known as "baisa buses") – basically minivans painted white and orange and seating up to around fifteen passengers, at a squeeze. These are mainly used by low-wage expats from the Indian subcontinent and are easily the cheapest way of getting around, although it can often be difficult to work out where micros run. Vehicles aren't signed, so it's just a question of asking around (or waving at anything that passes) until you find one going where you want to go. Outside Muscat, drivers are unlikely to speak more than a few words of English.

By taxi

Within larger towns, the easiest way of getting around is by **taxi**. These are easily recognizable thanks to their white and orange livery, and usually fairly easy to find – just flag one down at the roadside. At the time of writing, the government had just announced plans for all taxis in the country to follow a **meter**, although fares had not yet been decided on. The exception to this is Muscat's new metered airport taxis, which were introduced in 2018 by state transport company Mwasalat. The metered fares for the airport taxis start at 1.9 OR, plus a further 300bz/km from 6am–10pm, Mon–Thurs, Sat & Sun; and start at 2.3 OR, with a further 350bz/km, at all other times, including Fridays. By the time you read this, similar fares may well have been standardized across the city or indeed the whole of Oman.

At the time of research, though, most taxis remained unmetered. If this is still the case you'll have to agree the **fare** before you set out – bargain hard. Locals would expect to pay no more than 1–2 OR for trips within most cities (or up to around 5 OR for long trips within Muscat), although foreigners are likely to pay significantly over the odds – anything up to double these prices, depending on your bargaining powers. All taxi **drivers** are Omani (the profession is reserved for Omani nationals). In Muscat, virtually all speak at least basic English; outside Muscat, they may speak Arabic only.

Taxis can also operate on a **shared** basis, with three or four passengers splitting the fare. Shared taxis operate both within towns and also on longer-distance routes between towns, offering a convenient alternative to buses. The system works on an ad hoc basics, however, so you'll have to scout around locally to find out where the best places to pick up a shared taxi are, and you may feel that it's more bother than it's worth.

By plane

There are three **domestic air services** within Oman at present: between Muscat and Khasab in Musandam (see page 152); between Muscat and Salalah (see page 210); and between Muscat and Duqm on the east coast (see page 198). Periodically, airlines including Oman Air (Ⓦ omanair.com) and SalamAir (Ⓦ salamair.com) offer flights from Muscat and Salalah to Sohar, although they were not doing so at the time of writing.

By ferry

There is currently only one long-distance boat service in Oman: the high-speed **ferry** service between Shinas and Khasab or Dibba in Musandam (see page 153), operated by the National Ferries Company (NFC). There is also an NFC service between Shana on the east coast and Masirah Island (see page 196). A new NFC service around the southern coast between the Hallaniyat islands, Shuwaymiyah and Hasik has been in the pipeline for several years, although there was no sign at the time of research that it was anywhere near becoming a reality.

Accommodation

There are hotels in all major cities and towns in Oman, although outside Muscat standards are middling and you're not exactly spoilt for choice. Prices, too, tend to be rather expensive for what you get.
There are relatively few **tourist hotels** aimed specifically at foreign visitors. Far and away the best selection is in Muscat (see page 66), which boasts some of the most memorable hotels in the region.

Most smaller towns boast a simple one- or two-star **local hotel** (usually in the range of 20 OR/£40/US$52) aimed at Omani travellers. These are usually functional and somewhat basic places – most are passably comfortable and generally clean, though in the worst places you may have to put up with rock-hard mattresses, dodgy electrics and the occasional cockroach.

Camping is another possibility, and pitching a tent in a remote mountain wadi or on an unspoilt beach can be a memorable experience. There are no restrictions on wild camping in Oman, assuming the area you pitch your tent in is clearly uninhabited and uncultivated. If you want to camp anywhere close to a village or other signs of human habitation, you should ask permission first.

A more upmarket alternative is to spend a night or two in one of the country's various **desert camps**, mainly found in the Wahiba Sands (see page 190).

Rooms and facilities

All hotel rooms in Oman boast the two essentials of modern Gulf living: air conditioning and a TV. Most places also give you a fridge, while hot water should also come as standard, although it doesn't always work reliably in the cheapest places (in budget places you'll usually have to turn the water heater on at least ten minutes before you hope to shower).

Some budget hotels also boast a simple in-house restaurant (and if there isn't one in house, there are likely to be other options close by). If you want a bar, licensed restaurant or swimming pool, however, you'll have to head somewhere a bit more upmarket. If you're driving yourself around, you'll find most hotels have free parking – very helpful, particularly in Muscat.

Hotel nightlife

One peculiarity of accommodation in Oman is that many mid-range hotels double as local night-spots and drinking venues. Numerous hotels boast in-house **live-music bars** – essentially places where young, heavily made-up ladies dressed in (by Omani standards) relatively revealing clothing stand up on stage in front of a largely male audience and pout, simper and sing (and possibly dance as well). These venues usually host either Arabic or Indian performers; it's not uncommon for a single hotel to have two or three such venues, usually tucked away somewhere discreet, like the basement, and often reachable only from an entrance outside the hotel itself. Rooms in most hotels are reasonably well insulated from the massive amounts of noise generated in these places, although it's still worth trying to get a room as far away as possible to avoid being kept awake half the night.

Also popular with local Omanis (despite traditional Muslim strictures against the drinking of alcohol) are the so-called **sports bars** to be found in various

---

ACCOMMODATION PRICES

The **rates** given throughout the Guide are for the cheapest double room in high season. They include **taxes** of 17 percent – you should always check whether these charges are included when a hotel quotes you a price, as often they will not be. Rates vary from 12 OR (£22/$31) in the very cheapest places to 150 OR (£280/$400) and above at Muscat's top hotels. Cheaper places tend to quote a "nett price" (as it's described locally, meaning inclusive of all taxes); more upmarket places often quote prices before tax.

Local hotels tend to maintain the same prices throughout the year. Rates at more upmarket tourist-oriented places are usually quite flexible and tend to change according to demand, usually most expensive during the **winter** months, and falling by as much as thirty percent during summer.

Small, local hotels normally include **breakfast** in their quoted prices as standard. At mid- and upper-range places, you will often be quoted separate prices for a room with and without breakfast.

hotels. These range from fairly civilized pub-style bars with TVs showing football through to raucous backrooms stuffed with pool tables and usually selling the cheapest beer in town – a good place to hang out with the locals, although even in the top-end hotels these sports bars manage to have a pretty downmarket atmosphere. The same can be said of their nightclubs, many of which (such as those formerly found in Muscat's *Grand Hyatt* and *Sheraton*) have been closed down, as they were perceived to have been attracting a less than desirable clientele.

Food and drink

Food in Oman is mainly a question of eating to live, rather than living to eat. The country's culinary traditions offer an interesting blend of Arabian and Indian influences, although the stuff served up in most local cafés and restaurants generally consists of a predictable selection of shwarmas and biryanis, with maybe a few other Middle Eastern meze and grills or Indian curries. Honourable exceptions exist, of course, but outside Muscat, good places to eat are few and far between.

Cafés and restaurants

There are plenty of places to eat in Oman, although few have any airs and graces. The basic eating venue is the **café**. At their simplest, these can be nothing more than a functional little room with plastic furniture and a strictly limited range of food and drink – perhaps one type of shwarma and one kind of biryani, washed down with cups of Lipton's tea. Better places will have bigger menus offering a range of Arabian- and/or Indian-style dishes, perhaps along with some fish, plus a few simple European dishes such as a burger and chips. You can usually get a filling meal at any of these places for around 1.5 OR, although culinary surprises are rare.

Restaurants are relatively thin on the ground – and the vast majority are located in hotels. These might have slightly fancier decor and a somewhat wider range of cuisines (including Indian, Chinese and European dishes) at inflated prices, although culinary standards are often no higher than those in local cafés – and often worse.

Cafés and restaurants do well enough for both lunch and dinner, although the only reliable source of Western-style **breakfasts** is hotel restaurants; even then, it tends to be a safer bet to go for the Indian

options, which are unusually extensive at breakfast buffets. More upmarket cafés may be able to rustle up some eggs or an omelette plus toast, although otherwise you'll probably be limited to traditional Indian-style breakfasts of dhal and bread.

Restaurants and cafés of all standards tend to **close** during the afternoon, from around 3 to 6pm.

What to eat

Most of the food served up in Omani cafés and restaurants comprises a mix of Arabian standards (shwarma, kebabs and meze) alongside the ubiquitous biryani and other lacklustre Indian and Pakistani-style fare.

Arabian (aka "Lebanese") food is based mainly on grilled meats. If you want to eat cheaply and well in Oman, your best bet is the humble **shwarma**, spit-roasted chicken and/or beef carved off and served wrapped in bread with salads – the Gulf version of the doner kebab (also served laid out on a piece of bread on a plate with chips and salad – the so-called "shwarma plate"). A simple shwarma sandwich usually goes for under 0.4 OR, and two or three make a satisfying light meal. The fact that the meat is being spit-roasted in public also means that you can see what you're getting and how it's being cooked.

Other Lebanese- and Turkish-style grilled **kebabs** are also reasonably common and often as good as anything in the country – places styling themselves as "Turkish" cafés/restaurants are often the best for this sort of food. Common dishes include the Lebanese *shish taouk* (chicken kebabs served with garlic sauce) and Turkish-style *kofte* (minced spiced lamb) kebabs. Most kebabs are served with Arabian-style **flatbread** (*khubz*) and a bowl of hummus, while some places also offer other classic Lebanese **meze**.

Along with the biryani (see page 31), lots of cafés offer various **pseudo Indian and Pakistani** dishes – anything from Pakistani-style meat curries through to Indian vegetarian classics like *mutter paneer* – although these (the vegetarian dishes especially) can often be astonishingly bad, and it's probably best avoiding ordering curries except in proper Indian restaurants.

Traditional **Omani dishes** provide an interesting, lightly spiced blend of Indian and Arabian culinary cultures, although they only rarely make it to restaurant menus. The nationwide *Bin Ateeq* chain (see page 70) is doing its best to revive local culinary traditions, while in Muscat places like *Kargeen* and *Ubhar* (see page 72) serve up old-fashioned creations like *harees laham* (lamb with wheat in cow ghee) and *shuwa* (slow-roasted meat cooked in a clay oven).

Chicken (*dijaj*) is the staple ingredient in most biryanis, kebabs and curries, although various other types of meat are also available, going under the name **laham** (literally "meat"), which usually means beef or lamb, but might also conceivably mean goat or, in Salalah, camel.

There's lots of top-quality **fish** available along the coast, although to see it done justice you'll have to shell out for a meal at one of Muscat's upmarket seafood restaurants – or go to Dubai, which is where a lot of the catch ends up. The local kingfish (*kenadh*), shark (*samak al qersh*) and lobster (*sharkha*) are particularly good.

Outside Muscat and Salalah, **vegetarians** are likely to struggle. Your most reliable chance of getting fed is to find a café serving Indian vegetarian food, although a fair few Lebanese-style meze are also vegetarian. Alternatively, you can always put together some sort of a meal out of a bowl of hummus, a plate of bread and some salad.

Desserts and accompaniments

The classic Omani dessert is **halwa**, the local version of the much-travelled sweet which is made, in widely different forms, across Europe, the Middle East and Asia. Omani *halwa* is wheat-based, which gives it a quite different taste and texture to the nut-based *halwas* made in Eastern Europe, Greece and Turkey. It is traditionally made from semolina, ghee (butter), sugar and rose-water, flavoured with cardamom and almonds and slow-boiled over a wood fire. You'll see *halwa* for sale all over the country, either in traditional ceramic bowls or in more functional plastic tubs stacked up in the fridges of cafés and grocery shops. It's worth a try, although something of an acquired taste: a rather sickly mush, somewhere in texture between porridge and blancmange.

Dates (see page 133) are another Omani staple, traditionally served with coffee – the national symbol of hospitality. Dates come in a wide range of varieties, both from Oman and neighbouring countries, with subtle variations in taste, size and colour. They're available in souks and supermarkets across the country, as well as at more upmarket chains such as Bateel (see page 75); they make a great gift or souvenir.

Drinks

Perhaps the most distinctive local drink is traditional **coffee** (*gahwa*) – although this doesn't bear much resemblance to European coffee. Arabic coffee is traditionally served in tiny handle-less cups, without milk and (often) sugar but flavoured with spices, usually including cardamom and/or cloves – intense, aromatic and slightly bitter. The serving and drinking of coffee is an important element of traditional Omani hospitality, and it's not uncommon even now to enter a hotel lobby or other public place and see a coffee-pourer wandering about with a traditional metal coffeepot (*dallah*) and tray of dates. If offered

---

THE OMANI BIRYANI

A staple of Omani cooking, the **biryani** doesn't bear a great deal of relation to its fancier Indian and Persian cousins, usually being little more than a leg of chicken buried in rice flavoured with a few whole spices and bits of roasted onion. As a staple dish, it's usually good value and often quite tasty. Other similar biryani-style dishes you may encounter include the Afghan-style **kabuli** (or *qabooli*), the Saudi **kabsa** (*kebsa, kibsa* – also known as *maqboos* or *machbus*) and the Yemeni **mandi**. In theory, each of these regional variants has its own distinct character and manner of preparation (the meat used in *kabsa* and *mandi*, for instance, is traditionally slow-cooked in a tandoor oven dug in the ground, although obviously this is unlikely to be the case in your local Omani café). In practice, however, these dishes are prepared in so many different ways that it's impossible to generalize about exactly what to expect, beyond a basic combination of meat and rice, mildly spiced.

---

coffee in a social situation, it is considered polite to accept one cup as a symbol of accepting the offered hospitality, even if you don't really want it. Your cup will be refilled whenever you empty it, although it's considered impolite to take more than three cups. When you've finished, shake the cup gently from side to side and say *"Bas, shukran"* ("Enough, thank you").

More conventional coffee, often described as **Nescafé** (or "Nescoffee"), is also available, as is tea (*shay*; usually a Lipton's tea-bag). **Fruit juices** are also often good, especially in local shwarma cafés and other Lebanese establishments. You may also come across **laban** (buttermilk).

Alcoholic drinks are relatively difficult to come by outside of Muscat, and often punitively expensive; even Salalah, for instance, the country's second-biggest city, boasts barely a handful of functioning licensed venues. **Beer** is usually a stereotypical selection of European lagers (Heineken, Carlsberg, Amstel, Tuborg and so on), either canned or on tap. A 50cl can of beer usually costs around 2 OR, or at least 3 OR for a draught pint – significantly more in upmarket places. **Wine** is available at the country's upmarket hotel restaurants, although at a predictably hefty price.

The media

Like most other countries in the region, Oman isn't particularly noted for its freedom of speech, a fact reflected in its rather turgid media, which still serves more as a PR and propaganda vehicle than a forum for genuine debate and analysis.

Newspapers

The Omani press is unlikely to set pulses racing. All publications are kept heavily under the thumb of the state, and coverage of events in Oman consists of little more than dutiful PR puff about the meetings of assorted government bigwigs, industrial developments and the latest production statistics. Coverage of events abroad (which doesn't need to be censored) tends to be of a significantly higher quality, however. The *Oman Observer* (Ⓦ omanobserver.om) is perhaps the best of the country's four English-language dailies; the others are the *Times of Oman* (Ⓦ timesofoman.com), the *Oman Tribune* (Ⓦ omantribune.com) and the *Muscat Daily* (Ⓦ muscatdaily.com).

Television and radio

The state broadcaster, Oman TV, broadcasts in Arabic only, with the exception of occasional short bulletins in English, although the **televisions** provided in hotel rooms generally carry a range of satellite channels, usually including BBC World News and CNN. The country has a handful of **English-language radio stations**, including BBC World (93.5). Hi FM (95.9 FM; Ⓦ hifmradio.com) serves up a bland diet of mainstream western pop and inane chat. There's also the longstanding state-run talk channel Radio Sultanate of Oman (90.4), while T FM (95.4) started broadcasting in January 2018 as the voice of the Times of Oman. You can't usually pick these stations up outside Muscat, however, which might be a good thing. Elsewhere in the country the radio airwaves can be disconcertingly empty.

Festivals

The highlight of Oman's festival calendar is the large-scale annual Muscat Festival and its smaller cousin in Salalah. For a more traditional insight into the country's religious culture, visiting Oman during one of the annual Islamic festivals is especially rewarding

– Ramadan is a particularly interesting time to visit, assuming you're prepared to put up with a certain level of practical inconvenience.

A FESTIVAL CALENDAR

Muscat Festival Late Jan to late Feb ⓦ muscat-festival.com. The highlight of the festival calendar, with a wide-ranging programme of events offering a mix of traditional arts, culture and heritage (including a special Oman Heritage and Culture Village in Qurum Park) along with fun events like the Muscat Fashion Show, Oman Food Festival and concerts at the Qurum Park Amphitheatre.

Ramadan Scheduled to run from approximately May 6 to June 4, 2019; April 23 to May 23, 2020; April 13 to May 12, 2021; precise dates vary according to local astronomical sightings of the moon. The Islamic holy month of Ramadan represents a period in which to purify mind and body and to reaffirm one's relationship with God. Muslims are required to fast from dawn to dusk, and as a tourist you will be expected to publicly observe these strictures, although you are free to eat and drink in the privacy of your own hotel room, or in any of the carefully screened-off dining areas which are set up in hotels (mainly in Muscat). Alcohol is also served discreetly in some places after dark, but not during the day. Eating, drinking, smoking or chewing gum in public, however, are definite no-nos, and will cause considerable offence to local Muslims; singing, dancing and swearing in public are similarly frowned upon. In addition, live music is also completely forbidden during the holy month (though recorded music is allowed), while many shops scale back their opening hours. Fasting ends at dusk, at which point the previously comatose country springs to life in a celebratory round of eating, drinking and socializing known as Iftar ("The Breaking of the Fast"). The atmosphere is particularly exuberant during Eid Al Fitr, the day marking the end of Ramadan, when everyone lets loose in an explosion of celebratory festivity.

Renaissance Day July 23 Celebrating the 1970 coup which brought Sultan Qaboos to power and signalled the start of the Oman Renaissance (see page 244).

Salalah Tourism Festival (also known as the Khareef Festival) July 15 to Aug 31. Held during the months of the *khareef*, featuring assorted cultural attractions, sporting events, concerts and shopping promotions.

Eid al Adha Estimated dates: August 1, 2019; July 30, 2020; July 19, 2021. Falling approximately 70 days after the end of Ramadan, on the tenth day of the Islamic lunar month of Dhul Hijja, the "Festival of the Sacrifice" celebrates the willingness of Abraham (or Ibrahim, as he is known to Muslims) to sacrifice his son Ismail at the command of God (although having proved his obedience, he was permitted to sacrifice a ram instead). The festival also marks the end of the traditional pilgrimage season to Mecca. Large numbers of animals are slaughtered during the festival. No alcohol is served on the day of the festival or on the day before.

National Day November 18. The Sultan's birthday is celebrated with fireworks and the decking out of Muscat's Sultan Qaboos St in tasteful green and red lights – an inadvertently Christmassy evocation for Western visitors.

Sports and outdoor activities

Oman's wild mountain and desert landscapes offer enormous potential for outdoor activities and adventure sports – potential which is slowly beginning to be realized, although the field remains in its infancy. The country is also a leading diving destination, with some of the region's most pristine underwater landscapes and marine life.

Hiking

The most obvious – and perhaps most rewarding – of the country's outdoor activities is **hiking**. An extensive network of hiking trails exists across the country, particularly in the Western Hajar (see page 94), with reasonably well-marked trails winding around and through some of Oman's most spectacular mountain ridges, wadis and canyons. Walks range from high-altitude treks along the mountain ridges through to exhilarating and challenging canyon walks, which usually involve scrambling over boulders and wading (and sometimes swimming) through rock pools and watercourses.

None of the treks should be attempted lightly. It's imperative to carry sufficient water and also to keep a watchful eye on the weather if trekking through wadis (especially narrower canyons). Rainfall in the mountains can be sudden and dramatic, leading to violent and potentially fatal flash flooding.

Twelve of the best routes are covered in *Oman Trekking*, published by Explorer.

Adventure sports

There is a range of **adventure sports and activities** around the country. Activities include canyoning (the rough scramble up Wadi Bimah is especially popular), caving, abseiling, rock-climbing or tackling one of the country's three *via ferratas* (Wadi Nakhr, Snake Canyon and Bandar Khayran). Mountain biking and kayaking are other possibilities. Leaders in the field are the Muscat Diving & Adventure Centre (ⓦ holiday-in-oman.com), while Gulf Leisure (ⓦ gulfleisure. com) also run a similar range of offerings.

Diving and snorkelling

Oman offers some of the region's finest **diving**, with good **snorkelling** too. Compared to other parts of the region, most of the coastal waters remain unspoilt, home to fine coral gardens and a few wrecks, and attracting some spectacularly large marine life.

It's possible to go diving straight from **Muscat**, which has a surprisingly extensive roster of dive centres (see page 62). Many operators here can also arrange trips to the spectacular **Daymaniyat Islands** (see page 129) up the coast north of Barka. Further afield, **Musandam** (see page 157) is perhaps the finest diving destination in the country, while there are further excellent dive sites along the south coast, especially around **Mirbat** (see page 210).

Most of the country's dive centres are run by European and North American expats; all offer a fairly standard range of dives, along with PADI courses, while many places also run **snorkelling** trips and assorted **boat cruises**.

Spectator sports

There's little in the way of organized sport in Oman, although if you're lucky you might catch a glimpse of one of the country's traditional competitive pastimes like **bull-butting** (see page 119) and **camel racing** – the latter is held at many locations around the country, especially on public holidays and National Day, although it's difficult to pick up information about forthcoming events. Try asking locally to find out if anything's planned. Beaches along the country's coastline often have goalposts and are popular spots for impromptu **football** matches.

Currently, the only formal annual sporting event is the **Tour of Oman** (Ⓦtourofoman.om) cycling race. Held over six days in February at locations around Muscat and the Western Hajar, it attracts a strong field of international riders.

Culture and etiquette

Foreigners are generally made to feel very welcome in Oman, although in return you'll be expected to abide scrupulously by Omani cultural norms. This remains a deeply traditional – and in many ways very conservative – country, and despite its sometimes superficially westernized appearance and growing openness to tourists, old attitudes run extremely deep.

Away from the main tourist centres, foreigners remain a source of considerable interest – often occasioning a certain amount of benign curiosity

and clandestine staring. This is almost always friendly, and a smile, wave or (best of all) a cheery *salaam aleikum* (see page 256) will usually break the ice and lead to a conversation with whatever bits of a shared language you can muster.

Visiting traditional **Omani villages**, it's worth remembering that you are entering what is generally considered the private space of the locals who live there. Discretion is the order of the day, and the onus is on you, as the outsider, to behave in a friendly and open manner, and to exercise sensitivity when taking photographs (see page 40). A few pre-prepared phrases of pidgin Arabic (see page 256) should help smooth the progress of any visit.

Dress

Dressing appropriately is perhaps the single most important thing to remember. Women should wear loose clothing, with arms and shoulders covered. Skirts, if worn, should reach at least beneath the knee, although wearing trousers is probably a better option. It's also useful to carry a shawl to cover your hair in more conservative areas. Dress codes are less crucial for men, although many Omanis will look rather askance at blokes dressed in tight or thigh-length shorts or singlets – below-the-knee shorts are probably OK, although it's best to err on the side of caution and wear trousers, even if it means foregoing a tan. For both men and women, it helps to dress conservatively, especially in rural areas. Ripped jeans, dodgy T-shirts with inappropriate slogans or images and elaborate piercings are unlikely to play well in a rural village in deepest Sharqiya. Inside foreign-oriented tourist hotels more Western standards prevail, although it's still polite not to wander around in a bikini away from the pool or beach.

Religion

The vast majority of Omanis are **Muslims**; however, the type of Islam which predominates here is different from that in neighbouring Saudi Arabia and the UAE. Around 75 percent of the Omani population belong to the Ibadhi school of Islam, which has been noted for its tolerance of other religions but remains a deeply traditional sect nonetheless. A further 10 percent identify with other forms of Islam, while the remaining 15-or-so percent of the population are made up of small communities of Hindus (largely members of the Indian expat community), Christians, and even smaller Sikh and Buddhist communities. Freedom of religion is enshrined in law in Oman, although in practice it is only in and around Muscat that there is any significant non-Muslim religious activity. In addition, non-Muslim groups are subject to greater regulation by the government – strictly speaking, for example, they are only allowed to publicly practise their religion in government-approved places of worship. In general, though, Oman is a more religiously tolerant society than some of its neighbours in the Gulf. Certainly, as a tourist, you are highly unlikely to come across any form of religious discrimination. That being said, if the topic comes up in conversation, as a Westerner it's easier to identify as a Christian than to profess atheism or agnosticism.

Drinking culture

Oman's **alcohol** culture is largely – although by no means exclusively – confined to Muscat and to the expat community. In the capital, it's not hard to come by a drink, although it tends to be prohibitively expensive (see page 73) and normally involves visiting either a licensed restaurant or one of the city's high-end hotels. Drinking in public or on the street is a sure-fire way to find yourself behind bars – don't do it. The law takes a similarly dim view towards any public displays or evidence of drunkenness. Even so, drinking laws are less strict than elsewhere in the Gulf, and you may be surprised at the number of Omani men in traditional dress you see drinking in bars.

Behaviour

As throughout Arabia, it pays to keep your cool. Expressions of overt anger and any raising of the voice should be strictly avoided, whatever the situation. It's also worth knowing that even innocuous **hand gestures** are punishable under Omani law, if deemed offensive. Exact definitions are somewhat elastic, although it's a lesson well worth absorbing, particularly if driving, when the urge to flap your hands in exasperation (or give the idiot in the Toyota Landcruiser who has just cut you up at 150km/h the finger) may become overwhelming.

Taboo subjects

Conversations in Oman generally run along well-regulated lines – your country, age, marital status, number of children (if any), religion, profession, reasons for visiting Oman and impressions of the country being the usual topics.

Pride in their country is strong among Omanis, and criticisms of the nation of any type will not be well received (unless, perhaps, you are simply agreeing with an opinion expressed by your host). Negative statements about Islam should be even more strenuously avoided. In addition, if asked your own religion, it's easiest to profess Christianity, even if in fact you believe in nothing of the sort, given that concepts of atheism, agnosticism and alternative religions are not widely understood. Political discussion – except of the most general and harmless kind – also remains a sensitive subject to be approached with extreme care, while criticisms of Sultan Qaboos are a definite no-go.

Women travellers

Women travelling in Oman should experience few problems, although the sight of unaccompanied Western females, either solo or in pairs, is still something of a novelty in most parts of the country. Hassles are rare (assuming you dress conservatively – particularly crucial if travelling without a male companion), albeit not unknown, particularly in Muscat. On the downside, solo women travellers may feel particularly isolated, given that most Omani men will, out of respect, tend to studiously ignore you, while it's difficult to make friends with Omani women, at least without local contacts.

Shopping

Oman offers a wonderful range of traditional Arabian products both natural and manufactured, ranging from inexpensive bags of aromatic frankincense and tubs of bukhoor through to elaborately wrought khanjars and chunky Bedu jewellery.

Where to shop

Many of the items described below can be found in **souks** all over the country, although for the finest array of Omani goods under one roof nothing beats a visit to the legendary Muttrah Souk (see page 47) in Muscat. The souks at Nizwa (see page 88) and Salalah (see page 207) also offer an excellent selection of merchandise – Nizwa is particularly celebrated for its handicrafts, while Salalah is perhaps the best place in the country to pick up samples of the greatly prized Dhofari frankincense. **Prices** are rarely fixed, however, and **bargaining** is very much the order of the day.

MEETING AND GREETING

Traditional Arabic **greetings** serve as an important oil in the machinery of everyday Omani life (see page 255) – the elaborate, almost courtly, formality with which Omanis greet one another in even the most prosaic of circumstances (your driver stopping to ask for directions, for example) offers a fascinating insight into the forms of decorum that still regulate Omani life.

Physical modes of greeting are also important. Close male and female friends and relatives will kiss one another on either cheek, although between male strangers the standard form of physical greeting is a handshake. Members of the opposite sex do not generally touch – do not offer your hand to an Omani of the opposite sex unless they offer you theirs first.

Invitations to **visit an Omani home** are common – don't be surprised if your driver asks you back to his house at the end of a tour for coffee and dates. If invited for a formal meal, it's polite to take some form of small gift, ideally gift-wrapped – chocolates or dates are ideal. Remember to take your shoes off when entering any Omani house. Once inside, it's considered polite to take whatever form of food or drink is offered, since refusal may be construed as dissatisfaction or disapproval. Coffee-drinking has its own etiquette (see page 30).

For a more contemporary, but in many ways equally rewarding, shopping experience, head to one of the many **Lulu Hypermarkets** which dot the country (the one between Muttrah and Ruwi in Muscat is convenient, and particularly good). A browse through the aisles here uncovers a fascinating array of local, Arabian and Asian produce, usually at bargain prices – anything from tubs of dates, jars of Yemeni honey, big packets of cut-price spices and great piles of outlandish vegetables through to traditional Indian tiffin-boxes and bars of sandalwood soap. Many of these products retail at far higher prices in the souks.

Aromatics

Oman is famous for all things fragrant – frankincense, *bukhoor*, myrrh and traditional perfumes – a cheap and portable memory of the sultanate.

Frankincense

Oman's most celebrated natural product is **frankincense** (see page 208), widely available in souks all over the country, although you'll find the best selection in Muttrah Souk in Muscat and Al Haffa Souk in Salalah. Frankincense is sold in various **grades**, referred to by

a confusing variety of names. Cheapest is the rather blackish, low-grade stuff from Somalia. Local Omani frankincense is generally considered superior, though again there are many different qualities on offer, ranging from the generic, yellowish lumps of stand-ard-grade frankincense through to the highly prized "silver" frankincense (also sometimes referred to as *hojari*, *hawjari* or *hugari*). As a general rule of thumb, the larger the chunks of frankincense resin and the clearer and lighter the colour, the better the quality. That from Dhofar is usually reckoned to be the best, although even here aficionados distinguish between different types of frankincense grown in different locations around the region.

Prices range from a rial or two for a bag of Somali frankincense through to 7–10 OR for higher-quality Salalah produce. Various types of **frankincense burner** (*mabkhara*) can also be found in shops around the country, ranging from functional little wooden and metal designs costing just a couple of rials through to brightly painted pottery frankincense burners from Salalah. Boxes of the tiny charcoal blocks used to burn the stuff are also widely available.

Bukhoor and myrrh

Almost as ubiquitous as frankincense is **bukhoor**, a distinctive local aromatic usually sold in cute little golden tins – a modern version of the traditional *mukkabbah* (see page 88) – or in larger plastic jars, when it's easily mistaken for tea. *Bukhoor* is made from perfumed woodchips soaked in oil and blended with various perfumes in a range of styles. Traditional *bukhoor* will typically contain some combination of musk, frankincense, *oud* and sandalwood, although other ingredients are also sometimes added, creating a wide range of scents.

TOP 5 OMANI SOUVENIRS

Dates from Bateel, Muscat. See page 75
A tub of halwa from Seeb's old souk. See page 116
A bottle of rose-water from Jebel Akhdar. See page 93
A bag of frankincense from Salalah. See page 207
A khanjar from Nizwa souk. See page 88

Like frankincense, *bukhoor* is burnt using a charcoal burner (and works fine in a frankincense burner), although a tin of the stuff with its lid off will do very well as a kind of traditional Omani air-freshener. Prices vary according to the quality of the ingredients used, although 2–3 OR is usual, despite what some optimistic shop owners might tell you.

Myrrh is another popular local aromatic, although less widely available than frankincense and *bukhoor*. It's produced by cutting the bark of a myrrh tree, collecting the resultant resinous sap and then burning it. Although Oman produces small quantities of myrrh, the stuff for sale in the country's souks will most likely have come from Somalia or Yemen. A small tub should cost a couple of rials.

Perfume

Traditional Arabian **perfumes** (*attar*) are another local speciality, although the flowery, oil-based scents are somewhat overpowering compared to subtler European-style fragrances. Fine Arabian perfumes are usually founded on a base of essential oils derived from *oud* (aloes, or agarwood) leavened with other local fragrances, often including frankincense. As well as pre-packaged scents, most perfume shops (such as the nationwide Al Haramain chain) can mix up bespoke perfumes from the long lines of glass bottles kept behind the counter. For the ultimate in Omani perfumeries, check out the Amouage factory just outside Seeb (see page 117).

Handicrafts

Oman boasts a wealth of artisanal traditions, ranging from the country's famed metalworking (seen in elaborately detailed *khanjars* and Bedu jewellery) through to traditional wooden walking sticks, pottery and clothes.

Khanjars

Perhaps the most tempting local souvenir is the **khanjar**, the traditional curved dagger which can be found around the Gulf, although those from Oman are often reckoned to be the finest. Modern replica *khanjars* are widely available, often sold ready-framed in small glass cases from as little as 10–15 OR; some are also given an artificially antique appearance through the use of black silver. These are often of poor quality, however, and don't begin to compare with the superb antique *khanjars* you'll find for sale in Muttrah and Nizwa souks and a few other places around the country. No two antique *khanjars* are ever completely alike, and many display wonderfully intricate metalworking on their hilts and scabbards, along with deer-horn hilts (modern

khanjars use plastic). Traditional Nizwa *khanjars* are characterized by their incredibly detailed silverwork, while those from Sur traditionally use gold thread to pick out designs. You'll also see plenty of antique Yemeni *khanjars* in Muttrah and Nizwa. These have leather rather than metal scabbards and generally show significantly lower standards of craftsmanship, although they are also very appealing in their own, slightly rustic, way, and significantly cheaper than their Omani equivalents. Prices for a genuine, high-grade Omani *khanjar* aren't cheap, and you won't get much for under 75 OR – it pays to shop around carefully.

Pottery

Omani **pottery**, most of it manufactured in the workshops of Bahla (see page 107), is also widely available, particularly in Nizwa Souk, and includes a range of traditional pots and frankincense burners along with more touristy creations (miniature clay forts and watchtowers, for example).

Jewellery

Gold, **silver** and **jewellery** are also well represented. Oman is a particularly good place to pick up examples of distinctive antique **Bedu jewellery** – chunky necklaces, bracelets and anklets in elaborately worked silver. Traditional necklaces often sport the distinctive Maria Theresa Thaler coins which formerly served as the major currency in the Gulf, as well as cute boxes designed to hold fragments of Qur'anic text, meant to ward off the evil eye. Traditional Gulf-style gold bracelets are another eye-catching purchase – the Gold Souk section of Muttrah Souk is the place to go for these.

Other handicrafts

The traditional wooden **walking stick** is another popular souvenir, as are wooden **toy rifles**. Assorted **clothes and textiles** can also be found. An embroidered Omani cap makes a particularly cute souvenir, or you could go the whole hog and invest in a turban and dishdasha. Women will find a chintzy range of colourfully embroidered dresses, trousers and blouses, including local versions of the classic Indian *shalwar kameez*. Oman isn't a carpet-producing centre, although a few shops in Muttrah and Qurum in Muscat offer a decent range of Iranian, Afghan and other **rugs and kilims** at prices lower than you'd pay in the West. The country's large subcontinental population means that there's a good range of **Indian handicrafts** on offer (particularly in Muttrah), including Rajasthani-style patchwork and tie-dye fabrics, and Kashmiri pashminas.

Travelling with children

Children form a central part of Omani life: treasured, fussed-over and generally integrated into most social situations. Families are usually large, and even quite young children are habitually included in social gatherings and night-time excursions at an hour when their Western counterparts are tucked firmly up in bed. For visitors with children, this means that your kids will generally be welcomed wherever you go (except perhaps in a few of Muscat's more exclusive restaurants and bars), and may well prove a bridge between you and the Omanis in whose company you happen to find yourself.

There are hardly any dedicated **children's attractions** in Oman, except the Children's Museum in Muscat (see page 58), although kids will enjoy many of the country's mainstream attractions. Exploring forts can be fun, while some of the less strenuous mountain walks (or parts of walks) may also appeal. Turtle-watching at Ras al Jinz is a guaranteed hit, as are dhow cruises amid the dolphins of Musandam. Desert activities such as camel-riding are also good for older kids.

The main child-related hazard in Oman is the **sun**. Children are particularly susceptible to the effects of sunburn and heatstroke and should be wrapped up carefully and made to drink plenty of fluids.

Outside Muscat, it can prove tricky to find supplies of nappies and other essential items for babies and toddlers. It's best to bring everything you might need with you from home.

Travel essentials

Costs

Unfortunately, a visit to Oman doesn't come cheap. The major expenses are accommodation and transport/tours. The very cheapest **hotel** rooms start at around 12–15 OR per night (£22–28/US$30–40), at least double this for mid-range places, and anything from 75 OR (£140/$195) and upwards for top-end places.

The lack of reliable public **transport** options means that to see the country properly you'll have to at least hire your own car (from around 15 OR/£30/$40/day), hire a car plus guide-driver, or go on a tour. The fact that so many of the country's highlights require 4WD adds further fiscal punishment, meaning either hiring your own 4WD (from around 32 OR/£60/$80/day) or, more realistically, taking a 4WD with guide-driver (from around 80 OR/£150/$210/day). At least petrol is cheap.

Once you've paid for lodgings and transport, other costs are relatively modest. **Eating** can be very cheap (if only because of the lack of proper restaurants), although the price of alcohol (if you can find it) is punitive. **Entrance fees** to the country's various forts and museums are extremely modest – seldom more than 1 OR.

Staying in the cheapest hotels, eating at local cafés, driving yourself and foregoing beer, you might scrape along on a bare minimum of 40 OR (£75/$105) per day per couple, without tours. Realistically, however, you're probably looking at around double this figure once you factor in the cost of taking a couple of off-road tours or a boat trip in Musandam. And of course it's very easy, in Muscat especially, to spend a lot more than this if staying in nice hotels and eating (and drinking) at good restaurants – in which case you could easily push this figure up to several hundred rials per day.

Many more upmarket hotels and restaurants levy a 17 percent **tax** (comprising an 8 percent service charge plus 9 percent government tax) on food and rooms. This is usually but not always mentioned in published room rates and menus – if in doubt, check. Cheaper places usually quote prices inclusive of taxes (the "nett" rate).

Crime and personal safety

Oman is an extremely safe country. Violent crime is very rare, and even petty crime such as burglary and pickpocketing is significantly less common than in most Western countries.

It pays to be sensible, even so. Make sure you have a good travel **insurance** policy (see page 39) before you arrive, protect all personal valuables as you would anywhere else, and take particular care of personal possessions in crowded areas such as Muttrah Souk.

If you are unfortunate enough to become the victim of theft, you'll need a police report for your insurance company, obtainable from the nearest police station. Don't count on finding any English-speaking officers, however; taking an Arabic speaker with you will probably be a major help.

Far and away the major threat to personal safety in Oman is **traffic**, whether you're a driver, passenger or pedestrian (see page 25). As a **pedestrian**, bear in mind that traffic will not necessarily stop – or even slow down – if you start crossing the road, and may also be travelling a lot faster than you might expect.

The British Foreign and Commonwealth Office (FCO) advises that terrorists are likely to try to carry out attacks in Oman, based largely on the fact that the country is in the Gulf region. Oman is generally very safe in this regard, but, as ever, it pays to be vigilant. The latest FCO advice can be found at ⓦ gov.uk/foreign-travel-advice/oman/terrorism. Under no circumstances should you attempt to cross the southern border into Yemen. The FCO advises against all travel to Yemen, including the mainland and its islands.

Customs regulations

Oman has strict and rather complex **customs** regulations, which it's worth being aware of before you travel. Non-Muslim visitors over the age of 21 are allowed to import up to two bottles (max. two litres), or 24 cans, of alcoholic beverages. It is permissible to bring in up to 400 cigarettes and 100ml of perfume. DVDs are limited to ten per person; any DVDs or CDs you bring in may be checked for their content first. A yellow fever vaccination certificate is required for travellers arriving within six days from infected areas in Africa and South America. Travellers carrying prescription drugs should take a letter from their doctor stating that they are obliged to take this medicine.

Electricity

UK-style **sockets** with three square pins are the norm. The country's current runs at 240 volts AC, meaning that UK appliances will work without problem directly off the mains supply, although US appliances will probably require a transformer.

Health

There are no serious **health risks** in Oman (unless you include the country's traffic). All the main cities in the country are equipped with modern hospitals and well-stocked pharmacies. **Tap water** is safe to drink, while even the country's cheapest cafés maintain good standards of **food hygiene**. One possible health concern is the **heat**. Summer temperatures regularly climb into the forty-degree Celsius range, making sunburn, heatstroke and acute dehydration a real possibility, especially if combined with excessive alcohol consumption. Stay in the shade, and drink lots of water.

Bilharzia is another possible risk if swimming in rock pools in the mountains. This is a parasitic infection which can cause rashes, fever, diarrhoea,

and, in the long term, organ damage. There may be no symptoms, or they can take weeks to show up – visit your GP if you think you have any symptoms after swimming in fresh water.

Insurance

There aren't many safety or health risks involved in a visit to Oman, although it's still strongly recommended that you take out some form of valid **travel insurance** before your trip. At its simplest, this offers some measure of protection against everyday mishaps like cancelled flights and mislaid baggage. More importantly, a valid insurance policy will cover your costs in the event that you fall ill in Oman, since otherwise you'll have to pay for all medical treatment. Note, too, that most insurance policies routinely exclude various "adventure" activities. In Oman this will include adventure sports such as caving, abseiling and rock-climbing, and might conceivably also include trekking. If in doubt, check with your insurer before you leave home.

Internet

As in many places across the world with widespread internet access, internet cafés are more or less redundant and are far less widespread than they used to be, including in Muscat.

Internet access is available in pretty much all mid-range and all top-end **hotels**, usually via wi-fi and sometimes also via cable. A large proportion of restaurants will also have wi-fi available to guests. Almost without exception internet access is free in such establishments, although it's not unheard of for some hotels to charge extra for it.

In all but the most remote areas, you'll find fast and widespread mobile phone data coverage courtesy of Oman's main mobile phone providers, Omantel, Ooredoo and Friendi. Obviously this is an expensive way of getting online if you're using a foreign SIM card, but it's easy to pick up an Omani SIM at one of these companies' kiosks at the airport, or at countless stores nationwide.

The **country URL** for Oman is ".om" – which looks confusingly like a typo for ".com". If you find a .om address not working, try replacing it with .com, or vice versa.

Laundry

All hotels in Oman will provide some kind of **laundry** service, but it's often extortionately overpriced; expect to pay at least 200bz for even the smallest

ROUGH GUIDES TRAVEL INSURANCE

Rough Guides has teamed up with WorldNomads.com to offer great travel insurance deals. Policies are available to residents of over 150 countries, with cover for a wide range of adventure sports, 24hr emergency assistance, high levels of medical and evacuation cover and a stream of travel safety information. Roughguides.com users can take advantage of their policies online 24/7, from anywhere in the world – even if you're already travelling. And since plans often change when you're on the road, you can extend your policy and even claim online. Roughguides.com users who buy travel insurance with WorldNomads.com can also leave a positive footprint and donate to a community development project. For more information, go to Ⓦroughguides.com/travel-insurance.

item. The chains Snowhite and Kwik Kleen are slightly cheaper, while the best value is to be found in one of the countless local (often Indian-run) shops.

LGBT travellers

Oman shares the medieval attitudes prevalent around the Gulf with regard to **same-sex relationships**. Homosexuality remains illegal, and anyone caught in anything that might be classed as a homosexual act is technically looking at a spell in prison, although local police are unlikely to go after foreign gays and lesbians unless given good cause to.

As with other places around the Gulf, a scene does exist (particularly in Muscat), but it's extremely secretive. The only accessible online resource available at the time of writing is via Facebook (try searching for "Gay in Oman"), although the few groups currently in existence appear to be largely made up of men looking for one-night stands.

In practical terms, the good news is that, given the sexually segregated nature of Omani society, male or female couples travelling together are unlikely to elicit any particular attention, assuming you behave in a manner consistent with local standards. Same-sex couples shouldn't attract too much attention when checking into a hotel room together, assuming you stick to twin, rather than double, beds. Discretion is naturally the order of the day, at all times, and any public displays of affection or other unconventional behaviour should be strictly avoided, unless you know the people you are with very well.

Maps

The best **map** of the country is the *Reise Know-How Oman* map (1:850,000). It's printed on (nearly) indestructible paper and covers the country in clear and commendably up-to-date detail. For off-road maps, *Oman Off-Road*, published by Explorer, includes excellent satellite maps of 26 routes around the country.

Money

The Omani currency is the **rial** (usually abbreviated "OR", or sometimes "OMR"), subdivided into 1000 **baiza** ("bz"). Banknotes are denominated in 100, 200 and 500 baiza and in 1, 5, 10, 20 and 50 rials (there are two types of one-rial note, coloured either purple or red). Coins are denominated in 5, 10, 25 and 50 baiza. Exchange rates at the time of writing were 1 OR = £1.86, $2.60 and €2.10. For the latest exchange rates, go to Ⓦxe.com.

There are plentiful **ATMs** all over the country, virtually all of which accept foreign Visa and MasterCard; American Express is widely accepted, although not universally. Most ATMs have a daily cash withdrawal limit of 150–250 OR. You'll also find **banks** pretty much everywhere, all of which will change travellers' cheques and foreign cash. Many more upmarket hotels will also change cash and travellers' cheques, usually at poor rates.

Major credit cards are widely accepted in Oman, but smaller restaurants (and, very occasionally, hotels) sometimes work on a cash-only basis, so always carry some.

Opening hours and public holidays

Oman runs on a basically Islamic schedule. The traditional working week runs from **Saturday to Wednesday**, although some businesses also open on a Thursday morning, while Friday serves as the Islamic holy day (equivalent to the Christian Sunday). Usual **business hours** are 8am–5pm; government offices open 8am–2pm. **Banks** are usually open Saturday to Wednesday 8am–noon and Thursday 8–11.30am.

Shopping hours are slightly different. Shops in most souks generally open seven days a week, although most places remain closed on Friday mornings. Most places also shut down daily for an extended siesta from around noon or 1pm until 5 or 6pm, lending many smaller places a rather ghost-town ambience during the hot afternoon hours. Local **cafés** may stay open, although there's unlikely to be much food available past around 1pm (more upmarket restaurants tend to stay open until 2 or 3pm, but then usually close until around 7pm). Things fire back into life as dusk approaches, usually remaining busy until 9 or 10pm.

Museums tend to follow a similar pattern, opening Sunday to Wednesday from around 9 or 10am to 1pm and from 4 or 6pm to 7pm. Some remain closed for the whole of Thursday and Friday; others open, but only during the afternoon/evening. **Forts** broadly divide into two categories. Smaller forts tend to be open Saturday to Wednesday 8am–2pm; larger forts are generally open Saturday to Thursday 9am–4pm and Friday 8–11am.

There are eight **public holidays** in Oman. Three of these fall on the same day every year; the other five follow the lunar Islamic calendar and therefore change date by around eleven days every year, moving gradually backwards through the year.

PUBLIC HOLIDAYS

New Year's Day Jan 1

Mouloud (The Prophet's Birthday) Nov 10, 2019; Oct 29, 2020; Oct 19, 2021

Leilat al Meiraj (Ascension of the Prophet) April 3, 2019; March 22, 2020; March 13, 2021

Renaissance Day (see page 32) July 23

Eid al Fitr End of Ramadan (see page 32). June 5, 2019; May 24, 2020; May 13, 2021

Eid al Adha Feast of the Sacrifice (see page 32). Aug 12, 2019; July 31, 2020; July 20, 2021

National Day and birthday of Sultan Qaboos (see page 32) November 18

Islamic New Year Sept 1, 2019; Aug 20, 2020; Aug 10, 2021

Phones

The **country code** for Oman is ☎968. All Omani landline phone numbers are eight digits long, starting with ☎2. Area codes (eg ☎24 for Muscat) have now been integrated into the eight-digit format, and must be dialled irrespective of where you're calling from. **Mobile** numbers also follow an eight-digit format, but begin with ☎9. To call Oman from abroad you have to dial the country code plus full eight-digit number. The **emergency number** for police or ambulance is ☎9999.

Public phones are scarce in Oman. Check the relevant **mobile** (cell phone) charges before you leave home. European GSM handsets should work fine in Oman, although North American cell phones may not (except tri-band phones).

If you're going to be using your phone a lot, it might be worth acquiring a **local SIM card**, which will give you cheap local and international calls. The leading local phone operators are Omantel (ⓦomantel.om) and Ooredoo (ⓦooredoo.om), which have shops countrywide where you can pick up a SIM card (you'll need to show your passport when purchasing). The easiest way of doing things is with the pre-paid packages, which include a SIM card and a certain amount of credit which you can then top up. Funds can be added to your account using the widely available scratchcard-style recharge cards, available from many local shops – look out for the window stickers. Another option is Friendi (ⓦfriendimobile.com), who have a kiosk at the airport and offer similar services to the other two, although shops and recharge cards are less widely available.

Photography

Oman is a very photogenic country, although the often harsh light can play havoc with colour and contrast – for the best results head out between around 7am and 9am in the morning, or after 4pm. Don't take photographs of people without asking or you risk causing considerable offence, especially if taking photos of ladies without permission. In Arabic, "May I take your picture?" translates (roughly) as *Mumkin sura, min fadlak?* (to a man) or *Mumkin sura, min fadlik?* (to a woman). Men will probably be happy to oblige, women less so, while children of either sex will usually be delighted.

Post

Oman has an efficient and reliable modern **postal service**. Postcards and letters cost between 600bz and 800bz to Europe, Asia and North America, rising to as much as 12–16 OR for parcels weighing over 1kg, although if sending anything valuable you may prefer to use an international courier such as DHL or FedEx, who have offices in Muscat and Salalah. There are no reliable **poste restante** facilities in Oman. If you need to receive a letter or package, it's best to have it delivered to your hotel (and to warn them in advance of its arrival).

Smoking

Smoking is not permitted inside cafés, restaurants, bars, malls, offices and other public areas – although it's usually permitted on the outdoor terraces of bars and restaurants.

Time

Oman runs on **Gulf Standard Time** (GST). This is 4hr ahead of GMT (or 3hr ahead of British Summer Time), 9hr ahead of US Eastern Standard Time, 12hr ahead of US Pacific Time; 4hr behind Australian Western Standard Time, and 6hr behind Australian Eastern Standard Time. There is no daylight saving in Oman.

Toilets

There are not many **public toilets** in Oman (a notable exception is at the corniche-side entrance to Muttrah Souk). If you get caught short elsewhere, head to the nearest plausible-looking hotel, restaurant or café. Pretty much all tourist attractions, including museums and forts, also provide toilets. Most toilets in Oman are of Western-style sit-down design, although Asian-style squat toilets are also occasionally found.

Tourist information

There are no proper tourist information offices **in Oman** (apart from a small kiosk at the Muscat airport), and getting reliable local information can be a struggle. Your best bet is to talk to a local tour operators (see page 24). Staff at better hotels may also be able to provide local information, though this is decidedly hit and miss.

There are no proper Oman tourist offices overseas. In the **UK and Ireland**, tourist enquiries are handled by the PR company Four Communication (☎ 020 3697 4200, ✉ omanministryoftourism@fourcommu-nications.com).

USEFUL WEBSITES

🌐 **destinationoman.com** Longstanding website devoted to travel throughout Oman, packed with information on hotels, restaurants, tours and activities.

🌐 **muscatmutterings.com** Useful listings of forthcoming events in the capital plus links to other Oman-related blogs.

🌐 **omanobserver.com** Latest news from the country's leading daily newspaper.

🌐 **omantourism.gov.om** Official website of the Ministry of Tourism, with extensive information and features on all parts of the country.

🌐 **tourismoman.com.au** Official website from the Ministry of Tourism aimed at Australian visitors, but more user-friendly and useful to all visitors than the ministry's main site.

Travellers with disabilities

Unfortunately, visiting Oman presents major challenges for travellers with disabilities. Many of the country's leading attractions – including its rugged mountains and rickety old forts – are, by their very nature, largely inaccessible to visitors with impaired mobility. Muscat is the country's most accessible destination. Some of the city's upmarket hotels have

CALLING HOME FROM ABROAD

To make an international call, dial the international access code (in Oman it's 00), then the destination's country code, before the rest of the number. Note that the initial zero is omitted from the area code when dialling the UK, Ireland, Australia and New Zealand from abroad.

Australia international access code + 61
New Zealand international access code + 64
UK international access code + 44
US and Canada international access code + 1
Ireland international access code + 353
South Africa international access code + 27

specially equipped rooms, while leading attractions including Muttrah Souk and Sultan Qaboos Mosque are fully accessible (although you'll have to check with your hotel as to whether they can provide you with suitable transport). Outside the capital things become more difficult, but you may be able to arrange transport through one of the tour operators (see page 24). Muscat Diving and Adventure Centre (🌐 holiday-in-oman.com) and Oman Travel (🌐 omantravel.co.uk) are two recommended operators for travellers with disabilities.

Working and studying in Oman

Oman is so popular a destination among expats that they now account for almost half of the total popula-tion, and more than half – almost two thirds, in fact – of the population in Muscat. It's also a popular desti-nation among study abroad and gap year students.

STUDY, WORK AND VOLUNTEER PROGRAMMES

Anglo-Omani Society ☎ 020 7851 7439, 🌐 angloomanisociety. com. Longstanding society promoting Anglo-Omani relations, offering Arabic courses, grants for educational projects, and school teaching placements in Oman.

Center for International Learning ☎ 968 2443 4779, 🌐 ciloman.org. Muscat-based language school offering courses in Arabic and Middle Eastern studies.

Council on International Educational Exchange (CIEE) US ☎ 1207 553 4000, 🌐 ciee.org. Leading NGO offering study programmes and volunteer projects around the world.

Earthwatch Institute Europe ☎ 01865 318 838, US ☎ 1800 776 0188, Australia ☎ 03 9016 7590, 🌐 earthwatch.org. Scientific expedition project that spans over fifty countries, with environmental and archeological ventures worldwide.

Muscat

VIEW ACROSS OLD MUSCAT

1 Muscat

Oman's capital, and far and away its largest city, Muscat offers an absorbing snapshot of the country's past and present. Physically, much of the city is unequivocally modern: a formless straggle of low-rise, white-washed suburbs which sprawl along the coast for the best part of 30km, now home to a population of well over a million – almost a quarter of the country's total. It's here that you'll find Oman at its most contemporary and consumerist, exemplified by the string of opulent hotels which line the city's sand-fringed coastline, backed up by swanky restaurants and modern shopping centres, and honeycombed with a network of roaring highways. It's also unquestionably the commercial and administrative powerhouse of modern Oman, from the stately government buildings that line the main highway into town through to the high-rise office blocks of Ruwi's Central Business District.

Significant reminders of the city's past remain, however. These include, most notably, the engaging port district of **Muttrah**, home to the famous **Muttrah Souk**, and the nearby quarter of **Old Muscat**, which holds Sultan Qaboos's florid Al Alam Palace, as well as a stretch of salty seafront lined with old Portuguese forts, colourful mosques and assorted traditional Arabian buildings (many now converted to small-scale museums). These are the places where you'll get the strongest sense of Muscat's sometimes elusive appeal, with its beguiling atmosphere of old-time, small-town Arabian somnolence, quite different from the somewhat faceless modern suburbs to the west. Muttrah and neighbouring **Ruwi** also offer the city's most interesting streetlife, and the best view of the patchwork of cultures which make up the city: Omani, Indian and Pakistani, with an occasional hint of Zanzibari, Baluchi and Iranian thrown in for good measure – a living memory of the city's surprisingly cosmopolitan past.

West of Ruwi stretches the endless sprawl of modern Muscat's Legoland suburbs. Attractions here include the fine beach of **Shatti al Qurum**, close to many of the city's most appealing hotels and restaurants, while nearby **Qurum** is home to a string of interesting shops. A smattering of further low-key museums lies scattered here and there, while most visitors also head out to Ghubrah, on the western edge of the city, to visit the magnificent **Sultan Qaboos Grand Mosque**.

Brief history

Evidence of human settlement in the Muscat area dates back to at least 6000 BC, although the city's rise to national pre-eminence is a much more recent affair. Muscat's port was sufficiently important to merit passing references in the works of Greek geographers, including Ptolemy, and Pliny the Elder during the first century AD. For much of early Omani history though, it was overshadowed first by Sohar, to the

---

THE GRAND HYATT

Highlights

❶ Dolphin-watching Take a boat trip out for a glimpse of frolicking dolphin pods, and for unrivalled views of the area's rugged coastline. See page 62

❷ Muttrah Souk Oman's most absorbing souk: a labyrinthine tangle of tiny shops piled high with Arabian curios and exotica. See page 47

❸ Old Muscat Explore superb museums and admire Sultan Qaboos's eye-catching Muscat residence in the city's quietly stately old quarter. See page 51

❹ Bait al Zubair The best small museum in the city, with wide-ranging displays on Omani culture and crafts. See page 53

❺ Souq Ruwi Street The vibrant commercial heart of Muscat's "Little India", crammed with colourful shops and curry houses. See page 56

❻ Afternoon tea at the Grand Hyatt Sit back over a traditional English afternoon tea while enjoying the super-fuelled Arabian kitsch of one of Muscat's most extravagant hotels. See page 58

❼ Sultan Qaboos Grand Mosque Magnificent modern mosque rising above the western approaches to the city – and the only one in the country open to non-Muslim visitors. See page 60

HIGHLIGHTS ARE MARKED ON THE MAPS ON PAGES 46, 52 AND 55

1

north, and then Qalhat, to the south; one of the first European visitors to Muscat, Thomas Kerridge, writing in 1624 to the East India Company, described it as a "beggarly poor town".

Muscat suffered particularly at the hands of the **Portuguese**, who captured the town in 1507 and held onto it until 1650 – although ironically it was the Portuguese destruction of the nearby ports of Qalhat and Quriyat which cleared the way for Muscat's subsequent economic rise. The town began to flourish during the early Al Bu Said era (see page 236) in the second half of the eighteenth century when it established itself as the country's leading port and entrepot, while it also assumed increasing political significance during the reign of **Hamad bin Said** (1784–92), who moved the court to Muscat, where it has generally remained ever since. The city's economic position was confirmed during the nineteenth and twentieth centuries, thriving as a major centre for a range of economic activities including fishing, boat-building, slaving, arms-smuggling and general trade.

The sprawling metropolis you see today is a largely modern creation, although building regulations ensure that any new development remains attractively traditional. Until the accession of **Sultan Qaboos** in 1970 the town comprised simply the old walled town of Muscat proper (or "Old Muscat", as it's now known), home to the residence of the sultan and other notables, and the separate port of Muttrah, the centre of the town's commercial activity.

Orientation

Greater Muscat boasts an unusual geography and layout which can be somewhat perplexing at first impression. The entire city is extremely linear: a narrow ribbon of urban development spread out along 30km of coastline. As such, it's useful to think of Muscat not so much as a conventional city but rather as a collection of disparate towns and modern suburban developments without a single defining centre. Broadly speaking, the city divides into two parts: **modern Muscat**, which stretches in a largely formless expanse of monotonous suburbs from just east of the airport through the suburbs of **Ghubrah** and **Khuwair** and on to **Qurum**; and the **older**

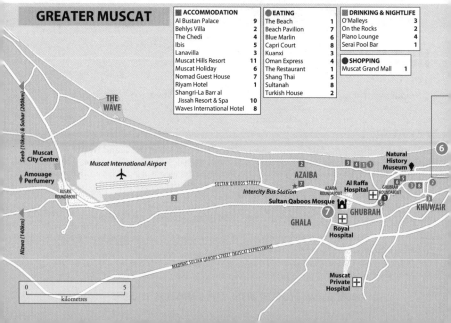

GREATER MUSCAT

■ ACCOMMODATION	
Al Bustan Palace	9
Behlys Villa	2
The Chedi	4
Ibis	5
Lanavilla	3
Muscat Hills Resort	11
Muscat Holiday	6
Nomad Guest House	7
Riyam Hotel	1
Shangri-La Barr al Jissah Resort & Spa	10
Waves International Hotel	8

● EATING	
The Beach	1
Beach Pavilion	7
Blue Marlin	6
Capri Court	8
Kuanxi	3
Oman Express	4
The Restaurant	1
Shang Thai	5
Sultanah	8
Turkish House	2

■ DRINKING & NIGHTLIFE	
O'Malleys	3
On the Rocks	2
Piano Lounge	4
Serai Pool Bar	1

● SHOPPING	
Muscat Grand Mall	1

parts of the city, comprising the three disparate districts of **Muttrah**, **Old Muscat** and **Ruwi**, divided from the rest of the city (and each other) by ridges of untamed, red-rock hills which give the eastern end of the metropolis a strangely lunar appearance in places.

The entire city is bisected from west to east by the main Highway 1, known as **Sultan Qaboos Street**, which runs from the airport to Shatti al Qurum and then splits (just beneath the rocky bluff topped by the *Mumtaz Mahal* restaurant – a useful landmark, since signage is poor) into two branches, with one arm, Qurum Heights Road, heading off to Muttrah and Old Muscat, and the other, Al Nahdah Street, to the centre of Qurum and then Ruwi. The **Muscat Expressway** runs parallel to Sultan Qaboos Street a couple of kilometres inland, joining up with Al Nahdah Street at Qurum.

Muttrah

Sweeping around a beautiful seafront corniche, **MUTTRAH** (also spelled Mutrah or Matrah) is the city's old commercial centre, and still far and away the most interesting part of the city. The area retains much of its mercantile importance thanks to the presence here of the large **Port Sultan Qaboos**, the city's **Fish Market** and the enduringly popular **Muttrah Souk**, as well as reminders of its past in the form of the old Portuguese **Muttrah Fort**.

Muttrah Souk

The main draw in Muttrah is the famous **Muttrah Souk**, probably the single most popular tourist attraction in the country. This is Muscat at its most magical: an absorbing labyrinth of narrow, perfume-laden alleyways packed with colourful little shops stacked high with tubs of frankincense and *bukhoor*, old silver *khanjars*, Bedu jewellery and other exotic paraphernalia – one of the few markets in the world where it's possible to buy gold, frankincense and myrrh all under a single roof. You could

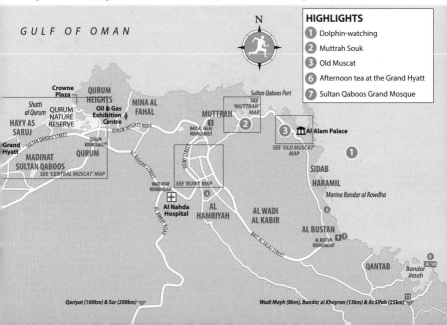

1

spend many enjoyable hours here, attempting to make sense of the maze and haggling over handicrafts; the traders here are unusually pushy by Omani standards, giving a sense that the atmosphere is somewhat contrived for the benefit of tourists. It's good fun, though, particularly when you venture away from the heavily touristed main drag into the tangled backstreets beyond.

Getting lost in the maze of Muttrah Souk is half the fun of a visit, and it's well worth wandering off at random and seeing where you finally end up – which will probably be a long way from where you expected to be. The directions given in the following account describe the basic layout of the place, although there's still plenty of room for entertaining error in between.

The entrances

There are **three main entrances** to the souk, one at the front on the corniche (marked with a miniature dome and a pedestrian crossing), and two close together at the rear on Muttrah Street. Alternatively, and in many ways more interestingly, you can enter the souk from **behind the Muttrah Gold Souk** building on the corniche, which puts you straight into the colourful tangle of alleyways at the heart of the Gold Souk area.

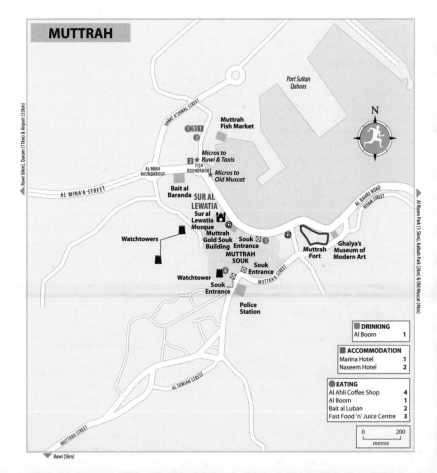

The main drag

The souk can be somewhat deceptive at first acquaintance: it's a lot larger, and a lot more confusing, than you might initially suspect. Heading in from the main entrance on the corniche it's possible to walk across the souk in under five minutes, following the main thoroughfare which bisects the area from north to south. This stretch – at its liveliest after dark – is where you'll find the souk's most touristy (and expensive) shops, lined with neatly restored old buildings under a fine wooden roof and thronged with an eclectic mix of robed Omanis and camera-toting coach parties.

The main north-south drag is divided by three diminutive covered squares. At the first of these, recognisable by its wooden-spoked ceiling which resembles a bicycle wheel, a side alleyway branches off to the left, leading to the closest of the souk's two rear exits. Continuing along the main drag you'll pass a second square (with stained-glassed *khanjars* on the ceiling) and then a third (with stained-glass coffeepots).

West to the Muttrah Gold Souk

The **Muttrah Gold Souk building**, which fronts the corniche a couple of hundred metres west of the main souk entrance, comprises a fascinating series of alleyways lined with shops stuffed with gold and silver jewellery.

To reach the Gold Souk from the square with the coffeepots on the ceiling, take the narrow alleyway on your right by the Muscat Pharmacy, then keep left as the alleyway splits at Ahmed Darwish Trading, and keep left again at the next fork, past Al Mina Perfumes.

Further alleyways head off in every direction, lined with increasingly run-of-the-mill shops and eventually shooting you out of the souk either back onto the corniche or into the tangle of narrow backstreets and tiny alleyways which honeycomb the area behind Sur al Lewatia (see page 51) and the *Naseem Hotel* – a fascinating, if disorientating, walk.

Muttrah Street

It's worth having a wander around the area immediately behind the souk and up along **Muttrah Street**. The whole neighbourhood is surprisingly untouristed, given its proximity to the souk, and remains one of Muscat's most traditional and interesting districts – a lively jumble of streets lined with little cafés and grocery stores and hemmed in by a lunar-looking horseshoe of red-rock hills, dotted with a string of watchtowers. It's possible to walk from here all the way up to Ruwi: carry on straight ahead past *Intaqiah* restaurant.

SHOPPING IN MUTTRAH SOUK

Pretty much anything and everything of Omani provenance can be found for sale in Muttrah Souk, including vast quantities of frankincense and *bukhoor*, herbs, *halwa*, spices and crushed rose petals and rose water from Jebel Akdhar (see page 98), alongside traditional perfumes, pashminas and Omani caps, robes and turbans. Many shops also sell old Bedu silver jewellery and *khanjars*, including museum-quality pieces which retail for hundreds of dollars, alongside pieces of "Omani silver" (anything from antique jewellery and Maria Theresa Thaler coins through to worthless modern junk) heaped up in tubs and sold by weight. The **Gold Souk** area is packed with shops selling gold and silver jewellery in a range of Arabian and European designs.

It's difficult to generalize about **prices**, although for more workaday items you're likely to pay significantly more here than in less touristed parts of the city. A tub of *bukhoor*, for example, which might be found in local supermarkets for less than a rial, usually goes for around 3–4 OR, while some rogue traders might try to sell you an equivalent for as much as 10 OR. It goes without saying that it's best to shop around, while virtually all shop-owners are amenable to **bargaining**.

1

Bait al Baranda

Mina Qaboos • Mon–Thurs, Sat & Sun 9am–1pm & 4–6pm • 1 OR

A five-minute walk west of Muttrah Souk lies **Bait al Baranda**, literally "The Veranda House" (the veranda actually being on the first floor). This fine old traditional Omani mansion was built in the late nineteenth century and was formerly home to the American Mission clinic, followed by the British Council. It now houses a museum devoted to the history of Muscat, although the main draw is the building itself, centred on an airy central courtyard-cum-atrium, supported on wooden columns.

The ground floor hosts temporary art exhibitions. Upstairs, well-presented displays cover the history of Muscat from the Stone Age settlements (c.10,000 BC) discovered at nearby Bowshar, Ras al Hamra and Al Wataya, through to modern times, with particularly good coverage of the colonial era and various maritime skirmishes between British and French forces, backed up with a smattering of old maps, navigational charts, prints and other documents.

The corniche

Bait al Baranda is a good place to begin exploring Muttrah's fine seafront **corniche**, which stretches from **Fish (As Samak) roundabout**, just below the Bait al Baranda, and continues for around 3km east along the Muttrah seafront and beyond towards Old Muscat. A paved pathway hugs the curve of the harbour and is dotted with shaded pavilions, where you can sit and watch the waves lapping the rocks below. It's all rather pleasant, and it's well worth making the effort to walk between Muttrah and Old Muscat rather than drive or get a taxi – the walk between Muttrah Souk and Bait al Zubair takes around 40 minutes.

The fish market

Right next to Fish roundabout stands Muttrah's swanky new **fish market**, opened in 2017, which combines traditional mercantile bustle with modern amenities for tourists and the local community – a neat microcosm of modern Oman. Several new facilities were under construction at the time of writing but should be open by the time you read this, and are projected to include offices, restaurants and cafés. Designed by Norwegian architecture firm Snøhetta, the building has quickly become a Muttrah landmark but exhibits an uncharacteristically contemporary aesthetic by Muscat standards, with its impressionistic, wave-like roof, apparently inspired by the flowing curves of Arabic calligraphy.

The market is busy every morning until around 9–9.30am with local fishermen and traders haggling over piles of freshly caught seafood.

Port Sultan Qaboos

Next door to the fish market stands **Port Sultan Qaboos**, one of Oman's largest ports, opened in the 1970s, whose gantries, silos and great piles of stacked-up containers dominate views from all around the harbour, and which also provides moorings for the vast cruise ships that dock here during their tours of the Gulf. Particularly impressive is the Sultan's luxury yacht, *Al Said*, one of the biggest and most powerful of its kind in the world.

The central corniche

East of Fish roundabout stretches the attractive central section of the corniche, an elegant curve of snow-white buildings hemmed in between the sea in front and the chain of craggy red-rock mountains which flank Muttrah to the rear. There's a particularly fine parade of traditional seafront **mansions** between Fish roundabout and the entrance to Muttrah Souk: venerable old whitewashed two- or three-storey structures with intricately carved windows and ornate wooden balconies.

Sur al Lewatia
Immediately past the mansions lies the large, blue-tiled Shia **Sur al Lewatia mosque**, next to which a small gateway leads into the walled Shia area of **Sur al Lewatia**; casual visitors are not welcomed here, and a local resident can usually be seen sitting at the gate turning back inquisitive tourists. A few further steps along the corniche brings you to **Muttrah Souk** (see page 47).

Muttrah Fort
High above the waters at the far eastern end of Muttrah harbour sits the modest **Muttrah Fort**. It's more facade than fort these days: a single high wall with a round tower at either end, balanced precariously atop a craggy ridge – it's particularly dramatic when illuminated after dark. You can climb the rough concrete steps up to the top for sweeping harbour views and a closer look at the crumbling fortifications.

Ghalya's Museum of Modern Art
Muttrah High St • Mon–Wed, Sat & Sun 4–11pm, Thurs & Fri 9am–midnight • 1 OR • ☎ 2471 1640, ⊛ ghalyasmuseum.com
Despite the name, **Ghalya's Museum of Modern Art** is more of an ethnographic museum, detailing the rapid pace of change in Omani society in the late twentieth century. You make your way through a maze-like warren of rooms, which have been lovingly appointed to resemble, say, a 1960s living room or 1970s kitchen; the attention to detail is exquisite, with plenty of authentic period items. There's also a small art gallery attached to the museum, housing modern works by Omani artists.

Al Riyam Park and around
Al Bahri Rd • Mon–Wed, Sat & Sun 4–11pm, Thurs & Fri 9am–midnight • Free
East of Muttrah Fort it's a fine, breezy walk along the attractively landscaped seafront, with assorted gardens, fountains and gold-domed pergolas en route, dotted with an extraordinary number of statues of fish. Ten minutes' walk brings you to a rocky headland poking out into the sea and topped with a pair of **watchtowers**; steps lead up to the watchtower nearest the sea (closed for building work at the time of writing).

On the opposite, land side of the road lies **Al Riyam Park**, a shady park with extensive children's play areas and a small funfair. The bizarre structure on the rocky outcrop overlooking the park is a supersized model of an **incense burner**, although it looks more like some kind of rococo spaceship. This iconic Muttrah landmark, formerly a viewpoint, is now closed to the public.

Kalbuh Park
Al Bahri Rd • Mon–Wed, Sat & Sun 4–11pm, Thurs & Fri 9am–midnight • Free
Beyond Al Riyam Park, you'll see the tower of Muscat Gate Museum (see page 54) poking up ahead. On your left is **Kalbuh Park**, a pleasant strip of palm-fringed grass in the lee of the cliffs, with a watchtower perched high above on a ridge at the far end and plenty of drinks kiosks. From here it's just another five minutes' walk on to Old Muscat.

Old Muscat
Clustered around a small bay at the far eastern end of the capital lies Muscat proper – often referred to as **Old Muscat** to distinguish it from the surrounding city to which it has now given its name. Despite serving as the home of the ruling sultan, Old Muscat retains the feel of a small and decidedly sleepy little town, quite distinct from the rest of the city, from which it's separated by a swathe of craggy mountains. That said, its status as the seat of governmental power is left in no doubt by the abundance of grand civic buildings which flank its tidy, palm-lined roads. In addition to the mountains, protection is afforded by the restored **city walls** which guard the landward approaches. Right up until the mid-twentieth

1

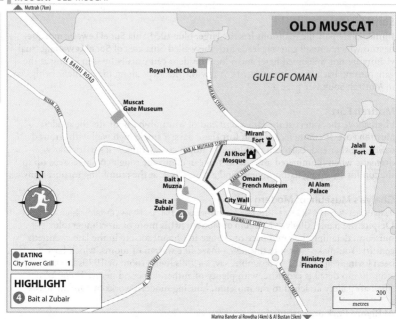

century the gates were closed three hours after dusk, and anyone venturing out onto the streets afterwards was obliged to carry a lantern with them – just one of the unusual local laws which also included a ban on smoking in the main streets and playing music in public.

Al Alam Palace

At the heart of Old Muscat is **Al Alam Palace** ("Flag Palace"), nominally the most important of the six royal residences of the ruling monarch, Sultan Qaboos, which are dotted around Muscat, Salalah and Sohar. Received local wisdom has it that these days the Sultan, who is thought to be in poor health, spends more time at his coastal residences. Built in 1972, the palace is Oman's most flamboyant example of contemporary Islamic design, with two long wings centred on a colourful, cube-like central building, its flat, overhanging roof supported by extravagantly flared blue and gold columns. The palace isn't open to the public, although you can get a good view of the facade from the iron gates at the front.

The palace complex is impressively stage-managed, approached via a long pedestrianized boulevard framed by two arcaded colonnades, with copious amounts of highly polished marble covering every available surface. On either side stretches a cluster of impressive **government buildings**: huge, snow-white edifices sporting crenellated rooftops, traditional wooden balconies and window shutters. Look right as you approach the palace and you'll also see a fine section of the original city **walls** snaking up the hillside, punctuated with three large watchtowers en route. Even by Muscat's standards, it's a serene spot, and it makes for a lovely stroll.

Mirani and Jalali forts

Immediately behind the palace lies Old Muscat's neat little harbour, flanked by a pair of rocky headlands on which sit the Portuguese forts of **Jalali** and **Mirani**. Like Muttrah Fort (see page 51), just down the road, these are quite unlike the traditional Omani

A MIRANI MARRIAGE

The virtual impregnability of **Mirani and Jalali Forts** has meant that those wishing to capture them have had to resort to some unconventional stratagems over the centuries. The most famous incident in the forts' colourful history – and the final *coup de grâce* to the Portuguese occupation in Oman (see page 233) – occurred in 1650. The Portuguese had already been driven from virtually every other part of the country and were now holed up in their Muscat strongholds. The commander of Muscat's Portuguese garrison, a certain Pereira, was besotted with a local Hindu girl, whom he wished to marry. Her father, Narutem, feigned obedience to Pereira's wishes and ordered preparations for a great **wedding celebration** at Mirani Fort, during which he proposed cleaning the water tanks, replacing the fort's contaminated gunpowder and restocking its provisions. At the moment when the fort had been stripped of all food and ammunition, Narutem gave the signal and Omani fighters attacked, eventually retaking the old city.

Ironically, less than a hundred years later the Omanis themselves would lose both Mirani and Jalali Forts to the Persian forces of Taqi Khan under perhaps even more embarrassing circumstances (see page 236).

forts you'll see elsewhere in the country: essentially just a sliver of wall plus flanking watchtowers squeezed into the tiniest of spaces on top of the rocks – seriously cramped, but virtually impregnable.

Mirani Fort stands directly behind the palace above the pretty blue-tiled Al Khor mosque. The fort wasn't open to the public at the time of research, but you can walk around the back of it for a good view of the rear of the palace and of the fort's major structure, a soaring five-storey tower, each storey slightly narrower than the one below, like an enormous telescope.

From here there are good views over to the similar **Jalali Fort**, which crowns the rocky ridge on the opposite side of the harbour, although it too lies out of bounds to the general public thanks to its location beyond the assorted government buildings next to the Al Alam Palace.

Old Muscat harbour

Past Mirani Fort you can walk a short distance along the water as far as the Royal Yacht Club, with pleasant views of the **harbour** itself, its two forts, and of further considerable fortification erected at the end of the headlands to either side of the entrance to the harbour. You'll also notice the names of assorted **ships** (HMS *Falmouth* and HMS *Perseus* prominent among them) on the cliffs opposite, painted onto the rockface by the crews of visiting vessels – like a kind of maritime visitors' book. According to legend, the young Horatio Nelson himself scrambled up the rocks here during a visit to Muscat in the 1770s, despite his fear of heights.

Bait al Zubair

Al Saidiya St • Mon–Thurs, Sat & Sun 9.30am–6pm • 2 OR • ⓦ baitalzubair.com

Of the various small museums scattered about Old Muscat, easily the most interesting is the **Bait al Zubair** (pronounced "Zubeer"), with wide-ranging exhibits relating to Omani culture, customs and craftsmanship, all collected over the years by the Zubair family, who still own and run the museum.

Bait al Bagh

The museum is spread across four separate buildings. The bulk of the collection is concentrated in the **Bait al Bagh** ("Garden House"), a large, white and not particularly exciting building dating from 1914, when it served as a former Zubair family residence.

1

Displays include antique *khanjars* and firearms, as well as assorted household articles ranging from coffeepots to kohl holders and a good selection of traditional clothing and jewellery (look out for the ingenious *salwa*, a style of necklace worn by unmarried girls – the main "jewel" is actually a recycled bicycle reflector). Exiting the rear door of the building brings you into the surrounding **gardens**, where you'll find a traditional *barasti majlis* and a *falaj*, along with an entertaining Omani-style model village.

Bait Dalaleel and Bait al Oud

Diagonally opposite the Bait al Bagh stands the **Bait Dalaleel**, where you'll find the museum's coffee shop along with a little cluster of rooms quaintly refurbished in traditional Omani style.

Opposite the Bait Dalaleel stands the **Bait al Oud** ("Grand House"), whose ground floor is used for temporary exhibitions of contemporary art. Upstairs, the **first floor** has interesting displays of old maps and wooden models of traditional dhows. Next door, a large room is stuffed full of an eye-catching array of household items from the original home of Sheikh al Zubair bin Ali. The **second floor** houses a random assortment of artefacts, including black and white photos from the late nineteenth century, early cameras, old Islamic coins and historic prints.

Bait al Nahdah and Gallery Sarah

The last of Bait al Zubair's main buildings is the **Bait al Nahdah**, a collection of Omani art designed as a celebration of the country's renaissance (al nahdah) since 1970 under Sultan Qaboos. Artwork from over fifty Omani artists is exhibited here across four floors; yet more can be found in the **Gallery Sarah**, also in the museum's grounds, which is dedicated to local contemporary art.

Omani French Museum

Qasr al Alam St • Mon–Thurs & Sun 8am–1.30pm, Sat 9am–1pm • 1 OR • ☎ 2473 6613

A couple of other museums and galleries lie scattered around the western end of Old Muscat. A five-minute walk around the block and through Al Kebir Gate brings you to the **Omani French Museum**, located in the former house of the French consul, Bait Faransa, a gift from Sultan Faisal bin Turki in 1896, during a period of rising French influence in the Sultanate (see page 240). The museum houses various mildly interesting historical exhibits covering the history of the French in Oman, although be advised that the place is aimed at French visitors, and there are only sporadic English translations to accompany the exhibits.

Muscat Gate Museum

Al Bahri Rd • Mon–Thurs & Sun 8am–2pm • Free • ☎ 9932 8754

At the western edge of the district, the **Muscat Gate Museum** occupies a single large room inside the restored gateway that spans the main road at the entrance to Old Muscat (staff tend to keep the heavy wooden doors shut at all times, making the place look closed even when it's open; push hard). The museum doesn't have much in the way of exhibits, bar a couple of small models, although the detailed boards covering the history of Oman and Muscat feature some interesting old pictures and black-and-white photographs, along with detailed explanations of the various historical periods involved.

National Museum of Oman

Al Saidiya St • Mon–Thurs, Sat & Sun 10am–5pm, Fri 2pm–6pm • 5 OR • ☎ 2208 1500

The Sultanate's shiny new flagship **National Museum of Oman**, opened in 2016, is a long-overdue replacement for the former national museum, housed in a single room

1

in a nondescript building in Ruwi. The new museum was worth the wait: a beautifully designed space that tells the story of Oman's cultural and natural history in microscopic detail and through enjoyable, informative exhibits. The quality throughout is superb, from the polished educational films to the fantastic exhibits. These include to-scale reconstructions of traditional plank-sewn boats, galleries dedicated to the history of the frankincense trade in Dhofar, and life-size replicas of the Bronze Age beehive tombs at Bat and Al Ayn. Also here is a modern art gallery, in a nod to the country's rapid and ongoing modernization. It's more expensive than most museums in Oman, but this should be on any itinerary, particularly if you are already in Old Muscat.

Ruwi

Some 3km inland from Muttrah lies **RUWI**, the de facto commercial heart of the city. It's relatively small beer compared to other urban areas around the Gulf, though if you've spent long in the quieter backwaters of Oman the district's blaze of neon,

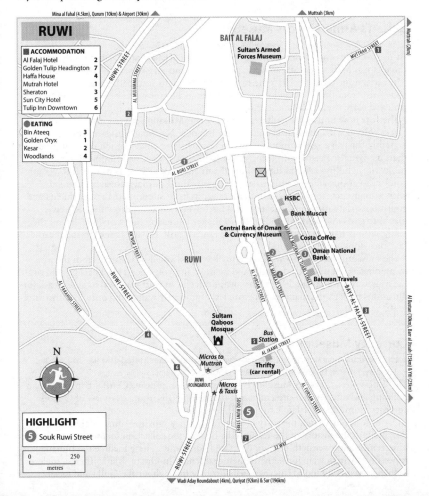

RUWI

ACCOMMODATION

Al Falaj Hotel	2
Golden Tulip Headington	7
Haffa House	4
Mutrah Hotel	1
Sheraton	3
Sun City Hotel	5
Tulip Inn Downtown	6

EATING

Bin Ateeq	3
Golden Oryx	1
Kesar	2
Woodlands	4

HIGHLIGHT

5 Souk Ruwi Street

0 — 250 metres

1

high(ish)-rise buildings and commercial hustle and bustle can come as something of a surprise, especially after dark, when the whole place has a real urban buzz – one of the few places in Muscat where you get a genuine sense of being in the capital city of a sizeable country. Ruwi is less attractive than many areas of the city, and there's not much in the way of tourist attractions, but it makes for a decent, central base, and is worth a visit if only to experience the rarefied atmosphere of the newly renovated *Sheraton*.

The southeastern side of the district is popularly known as Muscat's **Little India**, on account of the many Indian and Pakistani expats who live and work here, and parts of the area have a distinctly subcontinental flavour, with the city's best selection of cheap curry houses and dozens of colourful little shops, especially along the vibrant **Souq Ruwi Street**.

The western side of the district, often described as the **CBD** (Central Business District), is altogether more sedate, home to the rather grand headquarters of most of the country's leading banks, along with assorted travel agents, airline offices and a smattering of good restaurants.

Sultan's Armed Forces Museum

Al Mujamma St • Mon–Thurs & Sun 8am–1.30pm, Sat 9am–noon & 3–6pm • 1 OR • ☎ 2431 2648

At the northern end of Ruwi lies the old white **Bait al Falaj Fort**. Dating from 1845, the fort was built to guard a strategic point at the entrance to several valleys leading to Muscat and the coast. In 1915 the fort was site of a ferocious battle between rebellious tribesmen from the south and the forces of Sultan Taimur – a key encounter in Oman's troubled early twentieth-century history.

The fort now houses the **Sultan's Armed Forces Museum**, signed off Al Mujamma Street. Along with the Bait al Zubair and the new National Museum, this is arguably the most rewarding museum in the city, and covers much more ground than its name suggests, with informative exhibits on all sorts of non-military subjects, including Omani history, Ibadhism and navigation, as well as the country's various rulers and dynasties. The historical displays are accompanied with armaments from the relevant era, ranging from superb old Persian shields and enormous Arabian swords through to Martini-Henry rifles, Browning & Lewis machine guns and assorted mortars and rocket launchers. Upstairs, you'll find the really serious hardware including an anti-aircraft gun, missile launcher and a rather fearsome-looking cluster bomb.

The museum sits within a working army base, and you'll be escorted from the gate by an official; they are very friendly and helpful, and you'll get a brief background on the museum before being left to your own devices. On your way out, be sure to ask for directions back to the main road, or you risk innocently wandering onto the army base itself.

Currency Museum

Central Bank of Oman, Markaz Muttrah al Tijari Street • Mon–Thurs & Sun 9am–1pm; access is by guided tour only – go to reception; you'll need to provide photo ID, preferably a passport • 250bz • ☎ 2477 7777, ⓦ cbo-oman.org/coin_museum

The little-visited **Currency Museum** is located in the impressive Central Bank of Oman building and offers a well-presented and surprisingly absorbing overview of Omani currency from the pre-Islamic times to the present.

Dry as it might sound, the story of Omani currency provides some interesting insights into the history of the region. The bulk of the collection focuses on nineteenth- and twentieth-century coins and banknotes. These include the Indian rupee notes which were formerly used as legal tender in Oman, Maria Theresa thalers (which served as a kind of international currency throughout the Gulf) and locally

BLACK GOLD

East of Qurum Heights, the industrial district of **Mina al Fahal** is home to one of the country's major oil refineries, and the centre of operations for the government-owned **PDO** (Petroleum Development Oman; ⓦ pdo.co.om). If you want to find out more about the black gold, head for the **Oil & Gas Exhibition Centre** (Mon–Thurs & Sun 3am–3pm; free), run by PDO, which has a good array of educational exhibits on oil exploration and production, many of which are interactive, giving you the chance to try your hand at prospecting for oil, loading a tanker or launching an "intelligent pig".

produced *baiza* coins used for small sums – meaning that three different currencies were in simultaneous circulation right up until 1970, when Oman issued its first banknotes.

Other exhibits include a fine selection of pre-Islamic coins, stamped with some engaging portraits of the various rulers under whose jurisdiction they were issued. Pride of place goes to the first ever Islamic coin, one of only two in the world, minted in 700 AD during the caliphate of Ummayad ruler Bin Marwan.

Qurum

The suburb of **QURUM** (also spelled Qurm) is, from a tourist point of view at least, the heart of modern Muscat, and the place where you'll find the densest concentration of shops, upmarket hotels and good places to eat, as well as the city's best public beach, Shatti al Qurum. The centre of the suburb is marked by Qurum's lively **commercial district**, close to the junction of Sultan Qaboos Street and the Muscat Expressway, which is home to a cluster of lowbrow restaurants and small-scale malls dotted with some interesting shops. North of here lies the very upmarket suburb of **QURUM HEIGHTS**, with tree-lined streets and discreet, low-rise white villas surrounded by bougainvillea-filled gardens.

Shatti al Qurum and around

West of Qurum Heights stretches the attractive **Shatti al Qurum** (Qurum Beach), a fine swathe of golden sand which extends west to the neighbouring suburb of **Hayy as Saruj** and beyond, with views of the rocky **Fahal Island** (also known as Shark Island, one of the city's leading dive sites) offshore. If you want to sunbathe, you're better off sticking to the areas of beach around the back of the *InterContinental* or *Grand Hyatt* hotels, where the number of other sun-worshipping Westerners on the sands guarantees relative anonymity and hassle-free relaxation; elsewhere on the beach, female visitors may attract unwanted attention.

The eastern end of the beach is bounded by a small rocky outcrop, topped by the distinctive, cruiseliner-shaped *Crowne Plaza* hotel, while south of the beach stretches the low, green expanse of the **Qurum Nature Reserve**, protecting a rare surviving stretch of coastal mangrove forest (not open to the public).

The Jawaharat A'Shatti Complex and around

From below the *Crowne Plaza*, a pleasantly breezy road heads along the open seafront for around 1km to reach the cluster of hotels and restaurants centred around the *InterContinental* hotel. The main attraction here is the attractive **Jawaharat A'Shatti Complex**, a poky and old-fashioned little mall on the inside, although its exterior terrace, and that of the **Oasis by the Sea** restaurant complex opposite, has been colonized by a sociable string of restaurants, including the popular *D'Arcy's Kitchen* (see page 71).

The area around the InterCon, as it is known to all, is currently the subject of extensive redevelopment, with a new W Hotel set to shake up Muscat's luxury hotel scene and attract a younger, hipper crowd to Shatti al Qurum.

Bait Muzna

Way 2818 • Mon–Thurs, Sat & Sun 9.30am–7pm • ⓦ baitmuznagallery.com

The **Bait Muzna** art gallery displays original or limited edition artworks in a wide range of styles, usually either by local artists or with an Omani theme, with prices ranging from around 50 OR up into the thousands. Exhibitions rotate regularly and showcase a wide variety of genres and styles, from Arabic calligraphy to emerging artists from Dhofar. Workshops, seminars and photography courses are also on offer.

The Children's Museum

Way 2601, off Sultan Qaboos St • Mon–Thurs & Sun 8am–1.30pm, Sat 9am–1pm • 500bz • ☎ 2460 5368

On the south side of Qurum Nature Reserve next to Sultan Qaboos Street is the **Children's Museum**, located in the larger of two distinctive dome-shaped buildings. Inside you'll find an array of enjoyable interactive exhibits on sight, sound, the body and science – a guaranteed hit with kids, and fun for grown-ups too.

Qurum Natural Park

Al Qurum St • Mon–Thurs & Sun 9am–11pm, Sat 9am–midnight • Free

Adjacent to the Children's Museum is **Qurum Natural Park**, the biggest public park in the whole of Oman: some four hundred acres of manicured lawns, neat, paved pathways and bubbling fountains. It makes a serene backdrop for an afternoon's walk, and there are ample play areas for kids.

Grand Hyatt

Off As Sarooj St • ☎ 2464 1234, ⓦ muscat.grand.hyatt.com

West past the Jawaharat A'Shatti Complex, an attractive ten-minute stroll along the pedestrianized seafront walkway brings you to the rear of the **Grand Hyatt**, one of Muscat's most flamboyant hotels. Owned by a Yemeni sheikh, the rather peculiar exterior looks like the bastard lovechild of an Omani fort and a French château. It's worth going inside, though, for a look at the hotel's fabulous interior. This is pure Orientalist chintz at its most extravagant, with soaring gold and cream pillars, a great tumbling staircase, 25m-high stained-glass windows, plus assorted palm trees and Bedu tents. The whole place is best appreciated over a superior afternoon tea at the *Sirj Tea Lounge* in the shadow of the impressive bronze statue of an Arabian falconer on horseback, who glares out across the foyer – the whole statue actually rotates, imperceptibly, every hour, which explains why it never seems to be quite where you remembered it.

Khuwair

Heading west from Shatti al Qurum, the next suburb you reach is **KHUWAIR**, home to an impressive string of **government ministries** – large, white buildings with traditional architectural decorative touches – which line the northern side of Sultan Qaboos Street.

Natural History Museum

18th November St • Mon–Thurs & Sun 8am–1.30pm, Sat 9am–1pm • 500bz

In the same complex as the Ministry of Heritage and Culture, right next to the main highway, lies the modest **Natural History Museum**. This is worth a visit if you're

1

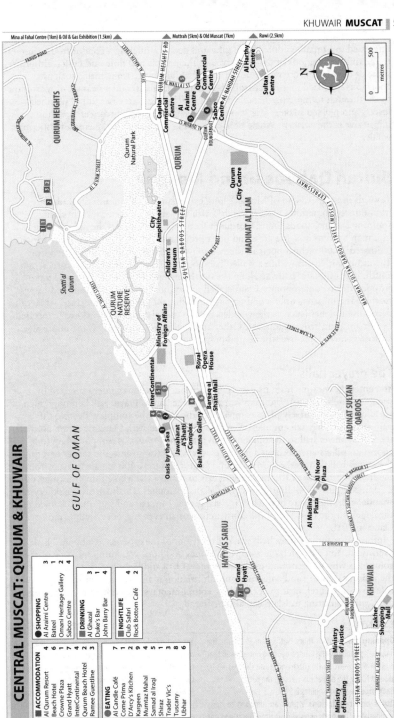

Mina al Fahal Centre (1km) & Oil & Gas Exhibition (1.5km) ▲   ▲ Muttrah (5km) & Old Muscat (7km)   ▲ Ruwi (2.5km)

CENTRAL MUSCAT: QURUM & KHUWAIR

TAHUD ROAD

QURUM HEIGHTS

QURUM
Natural Park

Shatti al
Qurum

GULF OF OMAN

QURUM
NATURE
RESERVE

QURUM

MADINAT AL ILAM

QURUM HEIGHTS RD

AL WAILLAI ST.

Capital
Commercial
Centre

Al
Araimi
Centre

Qurum
Commercial
Centre

Sabco
Centre

Al Harthy
Centre

Sultan
Centre

Qurum
City Centre

City
Amphitheatre

Children's
Museum

Ministry of
Foreign Affairs

Royal
Opera
House

Bareeq al
Shatti Mall

InterContinental

Oasis by the Sea

Jawaharat
A'Shatti
Complex

Bait Muzna Gallery

MADINAT SULTAN
QABOOS

HAYY AS SARUJ

Al Madina
Plaza

Al Noor
Plaza

AL MUNTAZAH ST

Grand
Hyatt

KHUWAIR

Zakher
Shopping
Mall

Ministry
of Justice

Ministry
of Housing

■ ACCOMMODATION
Al Qurum Resort	4
Beach Hotel	6
Crowne Plaza	1
Grand Hyatt	7
InterContinental	2
Qurum Beach Hotel	4
Ramee Guestline	3

● EATING
Al Candle Café	7
Come Prima	1
D'Arcy's Kitchen	2
Kargeen	9
Mumtaz Mahal	4
Samad al Iraqi	5
Shiraz	1
Trader Vic's	3
Tuscany	8
Ubhar	6

● SHOPPING
Al Araimi Centre	3
Bateel	1
Omani Heritage Gallery	2
Sabco Centre	4

● DRINKING
Al Ghazal	3
Duke's Bar	1
John Barry Bar	4

● NIGHTLIFE
Club Safari	4
Rock Bottom Café	2

Natural History Museum (1.5km), Sultan Qaboos Grand Mosque (7km) & Airport (18km) ▼

0 — 500 metres
N

1

interested in Omani wildlife, geography and geology, offering a good introduction to the different regions of the country, and their associated flora and fauna, although some of the displays are rather out of date. Exhibits range from curios such as enormous fossilized marine gastropods (prehistoric snails) and a neat set of mastodon teeth, through to more predictable offerings including glass cases full of petrified insects and pickled snakes, plus various stuffed animals and birds. Perhaps most impressive is the adjacent **Whale Hall**, containing the complete skeleton of a sperm whale.

Sultan Qaboos Grand Mosque

Towards the western end of Muscat's long urban sprawl, the suburb of **Ghubrah** (pronounced something like "*Hob*-rah", with throaty *h*) is where you'll find the stunning **Sultan Qaboos Grand Mosque**. Opened in 2001, this is the only mosque in Oman open to non-Muslims and one of the largest in the Gulf, with room for an estimated 20,000 worshippers in the two prayer halls and surrounding courtyard. The mosque itself sits within a walled compound with a minaret at each corner, plus a fifth, larger minaret halfway along the northern wall. The overall style is a kind of stripped-down contemporary Islamic, clad in vast quantities of white and red-brown marble. The minarets offer a nod towards traditional Egyptian architecture, while other decorative touches (such as the wooden ceilings and elaborate tilework) were inspired by Omani and Persian traditions. Other architectural details, such as the impressive latticed golden dome over the central prayer hall, are entirely original.

The prayer halls

You **enter** the mosque from its eastern end, through spacious gardens bisected by water channels. The first building you reach is the **Ladies' Prayer Hall** (although men are allowed in), relatively plain compared to the rest of the complex. Beyond this a pair of distinctively tall and narrow arches, embellished with Qur'anic script, connect the ladies' prayer hall to the opulent **main prayer hall** (*musalla*), supported on four enormous pillars and decorated in whites, greys and sea-greens. The **carpet** covering the prayer hall floor is the world's second largest and took 400 female weavers from the Iranian province of Khorasan four years to make – the whole thing measures 60 x 70m, contains 1.7 million knots and weighs 21 tonnes. The huge Swarovski crystal **chandelier** in the centre of the hall is a staggering 14m tall and was often claimed to be the largest in the world until the construction of an even bigger crystalline monster in Qatar in 2010.

Informative audio guides help you get more out of the experience, but are a little overpriced. You may prefer to save your money and hope you bump into one of the volunteers who hang around in the main prayer hall and happily chat to tourists about the mosque's history and construction. Information is also available at the Islamic Information Center, near the exit, where complimentary tea, coffee and a range of free publications relating to Islam can also be found.

ESSENTIALS
SULTAN QABOOS MOSQUE

Opening times Mon–Thurs, Sat & Sun 8–11am. The mosque's popularity and limited opening hours mean that it often gets overrun with coach and cruise ship parties by around 10am: the earlier you can visit the better.
Entrance Free; audio guides 2.5 OR.
Rules and regulations Visitors are required to dress appropriately: no shorts or uncovered arms. The attendants

are particularly strict about women's attire: women are required to cover their heads, and even long skirts will not suffice if they don't cover the ankles; a scarf covering the arms isn't enough, so wear something long-sleeved. *Hijabs* and *abayas* can be rented from 2 OR. Shoes must be removed before entering either prayer hall. Under-10s are not allowed into the main prayer hall.

South of the centre

1

The city **south of old Muscat** is much less developed than that to the north, with attractively landscaped roads winding through largely unspoilt mountains and a string of self-contained fishing villages shoehorned into the rocky little bays which dot the coast. There are no must-see sights here, although you might be tempted to drop into the lavish **Al Bustan Palace hotel** for afternoon tea, or to spend an evening over drinks and a meal at the vast **Shangri-La Barr al Jissah Resort**, which boasts some of the city's finest restaurants and bars.

Marina Bandar al Rowdha

A kilometre or so south of Old Muscat lies the village of Sidab, arranged around a neat little horseshoe harbour, and the contiguous village of Haramil. A further kilometre south of Haramil is the little harbour, usually packed with lines of posh yachts moored up in the **Marina Bandar al Rowdha**, home to the *Blue Marlin* restaurant (see page 73) and the departure point for all manner of boat trips.

Aquatic Exhibition of Marine Living Species

Marine Science & Fisheries Centre • Mon–Thurs & Sun 8am–2.30pm, Fri 4–6pm • Free • Follow the road down into the marina (where there's ample parking) – the aquarium is on your right at the bottom of the hill

The underwhelming **Aquatic Exhibition of Marine Living Species** aquarium boasts a few tanks of local marine life such as parrotfish, wrasse, surgeonfish, butterfly fish, triggerfish and pop-eyed mudcrabs, plus a few turtles in depressingly small tanks. Hours are erratic, and there's no guarantee anyone will be around to let you in. By the time you read this, it will have been spectacularly eclipsed by the new Oman Aquarium in Seeb's Palm Mall, which is set to be the largest aquarium in the Middle East.

The Sohar dhow

A kilometre south of the marina, now somewhat ignominiously beached in the middle of the roundabout at the entrance to the *Al Bustan Palace* hotel, lies a famous wooden dhow, the **Sohar**. The dhow was constructed in 1979–80 using traditional Arabian boat-building techniques (including the unusual method of "stitched" construction: literally sewing planks together using coconut twine) and then sailed to China by a team led by redoubtable British adventurer Tim Severin – a fascinating adventure described in his *The Sindbad Voyage*.

Al Bustan Palace

Al Bustan St, Al Bustan • ☎ 2479 9666, ⓦ albustanpalace.com

Follow the driveway from the *Sohar* dhow down to **Al Bustan Palace** itself. Opened in 1985, this is the oldest of Muscat's super-deluxe hotels and was for many years the jewel in the crown of the fledgling Omani tourism industry, regularly cited as the most opulent and visually spectacular hotel in the Gulf. More recent hotel openings in neighbouring Dubai and Abu Dhabi, not to mention increasing competition within Muscat itself, have rather eroded the hotel's unique appeal, while the quirky exterior – like a kind of hexagonal Arabian spaceship – is beginning to look decidedly passé. At the time of writing, however, extensive interior renovations were underway, due to be completed by September 2018. The new-look hotel will undoubtedly be as palatial as ever, with the new design drawing on traditional Omani culture.

1

DIVING, SNORKELLING AND BOAT TRIPS IN MUSCAT

There are a surprising number of **diving operators** in Muscat offering a range of trips and PADI courses. The closest **dive sites** are just south of the city along the coast at **Bandar Jissah** and **Bandar Khayran** (which is also where you'll find the popular *Al Munassir* wreck) and, slightly further afield, at **Fahal Island** (40min–1hr by boat). *Euro Divers* and *SeaOman* also do trips out to the **Daymaniyat Islands** (see page 128), about a two- to three-hour trip by boat each way. As throughout Oman, nutrient-rich waters attract a fine array of marine life, ranging from tiny nudibranchs to whale sharks. You stand a better chance of seeing larger sea life at the Daymaniyats and Fahal, since they're further offshore. The shop at *Extra Divers* at the *Shangri-La* stocks a wide range of diving gear.

All diving operators also run **snorkelling** trips to explore the coral gardens at Bandar Jissah, Bandar Khayran and Fahal Island, and most (plus a couple of other operators) also run **boat trips** around the coast. These include **dolphin-spotting boat trips** – you should have a better than ninety percent chance of seeing dolphins (mainly spinner, sometimes bottlenose); whale sharks and humpback whales are also very occasionally sighted. Some operators also offer **sunset cruises**, leaving at around 4.30pm and lasting a couple of hours.

DIVE OPERATORS

Euro Divers Capital Area Yacht Centre, Haramil (just north of Marina Bandar al Rowdha) ☎ 9819 4444, ⓦ euro-divers.com. Branch of a Swiss company, offering diving, snorkelling and dolphin-watching.

Extra Divers Qantab Bandar al Jissah ☎ 2485 3000, ⓦ extradivers.info. Part of the worldwide *Extra Divers* network, this is one of the city's leading dive centres, and also runs snorkelling and dolphin-watching trips. Find it in the *Shangri-La* resort complex.

SeaOman The Wave ☎ 2418 1400, ⓦ seaoman. com. Part of the Oman Sail stable of sailing schools, the professionally run *SeaOman* specialises in dive trips to the Daymaniyat Islands, which are easily accessible from its main outlet at The Wave development. There's another office at the *Millennium Resort Musannah*, up the coast from Muscat (see page 129).

BOAT TOUR OPERATORS

Coral Ocean Tours Bandar al Rowdha ☎ 9411 0088, ⓦ coraloceantours.com. This slick tour operator offers a variety of ways to experience Muscat's photogenic coastline, from dolphin-watching trips on one of their two luxury yachts to a sunset cruise on a traditional wooden *dhow*.

Sidab Sea Tours Bandar al Rowdha ☎ 9965 5783, ⓦ sidabseatours.com. With a similar programme of activities to *Coral Ocean Tours*, offering snorkelling, dolphin-watching tours and dhow cruises. Trips to the secluded inlet of Bandar Khayran are also available.

Bandar Jissah

Some 5km down the coast from the *Al Bustan Palace* lies the beautiful bay of **Bandar Jissah**, dotted with a couple of rocky islands and ringed with gently shelving cliffs and headlands, one of them hollowed through with a modest **sea arch** which tour boats usually take the opportunity to duck under. The beach here was formerly an unspoilt **turtle-nesting site** before the construction right on top of it of the massive *Shangri-La Barr al Jissah Resort* complex. Green and hawksbill turtles can still be seen nesting on the beach from November to March, and the resort employs a dedicated "turtle ranger" to look after them. Sadly, the beach is only accessible to hotel guests and diners, and the way in which one of Muscat's most compelling natural spectacles has effectively been appropriated by the resort and turned into an in-house attraction leaves a slightly sour taste in the mouth.

There is, however, rewarding diving and snorkelling here, plus accommodation and good food either at the *Shangri-La* or at the stylish *Muscat Hills Resort* nearby – the latter's eye-watering entry fee (10 OR), though, means it's only really worth it if you're diving.

Yiti

Some 20km from Muscat, at the end of the road past the Oman Dive Centre and *Shangri-La* resort, the tranquil little fishing village of **YITI** (or Yitti) makes a good

target for a picnic, with a spacious beach dotted with fishing boats and wading birds, and attractive views along the rocky coast. The beach is easy to spot from the road thanks to a huge, striking rock which rises dramatically from the firm sand, somewhat resembling a giant, petrified cockerel's comb. The whole place feels remarkably rural and traditional given its proximity to Muscat, although the beach is a popular landing spot for thrill-seeking paramotor pilots, which makes for an entertaining distraction but ruins the peaceful atmosphere somewhat. Yiti's backwater feel may truly become a thing of the past, though, if the proposed **Yenkit** project goes ahead. A US$2 billion "luxury integrated tourist resort facility" featuring five-star hotels and a golf resort was proposed way back in 2007, before economic difficulties meant that the scheme was shelved. At the time of writing, the royal-backed **Oman Investment Fund** was canvassing the public for opinions on the area's future direction, suggesting that the development may be back on in some capacity.

Bandar Khayran and As Sifah

Some 3.5km inland from Yiti, a road heads off left, winding through the mountains for 9km to reach the village of **BANDAR AL KHAYRAN** at the end of a beautiful rocky sea inlet fringed with sandflats and mangroves. This beautiful area of coastline provides a convenient, if less spectacular, alternative to the *khors* of Musandam (see page 155), for those who are basing themselves primarily in the Muscat area.

Beyond here, it's a further 14km to **AS SIFAH**, set around a bay hemmed in by low, rocky headlands and lined with another generous stretch of sand. The northern end of the beach is particularly popular. If you have 4WD you can continue 5km south along the graded coastal track to reach a further cluster of much quieter coves – a perfect spot for some wild camping.

Wadi Mayh

A twenty-minute drive south of Ruwi off the main road to Quriyat (see page 173) lies the idyllic **Wadi Mayh** – a wonderful stretch of untamed countryside in the shadow of the Eastern Hajar, offering a beguiling taste of rural Oman within an easy afternoon's drive of the capital. The wadi offers a perfect snapshot of traditional Arabia in miniature, its broad, gravel-strewn river bed interspersed with rock pools and flanked by craggy limestone cliffs, while an extended *falaj* connects the sand-coloured villages and date plantations which dot the valley – all remarkably unspoilt given its proximity to Muscat.

To **reach the wadi**, head south along the road to Quriyat from Wadi Aday roundabout in Ruwi. Around 23km south of Ruwi, a surfaced road heads off left into the wadi. The first half of the road (around 10km) is tarmacked, after which a graded track continues, eventually joining up with the road to Yiti.

ARRIVAL AND DEPARTURE   **MUSCAT**

BY AIR

Muscat International Airport (⊕ omanairports.co.om), still sometimes referred to by its old name of Seeb International Airport, lies on the western edge of the city, around 30km from Muttrah and Ruwi, and around 15km from the modern city-centre suburbs including Khuwair and Qurum. It's usually around a thirty-minute drive to Muttrah and Ruwi, or fifteen to twenty minutes to Khuwair or Qurum, although the trip can take significantly longer depending on traffic. The airport is also about a twenty-minute drive from Seeb (see page 115) to the west.

Airport facilities There are a few ATMs, plus Omantel, Ooredoo and Friendi kiosks at the airport if you want to pick up a local SIM card (see page 40), and a string of car-rental agents.

Taxis After years of price hikes which had put Muscat's airport taxis among the most expensive in the Gulf, a metered airport taxi was introduced in January 2018 courtesy of Mwasalat, a government-operated company that also run long-distance buses. Journeys start at 1.9 OR, plus a further 300bz/km from 6am–10pm, Mon–Thurs, Sat & Sun; and start at 2.3 OR, with a further 350bz/km, at all other times, including Fridays. A taxi should cost roughly 11 OR to Muttrah, 9 OR to Qurum, 14 OR to the *Al Bustan Palace*, and 16 OR to the *Shangri-La Barr al Jissah Resort*.

Micros Micros running between Seeb and Ruwi roundabout run directly past the airport, though the lack of space can be a problem with luggage. Unless you're absolutely skint, it's best to catch a taxi.

BY BUS

The main Mwasalat intercity bus station is in Azaiba (see map, p.46). For local buses, head to the Mwasalat station in Ruwi.

Destinations Buraimi (3 daily; 4hr 30min); Dubai via Sohar (3 daily; 6hr 30min); Duqum (1 daily; 7hr 30min); Jalan Bani Bu Ali (1 daily; 5hr); Jibal (1 daily; 5hr); Marmul (2 daily; 10hr 30min); Salalah (3 daily; 13hr); Sur (3 daily; 5hr); Yanqul (2 daily; 5hr).

BY MICRO AND SHARED TAXI

Various intercity micro services run to and from Muscat. These mainly depart from Rusayl roundabout, close to the airport at the junction of the Nizwa and Sohar highways, and reachable by micro from Ruwi roundabout. A steady stream of micros depart from Rusayl inland to Nizwa, north to Sohar, and other destinations en route, usually costing just a few rials. You may also find **shared taxis** here running along the same routes at slightly higher prices. Note that there's very little space inside a micro – something of a challenge when you're travelling with even a modest amount of luggage.

BY BOAT

The only other way of leaving Muscat is by taking the ferry service to Shinas or Musandam (see page 146).

INFORMATION

Tourist information There's no official source of tourist information in Muscat beyond a small tourist information kiosk at the airport. Your best bet is to talk to one of the local tour operators. Useful offices include Zahara, on Way 3305 in the Qurum 18 district, and Mark Tours on Al Iskan St in Ruwi and at the *Grand Hyatt* hotel.

Listings For listings, you're best off consulting local blogs like ⓦ muscatmutterings.com (which also has useful links to other local blogs). Information about theatre and opera

programmes, festivals and other cultural happenings can be found at the Oman Ministry of Tourism portal at ⓦ omantourism.gov.om. Comprehensive listings can be hard to come by, though; it's best to get in touch with specific venues.

Maps The best maps of the city are published by Dubai-based Explorer, either the handy, pocket-sized *Muscat Mini Map* (1.9 OR) or the excellent full-size *Explorer Muscat Map* (4.7 OR), which shows every street in the city.

GETTING AROUND

Greater Muscat is extremely spread out, and although parts of the city lend themselves to casual wandering, to explore the city in its entirety you'll need transport. Unfortunately, like virtually everywhere else in the Gulf, Muscat is determinedly car-centric, and public transport options are somewhat limited.

TAXIS

The most convenient way of getting around is to hop in one of the city's plentiful taxis, painted a distinctive orange and white. These can be found virtually everywhere, at any time of the day and night – indeed, it's difficult to walk anywhere in the city without being persistently honked at by passing drivers for custom. At the time of writing, orange-and-white airport taxis had been replaced with metered red-and-white ones from the state-run Mwsalam company, and plans were underfoot for Mwsalam to gradually take over all operations. This could take a while, but the metered fares (see below) will make taking a taxi a more predictable affair.

Fares All orange-and-white taxis are unmetered, meaning that you'll have to haggle over the fare before you set off – usually a frustrating business. Muscat's taxi drivers are an engagingly rogue-ish bunch: virtually all of them speak some kind of English, and they're often entertaining company to boot, although few are averse to making an extra rial or two out of visiting tourists. As a rough rule of

thumb, a taxi from Muttrah to Ruwi or Old Muscat should cost 1.5 OR, to Qurum 3 OR, and to the airport 10 OR (although note that all these prices double after midnight). In practice, as a foreigner, you'll probably end up paying anything from a third to twice as much, depending on the length of your journey and your bargaining powers. Trying to agree a reasonable fare outside the city's more upmarket hotels is a particularly frustrating experience. The metered fares for the Mwasalat taxis are as follows: journeys start at 1.9 OR, plus a further 300bz/km from 6am–10pm, Sat–Thurs; and start at 2.3 OR, with a further 350bz/km, at all other times, including Fridays. If you begin your journey at a shopping mall, which serve as hubs for taxis, the starting rates for journeys drop to 1 OR and 1.3 OR, respectively.

SHARED TAXIS

An alternative to hiring your own cab is to grab a seat in a shared taxi – roughly double the price of a seat in a microbus but significantly cheaper than hiring the whole vehicle yourself. Unfortunately, finding a shared taxi is

1

MUSCAT'S SPAS

There are several superb, international-standard **spas** in town. The Spa at *The Chedi* (see page 68) specializes in elaborate oriental-style treatments including body polishes, bathing ceremonies, beauty rituals and massages drawing on a range of Indian, Balinese, Thai and Arabian techniques. Chi – The Spa at the *Shangri-La Barr al Jissah Resort* (see p.00) has a similar Asian slant, along with locally inspired rituals including rasul, hammam, frankincense and rose body-wrap treatments. Neither comes cheap, however, with treatments at both places starting at around 45–50 OR/hr. The Six Senses Spa at the *Al Bustan Palace* offers a similar range of therapies but with a more traditionally Arabian approach, and slightly cheaper, with treatments starting at around 40 OR.

something of a challenge. The system operates on an entirely ad hoc basis, although if you see a semi-occupied taxi with a seat or two spare it's worth asking – just be aware that the taxi driver, seeing an interested foreigner, may evict the people already in the cab and try to get you to stump up the entire (inflated) fare yourself.

MICROBUSES

The only reliably cheap way of getting around Muscat is to avail yourself of the citywide network of microbuses – essentially white minivans, distinguished by an orange sign above the windscreen plus rosette on the side. These offer a generally swift and inexpensive way of getting around the city, assuming you don't mind being sardined into tiny seats amid a throng of workers and students.

Timings Micros are easiest to come by during the early morning and after dark. From midday through to late afternoon services are more sporadic.

Fares Fares are a bargain: at the time of writing it cost 200bz to go between Ruwi, Muttrah and Old Muscat, rising to around 500bz for longer rides across the city. Pay the driver as you leave the vehicle.

From Ruwi The hub of the micro system is Ruwi roundabout, from where microbuses depart to destinations across the city. Drivers stand on the pavement calling out their destinations; ask around until you find what you want, and note that micros to Muttrah depart from the opposite side of the roundabout.

From Muttrah From Muttrah, micros to Ruwi depart from Fish roundabout and, less regularly, for Old Muscat from the opposite side of the road.

From other parts of the city Elsewhere in the city the easiest way to pick up a micro is to head for one of the

major roundabouts along Sultan Qaboos Street; micros generally stop on the slip roads underneath roundabout flyovers. Make sure you're on the right side of the highway for the direction you want to travel in and, if in doubt, follow any likely-looking crowd of Indian or Pakistani workers, who can usually be found looking for transport until late at night.

SELF-DRIVING

Given the vagaries of public transport in Muscat, renting a car is an appealing option, assuming you're going to be moving around the city a fair bit – if not, it may well be easier and no more expensive to catch taxis. A couple of caveats apply, however. The first is the general standard of driving in the city, which is (by Omani standards) unusually aggressive, and occasionally downright homicidal, especially after dark, when Muscat's resident kamikaze petrolheads take to the streets. The second is the baffling complexity of the city's road systems and the lack of useful signage, meaning you're likely to spend considerable amounts of time going round and round like a laboratory hamster in some infernal road-traffic experiment. Equip yourself with a good map (such as Explorer's *Muscat Map*) and expect to get lost on a fairly regular basis.

Car rental The usual international car rental chains are at the airport; reserve in advance, especially for larger vehicles. Some hotels in the city have car rental desks, including the *Radisson Blu* (Thrifty), the *Crowne Plaza* (Dollar) and the *Grand Hyatt* (Mark). Thrifty also has a branch opposite the Ruwi bus station. Local operators have offices in Ruwi along Al Nahdah St; prices are usually cheaper, although vehicles may not be as modern or as reliable.

ACCOMMODATION

Muscat is the only place in Oman where you're even slightly spoilt for choice when it comes to accommodation, while the level of competition here helps keep **prices** a bit more honest than in other parts of the country. **Muttrah** is the place for budget accommodation – with the added attraction of placing you right at the heart of Muscat's most absorbing area. Accommodation in **Ruwi** is mainly aimed at business travellers, with a couple of budget options, with one notable exception: the long-awaited, re-opened *Sheraton*. There are a handful of mid-range places in the attractive suburb of **Qurum Heights**, along with a mix of mid- and top-end places further west around **Shatti al Qurum** and the suburbs of **Hayy as Saruj** and **Ghubrah**, plus a few mid-range, business-oriented options in nearby **Khuwair**. The area around

Ghubrah and **Azaiba** is also home to some low-key but appealing guesthouses. Sadly, many of the guesthouses have been closed down by the government, who are looking towards yet more five-star-plus resorts as the future of Omani tourism. The peaceful area **south of the city** is home to a few further hotels, including the opulent *Al Bustan Palace* and the vast *Shangri-La Barr al Jissah Resort*.

MUTTRAH

Marina Hotel Muttrah corniche ☎2471 3100; map p.48. This harbourside hotel offers decent value, with neat, if slightly dated, rooms and friendly service. Doubles also boast superb harbour views, though the twins and singles don't. The hotel is also home to the popular *Al Boom* restaurant (see page 70) and a licensed bar, often soundtracked by a truly awful live band. Room rates include breakfast. <u>30 OR</u>

Mutrah Hotel Muttrah High St ☎2479 8401, ⓦmutrahotel.com; map p.55. Oman's oldest hotel, around 20 minutes' walk inland from the corniche towards Ruwi, doesn't benefit from harbour views but is a decent choice. It offers perfectly comfortable and spacious (if slightly dingy) rooms, with purple walls and tiled floors, and a passable restaurant serving the usual mix of Arabian and subcontinental dishes. There's also a licensed bar, complete with pool tables, which is a convivial place to pass an evening. <u>30 OR</u>

★ **Naseem Hotel** Muttrah corniche ☎2471 2418, ⓔnaseemhotel@gmail.com; map p.48. A decent, if slightly overpriced, option, right in the thick of things and virtually within spitting distance of Muttrah Souk. Rooms (some with wonderful harbour views through big windows) are basic, but well maintained, while consistently friendly and professional service is another major bonus. Breakfast is available in the small in-house restaurant, but no other meals. <u>40 OR</u>

Riyam Hotel Way 2625 ☎9445 5068, ⓔinfo@riyamhotel.com; map p.46. This large, traditional hotel sits a little further from the action, but it's cheap, and Muttrah's souk and corniche remain in walking distance. It's not exactly tasteful – there's gold coving in the corridors, gold cladding around the lifts, and truly horrible mock-baroque beds and furniture – but it's comfortable enough. Rooms are spacious, many have their own balcony, and there's a small pool. <u>21 OR</u>

RUWI

Al Falaj Hotel Al Mujamma St ☎2470 2311, ⓦalfalajhotel.com; map p.55. This basic but agreeable four-star on the quiet northern edge of Ruwi is nothing exciting, but it's very comfortable and good value. The decent in-house facilities include a pair of spacious outdoor pools, a tennis court, and state-of-the-art gym. The *Tokyo Taro* Japanese restaurant, on the eighth floor, offers authentic Japanese food and decor to match, as well as fine views over the Ruwi sprawl. Other dining options include the ground-floor *Souq Café*, which hosts excellent themed nights. <u>24 OR</u>

★ **Golden Tulip Headington** Souq Ruwi St ☎2473 2000, ⓦgoldentulip.com; map p.55. This sleek new four-star breathes new life into Ruwi's otherwise anodyne selection of hotels, offering a stylish and comfortable stay at surprisingly good value. The rooms, all gleaming mahogany and black marble, are modern and spacious, although they could be quieter. There's a gym and massage rooms, and by the time you read this, there'll also be a rooftop pool and restaurant. <u>30 OR</u>

Haffa House Al Farahidi St ☎2470 7207, ⓦshanfarihotels.com; map p.55. Cosy four-star in a good, central location. Rooms are pleasantly furnished, with wall arches lending them an Arabian feel, while facilities include a swimming pool, massage centre and a basic gym. The *Four Seasons* restaurant serves decent international food, and the terraced *Samharam Café* shows sports and movies on a big screen. <u>30 OR</u>

Sheraton Bayt Al Falaj St ☎2237 7777 ⓦsheratonoman.com; map p.55. Housed in one of Ruwi's landmark buildings – a towering, midcentury monolith of brown and grey – this isn't much to look at from the outside, but once you're through the doors it's a different story. Re-opened in 2016 after a four-year renovation (and ten-year closure), The Sheraton has re-emerged as one of Muscat's most beautiful, and refreshingly restrained, hotels. Rooms are modern, tasteful and understated, the fitness and spa facilities are top-notch, and the beautiful *Tea Library* is a lovely place to spend an afternoon. If you can't afford to stay here, it's worth coming for dinner at the *Courtyard Restaurant*; its theme nights and seafood buffets are spectacular. <u>80 OR</u>

Sun City Hotel Al Jaame St, next to Mwasalat bus stand ☎2478 9801, ⓔhotel.suncity@hotmail.com; map p.55. One of Ruwi's cheapest options offers bright, clean and somewhat old-fashioned rooms overlooking the Mwasalat bus stand (convenient if you've got an early-morning intercity departure), and patchy internet (at a price of 800bz/hr). The upstairs "suites" (an extra 5 OR), which sleep three, are quite pleasant but still overpriced. <u>23 OR</u>

Tulip Inn Downtown Al Farahidi St ☎2486 4000, ⓦtulipinndowntownmuscat.com; map p.55. This comfortable three-star has an excellent location right in the thick of the Ruwi action, which is particularly helpful if you're arriving or leaving on an intercity Mwasalat bus. Rooms are generously sized, with even standard ones having space for a desk and a sofa, and have a jazzy blue-and-gold colour scheme fit for a pharaoh. Facilities include an outdoor pool, gym, and the ground-floor *Lobby Café*. <u>24 OR</u>

1

QURUM HEIGHTS

★**Crowne Plaza** Al Qurum St ☎2466 0660, ⓦcrowneplaza.com; map p.59. This pleasantly low-key four-star boasts one of the best locations of any hotel in the city, hugging the top of the rocky ridge at the southern end of Qurum Beach, and with sweeping views down the coast. Facilities include the good *Come Prima* Italian and *Shiraz* Iranian restaurants (see page 71), the alfresco *Edge* and the attractive *Duke's Bar* (see page 73). There's also a health club, gym and a decent pool set in pretty gardens, with a nice little secluded cove on the beach directly below. Rooms (with sea or land view) are on the small side, but given the location, price and facilities, this adds up to one of Muscat's most appealing packages. **66 OR**

Qurum Beach Hotel Al Qurum St ☎2456 4070, ⓔqbhotel@omantel.net.om; map p.59. This rather eccentric-looking, pebble-studded two-star offers the best value within walking distance of Qurum Beach. Rooms are pretty spartan, but fine, while the bar area is best avoided, particularly given you have the *Crowne Plaza* within easy reach. Generally, it's pleasant enough, although the big central atrium – an unexpected combination of hanging greenery, arabesque walls and what looks like a fire escape – is something of an acquired taste. **20 OR**

Ramee Guestline Al Qurum St ☎2456 4443, ⓦrameehotels.com; map p.59. This functional four-star doesn't offer much to write home about, but it's comfortable enough, even if the old-fashioned rooms could do with a revamp, and it's decent value in an expensive part of town. Other plus points include the *Keranadu* South Indian restaurant and *Mirchi*, its North Indian equivalent, which also offers Chinese and Arabian dishes. There are two lively options when it comes to evening entertainment: the American-themed *Rock Bottom Café* (see page 74) and the unimaginatively named Arabian nightclub, *Arabian Nights*. There's also a pool in a rather ugly interior courtyard hemmed in by high red walls. Book online for big discounts. **33 OR**

SHATTI AL QURUM AND HAYY AS SARUJ

Al Qurum Resort Back of Jawaharat A'Shatti Complex ☎2460 5945, ⓔreservations@alqurumresort.com; map p.59. An intimate little place, tucked away behind the *InterContinental* and right next to the beach. There's a decent-sized pool in the neat little gardens out back, a well-equipped gym and good restaurant, and a shisha lounge on-site. The resort's most notable feature is the lively *Route 66* bar, which is a fun place to come for live music most nights of the week – although the quality of the music is variable. It also does a good line in seafood, including, if you've a hankering, fish and chips. The resort's reasonable value if you can score one of the three very spacious sea-facing doubles with king-size beds; the four

twin-bedded rooms (including two sea-facing) are only slightly cheaper but much smaller and less appealing. Rates include breakfast. **55 OR**

Beach Hotel Way 2817 ☎2469 6601, ⓦbeachhotelmuscat.com; map p.59. Old-fashioned and overpriced, *Beach Hotel* is nevertheless an acceptable option if you're looking to stay within walking distance of Qurum Beach without breaking the bank. Rooms are generously sized, although they could be cleaner, and road noise can be an issue. Staff will do their best to help you, and fans of an Indian breakfast will find a decent spread. Overall, an okay option if the *Al Qurum Resort* is full. **55 OR**

★**Grand Hyatt** Off As Sarooj St ☎2464 1234, ⓦmuscat.grand.hyatt.com; map p.59. This enjoyably overblown hotel is one of Muscat's top addresses – although often significantly less expensive than its major rivals. Rooms are beautifully furnished and unusually spacious, arranged around the hotel's lovely (albeit rather small) gardens, bisected by an attractive serpentine pool-cum-river; there's also a public beach immediately to the rear of the hotel with plenty of sand to stretch out on, and where you'll also find the popular *Al Candle Café* (see page 71). The hotel is home to some of the city's top eating and drinking venues including *Tuscany* restaurant (see page 71), the three-storey *Safari* entertainment complex and the lovely *John Barry Bar* (see page 73). Facilities include a steam room, sauna and gym, with massage and other treatments available. **150 OR**

InterContinental Al Kharjiyah St ☎2468 0000, ⓦmuscat.oman.intercontinental.com; map p.59. This big dour concrete box of a hotel is easily mistaken for a multistorey car park from the outside, but is much nicer once you're through the doors. Rooms have land or sea views and are arranged around a stylish atrium up and down which glass-walled elevators silently shuttle, while the back of the hotel is enclosed by immaculate, expansive gardens, with two fine pools (one under a shady trellis) and a health club, a dive centre and an attractive swathe of public beach beyond. The French-Polynesian restaurant *Trader Vic's* and the *Al Ghazal* pub (see page 71) are popular with expats, and the *InterCon* remains something of a Qurum social hub. **140 OR**

KHUWAIR, GHUBRAH AND AZAIBA

Behlys Villa Way 4846, Azaiba ☎9934 5791, ⓦbehlys.com; map p.46. This little guesthouse is a convenient choice if you're getting the bus to or from the intercity hub in Azaiba, with basic but comfortable pastel-hued rooms, cats roaming the garden, and an outdoor pool. **40 OR**

★**The Chedi** Off 18 November St, Ghubrah ☎2452 4400, ⓦghmhotels.com; map p.46. One of Muscat's finest hotels, although compared to the size and extravagance of the city's other top-end options, this is a model of understated cool. The pseudo-tented

Arabian-style lobby offers a stylish nod towards its Gulf-side location, although the rest of the hotel is pure Asian designer Zen, with a minimalist decor of white pillars, feng shui-style water features and maze-like hedges. The huge canopied pool is a work of abstract art in its own right, and the whole place looks particularly magical after dark, when hundreds of candles flicker in the gardens. Rooms come with all mod-cons ranging from rain showers to Bose music systems, while facilities include no fewer than six restaurants (see page 72) and one of Oman's finest spas. The only caveats are that the grounds, though beautiful, are rather small, and the public beach at the end of the grounds is disappointing. **197 OR**

Ibis Dawhat al Adab St, next to Hotel Muscat Holiday, Khuwair ☎ 2448 9890, ⓦibis.com; map p.46. Aimed squarely at business travellers, with functional but modern and attractively designed rooms, plus restaurant (unlicensed), business centre and gym, but no bar (although there's one in the *Muscat Holiday* next door). **34 OR**

Lanavilla 37th St, Ghubrah North ☎ 7178 9660, ⓦlanavilla-oman.com; map p.46. Simple but very pleasant accommodation in an attractive modern house close to the beach. A breezy communal balcony overlooks the sea, as do some of the rooms, which are a little dated but perfectly comfortable nonetheless. There's a very homely feel about it all, and there's a pleasant garden too. **45 OR**

Muscat Holiday Dawhat al Adab St, next to Ibis, Khuwair ☎ 2439 9100, ⓦholidayhotelsoman.com; map p.46. Pleasant four-star, aimed mainly at business travellers although it manages to feel appealingly homely, from the plush, rather old-fashioned foyer through to the spacious and comfortably furnished rooms. Facilities include an in-house restaurant, live sport at the licensed *Churchill's Bar* and a good-sized, if otherwise unremarkable, pool. **43 OR**

★ **Nomad Guest House** Way 4468, Azaiba ☎ 9549 5240, ⓦnomadtours.com; map p.46. Homely guesthouse run by an affable British expat, with helpful staff, cosy rooms and a pleasantly sociable atmosphere; rooftop tents are a cheaper option in the winter months. *Nomad* also arrange a variety of tours, ranging from day trips to Wadi Shab to multi-night adventures in the desert. Tents **20 OR**, doubles **30 OR**

Waves International Hotel Dawhat al Adab St, Khuwair ☎ 2448 6999, ⓦwavesinternationalhotel.com; map p.46. Its four-star status may be a bit of a stretch, but this friendly, comfortable hotel is perfectly nice

and offers better value than its neighbours. Wi-fi is sporadic and you won't find a pool or gym, but there's great food, in big portions, at the restaurant and café. **22 OR**

SOUTH OF THE CENTRE

★ **Al Bustan Palace** Al Bustan St, Al Bustan ☎ 2479 9666, ⓦalbustanpalace.com; map p.46. Oman's most famous hotel (see page 61), this remains one of the most attractive places to stay in the city, thanks to its alluring, Arabian-nights interior and superb location on an unspoiled stretch of rocky coastline amid vast, palm-studded gardens, fringed with a fine swathe of private beach. The hotel was closed for extensive renovations at the time of research, but was due to reopen in September 2018. **252 OR**

Muscat Hills Resort (formerly the Oman Dive Center) Off Al Jissah St, Al Jissah ☎ 2485 3000, ⓦmuscathillsresort.com; map p.46. The most chilled-out place to stay in Muscat, spread out along a little private beach with accommodation in a string of pretty *barasti* (palm-thatch) huts. Huts are all a/c, although otherwise desert-island simplicity prevails; there are no TVs, and they're sparsely (but very nicely) furnished, and all come with verandas out front and attractively rustic stone-walled outdoor bathrooms to the rear. Slightly too many huts have been crammed into the available space, and it's a bit pricey for what you get, but even so this is still one of Muscat's nicer, and more unusual, places to stay. **90 OR**

Shangri-La Barr al Jissah Resort and Spa Off Al Jissah St, Al Jissah ☎ 2477 6666, ⓦshangri-la.com; map p.46. The largest of Muscat's top-end options, the vast *Shangri-La* resort sprawls for around a kilometre along one of the city's most beautiful stretches of coastline, squeezed in between rugged mountains and a generous swathe of beach. There are actually three hotels here: the family-orientated *Al Waha*, the fancier *Al Bandar*, and the palatial, ultra-exclusive *Al Husn* "private resort". Facilities include some of Muscat's finest restaurants and bars (see page 73), acres of sand, huge pools, an opulent spa and children's play areas. There are shops in the mock mudbrick "Omani Heritage Village" and adjacent Souk al Mazaar, where you can watch artisans at work. The complex as a whole has plenty of style, with a blend of Arabian chintz and Asian Zen-cool, although the sheer scale of the development has rather overwhelmed the pristine natural setting, and the security guards on every corner can make the whole place feel like some kind of five-star prison camp. Average rates run from around 135 OR at *Al Waha* up to 250 OR at *Al Husn*. **135 OR**

EATING

Muscat has far and away the best selection of places to eat in the country, albeit relatively modest compared to other capital cities in the region. There's a good spread of **upmarket restaurants**, mostly based within the various hotels in the city's more modern districts around Qurum. More down-at-heel options can be found in the older parts of the city: Ruwi

1

has the best range of cheap **curry houses** alongside slightly fancier restaurants, while Muttrah has the most enjoyable traditional **Arabian shwarma cafés**.

What to eat Muscat offers a rare chance to sample traditional Omani food at places like *Kargeen*, *Ubhar* or *Bin Ateeq*; you'll also do well for seafood, most of which comes fresh out of the local market at Muttrah. There's also a glut of good Indian restaurants thanks to the city's sizeable subcontinental population, along with a passable assortment of Italian, Chinese and Thai establishments, plus a couple of Iranian and Moroccan joints. Most restaurants close from 3–7pm.

Listings ⓦomanicuisine.com has some excellent in-depth critiques of various places around the city.

MUTTRAH

Al Ahli Coffee Shop Northern end of Muttrah Souk ☏2471 3469; map p.48. Squirrelled away inside Muttrah Souk, this popular little café attracts a mix of bargain-hunting Muscatis and souvenir-laden tourists alike. Good either for a quick drink or something more substantial, with a wide range of milkshakes and juices plus cheap sandwiches, burgers and shwarma. Mains 1–2 OR. Mon–Thurs, Sat & Sun 10am–1pm & 4–10pm, Fri 4–10pm.

Al Boom Marina Hotel, Muttrah corniche ☏2471 3100; map p.48. The main draw at this little hotel-top restaurant is the gorgeous views of the Muttrah corniche from the tightly packed tables lining the tiny outdoor terrace – arrive early to be sure of bagging a seat, or settle for a place in the more spacious but less spectacular interior. The short menu features an unexceptional mix of Indian, Arabian, Chinese and continental dishes, plus seafood fresh from the adjacent fish market. It also boasts the additional attraction of being Muttrah's only licensed restaurant. Most mains 4–5 OR. Daily 7am–10.30am, noon–3pm & 6pm–2am.

★ Bait al Luban Al Mina St ☏2471 1842; map p.48. Directly opposite the new fish market, this lovely restaurant is an altogether classier proposition than most of Muttrah's cheap and cheerful eateries. It's decked out in traditional Arabian style, with heavy dark-wood doors, wall arches and ornately wrought lanterns; you can choose to sit at a table, some of which overlook the harbour, or do things the old-fashioned way and sit on cushions around a low table on the floor. It's a great place to try classic Omani dishes as well as some novel takes on old classics, such as the *shuwa* lasagne. Mains from 6 OR. Daily noon–11pm.

Fast Food 'n' Juice Centre Muttrah corniche ☏9287 6036; map p.48. Busy, touristy café in a plum location right next to the entrance to Muttrah Souk – prices are slightly above average, although it's worth the premium for the breezy outdoor seating overlooking the corniche. Food includes all the usual snacks, burgers, sandwiches

and shwarmas along with more substantial grills, fish and pizza, plus juices, shakes and proper coffee. Mains from 3 OR. *Gulf Fast Food* next door is very similar. Daily 9am–10pm.

OLD MUSCAT

City Tower Grill Al Saidiya St; map p.52. The best of Old Muscat's virtually non-existent eating options, with a tourist-friendly menu of burgers, sandwiches, shwarmas, salads and juices, plus more substantial grills and biryanis. *Muscat Light Restaurant* next door has more of a mainstream Omani-Indian menu, with assorted biryanis and curries. Mains at both places around 1–2 OR. Daily 9am–midnight.

RUWI

Bin Ateeq Markaz Muttrah al Tijari St ☏2447 8225; map p.55. Part of a nationwide chain (with branches in Nizwa and Salalah), *Bin Ateeq* makes a commendable, if not entirely successful, stab at re-creating an authentic local dining experience. Food is traditional Omani, with a range of meat and seafood curries and biryani-style dishes served up in one of the dozen or so little traditionally furnished rooms into which the place is divided – you eat sitting on the floor. It's a nice idea, although the dining rooms are a bit drab (the TVs in each room don't do much for the atmosphere) and the food is average. Mains 1.4–2.5 OR. Daily 10am–11pm.

Golden Oryx Al Burj St ☏2470 6128; map p.55. An attractive upmarket (but unlicensed) Chinese restaurant, with a pleasantly soothing atmosphere and eye-catching decor – a bit like being inside an old wooden junk. The menu runs through a fairly mainstream selection of meat, fish and veg dishes, mainly Cantonese, with a few Szechuan options, plus Thai curries – competent rather than exceptional, although portions are huge. Mains 3.5–10.5 OR. Daily 10am–10pm.

Kesar Bank Al Markazi St ☏2470 7172; map p.55. For a cheaper alternative to *Woodlands*, head down the road to this superb vegetarian joint, where a vast array of delicious Indian dishes are on offer in a pleasant environment (mains from 2 OR). A range of Indian-Chinese dishes feature prominently on the menu; try the veg manchurian. Come at lunchtime for an even better deal on combo takeaway lunches (from 1.2 OR). Daily 9am–3pm & 6–11pm.

Oman Express Way 4359 ☏2483 1329; map p.46. Tucked away on a side road off Souq Ruwi St, this local favourite is the place to come for extremely tasty, and extremely cheap, South Indian food. 1 OR gets you the only thing on the menu: a bottomless thali of vegetarian curries, dahls and chutneys, with rice or chapattis; hovering staff are ever eager to provide you with seemingly unlimited refills. Daily 8am–11pm.

★ **Woodlands** Bank al Markazi St ☎2470 0192; map p.55. Ruwi's top dining choice, owned by the same people who run the excellent *Mumtaz Mahal* (see page 71), serving up excellent South Indian cuisine in a pleasantly rustic dining room with cane furniture and lots of potted plants. The restaurant specializes in feisty Chettinad cuisine from Tamil Nadu: spicy meat, fish and veg *poriyals*, *varuvals* and *kuzambu*. There's also a good selection of North Indian standards and South Indian snacks – *dosas*, *uttapam*, *vadas* and *appam*. Mains 3–6 OR. Also boasts a reasonable wine list, plus beer and other drinks. Daily 11am–3pm & 6pm–midnight.

QURUM AND QURUM HEIGHTS

Come Prima Crowne Plaza, Al Qurum St ☎2466 0660; map p.59. Small but suave Italian restaurant, in a minimalist modern dining room with white chairs, red glasses and big green pots – the food's best enjoyed, though, on the terrace overlooking the Gulf of Oman. The menu offers pasta and pizza (7–9 OR) plus more elaborate, modern-Italian-style mains (10–15 OR), with fresh, authentic ingredients and a flair for flavour. Daily noon–3pm & 7–11pm.

★ **Mumtaz Mahal** Off Sultan Qaboos St, next to the Children's Museum ☎2460 7103, ⓦmumtazmahal. net; map p.59. One of the city's best-loved restaurants, occupying a large and pleasantly airy dining room with picture windows offering fine views over the city below. The inventive menu features a mix of classic Mughlai and Punjabi dishes such as the signature *raan-e-mumtaz* (marinaded whole leg of lamb slow-cooked in a tandoor), alongside some original house specials and other dishes offering a nod towards South Indian culinary traditions, including assorted fish curries and the chef's special mutton pepper fry. The wine list is decent, and there's also live Indian classical music at weekends. Mains 4–11 OR. Mon–Thurs, Sat & Sun noon–3pm & 7pm–midnight, Fri 7pm–midnight.

Samad al Iraqi Al Wilaj St ☎2456 7151, ⓦsamadaliraqigroup.com; map p.59. For something a little different, head to this smart establishment for superb Iraqi food at very good value. The portions are huge – and that's before you get to the free bread, salads, and soups (plural). It's an international chain – there's an outlet on London's Kensington High St – but it's good value, and a beautiful environment to boot, with stained-glass arches, wooden balconies and brick-walled alcoves atmospherically lit by hanging lanterns. Most mains 4–6 OR. Daily 9am–midnight.

Shiraz Crowne Plaza, Al Qurum St ☎2466 0660; map p.59. This elegant restaurant serves up some of the best and most unusual Iranian food in the city,

including inventive *polos* (Iranian-style biryanis featuring ingredients such as orange-flavoured chicken, chicken and blackberry, and salmon & saffron), traditional stews (duck and pomegranate, shrimp and tamarind, green hammour) and meaty kebabs. Mains around 7.5–14 OR. Daily noon–3pm & 7–11pm.

SHATTI AL QURUM AND HAYY AS SARUJ

Al Candle Café On the beach at the back of the Grand Hyatt, Hayy as Saruj ☎9600 2233; map p.59. This breezy and very chilled-out little seafront café is best after dark, when a mellow crowd of local Omanis and other expat Arabs settles in over the cheap shisha (1.2 OR). Food comprises a short but well-prepared menu of burgers, falafel sandwiches and a few grills, plus assorted beverages including Turkish coffee and Moroccan tea. Mains around 2 OR. Daily 8am–midnight.

★ **D'Arcy's Kitchen** Jawaharat A'Shatti Complex ☎2469 9119; map p.59. This popular expat hangout does a fair impression of an English-style country teashop, with chintzy decor and waitresses in frilly white pinafores – even if they are from the Philippines. It's a bit naff, and the food's average, but its popularity makes for a good atmosphere. The menu features all-day breakfasts, salads, sandwiches and soups, plus more substantial burgers, pasta dishes and other mains (around 3–4 OR) ranging from fish and chips to stir-fries. Mon–Weds & Sun 8.30am–10.30pm, Thurs & Fri 8.30am–11.30pm.

Trader Vic's The InterContinental, Al Kharjiyah St ☎2468 0000 ⓦtradervicsmuscat.com; map p.59. This old favourite has long been a popular meeting place for expats and locals alike and is a convivial spot most evenings, with an extensive food menu and wide choice of cocktails (3–4 OR) to match. Ostensibly French-Polynesian, but in reality anything goes, with the ever-changing menu incorporating dishes from Mexico, Japan, China and beyond. The mix-and-match feel is amplified by the samba soundtrack, courtesy of an accomplished live trio. Dress code: smart casual. Mains 10–15 OR. Mon–Fri & Sun 6pm–12.15am, Sat noon–3pm & 6pm–12.15am.

Tuscany Grand Hyatt, off As Sarooj St ☎2464 1234, ⓦmuscat.grand.hyatt.com; map p.59. One of the top restaurants in the city, serving up a fine selection of authentic Italian cuisine under the leadership of the restaurant's Piedmontese chef, with seating in a rather solemn-looking dining area reminiscent of a domed Roman temple. The dress code is strictly formal. The menu features a small but carefully crafted selection of meat and fish mains, using authentic Italian ingredients alongside local seafood, plus superior pasta dishes and wood-fired pizzas. Pizza and pasta around 7–9 OR; mains 9–14 OR. Mon–Thurs & Sun noon–3.30pm & 7–11.30pm, Fri & Sat 7–11.30pm.

1

MUSCAT CAFÉ CULTURE

Hanging out over a freshly pressed juice or a cup of coffee in one of the city's local **cafés** offers a cheap and typically Omani experience – the coffee shops in and around Muttrah Souk and along the nearby corniche are particularly attractive places to shoot the breeze and watch the world go by. It's also worth heading to somewhere like *Al Candle Café* or *Kargeen* (see page 71) after dark and chilling out over a **shisha** and a cup of Turkish coffee. For a more upmarket variation on the same theme, **afternoon tea** in either the *Grand Hyatt* or *Al Bustan* are both enjoyable. Muscat's best afternoon tea, though, is to be had at the *Sheraton's Tea Library*, an elegant Chinese-inspired space where literally hundreds of teas from around the world wait to be enjoyed alongside snacks and light meals.

★ **Ubhar** Bareeq al Shatti Mall (due south of Jawaharat A'Shatti Mall) ☎ 2469 9826, ⓦ ubharoman. com; map p.59. One of Muscat's more original places to eat. The inventive menu features traditional Omani cuisine given a contemporary makeover, with dishes like camel biryani, shark *shuwa*, fish *machbus*, *harees* (chicken with wheat), plus novel desserts including frankincense ice cream and the signature "Ubhar's Dream" (*halwa* in puff pastry). There's also a choice of mainstream pastas, burgers and sandwiches. Most mains 4–7 OR. Daily 12.30–3.30pm & 6.30–11pm.

KHUWAIR AND GHUBRAH

The Beach The Chedi, off 18 November St, Ghubrah ☎ 2452 4343; map p.46. The second, and perhaps the best, of *The Chedi's* two main dining venues. Follow the candles through the Japanese-style hedges to this magical outdoor pavilion-style restaurant, right on the seafront, which manages to combine high contemporary Asian style with beachside informality. The menu features a fine selection of international seafood, plus a selection of oysters and caviar. Mains from around 15–40 OR. Open for dinner only, apart from Friday brunch (1–4.30pm; alcohol service from 2pm; around 70 OR/ person including as much champagne as you can drink – which will probably be quite a lot, given the price). Daily 7–10.30pm.

★ **Kargeen** Madinat Sultan Qaboos shopping complex, between Al Noor Plaza and Al Madine Plaza ☎ 2469 9055, ⓦ kargeen.com; map p.59. One of the most enjoyable places to eat in Muscat, occupying a rambling series of small buildings set amid large, shady gardens, with seating either inside or out, on wooden benches scattered with colourful cushions under the trees. The vast menu seems to have a little bit of everything, from crepes, pasta, pizzas, steaks, seafood, sandwiches, grills and no less than six types of shwarma through to traditional Omani-style mains including *shuwa* (slow-roasted meat) and other local specialities. Service can be decidedly random, however, so don't expect to get served in a hurry. There are now several other branches around town, but none is a patch on the original. Mains 4–9 OR.

Mon–Thurs, Sat & Sun 8am–midnight, Fri noon–midnight.

Kuanxi Dawhat al Adab St ☎ 2429 9998; map p.46. Resembling a sleek cocktail bar as much as a restaurant, this large, neon-underlit Chinese restaurant makes for a good mid-range alternative to Khuwair's Turkish cafés. The menu ranges from the predictable (crispy duck, kung pao chicken) to the baffling ("shrimps walking in forest"); the choice is vast, with portion sizes to match. The staff are very helpful and will gladly help you navigate the more esoteric reaches of the menu. Mains 4–7 OR. Daily noon–5pm & 6–11pm.

The Restaurant The Chedi, off 18 November St, Ghubrah ☎ 2452 4343; map p.46. The main restaurant in the idyllic *The Chedi* hotel – slightly cheaper than, although perhaps not quite as memorable as *The Beach*. There are four separate kitchens here, turning out accomplished Arabian, Asian, Indian and "Contemporary" (meaning modern European/international) food, backed up by a selection of more than three hundred wines. There's indoor seating, although you might prefer the lovely palm-studded courtyard outside. Most mains around 14–18 OR. Daily 7am–10.30am, noon–3pm & 7–10.30pm.

Shang Thai Muscat Grand Mall, Khuwair ☎ 2200 6644; map p.46. This elegant Thai restaurant is a cut above most of its immediate neighbours in the Muscat Grand Mall. The menu features a good range of well-prepared meat, seafood and vegetarian Thai classics (plus a few Szechuan and Hokkien dishes), served in big portions and with plenty of flavour. Mains 3–5 OR. Daily 10am–11pm.

Turkish House Off Al Hadiqa St ☎ 2448 8071; map p.46. This local favourite is justifiably popular for its lip-smacking kebabs, *koftes* and mezes, all accompanied by sumptuous fresh salads, bowls of hummus and *baba ghanouj*, and fresh-baked breads as long as your arm. It's also, less predictably, a fantastic place to sample the fresh bounty of the harbour. The place is owned by an ex-fisherman, and he clearly still knows his way around Muttrah market – the seafood platters are exceptional. Be sure to try the grilled squid. Mains from 3 OR. Daily 9am–midnight.

1

SOUTH OF THE CENTRE

Beach Pavilion Al Bustan Palace, Al Bustan St, Al Bustan ☎ 2476 4000; map p.46. On the beach at the *Al Bustan Palace* hotel, and one of the most beautiful locations in town. Not surprisingly, seafood is the speciality here, with a range of local and international offerings either fresh from Muttrah fish market or flown in, although there are also some meat alternatives. Non-guests will need to reserve in advance. Most mains are around 15 OR. Mon–Thurs, Sat & Sun 7–11pm, Fri 1.30–5pm & 7–11pm.

Blue Marlin Marina Bandar al Rowdha ☎ 2474 0038; map p.46. Attractive modern restaurant, with alfresco seating overlooking the marina. There's a good range of international breakfasts, snacks and mains ranging from sandwiches, burgers and pasta dishes through to more substantial seafood dishes using ingredients straight from the Muttrah fish market, all backed up by a decent drinks menu featuring cocktails, wine and beer. Try the tuna steak nicoise. Mains 4–11 OR. Daily 8am–11pm.

Capri Court Al Bandar, Shangri-La Barr al Jissah Resort ☎ 2477 6565; map p.46. Vying with the *Grand Hyatt's Tuscany* for the title of the best Italian in Oman, with an intimate and very chic dining room or tables on the terrace. The menu showcases both classic and contemporary Italian, and makes the most of regional produce from land and sea – try the Omani lobster linguine, or the red wine and lamb risotto. There's also an excellent (if expensive) wine list. Casual dress code. Mains 7–17 OR. Mon–Wed, Sat & Sun 7–11.30pm, Thurs & Fri 6–11.30pm.

Sultanah Al Husn, Shangri-La Barr al Jissah Resort ☎ 2477 6565; map p.46. One of the finest restaurants in the city, situated in the exclusive *Al Husn* section of the vast *Shangri-La* resort and named in honour of the *Sultanah*, which in 1840 became the first Omani ship to cross the Atlantic. The decor features sea views and subtle, marine-inspired designs, while the menu offers a range of top-notch à la carte meat and seafood – it describes itself as Spanish, but there are offerings from across the world, including Oman. There's a good but very pricey wine list and the food is predictably expensive, with mains starting at around 20 OR. Dress smartly. Daily 6.30–11am & 7–11.30pm.

DRINKING

Muscat has far more **licensed** pubs, bars and restaurants than anywhere else in Oman, mainly (but not exclusively) found in hotels. There are three main options: the swanky **bars** found in the city's upmarket hotels; the somewhat more downmarket English-style **pubs**, also found in most mid- and upper-range hotels; and the raucous **live-music bars** with live Arabian or Indian stage shows. Nowhere is drinking cheap, however, and the city's fancier bars can empty your wallet very quickly.

Al Boom Marina Hotel, Muttrah corniche, Muttrah ☎ 2471 3100; map p.48. Muttrah's only licensed restaurant (see page 67) is also a good place for a drink, if you can bag one of the terrace tables overlooking the corniche. Daily 7am–10.30am, noon–3pm & 6pm–2am.

Al Ghazal The InterContinental, Al Kharjiyah St, Shatti al Qurum ☎ 2468 0000; map p.59. Strangely Arabian name for a thoroughly British pub, with wood-panelled interior, a couple of pool tables and live sport on TV. There's live music nightly except Monday, plus quiz nights, pool and darts competitions, and karaoke. This has long been a popular expat hangout, and is rather more nicely done than Muscat's other British-style pubs. *Trader Vic's*, a French-Polynesian restaurant and cocktail bar (see page 71) is another lively *InterCon* hangout. Daily 6pm–3am.

Duke's Bar Crowne Plaza, Al Qurum St, Qurum Heights ☎ 2466 0660; map p.59. Spacious English-style pub-bar with a lovely stained-glass ceiling and views of palm trees through large picture windows. There's also big-screen sports, weekly quiz nights, and even roast dinners on a Friday. Daily noon–1am.

★ **John Barry Bar** Grand Hyatt, off As Sarooj St, Shatti al Qurum ☎ 2464 1234; map p.59. Recent renovations ensure the *John Barry Bar* retains its long-held place among Muscat's most stylish nightspots (with prices to match). There's more than a touch of the Rat Pack about the decor, which includes wide armchairs set around marble tables, a marble-clad bar to match, and an ever-tinkling transparent piano. There's also a menu of tapas-style light bites, a pleasant outdoor terrace overlooking the hotel's gardens, and live music which gives way to a late-night DJ every night of the week. Smart casual. Daily 4pm–2am.

O'Malleys Radisson Blu, Al Khuwair Way, Khuwair ☎ 2448 7777; map p.46. There's nothing particularly Irish about this "Irish pub" beyond a couple of Guinness posters on the walls, but there's a daily happy hour (6–9pm) and an abundance of big screens for sport, making it a popular spot in the otherwise rather sedate Khuwair neighbourhood. A DJ keeps things going into the small hours three nights a week (Tues, Thurs & Sat), ladies go free on Wednesdays and Fridays, and there's stand-up comedy on the first Saturday of each month. Mon–Thurs, Sat & Sun 6pm–3am, Fri 2pm–2am.

★ **Piano Lounge** Al Bandar Hotel, Shangri-La Barr al Jissah Resort ☎ 2477 6565; map p.46. Gorgeously svelte little bar, with very cool decor, shelves full of temptingly back-lit bottles and an accomplished pianist tinkling the ivories from her perch next to the bar. Sink back into one of

1

the big white armchairs, or head outside to the long outdoor terrace, with beautiful sea views. Daily 6pm–2am.

Serai Pool Bar The Chedi, off 18 November St, Ghubrah ☎ 2452 4343; map p.46. Beautiful outdoor

bar next to *The Chedi*'s stylish monochrome pool. There's a modest list of wines, cocktails, beers and mocktails, and you can also order a selection of food from *The Restaurant* (see page 72) next door. Daily 9am–11.30pm.

NIGHTLIFE

Nightlife in Muscat is a pretty low-key affair – it can often seem like the city's two most popular after-dark activities are driving at maniac speeds up and down Sultan Qaboos Street or piling into the nearest Lulu hypermarket for late-night shopping. Western expat and tourist nightlife tends to focus around drinking in one of the city's bars or pubs. **Listings** of forthcoming events are also hard to come by – have a look at the "Oman Nightlife" group on Facebook or check out Ⓦ muscatmutterings.com.

LIVE MUSIC

Quite a few of the city's pubs have live music most nights, ranging from the accomplished international cover bands (or occasional jazz acts) which play the city's five-star drinking joints through to the gyrating Filipina chanteuses who can be heard murdering classic tunes in the city's more downmarket pubs. For a quintessential slice of Omani nightlife, head to one of the live-music bars found in some of the city's mid-range hotels (such as the *Marina* and *Mutrah* in Muttrah and the *Ruwi* in Ruwi).

CLUBS

Many of the city's fancier hotels were once home to nightclubs, although increasingly these are being closed down in favour of bars, as it was perceived that they attracted an undesirable clientele and encouraged prostitution. That said, it's perfectly possible to find something going on every night of the week in Muscat, although all are either part of a hotel (non-guests are welcome) or double up as restaurants.

Club Safari Grand Hyatt, off As Sarooj St, Shatti al Qurum ☎ 24641234; map p.59. Small African-themed bar with poky, uninspiring decor and rather lacking in seats, although the live music, provided by a regularly changing roster of international bands, is usually among

the best in the city. The tiki-themed *Habana*, on the ground floor of the *Safari* complex, has pool tables and shows sport on big screens. Mon–Thurs, Sat & Sun noon–3am, Fri noon–2am.

On the Rocks Al Maardih St, opposite the airport ☎ 9798 3333; map p.46. This stylish spot near the airport is the closest that Muscat gets to a Western-style nightclub (although it also operates as a restaurant), and gets packed to the rafters with expats and locals alike at the weekend. The slick interior features funky, jagged ceiling tiles, veins of neon strip lighting zig-zagging the floors, and white, cuboid tables and chairs dotted like sugarlumps around the bar. The wide selection of alcoholic drinks includes an extensive cocktail menu. Mon–Wed, Sat & Sun 6pm–midnight, Thurs & Fri 6pm–2am.

Rock Bottom Café Ramee Guestline Hotel, Al Qurum St, Qurum Heights ☎ 2456 4443; map p.59. A less sniffy, more rough-and-ready alternative to Qurum's classier options over at the *Grand Hyatt*, home to a crowd of under-age, under-dressed drinkers and a determinedly American theme – think mounted Harley-Davidsons and decorative leathers. It has a reputation for getting quite raucous, although by Muscat's standards that's not saying much, and the band's usually quite good – just don't antagonize the bouncers. Daily noon–3pm & 6pm–3am.

ENTERTAINMENT

Big-name international popular **music acts** only occasionally pass through the city, during which the gardens at the *InterContinental* hotel are pressed into service as an impromptu concert arena. By far the highest quality place to see music is the beautiful Royal Opera House, a tourist destination in its own right.

Royal Opera House Al Kharjiyah St ☎ 2440 3300, Ⓦ rohmuscat.org.om. This vast, beautiful neo-Islamic building looms pristine over Sultan Qaboos St and has become a Muscat landmark since its opening in 2011. The Sultan, a great patron of the classical arts, built it to be the country's premier venue for opera and classical music, and today it hosts world-class performances and

serves as an education centre aimed at fostering the arts in Oman's younger generation. The best way to experience it is obviously to watch a show, but guided tours (Mon–Thurs, Sat & Sun 8.30am–5.30pm; 3 OR) are another way to marvel at the building up close, from the grand columns of its gilded lobby to the intricate masonry and woodwork which cover every surface.

SHOPPING

The majority of visitors to the city do all their shopping in **Muttrah Souk** (see p.47), although there are a few other places worth checking out. The most interesting area is the commercial district in central **Qurum**, around Qurum roundabout, where a cluster of old-fashioned malls harbour an interesting range of shops selling traditional arts and crafts, gold, jewellery and perfumes.

Al Araimi Centre Qurum Way 651, Qurum; map p.59. This poky little mall is a good spot to pick up local perfumes, with branches of the Gulf-wide Arabian Oud and Ajmal chains (although the English sign on the latter is bafflingly tiny); if you don't like any of the ready-made perfumes on offer, both these shops will help you create your own bespoke scent, mixed at your pleasure from the big glass jars behind the counter. Mon–Thurs 9am–1pm & 5–10pm, Fri 5–10pm.

Bateel Oasis by the Sea Complex (opposite the Jawaharat A'Shatti Complex), Shatti al Qurum ☎ 2460 1572; map p.59. If you're a lover of the date, this place has the best in the city, with a top-quality range of Saudi varieties either sold plain or stuffed with lemon, orange or almond, from 10 OR/kg. They also do a good range of chocolates, as well as beautiful gift boxes and date-derived drinks. There's another outlet in Muscat Grand Mall in Khuwair. Mon–Thurs, Sat & Sun 10am–1pm & 5–10pm, Fri 2–11pm.

Muscat Grand Mall Dawhat al Adab St, Khuwair ☎ 2200 0000 ⓦ muscatgrandmall.com; map p.46. This gleaming cathedral to all things commercial is indeed the grandest mall in the city, eclipsing the also decent Oman Avenues, just next door. On evenings and weekends the place is absolutely packed with Omanis of all ages, who come to eat and shop their free time away at over 150 outlets. Entertainment options include a cinema, climbing wall, and extensive play area for kids. Daily 8am–midnight.

Omani Heritage Gallery Jawaharat A'Shatti Complex, Shatti al Qurum ☎ 2469 6974; map p.59. Traditional Omani handicrafts including Bahla pottery, frankincense burners from Dhofar, rugs, caps, coffeepots and some attractive jewellery with traditional Bedu designs given a contemporary makeover. Relatively expensive, although at least the quality is assured. There is another branch in Muttrah, a few doors down from the *Fast Food & Juice Centre*. Mon–Thurs, Sat & Sun 10am–8pm.

Sabco Centre Way 651, Qurum ☎ 2456 6701, ⓦ sabcooman.com; map p.59. Home to one of the city's better selections of carpet and handicraft shops, including Village Arts & Crafts, Art of Loom and one of the nationwide branches of Al Haramain Perfumes, all of which line up to the right of the entrance, facing the street. Further jewellery, carpet and perfume shops line the road past the entrance, while inside the centre is a pleasant *Barista* coffee shop set in a fake tropical garden, a branch of Amouage (see page 117) and a handful of designer fashion outlets. Daily 10am–10pm.

DIRECTORY

Banks and money There are plentiful ATMs all over the city. Almost all accept foreign-issued Visa and/or MasterCards.

Embassies and consulates Virtually all the city's embassies are located in the diplomatic quarter of Hayy as Saruj, south and west of the *Grand Hyatt* hotel. Australia, New Zealand and Ireland are represented by their embassies in Saudi Arabia (although New Zealand and Ireland maintain an honorary consul in the city). Canadian consulate, 7th Floor Getco Tower, Way 2728, CBD, Ruwi (☎ 2470 3113); Ireland, Honorary Consul, Dr Mohammed Hassan Darwish, O.C. Centre, 8th Floor, Suite #807, Ruwi (☎ 2470 1282); UK embassy, Jamiat ad Duwal al Arabiya St, Hayy as Saruj (☎ 2460 9000, ⓦ ukinoman.fco.gov.uk); US embassy, Jamiat ad Duwal al Arabiya St, Hayy as Saruj (☎ 2464 3400, ⓦ om.usembassy.gov).

Health For an ambulance, call ☎ ☎ 9999. There's a well-developed network of public and private hospitals in the capital. Two of the main government hospitals are The Royal Hospital (☎ 2444 1999, ⓦ moh.gov.om) in Ghubrah south of the Sultan Qaboos Mosque, and Al Nahdha Hospital (☎ 2483 7800) in Ruwi near Wadi Aday roundabout. The main private hospital is Muscat Private Hospital (☎ 2458 3600, ⓦ muscatprivatehospital.com) in Bowshar.

Police Emergency number ☎ 9999. The most conveniently located police stations are in Muttrah, next to the southern entrance to Muttrah Souk, and in Ruwi at the northern end of Souq Ruwi St.

Post The main post office (Mon–Thurs & Sun 8am–4pm, Sat 8.30am–12.30pm) is at the northern end of Markaz Muttrah al Tijari St in Ruwi's CBD. FedEx have an office on Hellat Asud St to the southwest of Ruwi, and there's a DHL office on the lower floor of the Qurum City Centre mall.

The Western Hajar

NIZWA GOAT MARKET

The Western Hajar

Inland from Muscat, Highway 15 winds up into the craggy Hajar mountains, Oman's geological backbone, which extend all the way along the east coast of the country, from Sur to the Musandam Peninsula. The region southwest of Muscat is home to the Hajar's highest and most dramatic section, often described as the Western Hajar, or Al Hajar al Gharbi (as opposed to the somewhat lower and less extensive Eastern Hajar, covered in Chapter Five). The area is also sometimes referred to as Al Dakhiliya (literally, "The Interior"), one of the seven administrative regions into which Oman is divided and which encompasses the towns and mountains of the Western Hajar, as well as a large swathe of desert to the south.

The main focus for most visits to the region is the famous old town of **Nizwa**, the pre-eminent settlement of the Omani interior and formerly home to the country's revered imams. Nizwa also provides a convenient base from which to explore other attractions around the hills, with its mix of rugged mountainscapes and dramatic wadis along with historic old mudbrick towns and idyllic date plantations bisected with traditional *aflaj*. Leading attractions include the spectacular massifs of the **Jebel Akhdar**, east of Nizwa, and **Jebel Shams** to the west, the highest summit in Oman. There are also memorable traditional villages at **Al Hamra** and **Misfat al Abryeen**, plus a number of the country's finest forts, including those at **Bahla**, the largest in the country, and **Jabrin**, perhaps the most interesting.

Inland from Muscat

It's around 150km from Muscat to Nizwa (roughly 1hr 30min–2hr) along the modern dual carriageway of **Highway 15** that whisks you through the scenic pass. It makes for a fine drive up into the mountains and an even more exhilarating downward swoop when descending from Nizwa towards the coast.

The route covered by the modern highway is one of the most significant in Omani history, winding through a gap between the jagged, towering uplands of Jebel Akdhar on one side and the more modest peaks of the eastern Hajar on the other. This was once perhaps the most important commercial conduit in the country, and the principal trade artery between the highland capital of Nizwa and Muscat on the coast, its former importance signalled by the extraordinary surfeit of forts, watchtowers and fortified settlements which still flank the modern highway. These include the massed watchtowers and hilltop village of **Fanja**, the fort at **Bidbid**, the walled town at **Izki**, and the oasis-smothered valley and massed fortifications of **Sumail**, all of which offer rewarding diversions from the main road up into the hills.

Fanja

Some 30km from Rusayl roundabout along Highway 15, the town of **FANJA** is home to a dramatically situated old **walled village and watchtower**, perched high on a hilltop

The falaj p.83
Walks in the Western Hajar p.94
How green was my mountain p.95

The rose harvest p.98
Geology of the Hajar p.102

JABRIN CASTLE

Highlights

❶ Misfat al Abryeen Picture-perfect traditional mountain village, with a labyrinthine tangle of mudbrick buildings and an idyllic *falaj* set amid beautiful upland scenery. See page 103

❷ Nizwa Historic capital of the interior and Oman's most personable town, with a grand fort, an absorbing string of souks and an entertaining traditional goat market, where hundreds of locals congregate to haggle over livestock. See pages 85 and 89

❸ Jebel Shams Drive up the country's highest peak for spectacular mountain scenery and stomach-turning views looking down into Wadi Nakhr – Oman's "Grand Canyon". See page 104

❹ Jabrin Fort Fairytale fort, whose beautifully restored interiors offer a fascinating glimpse into Omani life in centuries past. See page 107

❺ Balcony Walk Oman's most celebrated hike, skirting 1000m cliffs along an old donkey trail to an abandoned village. See page 105

❻ Saiq Plateau The heart of the Jebel Akhdar, with a string of old-fashioned villages clinging to the edge of Wadi al Ayn. See page 95

❼ Wadi Bani Auf The classic Omani off-road drive, descending from the mountains to the coast via the dramatic chasm of Wadi Bani Auf. See page 101

HIGHLIGHTS ARE MARKED ON THE MAP ON PAGE 80

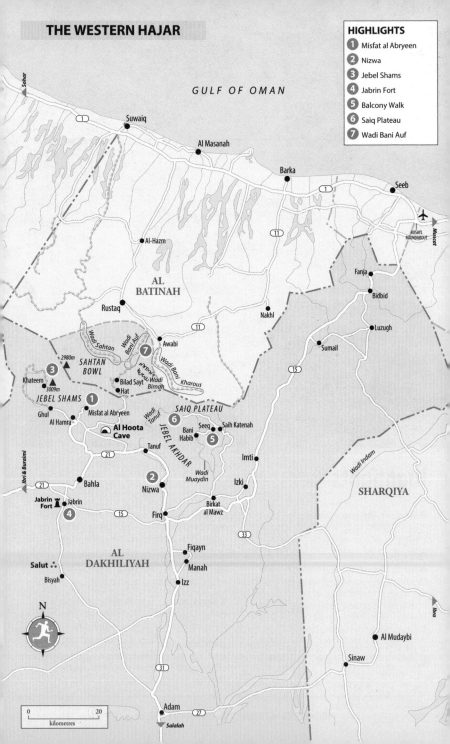

overlooking the modern town and providing commanding views over the valley below. The area's former strategic significance is signalled (as at Sumail, further up the road) by the extraordinary quantity of towers which stand watch from the surrounding hills. Entrance to the village is via a well-preserved gateway flanked by a very solid-looking stretch of stone wall. Inside, the old walled village comprises a decaying muddle of ruined mudbrick buildings plus, incongruously, a few modern concrete houses, still apparently inhabited. Where the view opens up to the valley below is a round, crumbling tower and a pair of well-worn cannons, still fired annually on Eid al Fitr to end Ramadan with a bang. It's only a few minutes of scrambling from here to reach the hilltop's highest tower, built in an unusual lozenge shape rather than the usual circle or square, and commanding 360-degree views over the surrounding hills, dotted with a dozen or so further watchtowers.

On the opposite side of the hilltop village is an attractive extension of Fanja – a tranquil, car-free valley that's home to a set of **hot springs**. Exiting the old village's main gateway, turn left and follow the road 100m or so to reach a small, whitewashed mosque. On its left side is a row of thermal pools, each walled off for privacy and free to access (though these should be avoided during prayer times). Even if you don't intend to bathe, it's worth a stroll through this peaceful, shady enclave of Fanja, packed with date palms and sugarcane and very little to interrupt the sound of the rustling *aflaj*.

ARRIVAL AND DEPARTURE   FANJA

By car from Muscat Follow the signs off Route 15 into Fanja. This road runs through the centre of the modern town, descending to a big modern bridge across the wadi. On the far side of the bridge you'll see a large round watchtower on your right. Take the small side road on your right after about 150m which loops back to the watchtower; it's easiest to park here and walk the rest of the way (around 15–20min), given the narrowness of the roads. Walk along this road for about 500m, then turn left up the narrow road just before the shop signed "Laundry"

and then right at the base of the cliff, following the road around to the old town's main gateway (on the opposite side of the hill).

By car from Nizwa Take the exit off Route 15 about 1km after Bidbid, then turn left to pass beneath the highway and right at the next roundabout. Follow this road another 3km, turning left just before the bridge to park beside the watchtower overlooking the wadi. For directions from here, follow the instructions above.

Bidbid

A few kilometres beyond Fanja, about 1km off Highway 15, the small town of **BIDBID** is worth a quick detour for its quaint **fort** (not open to the public). This is one of the prettiest small castles in the country: a rustic little structure, built with mudbrick walls on a stone base, with windows and rifle-slits cut lopsidedly out of the adobe, half-hearted little rounded battlements topped with cannons above and a large watchtower perched on a small rock outcrop beside. Unusually, the walls have been left unplastered following restoration, so you can see the pebbles and bits of straw mixed in to strengthen the mudbrick, adding to its rather homespun charm. A swiftly flowing *falaj*, in which villagers are wont to do their washing, runs around one side of the fort.

ARRIVAL AND DEPARTURE   BIDBID

By car from Nizwa Take the signed turn-off and follow the road into town until you reach a modest line of shops. Take the unsigned road on the left here just past a medium-sized white mosque, bear left over two oversized speed bumps and the fort is in front of you.

By car from Muscat There's no exit to Bidbid from the highway approaching from Muscat, though from Fanja

you can simply follow the main road south of the modern bridge for about 3km, after which you will pass beneath the modern highway and continue another 2km, turning left into town and following the directions from Nizwa given above. If you're not stopping in Fanja, continue along the highway for about 2km past Bidbid to turn around at the Ibra/Sur junction.

Sumail

Just over 20km beyond Bidbid, the town of **SUMAIL** (also spelled Samail) was historically one of the most important in the area thanks to its position at the head of a narrow pass through the mountains, the so-called **Sumail Gap**.

A stark change of scenery from the broad, barren floodplain to the west, the Gap stretches for about 10km northeast of town, lined with kilometre after kilometre of lush date plantations squeezed in below rocky ridges to either side, their summits crowned by dozens of watchtowers, walls and other fortifications – a picture-perfect slice of traditional Oman.

2

Sumail Fort

The castle is well-signed about 4km northeast of the Gap's western entrance; look out for the brown signs that will have you turn right immediately after crossing the first bridge across the wadi, then turn left after about 200m to arrive at the fort • Mon–Thurs & Sun 9am–1pm • 500bz

The largest and by far most imposing of the various fortifications dotting the valley, **Sumail Fort** is one of Oman's more unusual constructions. Its high, zigzagging walls are moulded around the contours of the rock outcrop on which it's built, its large tower at the summit of the outcrop is visible from almost anywhere in the valley and some modest living quarters are clustered around the gateway at the bottom. Much of the fort has been restored, and it's certainly worth the walk to its upper battlements if you're fortunate enough to arrive when it's open. Otherwise, the exterior is impressive enough, and the beautiful doors at the main entrance are worth a look.

Tomb of Mazin bin Ghaduba

Well-signed about 300m west of the turnoff to the castle • Free

Mazin bin Ghaduba, an early companion to the Prophet Muhammad and a resident of Sumail, is believed to have been the very first Omani to embrace Islam. The recently-restored mosque that he built about 2km southeast of the castle is also considered to have been the country's first when it was erected – just eight years after the *hijra*, the departure of Muhammad and his followers from Mecca to Medina. While the mosque is off-limits to non-Muslims, bin Ghaduba's colourful, open-air **tomb** is not – it sits just off the main road about 300m east of the castle on the north side of the wadi. Dress conservatively.

Bait al Sarooj

Signed to the left of the main road about 4km east of the castle turnoff; after about 200m the house will appear on your left • Mon–Thurs & Sun 8am–2pm; if it's closed you can call Farouk (☎ 9537 6880), who lives nearby, to come and unlock the gate • Free

Further up the road beyond the fort is **Bait al Sarooj** ("The Sarooj House" – *sarooj* being the traditional Omani-style plaster which was formerly used to protect the exterior of mudbrick constructions), completed by Sheikh Saud bin Ali al-Jabri in the late seventeenth century as an endowment for his male children. The rather plain exterior is enlivened with a beautifully carved wooden door imported long ago from Zanzibar, but far more memorable is the interior: beyond yet another ornate Zanzibari door is a small labyrinth of smooth-surfaced, arched passageways, for the most part well-restored, and you can follow the dark stairwell all the way to the roof terrace. For better valley views you can scramble up to the pair of watchtowers that caps the rocky ridge above.

On to Muscat via Luzugh

If you've made the detour to Sumail and are heading down to Muscat there's no need to retrace your steps back to Highway 15. It's just as quick, and considerably more pleasant, to continue on along the road down the Gap and on to **Luzugh**, from where another back road heads north, eventually rejoining Highway 15 just south of Bidbid.

ARRIVAL AND DEPARTURE   **SUMAIL**

By car from Muscat or Nizwa Follow the signs off Highway 15 into Sumail and through the ugly modern sprawl of Al Madrah. After about 3km you'll see Al Karama Hypermarket on your right; from here the road swings left through the pass.

THE FALAJ

One of the most distinctive sights in the Omani mountains is the **falaj**: the traditional system of narrow, mud-walled water channels used to irrigate fields and date plantations, and to provide villages and towns with reliable water supplies. The **origins** of the system go back into the mists of prehistory (the name itself perhaps derives from an old Semitic word meaning "distribution"; the true Arabic plural is *aflaj*, although "*falajes*" is often used instead). One theory holds that it was introduced by the Persians – who had developed a similar irrigation system, known as the *qanat* – in around the sixth century BC, although there is evidence that *falaj*-like irrigation systems were present in Arabia even before then.

Estimates of the **total number** of *aflaj* in Oman vary from five thousand to well over ten thousand, of which perhaps as many as four thousand are still in use. Traditionally, the reliability and size of the local *falaj* was the key factor underlying the size and prosperity of settlements in Oman. Nizwa, for instance, flourished thanks to its abundant water sources, including the mighty Falaj Daris. By contrast, if a *falaj* ceased flowing, it usually spelled the end of the village that relied on its water. Mosques can also often be seen near important sections of a *falaj*, offering a reliable source of water for ritual ablutions before prayers, while most of the country's larger forts also boasted their own dedicated *falaj*, often flowing from an underground source directly into the building and guaranteeing a steady supply of water in the event of a siege. *Aflaj* remain an integral part of the traditional Omani date plantation or village – even today, many locals still use them to wash clothes in or even, in larger ones, to take a bath.

CONSTRUCTION AND OPERATION

The communal effort and expense involved in constructing and maintaining a *falaj* was a heavy burden on traditional Omani society, although it also helped foster social cohesion and a sense of shared responsibility. Locating a suitable water source using the services of a specialist water diviner was the first challenge. There are two basic types of *falaj*: a **ghaily falaj**, drawn from a water source above ground such as a river bed or mountain spring, or, more commonly, an **iddi** or **daudi falaj**, drawn from an underground well, anything up to 50m beneath the surface – many *falaj* start with extensive tunnels before they emerge into the light of day. Creating such subterranean conduits was obviously a major engineering feat, as was constructing the **channels** themselves. In order to make sure the water keeps running, these are built on a constant, if often imperceptible, downward gradient from source to destination (although in places – such as the mountain villages of the Saiq Plateau – you'll see channels tumbling steeply down the hillside between layers of agricultural terracing).

The **operation** of the typical *falaj* is another highly developed part of the Omani social fabric. *Aflaj* are collectively owned, with villagers holding shares which give them the right to a certain amount of water. Water is diverted into adjoining fields by unblocking holes in the sides of the channel for a certain amount of time (traditionally calculated by the movement of stars at night and by sundials during the day, although nowadays virtually everyone just uses a clock). Large villages usually employ a full-time manager (*aref*) to oversee the running of the *falaj*, assisted by an agent, who looks after repairs and maintenance.

UNDER THREAT

Unfortunately, an increase in unregulated use, as well as lowering water tables due to the sinking of private boreholes, is now threatening the aquifers upon which the *aflaj* have long depended. Other looming threats include the disappearance of expertise (as young Omanis head to the city rather than learn the arts of maintaining and repairing *aflaj*) and the economic reality that date plantations aren't nearly as lucrative as they once were.

Izki

South of Sumail, the mountain scenery flanking Highway 15 becomes increasingly dramatic. To the west rise the towering uplands of the Jebel Akdhar, with their huge slabs of tilted limestone. To the east stretch the much smaller and more irregular ophiolite hills which mark the edges of the Eastern Hajar.

Just under 50km beyond Sumail, a few kilometres off the main highway, lies the town of **IZKI**, overlooking the broad **Wadi Halfayn**. Izki is popularly claimed to be the oldest

2

town in Oman, and was also formerly notorious for its tribal intrigues, being divided into Yamani and Nazari villages; up until recent decades, relations between the two communities remained strained and suspicious – a longstanding example of one of Oman's most ancient ethnic divides.

Modern Izki is a large and formless place which straggles alongside the main highway for more than 5km. The main attractions are the ruins of the old walled **town** and adjacent **fort**, situated on a bluff overlooking Wadi Halfayn, with the mountains to either side.

The old town

The **old town** consists of two settlements on either side of the fort. To the north is the old Yamani town – particularly beautiful as its extensive complex of disintegrating mudbrick buildings is enclosed within a rectangle of impressively solid walls, built on raised stone foundations; the walls have survived the years relatively intact, unlike many of the buildings within. Entrance to the old town is via the large **gateway** on the wadi-facing side of the town nearest the date plantations. Next to the gateway stands a well-preserved mosque on a raised platform, with a pair of fine arches, an unusually large *mihrab* and a red-painted wooden roof decorated with fragments of Qur'anic text within.

You can spend a peaceful twenty minutes nosing around the remains of the old streets, laid out on an approximate grid plan, with a wide main thoroughfare running dead-straight through the middle. Many fine buildings still survive in various states of dereliction; a number preserve their original carved wooden doors and beamed roofs. At the far end of the village stands a second, unusually large, mosque. The roof has long since vanished, but the interior survives partially intact, with two long lines of stone arches on chunky circular columns and a rustic *mihrab* and *minbar*.

Just south of here are the similarly crumbling remains of Izki's large **fort**, its impressive central keep (including one round tower built, unusually, entirely of stone) set within a square of collapsing walls. Following the road past the fort as it dips back down from the ridgetop brings you to a further fine collection of abandoned mudbrick houses – the old Nizari town – now surrounded by modern buildings. On its southern edge is **Jarnan cave**, a gaping hole in the rock said to have hidden a golden calf at the time of Islam's arrival, though it has long since disappeared.

Falaj al Malki

Izki is also home to the **Falaj al Malki** (or Mulki), thought to be the oldest in the country, whose tributaries water the date plantations beneath the old town – the entire *falaj* consists of a network of around 360 channels (although only two are now in use), drawing water from a source 20m below ground. In 2006 this became one of five Omani *aflaj* protected as a UNESCO World Heritage Site. Unfortunately, the water flow here isn't what it used to be (see page 83).

ARRIVAL AND DEPARTURE   IZKI

By car From Muscat (1hr 20min; 122km), take the exit off Highway 15 signed Izki and Qaroot al Janubiah then go straight through the roundabout, following the main road into town for about 2km. Izki is well-signed off to the left of here about 2km through the oasis and up towards the ridge where you'll find the old town and fort. From Nizwa (35min), head east of the Firq intersection, passing straight through Birkat al Mawz, after which Izki will be signed off to the right (2km).

Birkat al Mawz

Some 11km beyond Izki is the small town of **BIRKAT AL MAWZ**, slightly over an hour from Muscat, and just 25km east of Nizwa. Birkat al Mawz (literally "Pool of Bananas", which are still grown in the oasis here) is of interest mainly as the starting point for the stunning road up to the Saiq Plateau (see page 95), although there are a couple of sights in the town itself. The main attraction is the town's fort, the **Bait al Ridaydha**.

This is a relatively modern structure, the original having been destroyed by the British during the Jebel War (see page 242); though renovated some time ago, the fort remains closed indefinitely, though there are rumours that it will eventually reopen to the public. The impressive **Falaj al Khatmeen** (one of five *aflaj* across the country that were collectively listed as a UNESCO World Heritage Site in 2006; sometimes spelled Khatmayn) flows through the middle of the fort, emerging at the front in a raised, walled channel which continues on past a small stone-built mosque and watchtower.

Birkat al Mawz is a convenient place to **rent a 4WD** to go up Jebel Akhdar (see page 93). If you want to stay hereabouts, the *Golden Tulip* hotel (see page 90) is just 5km down the road in the direction of Nizwa.

Old Birkat

Largely obscured by the modern town is **Old Birkat**, just east of the centre – one of the region's most atmospheric abandoned villages, with a higgledy-piggledy pile of ruined mudbrick houses stacked up virtually on top of one another on a steep hillside, with a *falaj* (still flowing) running through the middle and a watchtower perched at the top. It's possible to climb (with care) all the way up to the jagged remains of an old watchtower above the village – following the main pathway between the houses, and then a series of steps between and within the ruined structures – where you'll be rewarded with good views across the valley, including a handful of other towers dotting the surrounding hills and a smaller, picturesque set of ruins just across the palm grove to the east.

ARRIVAL AND DEPARTURE — OLD BIRKAT

By car Old Birkat is surprisingly well hidden among the backstreets of the modern town. To find it, continue along the main road through town, about 500m east of the turn-off to the castle. Look out for the small shop signed "Rental Business and Professional Machinery Equipment" on your right. A narrow road heads north from here for about 100m to reach the old village. It's best to park about 50m on from the shop beside the patch of open date plantation on your right.

Nizwa

The principal city of the interior, **NIZWA** played a key role in the history of Oman for well over a thousand years, from the earliest days of Islam through to the 1950s, when the country was finally unified under the rule of Sultan Said bin Taimur. For much of this time, the city served as the capital of the interior and seat of the country's ruling imams, the religious leaders who presided over an independent state quite separate from the sultans of Muscat down on the coast. As such, Nizwa had until quite recently a reputation for tribal belligerence and religious conservatism verging on fanaticism. Ibn Battuta, visiting Nizwa in 1329, described the Omanis as "a bold and brave race … the tribes are perpetually at war with each other", while Wilfred Thesiger, travelling through the area some six centuries afterwards in the late 1940s, was advised by his Bedu companions to avoid the town on pain of arrest, imprisonment or worse.

Ironically, in the seventy years since Thesiger's aborted visit, Nizwa has reinvented itself as one of Oman's most welcoming destinations for foreign travellers. It's a thoroughly enjoyable place to while away a few days, not least for its convenient position, set within easy striking distance of pretty much anywhere in the Western Hajar, one of Oman's most rewarding regions. Nizwa's old town – a picture-perfect huddle of old-fashioned sandstone buildings clustered around a magnificent **fort** and mosque, flanked by a quaint tangle of traditional **souqs** – in many ways lives up to the sort of mental pictures which most foreigners have of Arabia. It's not entirely authentic, of course: the entire town was massively restored, rebuilt and generally scrubbed up in the 1990s, and now looks a lot neater than it ever did in its traditional heyday (at least excepting the wonderful old quarter of Al Aqr) – you'll see more tourists here than anywhere else in the country outside Muttrah Souk in Muscat.

Though perhaps overdone in parts, Nizwa's old centre retains a decidedly traditional, village-like atmosphere, particularly after dark, when the day-trippers have largely disappeared and locals come out to sit on the streets and share news and gossip. Things are particularly colourful during the Friday Goat Market (see page 89), when Bedu women in traditional face masks descend on town, accompanied by old-timers in lopsided white turbans, with perhaps a traditional *khanjar* shoved into their belts and a rifle slung jauntily over their shoulders.

Brief history

One of the oldest cities in Oman, Nizwa owes its importance to its strategic location at the crossroads of trade routes between the Buraimi, Muscat and Dhofar, as well as its proximity to unusually abundant water sources (the town's Falaj Daris is the largest in the country). Known as "The Pearl of Islam", Nizwa served as capital of Oman under the Julanda dynasty in the sixth and seventh centuries AD – according to legend it was in Nizwa that the Julanda leaders became the first Omani converts to Islam in 630 AD.

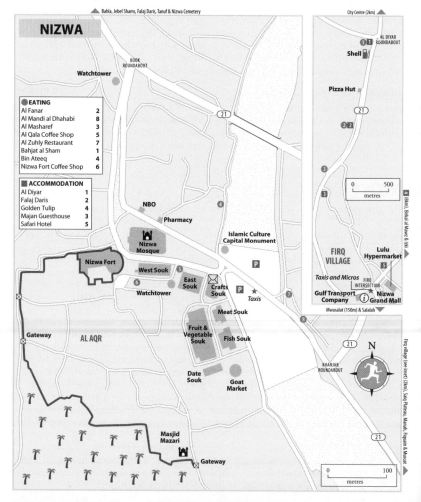

NIZWA

Bahla, Jebel Shams, Falaj Daris, Tanuf & Nizwa Cemetery

City Centre (2km)

● **EATING**

Al Fanar	2
Al Mandi al Dhahabi	8
Al Masharef	3
Al Qala Coffee Shop	5
Al Zuhly Restaurant	7
Bahjat al Sham	1
Bin Ateeq	4
Nizwa Fort Coffee Shop	6

■ **ACCOMMODATION**

Al Diyar	1
Falaj Daris	2
Golden Tulip	4
Majan Guesthouse	3
Safari Hotel	5

The town was chosen as capital in 793 AD at the beginning of the second imamate (see page 232), as its inland position made it a safer base for the imams than coastal Sohar, the previous capital, which was prone to attacks by the seafaring Persians. Nizwa subsequently remained the pre-eminent town of the interior for almost a millennium until challenged by Rustaq, to which the Ya'aruba imams decamped in 1624. Religion aside, Nizwa also developed into a major craft centre, home to skilled artisans working in silver, copper and leather.

Nizwa was caught up in the **Jebel War** (see page 242) – in the early 1950s the city's historic fort even suffered the indignity of being bombed by the British RAF. Since 1970, it's been transformed into a modern city and opened to the world via the modern highway linking Muscat. The 1990s saw major renovations of the fort and souks as well as an influx of students with the opening of a pair of polytechnics – followed shortly thereafter by the University of Nizwa in 2002. In recognition of its achievements – historical and ongoing – it was named the Capital of Islamic Culture in 2015 (along with Almaty and Cotonou). The southern stretch of town has grown particularly unrecognizable in recent years, now marked by a long strip of high-rise homes, flashy car dealerships, a Lulu Hypermarket and the massive Nizwa Grand Mall.

2

Nizwa Fort

Mon–Thurs, Sat & Sun 9am–4pm, Fri 8–11am • 5 OR

At the very heart of the town, squeezed in tightly between souks and mosque, squats Nizwa's mighty **fort**. The fort is said to date back to the days of the ninth-century imam Al Salt bin Malik, although the present structure dates from the later seventeenth and early eighteenth centuries – part of the large-scale Ya'aruba building programme which also saw the construction of nearby Jabrin and Al Hazm forts.

The main tower

The complex actually consists of two separate elements: the "fort" proper (*q'ala*), essentially a single huge round tower; and the attached "castle" (*hisn*), containing the imam's residential quarters, the entire complex enclosed within a large, walled compound. The **fort-cum-tower** was constructed between 1649 and 1661 by the second Ya'aruba imam, Sultan bin Saif al Ya'aruba. This is the largest such structure in the country, 30m high and 36m in diameter – a fearsome symbol of military power which compensates for Nizwa's defensively vulnerable location in the middle of a wadi. The inside of the tower is filled to a depth of 15m with rocks and rubble, while the rounded walls are designed to withstand cannon fire, a combination which lends the entire structure unusual strength – anti-tank rockets, fired against the tower during the 1950s Jebel War (see page 242), are said to have simply bounced off the walls.

The interior

The **interior** of the tower is an excellent example of the defensive ingenuity of Oman's military architects. Access to the roof is provided by a single narrow, zigzagging staircase protected by five spiked metal doors with a "murder hole" overhead (look up to see the narrow slits above), down which boiling date syrup could be poured or heavy objects dropped, as well as water, in the event that hostile forces attempted to set fire to the fort. In the unlikely event that attackers did manage to force the doors, they were likely to fall into the deep holes, or "pitfalls", located immediately beyond. Fortunately for modern tourists, these are now glassed over, and light up helpfully as you approach.

The rooftop terrace

At the top is a huge **rooftop terrace**, designed to provide a high, stable platform for the fort's twenty-odd cannon, which sit ranged around the perimeter, capable of providing 360-degree fire over considerable distances. Here you'll also see the openings of the various murder holes, along with a couple of wells and a vertiginous flagpole – pity (or admire) the fool who is tasked with changing the three light bulbs at the very top. A further 10m-high battlemented wall encloses the terrace, ringed with a walkway from which the garrison could fire on the enemy with rifles in the event that they got close enough to the fort without being blown to smithereens by the cannon. It also commands a bird's-eye view over the town and sprawling oases – a convenient vantage point from which to keep an eye on passing trade.

The residential quarters

Next to the tower stand the fort's extensive **residential quarters**, which acquired their present shape during the rule of imam Nasir bin Murshid al Ya'aruba in the early seventeenth century – a confusing little labyrinth of rooms, passages and stairwells. Rooms on the **ground floor** house an absorbing sequence of displays on just about every aspect of traditional Nizwa life: the *falaj*, silver and copper-working, forts, the Omani imams, keys, padlocks, the souk, mosques, all copiously illustrated and excellently explained, along with a couple of interesting old films.

A series of four rooms kitted out with traditional furnishings occupies most of the **first floor**, unusually spacious and high-ceilinged. Steps lead up to the roof from here for further views over the complex.

Nizwa Mosque

Virtually in the shadow of the fort walls lies Nizwa's second major landmark, the **Nizwa Mosque** or **Friday Mosque** (officially the Sultan Qaboos Mosque; non-Muslims not permitted inside), with its distinctive – and much photographed – brown-tiled dome and minaret, best seen from the fort walls.

The souks

Most shops open for business around 8am but close between 10am and 11am and don't reopen until around 5pm

Stretching around the southern side of the mosque lies Nizwa's absorbing sequence of **souks**, one of the most interesting in the country. The souks were extensively renovated during the 1990s and now look picture perfect (apart from the East Souk) – a bit overly sanitized, but undeniably pretty.

The souks nearest the fort are the most touristy, showcasing Nizwa's celebrated artisanal traditions. The town is one of Oman's major **craft centres**, particularly famous for its silver jewellery and *khanjars*, as well as copperware, leatherwork and *mukkabbah*, the traditional round airtight containers with fluted lids, made from copper, which were used to store volatile items like frankincense and *bukhoor*. The number of tourists passing through tends to inflate prices – you might find cheaper Nizwa silverware in the Muttrah Souk in Muscat – although things are quieter later on in the day and after dark.

The West and East souks

Opposite the castle, the attractive **West Souk** houses a mix of quaint shops with big wooden doors; some are devoted to touristy items like *khanjars* and walking sticks, others to more workaday items. East of here, the small **East Souk** is the most atmospheric in Nizwa, and the only one to have escaped restoration, with tiny shops clustered beneath crumbling mudbrick arches and columns, with weathered old wooden beams overhead propping up a makeshift corrugated-iron roof and Nizwa's most venerable collection of shopkeepers, some of whom appear to be almost as old as the buildings they sit in. Offerings here are fairly humdrum, featuring assorted foodstuffs, miscellaneous hardware and household items, although there are also a couple of photogenic spice stalls at the far end.

The Crafts Souk and around

At the eastern end of the East Souk a miniature square is lined with shops displaying shelves full of quaint **Bahla pottery**; you can also see a short section of the old city **walls** here, running south from the pottery stalls along the back of the fruit and vegetable souk. Past here, the tiny **Crafts Souk** houses a further handful of shops stocking all the usual staples of the Omani souvenir hunter including *khanjars*, old Bedu silver jewellery, coffeepots, walking sticks, *mandoos* (traditional wooden chests) and old-fashioned rifles.

The food and livestock souks

The southern end of the souk area is more functional, with specific areas devoted to fish, meat and dates, plus a colourful **Fruit and Vegetable Souk**, with piles of produce and a string of stalls along the western end selling tubs of *halwa*.

Immediately south of here is the **Goat Market**, home to Nizwa's famous **Friday Market** where locals come to trade livestock – cows and goats in particular – which is sold by auction. The market starts at around 7am and finishes at around 11am in time for *sala al Jum'ah*, the congregational Friday prayers. Animals are walked around the circular stand at the centre of the market and auctioned off to the highest bidder, a lively scene featuring hundreds of locals, a fair few tourists, and an overwhelming smell of animal poo. Things can get particularly lively during the cattle auctions, as some of the more restive animals (including some rather large bulls) attempt to break free of their handlers and charge to freedom through the surrounding throng.

Al Aqr and the city walls

To get a sense of how Nizwa looked in the days before it was buffed up for the tourists, head to the old walled quarter of **Al Aqr**, within spitting distance of the fort and souks, though it sees surprisingly few tourists. To reach the heart of the quarter, head south from the fort entrance. On your right will pass a marvellous traditional Omani townscape of imposing two- and three-storey houses in various stages of decay – although a surprising number are still in use, many of them inhabited by the town's sizeable Pakistani community.

It's a wonderful place for idle wandering along the narrow, shaded streets which honeycomb the area, looking out for the colourful doorways and finely carved wooden windows which still adorn many of the houses. There are also a couple of very old mudbrick mosques hereabouts: boxlike structures, lacking the usual minaret, with only a small pepper-pot dome of the roof betraying the buildings' function. The finest is the **Masjid Mazari** on the southern side of the district (no English sign; it's opposite Basateen Hai Alain Laundry), raised up on a high terrace, with access via a narrow flight of steps from street level.

Bounding the edge of Al Aqr is a section of Nizwa's surprisingly extensive and well-preserved **city walls**. These begin around the back of the fort (with whose own walls they link up) and continue for the best part of 1km, dotted with a fine sequence of crumbling gateways and watchtowers – Nizwa at its most memorably time-warped.

Nizwa cemetery

About 1km northwest of the centre (head north along the Bahla road then take the turning on the left signed Hay al Ain immediately in front of a large watchtower)

An even more ancient relic of Nizwa's past can be found at the old **Nizwa cemetery** on the edge of town. The cemetery is huge, stretching for around 1km along either side of the road, and dotted with thousands of graves dating back to the arrival of Islam; many of the religious scholars and *qadis* (judges) for whom the town was once famous are said to be buried here. The actual gravestones themselves are extremely modest, typical of the Islamic tradition in general (and the Ibadhi tradition in particular), which discourages the construction of elaborate funerary monuments. Most are little more than simple, uncarved fragments of stone set upright in the ground, and at first sight the whole place can look more like some strange kind of rock plain than a man-made cemetery – an unusual and strangely haunting glimpse into Nizwa's distant past.

ARRIVAL AND GETTING AROUND   NIZWA

By car Nizwa is 1hr 30min–2hr drive from Muscat along Highway 15, and about the same coming from Ibri or Ibra.

By bus and micro to Muscat For bus and micro services to Muscat, it's usually quickest to head out to the southwest corner of the busy Firq intersection, some 5km south of town, where there is a steady stream of passing traffic, much of which bypasses the town itself. Here you'll find the local office for Mwasalat (☎ 2521 8474, ⓦ mwasalat.om), which links Nizwa to both Azaiba in Muscat (1hr 40min–2hr 40min; 8 daily) and Salalah (11hr; 3 daily; more during the *khareef*) – check the website for up-to-date departure times. As of the time of writing there were also two Mwasalat buses to Muscat city centre, parking just opposite the souks (departing from Muscat 8.20am and 2.50pm and from Nizwa at 8.30am and 4pm; 2hr 40min). Several other bus companies in Firq offer similar services, among them the Gulf Transport Company (☎ 2543 1458).

On foot Unlike virtually every other town in Oman, Nizwa's centre is small enough to walk around. However, the town as a whole stretches about 15km along the main highway, so getting from most accommodation to the old city requires a set of wheels.

By taxi and local micro Plentiful taxis can be found in the vast car park just east of the souk, which is also the best place to pick up local micros. Between here and the Firq intersection you'll pay around 500bz for a shared taxi and 300bz for a micro.

INFORMATION AND TOURS

Tourist information There's an official tourist office (Mon–Thurs & Sun 7.30am–2.30pm; ☎ 2534 0165) on the southwest corner of the Firq intersection, just behind the hospital, offering stacks of brochures, lists of accommodation and little besides.

Tours For a car and/or guide, it's best to head to one of the better hotels.

ACCOMMODATION

Disappointingly, there are no places to stay in the centre of Nizwa itself. The *Nizwa Heritage Inn*, set 100m south of the fort, may become the first to change the situation, though its date of opening remained uncertain at the time of research. The following hotels are ranged along the main highway to Muscat, south of the centre.

Al Diyar 2.5km from the centre, next to the Al Diyar roundabout ☎ 2541 2402, ⓦ aldiyarhotel.com; map p.86. This plain modern hotel is one of the nicer places to stay in Nizwa, and the closest to the centre. Its 120 rooms are spacious and nicely furnished, some with balconies, though they come with shower only. There's also a small pool, and passable food at the attached *Bahjat al Sham* restaurant (see page 91). **40 OR**

★ **Falaj Daris** 4km from the centre ☎ 2541 0500, ⓦ falajdarishotel.com; map p.86. Designed like a miniature fort with discreet Omani touches, this well-run three-star is easily the most appealing place to stay in Nizwa. Rooms are nicely furnished (though with rather poky bathrooms) and arranged around a pair of attractive courtyards. Facilities include a gym, two pools (one "cool", the other at normal outdoor temperature), plus a kids' pool and a bar (for guests only). The in-house (licensed) *Al Fanar* restaurant (see page 91) is easily the best in town. They can also arrange a vehicle with driver-cum-tour guide for mountain excursions. **68 OR**

Golden Tulip 18km from the centre, 5km from Birkat al Mawz (see page 84) ☎ 2543 1616, ⓦ goldentulipnizwa.com; map p.86. This recently renovated four-star is the most upmarket place to stay in the Nizwa area, with rooms arranged around a pair of enclosed courtyard gardens; all come with balconies and are comfortable enough, if a bit chintzy, and some have little patios facing the hotel's immaculate pool. Other facilities include a nice English-style pub, sports bar, pool bar and gym. The setting, however – in a windy and exposed spot next to the Muscat highway more or less in the middle of nowhere – has limited appeal apart perhaps from being close to the road to Jebel Akhdar. Staff can arrange 4WDs with driver-cum-guide for this and other trips, although at rather pricey rates. Large discounts available during the summer. **70 OR**

Majan Guest House 5km from the centre ☎ 2543 1910, ⓔ majangh@hotmail.com; map p.86. This neat and cosy "guesthouse" (although it's really just a homely sort of hotel) is probably the nicest semi-budget option in town, with clean and cheerily furnished rooms. There are no in-house amenities, although the sociable *Al Masharef* café is just a five-minute stroll away, and the restaurant at *Falaj*

Daris hotel (and its adjacent bar) are also within walking distance (around 15–20min) or a short drive. **30 OR**

Safari Hotel 8km from the centre, just east of the Firq intersection on the side road to Birkat al Mawz ☏ 2543 2150, ⊛ safari-hotel.info; map p.86. Some way from the old town centre, this three-star sits just opposite the city's brand new hypermarket and mall, with well-worn but clean rooms, a small pool and a fitness centre. Official rates are a tad expensive for what you get, though significant discounts are usually available online. **40 OR**

EATING

There are few culinary delights in Nizwa. Apart from the pleasant *Al Fanar* restaurant at the *Falaj Daris* hotel, you're limited to a string of no-frills cafés in the centre and along the main road south of town and to the *Nizwa Grand Mall*'s food court. For picnic supplies it's best to head to the deli at *Lulu Hypermarket*. For drinking, the only licensed venues in town are at the *Falaj Daris* and its adjacent pair of (unassociated) noisy, local bars – one geared towards Arabs and the other towards South Asians.

★ **Al Fanar Restaurant** Falaj Daris hotel, 4km from the centre ☏ 2541 0500; map p.86. Easily the best place to eat in town (and the only one that's licensed), with seating in the bright dining room or in the pretty courtyard outside, set on a terrace around the hotel pool and with fairy lights twinkling in the trees after dark. The menu runs through all the usual staples, including mixed meze (4.20 OR) to start with followed by a choice of Indian, Chinese and Continental standards, plus a few Omani options – try the tasty *kabsa dijaj*, chicken pieces buried in a mound of cardamom-scented orange rice with coriander on top. Note, however, that there may only be a buffet available some nights if the hotel is full. Daily 6.30am–11pm.

Al Mandi Al Dhahabi Town centre, 100m east of the souk ☏ 9201 2015; map p.86. The largest and most inviting of the slew of restaurants lining the road opposite the souk complex, with a decent offering of East African favourites like *ugali* and *mhogo* (cassava; 2–2.2 OR) with fish, as well as plenty of local biryani-style dishes including *mandi* and *kabooli* (1.8–2.2 OR). Dine inside amid the garish decor or out on a terrace overlooking the souk and castle, pleasantly lit up at night. Mon–Thurs, Sat & Sun 10am–midnight, Fri 6am–noon & 1pm–midnight.

Al Masharef 5km south of the centre ☏ 9560 5335; map p.86. Cheery Turkish restaurant – particularly good for grills and shwarma (from 275bz), while there's also a good selection of Lebanese-style pastries and fruit juices. There's plenty of outdoor seating, and usually a big screen rigged up showing live football – a popular evening hangout among locals. As the car park can become quickly jammed with takeaway traffic, it's often best to park just north of the restaurant. Daily 8am–midnight.

Al Qala Coffee Shop Town centre, between the East and West Souks; map p.86. Built into the side of the archway linking the East and West Souks, this friendly hole-in-the-wall café offers a good pit stop for hot and cold drinks (coffee with dates 1 OR) while exploring the town, with shady outdoor seating under the trees, and plenty of people-watching opportunities. Daily 6am–8pm.

Al Zuhly Restaurant Town centre, 100m east of the souk; map p.86. Unpretentious streetside joint with fine views of the town from its outdoor seating and plumes of smoke from the kebab grills outside. The inexpensive menu features the usual meat and fish curries, masalas and biryanis, although you're probably better off sticking to the tasty shwarma sandwiches and plates (from 250bz) – the chicken is a lot better than the beef. Expect to eat your meal to a soundtrack of locals driving up and honking their horns for in-car takeaways. Daily 6am–midnight.

Bahjat al Sham Al Diyar hotel, 2.5km from the centre ☏ 2541 2402; map p.86. Set in the pleasant *Al Diyar* hotel, this functional restaurant resembles the changing room at a municipal swimming pool. There's a wider-than-average selection of food, however, including a small selection of Lebanese meze, assorted "Gulf food" (chicken, mutton, fish biryanis and *maqboos*), lots of grills such as *shish taouk*, plus a few Indian dishes (butter chicken masala 2.3 OR), some of them vegetarian, and allegedly even pizzas. There's also a good buffet spread when the occasional group passes through (6 OR). Daily noon–11.30pm.

Bin Ateeq Next to the wadi just east of the mosque ☏ 2541 0466; map p.86. Identikit Nizwa branch of the countrywide chain (see page 70). Daily noon–midnight.

Nizwa Fort Coffee Shop Town centre, opposite the entrance to the fort ☏ 2541 2825; map p.86. Though perhaps an odd fit for the heart of old Nizwa, this sleek and spotless new café and restaurant offers an air-conditioned break before or after climbing around the fort – serving Italian coffee, fresh juices and an array of sandwiches and meat skewers (from 1.5 OR), as well as a local breakfast of lentil curry and khubz (1.5 OR). Daily 9am–5pm.

DIRECTORY

Health Al Qalaah Pharmacy (daily 9am–1pm & 5–10pm) is just north of the Friday Mosque.

Post The post office is on the north side of the Crafts Souk (Mon–Thurs & Sun 8am–3.30pm & Sat 8.30am–12.30pm).

North of Nizwa

There are several rewarding sights just up the main highway to the **north of the city**. Before you've even completely left the town you'll reach the manicured gardens of **Falaj Daris Park**, which offer a glimpse of a section of Oman's largest *falaj*. Further up the highway, the valley bends west, leading to the crumbling remains of the evocative old mudbrick town of **Tanuf**, behind which begins the pretty canyon of the same name.

2

Falaj Daris

To reach the falaj, head out on the road to Bahla: a blue sign on your right around 7km from Nizwa's centre points downhill to the right, where it's about 100m off the main road • Open 24hr • Free

One of the keys to Nizwa's former prosperity was its plentiful water supplies – there were formerly 134 *aflaj* in the Nizwa *wilayat*, of which over a hundred are still in use. The biggest of the lot is the mighty **Falaj Daris**, the largest *falaj* in Oman, and one of the five collectively listed as UNESCO World Heritage Sites in 2006. A short section of the *falaj* to the north of Nizwa has now been restored and turned into a popular little park and picnic area.

The *falaj* here is impressively large, big enough to take a bath in places, which you'll probably see locals doing, and has been preserved in more or less its original condition, built up with stones (although some sections have been patched up with ugly concrete blocks). Unfortunately, only around 200m of *falaj* is actually visible here before it disappears underground at either end, while the suburban park, complete with kids' playground and a junior quadbiking centre, doesn't add to the atmosphere.

Tanuf

12km north of Nizwa; follow the brown sign off the Nizwa–Bahla highway signed Wadi Tanuf (if approaching from Bahla, ignore the blue sign to Tanuf about 5km further along by the Al Maha petrol station and continue until you reach the brown sign) • Open 24hr • Free

Pressed against the foot of Jebel Akhdar is the atmospherically ruined old town of **TANUF**, a large swathe of fragmentary mudbrick buildings that sprawls over the best part of a kilometre next to the modern village. This is all that's left of the original town, which was bombed by the RAF during the 1950s Jebel War (see page 242) at the request of Sultan Said bin Taimur, who wished to crush the power of local warlord Suleyman bin Himyar al Nabhani, the self-styled "King of the Jebel Akhdar". Not much remains beyond the occasional wall or eroded tower, apart from a small mosque, which survives with internal arches and *mihrab* intact, although the whole site is eerily beautiful, in a rather melancholy way.

Wadi Tanuf

Immediately beyond the old town the road heads into the fine narrow gorge of **Wadi Tanuf**, best known nowadays as the source of the popular Tanuf mineral water, which is bottled from a spring here and sold countrywide. Look to your left and you'll see a remarkable elevated *falaj*, built into the base of the mountain several metres above the floor of the wadi – in wet weather the *falaj* sometimes overflows and cascades down the rock, creating a spectacular little impromptu fountain.

Wadi Qashah

A rough track (4WD only) continues down the gorge for a further 5km or so, hemmed in by increasingly sheer cliffs, leading into **Wadi Qashah** and the tiny mud-brick village of Al Far. The track ends here, although it's possible to continue even further up the narrowing canyon on foot, aiming for the abandoned village of Al Rahbah (around 1hr 30min one-way).

South of Nizwa

South of Nizwa, and within easy striking distance of the town, lies the quaint little **Al Fiqayn Fort** and another extensive ruined mudbrick town at **Manah**. Past here you leave the mountains behind, entering the great swathe of largely flat and featureless gravel desert which blankets the south of the country, bisected by **Highway 31** as it begins its long and lonely journey to Salalah, almost 1000km distant.

Al Fiqayn Fort

18km south of Nizwa • Daily 7.30am–2pm • Free

Set amid a cluster of date palms comprising the northeastern outskirts of modern Manah, the sleepy village of Fiqayn (alternatively spelt Faiqain, Fiyquin or Feequian) is home to the attractively restored **Al Fiqayn Fort**. Despite its name, this is a fortified house (*sur*) rather than a traditional fort, an unusually tall and narrow structure which towers over the crumbling remains of the old mudbrick village.

Inside, 66 steps climb up past a sequence of small, bare rooms to the rooftop terrace; look out for the series of circular openings in the middle of each floor, running the entire height of the building, which were formerly used for drawing up buckets of water and other supplies. You can't actually see much from the **rooftop terrace** thanks to the high walls which enclose it – unless, that is, you fancy climbing up the watchtower that crowns the building via a series of perilous handholds projecting from the outer wall.

ARRIVAL AND DEPARTURE   AL FIQAYN

By car From Nizwa, head to the Firq intersection and drive 5km south along Highway 31 until you reach the left turn with a blue sign to Manah and Karsha and a brown sign to the fort itself. Head some 8km along this road and then take the turning on the right marked with a blue sign to Al Feequain and a brown sign to Al Fiyquin Fort and drive through the village to reach the fort, clearly visible above the surrounding houses.

Manah

Only a couple of kilometres south of Fiqayn lies **MANAH**, home to one of the country's most impressive ruined towns, which sprawls for 1km or so around the edge of modern Manah. Unfortunately, the extensive site remains closed for restoration, although you can still get a decent sense of the ruins of the mudbrick houses, dotted with a number of impressive stone watchtowers, including one particularly tall and slender square tower whose top has crumbled dramatically away like a rotten tooth.

ARRIVAL AND DEPARTURE   MANAH

By car The most direct route from Fiqayn to Manah runs south along extremely narrow roads hemmed in by mudbrick walls. Better to avoid these by heading back to the main road and continuing about 2km past the turn to Fiqayn, passing a large mosque on your left to reach a roundabout at the entrance to the town. Turn right here (signed to Al Sooq) and continue for 1.5km until you see the ruins rising on the left-hand side of the road behind the modern shops.

Jebel Akhdar and the Saiq Plateau

Northeast of Nizwa rises the great limestone massif of the **Jebel Akhdar**, centred on the **Saiq Plateau** (pronounced "Sirq", and often spelt Sirq or Seeq). This is one of Oman's more unusual natural curiosities: an extensive upland plateau, lying at an altitude of around 2000m and ringed by craggy summits to the north and the vertiginous gorge of Wadi al Ayn to the south. The plateau has been extensively farmed

2

WALKS IN THE WESTERN HAJAR

The Western Hajar boasts virtually limitless **trekking** possibilities, with spectacular mountain scenery and a well-established network of trails – many of them along old donkey tracks through the mountains. Many of these paths have been officially recognized as public trekking routes by the Oman government; some have been waymarked with yellow, white and red flags painted onto rocks en route to assist with route-finding, although you may still prefer to enlist the services of a specialist guide to make sure you don't get lost in what is often inhospitable terrain. The high altitude of many of the treks means that temperatures are pleasantly temperate, although it's wise not to underestimate the possible challenges of even relatively short hikes. Carry ample supplies of water and warm waterproof clothing at all times – weather conditions can change with spectacular suddenness on the face of the *jebel*.

For an excellent overview of some of the most rewarding routes, pick up a copy of **Oman Trekking**, published by Explorer, which details some of the country's finest hikes, including ten in the Western Hajar, and one through Wadi Tiwi in Sharqiya. Unfortunately, virtually all the treks are linear rather than circular, meaning that you'll either have to retrace your steps or arrange for transport to collect you at the end of the walk. The following are the best of the Western Hajar routes.

AROUND JEBEL SHAMS AND WADI N AKHR

Route W4 Al Qannah Plateau to Jebel Shams. This extended and challenging hike (specialist guide needed) follows the sheer cliffs ringing the top of Wadi Nakhr (Oman's "Grand Canyon") to the summit of the country's highest mountain, with views into Wadi Sahtan and Wadi Bani Auf en route. 9.5km; 5–6hr one-way.

Route W6 Al Qannah Plateau to As Sab. Probably the most famous walk in Oman, popularly known as the "Balcony Walk", this spectacular trek follows an old donkey trail inside the rim of Wadi Nakhr to the abandoned village of As Sab (aka Sab Bani Khamis). Links up with route W6a. 3.5km; 1.5hr one-way.

Route W6a Al Qannah Plateau, Wadi Ghul to Al Khatayam. Moderate trek following an old donkey path above the southern end of Wadi Nakhr. Links up with route W6. 6km; 3–4hr one-way.

AROUND WADI BANI AUF

Route W8 Bilad Sayt to the junction of W9 and W10h. Challenging high-level walk which climbs from the beautiful village of Bilad Sayt up the northern flank of the Western Hajar above Wadi Bani Auf. 5km; 3–4hr one-way.

Route W9 Misfat al Abryeen. Long trek along old donkey trail starting at the beautiful village of Misfat al Abryeen, with views into Wadi Bani Auf en route. Links up with routes W8 and W10h. 9km; 5–6hr one-way.

Route W10h Sharaf al Alamayn to the junction of W8 and W9. Relatively easy high-altitude walk from the village of Sharaf al Alamayn along the top of the mountains. 3.5km; 1.5–2hr one-way.

AROUND JEBEL AKHDAR

Route W18b Seeq to Al Aqr. An easy but spectacular walk through the traditional villages lining the edge of the Saiq Plateau, following the rim of the cavernous Wadi al Ayn. 4km; 2hr one-way.

Route W24a & W25 Wukan to Hadash via Jebel Akhdar. Challenging and extremely exposed high-altitude trek around the northern edge of the Jebel Akhdar above the Ghubrah Bowl. Links up with trek W24b to form a circular route, just about doable by very fit walkers in a single day. 14km; 7–10hr one-way, 10–13hr circular walk if combined with Route W24b.

Route W24b Hadash to Wukan via Al Qawrah. Short but challenging walk through a trio of mountain villages. 4km; 2.5–3hr one-way.

---

for at least a thousand years thanks to its temperate Mediterranean climate, which allows for the cultivation of many types of fruit which cannot survive the heat of the lowlands: peaches, pears, grapes, apples and pomegranates all flourish here, along with a wide range of vegetables and the area's famed roses (see page 98). The plateau is particularly beguiling during the hot summer months, and deliciously cool after the heat of the plains below.

Not long ago this was one of the most inaccessible inhabited regions in Oman, requiring a gruelling six-hour hike up Wadi Muaydin. The opening of the modern tarmac road cut the trip down to a smooth forty-minute drive from Birkat al Mawz, while the building spree that followed has transformed much of the plateau. The sprawling modern town of **Saih Katenah** is the main local eyesore, while the presence of a large military camp and firing range at the top doesn't help either, accompanied by endless barbed-wire fences and assorted military hardware. Meanwhile, some of the best mountain viewpoints now fall within the grounds of lavish hotels, most notably the five-star *Anantara Resort* (see page 98). Despite these developments, the plateau remains one of the most beautiful places in the Western Hajar, dropping into the huge natural chasm of **Wadi al Ayn** and ringed by the idyllic traditional villages of **Al Aqr** and **Al Ayn**.

Wadi Muaydin

To reach the wadi, take the Jebel Akhdar road from Birkat al Mawz about 4km, then take the left fork (just under 2km before the police checkpoint for Jebel Akhdar)

Just north of Birkat Al Mawz, you enter the dramatic **Wadi Muaydin**, the starting point for a steep six-hour hike up to the top of the plateau, passing rock pools beneath impressively stratified cliffs en route. It was once among the principal routes up into the mountains, and remains far more direct than the modern road, which loops its way circuitously up the back of the hills.

It's probably best to find a guide if you fancy tackling the hike up to the plateau – most reliably done via a travel agent in Muscat, although you could try asking around among the drivers who hang out in front of Bait al Ridaydha in Birkat al Mawz (see page 84). The initial section of the wadi is also driveable (even in a 2WD) for the first 5km or so along a good graded track between towering limestone walls – a good place to get your rental car dirty.

The Saiq Plateau

32km from Birkat al Mawz along a twisty highway; about 6km from Birkat al Mawz, a police checkpoint turns back all but 4WD cars

Just beyond the police checkpoint just north of Birkat al Mawz, the road begins to hairpin dramatically upwards into the hills, with huge sweeps of rocky mountainside dotted with the small, hardy shrubs and trees – *butt*, wild olive and the occasional stately juniper – which manage to suck a living out of the bare rock. The mountains are a study in naked geology, formed out of huge slabs of limestone which have been tilted sideways over millions of years to produce the evenly sloping mountainsides and neat right-angle summits you see today, and whose colour changes according to the light from a sere, green-grey with occasional splashes of brownish-orange – a striking contrast to the much

---

HOW GREEN WAS MY MOUNTAIN

The name Jebel Akhdar means "The Green Mountain", a somewhat unlikely moniker, given the massif's largely inhospitable terrain, with vast expanses of bare rock on which only the hardiest shrubs and ground plants are able to survive. The most convincing explanation for the unlikely name is that it refers to the days when the Saiq Plateau and other parts of the surrounding mountains were covered in a dense carpet of agricultural terracing, small pieces of which can still be seen today below the villages of Al Ayn and Al Aqr. An alternative if slightly less convincing theory holds that the name derives from the colour of the limestone from which the mountains are formed, and which can take on a decidedly greenish coloration in certain lights – in complete contrast to the reddish ophiolite hills which surround the plateau to the east and south.

Further ambiguity surrounds the present use of the name. On maps, the name **Jebel Akhdar** is generally used to refer to the entire section of the Hajar mountains running west from the Sumail Gap as far as Jebel Shams. In practice, however, most locals (and local road signs) use the name to describe the area of mountains immediately north of Nizwa, around the Saiq Plateau (which is the sense used in this guide). The area further west, beyond Al Hamra, is usually described as **Jebel Shams** (see page 104).

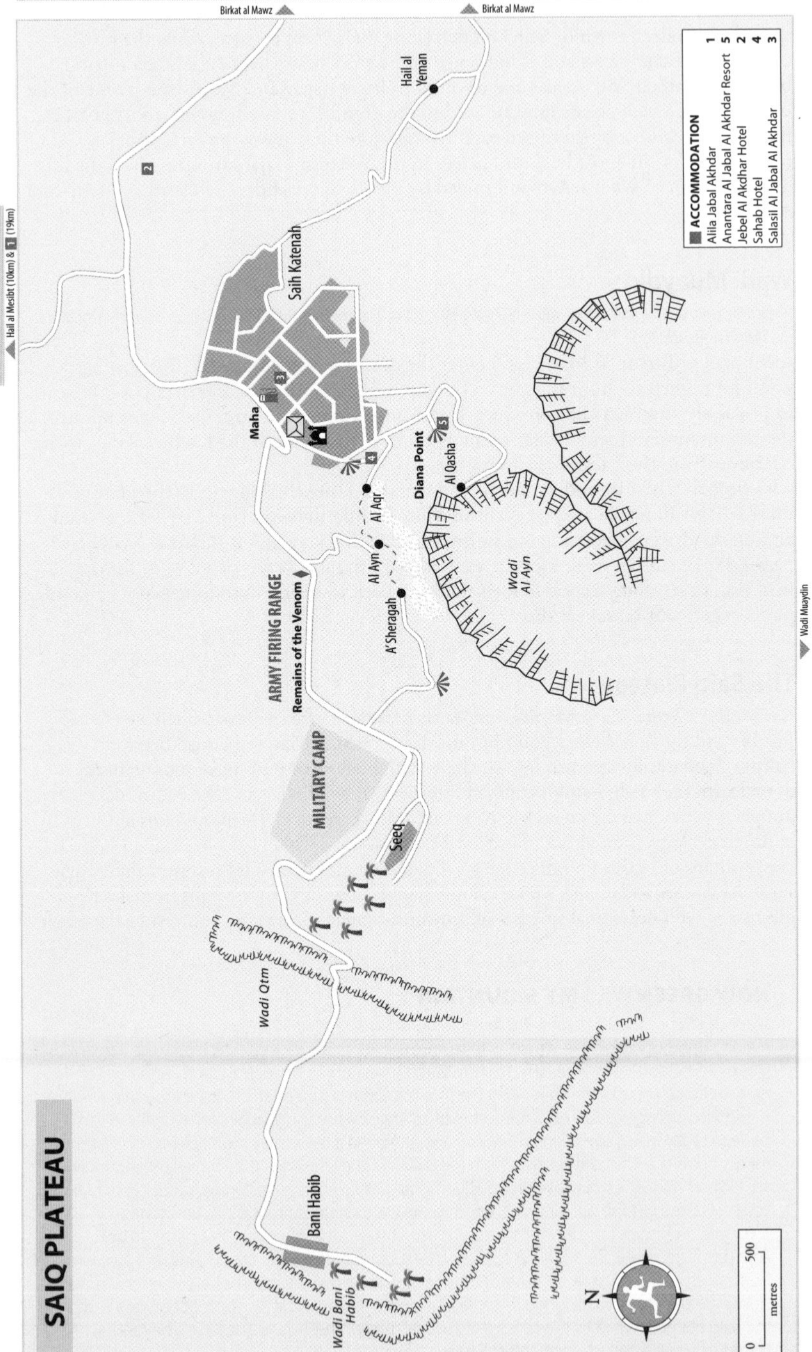

SAIQ PLATEAU
ACCOMMODATION
Alila Jabal Akhdar 1
Anantara Al Jabal Al Akhdar Resort 5
Jebel Al Akdhar Hotel 2
Sahab Hotel 4
Salasil Al Jabal Al Akhdar 3
Birkat al Mawz
Birkat al Mawz
Hail al Mesibt (10km) & 1 (19km)
Wadi Muaydin
Hail al Yeman
Saih Katenah
Maha
Diana Point
Al Qasha
Al Aqr
Al Ayn
A'Sheragah
Wadi Al Ayn
ARMY FIRING RANGE
Remains of the Venom
MILITARY CAMP
Seeq
Wadi Qtm
Bani Habib
Wadi Bani Habib
N
0
500
metres

smaller and more irregularly shaped reddish ophiolite hills below. A series of viewpoints on the road up allows you to stop and admire increasingly expansive views.

Saih Katenah
Back on the main road, a further ten minutes' drive brings you to the top of the plateau and its major settlement, the unattractive town of **SAIH KATENAH** – a surprisingly extensive place this high up in the hills, complete with a large modern mosque, petrol station, post office and a selection of mostly upscale hotels along its western fringe.

Wadi al Ayn and Diana's Point
On the far side of Saih Katenah lies the spectacular **Wadi al Ayn** (although throaty local pronunciation can make it sound something like "al Rin"), a wonderful, Grand Canyon-like chasm which ploughs through the heart of the plateau. By far the most celebrated spot for taking in the view is just west of town at **Diana's Point** – named in honour of the lonely Princess of Wales, who stared into the abyss here during a state visit in the 1980s. The first of many memorable viewpoints over the gorge, it now lies within the **Anantara Resort** (see page 98). It's well worth a stop here even it's only to gaze out from the stylish viewing platform perched over the edge of the cliff.

Al Aqr and Al Ayn
Just to the west of Diana's Point, a trio of remarkable hanging villages clings perilously to the edges of the chasm, with an intricate layer-cake of terraced fields edging their way down into the gorge. The first is the village of **AL AQR**, famous for its rose gardens (see page 98) and one of the prettiest villages in the country, with a cluster of little houses, walled gardens bisected with *aflaj* and an amazing viewpoint over Wadi al Ayn below. A short distance beyond lies the similarly picturesque village of **AL AYN**, perched on an unusual rock-spur projecting out from the escarpment (known to geologists as a "travertine cone", formed over hundreds of thousands of years by the evaporation of mineral-rich springs). It's possible to walk between Al Aqr and Al Ayn in around twenty minutes along a pretty little trail, following the yellow, white and red flags painted onto the rocks. This is part of the longer **hiking route** W18b (see page 94), which continues on to the village of Seeq (not to be confused with the modern town to the east) – around two hours' walk one-way.

Ash Shirayjah
To reach the next village, head back to the main road and turn left towards Bani Habib. Here you'll notice the scant, twisted remains of a British Venom jet, fenced off just a few metres to the right (north) of the main road. Nearby lies the unmarked grave of the pilot, RAF Lieutenant Owen Watkinson, who crash-landed here on 30 August, 1958, towards the end of the Jebel War (see page 242). Beyond here, the main road continues past an army firing range and then a side turn to the village of **Ash Shirayjah**, more modern and less interesting than Al Ayn and Al Aqr, though with further spectacular views into the gorge below. Note that the final section of road down into the village is perilously steep and it's best not to attempt it if you're driving yourself. Park at the top, just before the houses begin.

Across the Seeq Plateau to Bani Habib
Past Ash Shirayjah, the main road continues west across the plateau, flanked by an ugly military camp which stretches alongside the road from the Ash Shirayjah turning as far as **Seeq**, after which the plateau is named – another surprisingly large (but largely modern) village tucked away in a hollow. Past here the road twists down through the narrow, palm-filled **Wadi Qtm** and on to the uninspiring modern village of **BANI HABIB**, where the main road across the plateau terminates. Park your vehicle at the end of the road and follow the stone steps leading down into a lush narrow wadi filled with fruit trees and flowering shrubs – a solid mass of greenery amid the bare surrounding rock.

2

THE ROSE HARVEST

The Saiq Plateau – and the small village of Al Aqr (see page 97) in particular – is famous for its **rose gardens**, probably brought to Oman from Persia, where rose cultivation has a long history. The damask rose (*Rosa Damascena*) flourishes here thanks to the plateau's temperate climate; the gardens are at their most colourful for a few weeks in April, when the flowers come into bloom.

Aesthetics aside, the Saiq Plateau's rose gardens are also of considerable economic value thanks to their use in the production of the highly prized Omani **rose-water**. The petals of the fully grown roses are carefully plucked (usually early in the morning, when the weather is coolest, to help preseve their intense aroma) and then taken off for processing. This remains a largely traditional affair. The petals are stuffed into an earthenware pot with water, sealed up in an oven (traditionally heated using *sidr* wood, although nowadays it's more likely to be gas) and boiled for about two hours. The resultant rose-flavoured steam condenses into a metal container inside the pot, which is then repeatedly filtered to produce a clear liquid. Demand for the area's rose-water usually outstrips supply. Genuine Omani rose-water is itself an important ingredient in Omani *halwa* (see page 30), while it can also be added to drinks and food. Locals believe that it's also good for the heart, and can ease headaches if rubbed into the scalp.

Turn left here and scramble along the wadi floor for about 50m and you'll see some rough steps on the far side. It's possible to climb up these to reach part of the old village, its abandoned houses made of stone rather than mudbrick. From here there are memorable views over the rest of the old village, clinging to the edges of the narrow, steep-sided wadi, running between sandstone cliffs.

ARRIVAL AND TOURS   THE SAIQ PLATEAU

By car There's no public transport to the plateau, and 2WDs aren't allowed up, meaning that you'll have to hire a 4WD to visit. It's a 40min drive to the modern town of Saih Katenah, and you could easily drive yourself if you have a 4WD, although the drivers double as guides and will show you places and viewpoints you might otherwise well miss.

By guided tour The cheapest option is to get yourself to Birkat al Mawz (see page 84) and pick up a car with driver-cum-guide there. A few drivers with cars can usually be found hanging around the square in front of the fort; stand around looking lost for a couple of minutes, and someone will probably come and talk to you (or, failing this, try one of the car rental places at the entrance to the village). The current going rate is 35 OR for a tour of the plateau from here. These last around three to four hours, although drivers are pretty relaxed timewise and won't rush you. Alternatively, you may be able to arrange a tour through your hotel in Nizwa.

ACCOMMODATION

Over the past five or so years, a handful of plush **resorts** have appeared on the plateau, as have some relatively affordable options. Apart from *Salasil*, all those listed below have good **restaurants** on-site. Alternatively, there are plenty of pretty spots to **camp**, including several designated picnicking areas – though at the latter you can expect company at night.

Alila Jabal Akhdar 20km northeast of Saih Katenah; take the turnoff to the right about 2km before the Maha petrol station; ☎ 2534 4200, 🌐 alilahotels.com/jabalakhdar; map p.96. Secluded in a remote corner of Jebel Akhdar, this gorgeously designed resort is worth the extra travel time. In appearance it isn't quite as over-the-top as the *Anantara*, its dark stone fusing nicely with the rocky surrounds, though it nevertheless boasts comparable luxuries, from the stylish rooms and villas to the beautiful, curving infinity pool reflecting pristine mountain views. There's also a spa, complimentary morning yoga classes and a fine licensed restaurant and lounge bar. Doubles 255 OR, villas 375 OR

Anantara Al Jabal Al Akhdar Resort 1km south of main road in Saih Katenah; turn left 250m past the Maha petrol station ☎ 2521 8000, 🌐 jabal-akhdar.anantara.com; map p.96. Opened with much fanfare in October 2016, this star resort has hoped to challenge *Alila* as king of the *jebel*. Some of the best views to be found in the Western Hajar can be enjoyed from its elegant dining platform, extending past a long infinity pool to the very edge of the cliff at the famed Diana's Point. On site are six restaurants (most of them licensed) and a set of hammams, while most rooms have canyon views through giant windows, and each private villa comes with its own plunge pool and gardens. Built as it is on such a grand scale, with its painstaking blend of modern and traditional motifs, it all comes off a bit Disney-like, though you don't come here to be underwhelmed. Doubles 200 OR, villas 375 OR

AL HAMRA

Jebel Al Akhdhar Hotel About 1km east of Saih Katenah ☏ 2542 9009, ⓦ shanfarihotels.com; map p.96. This friendly, well-run hotel makes a pleasant place to hole up for a night or two, with bright and cheery rooms, clean and very comfortably furnished. Meals are available in the attractive restaurant (licensed) under a stained-glass dome, and staff can provide details and sketch-maps of local walks and attractions, and summon local guides on request. <u>50 OR</u>

Sahab Hotel 650m south of main road in Saih Katenah; turn left 250m past the Maha petrol station ☏ 2542 9288, ⓦ sahab-hotel.com; map p.96. Ageing but still charming hotel with grounds cascading towards the edge of the Saiq Plateau. In stark comparison to its hideous neighbour (under stalled construction)

immediately to the south, it manages to blend in somewhat with the mountain. Rooms come with pleasant little patios and garden views, while a few (84 OR) enjoy the panoramic mountain vistas for which the hotel was built, and there's a pool, a somewhat staid (unlicensed) restaurant and friendly staff eager to offer information and tours. <u>60 OR</u>

Salasil Al Jabal Al Akhdar 100m southeast of Maha petrol station ☏ 9947 2516; map p.96. Short of camping, this humble rest house is the most affordable option on the mountain, overlooking a big gravel car park just south of the Maha petrol station. It's doesn't quite ooze with charm, though the staff offer a warm welcome and rooms are clean and spacious enough – sufficient for a night or two, particularly if you'll spend the day out hiking. <u>20 OR</u>

Al Hamra and around

Tucked in at the foot of the mountains some 40km northwest of Nizwa (and 20km north of Bahla) lie several of the region's most memorable attractions, including **Al Hamra**, one of Oman's most venerable traditional towns, and **Misfat al Abryeen**, one of its prettiest villages, while it's also worth making a short detour to the impressive **Al Hoota cave** nearby.

Al Hamra

Magical **AL HAMRA** is one of the best-preserved old towns in Oman, with a warren of stony, rubble-strewn alleyways lined with endless traditional mudbrick houses tumbling down the hillside to the idyllic oasis below; it's hauntingly time-warped, although as throughout the rest of Oman these old dwellings are now being systematically abandoned.

Bait al Safah

Main Street • Daily 9am–5pm; closed June–Aug • 3 OR (2 OR if accompanied by a guide) • ☏ 9901 0373, ⓦ baitalsafah.com

Much of the pleasure of a visit to Al Hamra simply consists of getting lost amid the winding streets, although there is one low-key attraction to head for, set along the main dirt road running along the bottom of the old town. A kind of living museum of old Oman, **Bait al Safah** occupies an exquisitely restored traditional house, done up with traditional furnishings and old artefacts – pots, coins, swords, and the like. It gives a nice (although perhaps rather sanitized) impression of what these houses might originally have looked like, while a few jolly old ladies from the town sit around baking bread, grinding coffee and flour, and so on.

ARRIVAL AND DEPARTURE   AL HAMRA

By car The turning to Al Hamra, and also Al Hoota Cave, is off the main Nizwa–Bahla highway by the shops with the big Toyota sign on top. Head along this road for 12km to reach the roundabout on the outskirts of Al Hamra by the Shell garage. Go straight across this roundabout (signed towards Al Hoota Cave), and then straight across a second roundabout (signed Center City). Follow this road as it curves left through the new town, passing a

brown sign on your right to Misfat al Abryeen (see page 103). Ignore this turning, continuing straight ahead until you reach a fork in the road by a mosque at the edge of the old town. Take the right-hand fork, which climbs up to a ridge above the old town (you'll see lots of mudbrick houses on your left). Park somewhere along here and walk down into the old town.

Al Hoota Cave

Well-signed around 9km east of Al Hamra (see directions above) • Tues, Thurs, Sat & Sun 9.30am–noon & 2–5pm, Fri 9.30am–11am & 2–5pm • Access to the cave is by guided tour only; these last 45min and depart roughly every 30min, with the last tour at 5pm daily • 6.5 OR • ☏ 2439 1284, ⓦ alhootacave.com

The spectacular **Al Hoota Cave** (also spelt Al Hota) offers a rare opportunity to look underneath Oman's remarkable geological surface. Though under indefinite repairs at the time of research, a quaint little electric **train** typically shuttles visitors between the entrance and the cave itself, about 300m distant. The caves are some two to three million years old and stretch for about 5km in total, of which 500m is open to visitors, accessible via a metal walkway with handrails all the way around (plus a few flights of stairs). The open section is impressively large: a huge, sepulchral cavern, though the stalagmites and stalactites are unimpressively gloopy, like the melted stumps of enormous candles. At the far end steps lead down to the edge of a **lake**, the largest of four in the caves – a rather spooky expanse of water stretching away under a low rock ceiling. The lake is 900m long and up to 10m deep in places, and is home to a unique species of blind fish, although you probably won't see any. Fortunately, you can spot them back in the upstairs geological exhibit at the visitor's centre, where there's also a pleasant café.

Wadi Bani Auf

Beyond Al Hoota Cave lies the start of the spectacular descent of the Western Hajar down a sheer escarpment through **Wadi Bani Auf** (or Awf), widely considered the most memorable off-road drive in the country. This is Oman at its most nerve-janglingly dramatic, with stupendous scenery and a rough, vertiginous track which challenges the skills of even experienced off-road drivers – not to be attempted lightly, and best avoided during or after rain.

The entire off-road section between Sharafat al Alamayn and the main road at Awabi (see page 124) takes around 2–3hr. The track is regularly graded but gets very churned up after spells of bad weather. It's also possible to tackle the route in reverse, driving up from the Batinah, although the driving is easier and the views generally better heading downhill.

Sharafat al Alamayn

The route starts between Al Hamra and Al Hoota Cave – follow the signs to Hat and Bilad Sayt. The first section is along good tarmac road which twists up to the top of the escarpment and the wonderful viewpoint of **Sharafat al Alamayn**, one of the finest panoramas in Oman, with views across the entire Western Hajar and down towards the coast below – it's worth the trip up in a 2WD even if you don't plan to continue.

The fine **hiking route** W10h (see page 94) heads west from here along the top of the ridge, connecting with route W9, which heads up to the top of the *jebel* and Mifat al Abryeen, and route W8, which descends to the village of Bilad Sayt.

Hat

Past Sharafat al Alamayn the tarmac ends and a rough track begins worming its way down the almost vertical escarpment, offering spectacular views all the way. It's around thirty minutes of bumping and grinding from here to the village of **HAT**, which you'll see off the track on your right, watered by a spectacular *falaj* which comes tumbling down from the mountains.

Bilad Sayt

Past here the track continues across a very rough wadi bed – difficult going even in a 4WD, and not to be attempted after rain. Another ten to fifteen minutes down the track brings you to the village of **BILAD SAYT**, 2km down a (signed) side-turning off the main track. Tucked away in the folds of the mountains, this Shangri-La-like settlement is one of the most famous traditional villages in Oman, although its size and relative modernity

2

GEOLOGY OF THE HAJAR

Geology is all around you in Oman in a way that's matched by few other places on earth. For professional geologists, the country is one of the most interesting on the planet, and even casual visitors cannot fail to be intrigued by the spectacular rock formations which fill every corner of the Hajar mountains, where the lack of vegetation and soil cover leaves millions of years of complex geological processes exposed, often with textbook clarity.

Much of Oman's geological interest (and, by extension, its spectacular mountain scenery) is the result of its location at the southeast corner of the **Arabian continental plate** where it meets the Eurasian (aka Asian) oceanic plate. As the Red Sea grows wider, Oman is being pushed slowly north and forced underneath the Eurasian plate (a rare example of a continental plate being "subducted" by an oceanic plate), a geological pile-up which has created the long mountainous chain of the Hajar.

Most of the rocks now making up the Hajar mountains were actually formed **underwater**. As the Arabian plate was driven underneath the Eurasian, large masses of what was originally submarine rock have been pushed on top of the mainland ("obducted"), sometimes travelling hundreds of kilometres inland – which explains the incongruous abundance of marine fossils found buried near the peaks of some of Arabia's highest mountains. Most of the main part of the range is made of up various types of limestone, ranging from older grey and yellow formations through to outcrops of so-called geological "exotics" – pale, whitish "islands" of younger limestone, such as Jebel Misht and Jebel Khawr, north and south of Al Ayn (see page 97) respectively.

Surrounding the limestone are Oman's celebrated **ophiolites** – rocks from the oceanic crust which have been lifted out of the water onto a continental plate. These are of particular interest to geologists in that they reveal processes which are normally buried kilometres underwater. They also provide Oman with one of its most distinctive landscapes, forming the fields of low, irregular, crumbling red-rock mountains which you can see along the Sumail Gap, around the Rustaq Loop and in many parts of the Eastern Hajar.

If you're interested in exploring further, pick up a copy of Samir Hanna's *Field Guide to the Geology of Oman* (see page 254).

(complete with a big red-and-white pylon, telephone wires and a large modern school) come as something of a surprise given the remote and inhospitable location. The core of the village remains magical, however, with a picturesque pile of small houses, crowned with a tiny fort, sitting above a lush swathe of immaculate terraced fields.

Wadi Bimah

Another fifteen minutes beyond Bilad Sayt you'll see a deep gorge in the mountains below you on the right. This is **Wadi Bimah**, or **"Snake Gorge"**, as it's popularly known, an impossibly narrow crack running through the surrounding mountains. The entrance to the gorge lies a couple of kilometres further down the track, about twenty minutes beyond Bilad Sayt. It's possible to scramble into the gorge over the jumble of boulders lining the wadi floor, although the gorge should be avoided if there's any hint of rain – people have drowned here in flash floods, during which the wadi can fill up with frightening speed.

Wadi Sahtan and the Sahtan Bowl

Past Wadi Bimah the track finally levels off, running through a narrow pass between red cliffs before reaching the junction with the side-track leading into **Wadi Sahtan** and the extensive **Sahtan Bowl**, a large natural hollow in the hills, rather like the Ghubrah Bowl (see page 123), dotted with old-fashioned villages. The area is particularly famous for its **honey**, and many of the locals still keep bees. From here, it's a short drive back to the main road near Awabi (see page 124).

ACCOMMODATION

WADI BANI AUF

Al Hoota Rest House About 1km down the road before you reach **Sharafat al Alamayn** ☎ 9282 2473, @ hootaoman@hotmail.com. Simple lodgings in a mix of spacious modern chalets and rooms, set in a pleasant spot above the mountains. The helpful owner has a wealth of information, the restaurant is decent and rooms are clean enough, though the rest house itself is a bit cheerless and rather expensive for what you get. Half board costs an extra 15 OR per person. 85 OR

Shorfet Al-Alamin 300m west of the Sharafat al Alamayn ☎ 9944 9071, ⓦ shorfetalalamin.com. Newly-opened, friendly hotel in an arcaded compound surrounded by walls (a vain attempt to keep out the goats, perhaps) near the very top of the mountain ridge, with a few dozen somewhat drab hotel rooms in the centre and a handful of bamboo cottages around the edges – all come with BBQ facilities out front and there's a cosy if sometimes crowded common area where breakfast and dinner are served. Half board costs an extra 10 OR per person. 40 OR

2

Misfat al Abryeen

Sleepy **MISFAT AL ABRYEEN** (often abbreviated to Misfat, or Misfah) is one of the prettiest traditional villages in Oman, a picturesque huddle of old ochre-coloured stone buildings looking, from certain angles, a bit like a medieval Italian hill village. Arriving at the small parking area at the edge of the village you'll see only a single street climbing steeply up the hillside. Dive down one of the side alleys, however, and you'll find yourself amid a marvellous warren of twisting lanes, covered passages, gateways and meandering flights of steps – all of which bring you down, sooner or later, to the *falaj* which runs below the village, surrounded by lush bougainvillea, banana palms and other greenery. Back in the centre, it's also possible to scramble up the rocky hillside to the picturesquely ruined **watchtower**, said to be over a thousand years old.

The falaj

Once you've explored the village, head back to the main road, walk up the hill and then down the steps on the far side to rejoin the **falaj** as it exits the village running through a rocky, steep-sided gorge crowded with date palms and tiny terraced fields. You can walk along the *falaj* walls or the footpath which runs just above it for about 1km up into the gorge until the *falaj* disappears into a large rock. En route, notice the regular gaps in the side of the *falaj* from where subsidiary channels run off into fields below; these are kept blocked up with stones, which are removed when the adjacent fields need irrigating.

If you want to see more of the surrounding area, **hiking route W9** (see page 94) heads west of here across the top of the hills.

ARRIVAL AND TOURS
MISFAT AL ABRYEEN

By car Take the turning from Al Hamra (see page 100), then follow the road for around 8km; the road is narrow and twisty, but fine for a 2WD.

Tours Canyon Adventures and Tours (☎ 9941 2660, ⓦ canyonadventurestours.com) bounces between both guesthouses in town, with highly popular 3hr cultural tours that take you around the village offering fascinating insights on life in pre-1970 Misfat (25 OR), as well as cycling trips and full-day guided hikes up the W9 route to or from Bilad Sayt or Sharafat al Alamayn (85 OR).

ACCOMMODATION

Misfat may be the Western Hajar's most tranquil spot for whiling away a few days in the oasis' shade, and thanks to a pair of friendly and roughly comparable **guesthouses** in the old town, it's never been more accessible. At the time of research there were also rumours of a dedicated campsite coming to the village.

Al Misfah Hospitality Inn Just beside the road at the town entrance ☎ 9110 4466, ✉ misfah.inn@gmail. com. Brand new family-run guesthouse in a set of restored buildings in the upper part of town. True to their original design, the seven lantern-lit rooms all come with shared bathroom and don't have a whole lot of natural light, but are cosy enough, including a trio of three-bed rooms (70 OR). There's also a welcoming communal sitting area, where there's always complimentary tea, dates and cardamom-scented coffee, and the adjacent terrace hosts a nightly buffet dinner, with traditional dishes often prepared by the owner himself. Rates include half board. 50 OR

★ **Misfah Old House** Signed down the steps about 3min beyond the main gate into the old town ☎ 9361 1500, ⓦ misfaholdhouse.com. The town's original guesthouse, this remains the more relaxing of the two, set a bit further down from the road and thus deeper into the oasis. There are a dozen simple rooms with big windows overlooking the palm groves and mattresses laid out on wooden floors – two of the rooms have attached bathrooms (60 OR) while the rest share facilities. There's also tea and coffee ad infinitum in a pleasant common area and breakfast and dinner buffets served on a terrace up above. Rates include half board. 55 OR

Jebel Shams

The mountains to the northwest of Nizwa are much less developed than those on the Saiq Plateau, which makes for more continuously spectacular scenery, although there's no equivalent here to the Saiq Plateau's dramatic hanging villages. The highpoint (in every sense) of a visit out here is the drive up the flanks of **Jebel Shams** (3009m), the highest mountain in Oman.

Wadi Ghul and Ghul village

12km west of Al Hamra on the road to Jebel Shams

The road up Jebel Shams starts by running past the entrance of the narrow, steep-sided **Wadi Ghul**, which connects with the spectacular Wadi Nakhr directly below the summit of Jebel Shams. It's possible to **walk** up to Wadi Nakhr along hiking route W6/W6a (see page 94), which climbs from here up along the cliffs above the wadi to the village of Khateem.

At the entrance to the wadi you'll see the remains old **Ghul village**, a collection of ruined mudbrick houses clinging to the hill on the far side of the river bed, above lush date plantations, and disintegrating back into (and becoming increasingly indistinguishable from) the orangey-coloured rocks of the hillside whence it came. The modern village faces it on the other side of the wadi. You can explore the oasis at the bottom of the hill, with a *falaj* running between tiny banked-up plots, although there's no longer any safe way of scrambling up to the old buildings and fortifications on the hilltop above. The name *ghul* means, literally, "ghoul" – a devilish kind of jinn (the English word is derived from the Arabic, which also gave us the name of the star Algol). Quite why the village is named thus is unclear, although it may conceivably have something to do with the supernatural behaviour of the nearby jinns of Bahla (see page 106).

Wadi Nakhr

The first viewpoint is 40km from Al Hamra (28km from Ghul)

Beyond Ghul, the road begins to wind steadily up the western flanks of Jebel Shams. It's surfaced for most of the journey, though towards the top there's a seven-kilometre stretch where the tarmac gives, happily reappearing about three kilometres before the parking area for the first magnificent viewpoint over **Wadi Nakhr**. Sometimes referred to as Wadi Ghul (to which it's joined), this breathtaking chasm is more popularly known as the **"Grand Canyon"** of Oman, and gazing down into its abyss is the main reward for the trip. The landscape hereabouts is very similar to that on the road up to the Saiq Plateau, with huge sedimentary limestone formations, their colours ranging from chalky greys and greens through to sandstone oranges and reds. En route you'll also notice the distinctive outline of **Jebel Misht** (see page 143) standing in proud isolation away to the west.

Khateem

The paved road disappears once again about a kilometre after the first viewpoint, just beyond the *Jabal Shams Resort* (see page 105). From here, a dirt track runs about four kilometres further to the windswept hamlet of **KHATEEM** (also spelt Khatayam), just a handful of tiny houses clinging to the edge of the canyon. Getting out of your vehicle you'll probably be greeted by locals trying to sell you some of the area's traditional black-and-red rugs, or smaller woven trinkets made from the horns or fleece of the long-haired goats which browse the mountains hereabouts.

The Balcony Walk

Khateem is also the starting point for the spectacular **Balcony Walk**, part of hiking route W6 and clearly waymarked with the usual red, white and yellow painted flags (see page 94). This is probably the most famous hike in the country, winding around the cliffs halfway up the rim of Wadi Nakhr to the abandoned village of As Sab. The scenery here is some of the most dramatic anywhere in Oman: a kind of huge natural amphitheatre, with kilometre-high cliffs, the tiny village of Nakhr way below in the shadowy depths of the canyon and birds of prey – such as the Egyptian vulture, with its distinctive black-and-white-striped wings – hovering silently on the thermals overhead. Count on around three hours for the return journey from Khateem to As Sab, although even a ten-minute walk from Khateem offers memorable views and a good taste of the scenery hereabouts.

The summit

The road to the **summit** itself (topped by a golfball-style radar installation) is off limits due to military use, although you can still walk up to the southern summit (2997m), known as Qarn al Ghamaydah, along hiking route W4 (see box, page 94), with marvellous views into Wadi Nakhr, Wadi Sahtan and Wadi Bani Auf en route.

ARRIVAL AND TOURS — JEBEL SHAMS

By car Considering the rough stretches of road towards the end of the track, 4WD is highly recommended, though not essential in dry weather.

Tours It's possible to arrange a 4WD with guide for the trip up Jebel Shams through the nicer hotels in Nizwa and the guesthouses in Misfat al Abryeen. Husaak (☏ 9712 3324, ⓦ husaak.com), based at *Sama Heights Resort*, arranges all-inclusive hikes around Jebel Shams and Wadi Nakhr (from 29 OR per person in a group of four), while *Canyon Adventures* (see page 103) in Misfat offers day tours of Jebel Shams for 45 OR per person.

ACCOMMODATION

Rather surprisingly, there are a couple of **places to stay** right on top of the mountain, either of which offers an excellent base for walks around the mountain. If you're equipped for **wild camping**, there are some spectacular spots just off the road above the gorge – but be warned that it gets surprisingly chilly at night.

Jabal Shams Resort At the end of the paved road, about 1km past the first viewpoint ☏ 9938 2639, ⓦ jebelshamsresort.com. The best of Jebel Shams' two accommodation options, with a stunning location and extremely helpful staff. Some of the attractively furnished chalets boast superb mountain views through big French windows, while there are also some cosy mountain lodges and a massively overpriced Arabian tent with mattresses on the floor. Rates include half-board, with meals served in a trim little (unlicensed) restaurant, and there's a heated pool on-site. You can bring your own tent and camp here too (paying an extra 8 OR for breakfast and dinner). Camping (per person) 10 OR, Arabian tents 50 OR, mountain lodges 60 OR, chalets 70 OR

Sama Heights Resort 2km before the first viewpoint ☏ 2448 9853, ⓦ samaresorts.com. This sprawling camp is located in a natural hollow in the hills, a setting that provides a measure of shelter but also means that there are no views. Closest to the road is a row of passable tents with attached bathrooms, proper beds and air coolers, while the rest of the camp is more luxurious, with spacious if somewhat cheerless bungalows and grand chalets with huge windows overlooking the camp. There's also a pleasant common area and (unlicensed) restaurant. All rates are half-board. Arabian tents 45 OR, bungalows 60 OR, chalets 120 OR

2

Bahla

Some 40km west of Nizwa, the small town of **BAHLA** is famous for its gigantic fort and its distinctive earthenware pottery. Recently opened to the public after extensive restoration works, the **fort** is one of the most splendid and worthwhile in all of Oman. Bahla's crumbling **old town** and **city walls** are also worth a look, as is the engaging little **souk**. The town also has a certain reputation as the favoured haunt of mischievous jinns and other supernatural phenomena – a kind of Omani Glastonbury.

The fort

Mon–Thurs & Sun 9am–4pm, Fri 8–11am • 500bz

There's nothing subtle about Bahla's **fort**. One of the biggest in Oman, its immense walls and irregular skyline of assorted towers, bastions and crenellations loom massively above the modest modern town, looking like some kind of gigantic medieval factory. As with many of Oman's forts, Bahla is believed to have been established in pre-Islamic times, though the present structure dates back to the days of the Banu Nabhan, the dominant tribe in the area between the twelfth and fifteenth centuries. It was largely rebuilt during the seventeenth century, though by the twentieth century had fallen into such into an advanced state of disrepair that it was in danger of collapsing entirely. In 1987, it was listed as a UNESCO World Heritage Site and closed for the huge renovation works which were wrapped up in 2012.

The oldest and perhaps most interesting section lies on the southeast corner, a citadel built during the Nabhani dynasty and known as Al-Qasaba. A fort within a fort, its grand entry gate rises from the castle's courtyard, while just beyond is an impressively carved mihrab, a fine early example of muqarnas, the distinctly Islamic style of honeycomb vaulting. You can climb to the top of the five-storey structure to check out the shelves of its once impressive library and enjoy the views from its trio of towers.

The mosque and old town

It's worth exploring the area running down to the wadi below the fort on the western side of town. Start at the **mosque** sitting directly south of the fort on top of a large raised terrace – a plain, mudbrick box. Believed to be one of the oldest mosques in the country, its interior remains closed to the public, and therefore the only way to glimpse its exquisitely carved fourteenth-century mihrab is by visiting the photo display in the castle's Bait al-Qaed. The mosque's terrace, however, offers probably the best view of the fort in town, as well as a bird's-eye view over the extensive remains of **old Bahla**, a dense cluster of mudbrick houses in various states of disrepair, bounded by a couple of old gateways and the remains of old defensive walls and towers. Some of the buildings are surprisingly grand, including a number of very fine, but very decayed, three-storey houses, many of which retain their solid original wooden doors (or colourful modern metal replacements). The houses are largely uninhabited now and, as with so many similar places throughout Oman, it's difficult to imagine the ruins surviving for much longer.

The city walls

Continuing away from the fort brings you to even more considerable remains of Bahla's **city walls**, which stretch for some 12km around the fort, town and surrounding date plantations. The best-preserved section is down along the wadi. Walk down along the main road towards Jabrin until you reach the bridge over the wadi, look left, and you'll see an impressive line of fortifications stretching away in the distance, well over 5m high in places. There's also another stretch of walls on your right as you drive into town from Nizwa, shortly before you reach the fort.

The souk and around

Daily 7–11am & 4–6pm

Back near the fort on the other side of the main road lies the town's **souk**, one of the more attractive in the north, with dozens of little shops lined up within a cluster of arcaded buildings. The souk was once home to a famous old **tree** (now sadly gone), said to be the home of a jinn, which locals tied down with chains for fear that the resident supernatural spirit might fly off with it.

Al Adawi Clay Pots Factory

Bahla is also well known for its **pottery**, said to owe its superior quality to the unusual excellence of the local clay (collected from the local wadi) and the skill of the town's artisans, although you won't see much in town – most of it is sent off to the souk in Nizwa. Follow the road through the souk and out the far side into an attractive area of date plantations for about 1km to reach the **Al Adawi Clay Pots Factory**, marked by three domed, clay kilns. Here you can see the pots being made, and also buy them at prices significantly below what you'll pay elsewhere. Even if you're not interested in pots it's an attractive walk, along narrow shady streets dotted with the occasional old mudbrick house or fortification.

ACCOMMODATION **BAHLA**

Bahla Hotel Apartments 5km north of Bahla Fort ☏ 2542 1017, ⊕ bahlahotelapartments.info. Set just off the main highway equidistant from Bahla Fort and the turnoff to Al Hamra, this functional hotel is well-situated as a base for exploring Bahla and beyond. Rooms are clean and comfortable enough, with little balconies overlooking the road, and there's a decent breakfast buffet (for an extra 3 OR) and a good restaurant out front. 15 OR

Jabrin Fort

Around 7km southwest of Bahla • Mon–Thurs & Sun 9am–4pm, Fri 8–11am • 500bz

The small town of **Jabrin** (also spelled Jabreen, Jibreen, Gabrin, Gibrin and so on) is best known for its picture-perfect **fort**, nestled amid palm trees. If you only visit one fort while you're in Oman, this is the one to choose. The main building is surrounded by high walls and a gravel courtyard, home to a small mosque; you can also see the deep *falaj*, which formerly provided the castle with water (and which flows right through the building), to the rear. The **interior** is absorbingly labyrinthine, with dozens of little rooms packed in around a pair of courtyards. Essentially, the building divides into two halves, which, for the sake of clarity, are described below as the **northern** and **southern wings**, although you won't find this terminology used in the fort itself.

Brief history

The fort dates mainly from around 1670, one of several built during the Ya'aruba building boom of the later seventeenth century, constructed at the behest of the future imam **Bil'arab bin Sultan bin Saif** (reigned 1680–92), who lies buried here in a crypt beneath the fort. Further alterations were made to the castle during the eighteenth century by imam Muhammad bin Nasr al Ghafiri (reigned 1725–27), and the whole thing was restored between 1979 and 1983.

The northern wing

Walk through the entrance and you'll find yourself in the fort's extraordinarily deep and shady central courtyard. A right turn here brings you immediately into a second courtyard at the centre of the northern wing, centred around a similarly narrow and deep courtyard, with beautifully carved windows and wooden balconies above.

The ground floor

Rooms on the **ground floor** are devoted to practical matters. These include a huge date store (with distinctive corrugated stone floor; sacks of dates were stacked up here, and the resultant juice collected in the channels running across the floor), a kitchen area (with the adjacent *falaj* providing constant running water), and a guard room with a microscopic jail sunk into the floor, like a cupboard in the ground.

The rooftop

From next to the date store, steep steps lead directly up to the rooftop, passing an entrance into the low-ceilinged guard tower en route. Emerging onto the rooftop, note a second flight of steps immediately to your right which descend back into the fort, and to which you'll return in a moment.

The **rooftop** itself is covered in a further jumble of buildings and towers. The largest structure is a fine pillared mosque, with traces of old painting on its arches and a finely painted ceiling. Steps lead up onto the roof of the mosque, the highest point of the whole fort, with superlative 360-degree views. A Qur'anic school (*madrasah*) stands next door.

The first floor

Take the steps mentioned above back down to reach the fine set of rooms on the **first floor**, signed as "Conference Room, Dining Rooms & Courtroom"; all unusually spacious and high-ceilinged compared to most apartments within Omani forts (as are similar rooms in the southern wing). These include the large **courtroom**, with scales of justice hanging from the wall and a small opening at the far end of the room through which those convicted were forced to crawl out before being taken away for punishment.

Next door is a **dining room** and the so-called "conference room", a curious translation for what is simply a traditional **majlis**, or meeting room, with carpeted floor, cushions around walls, shelves lined with old swords, pots, kettles and a fine pair of wooden doors and painted ceiling hung with three big brass lamps. The high ceiling and line of floor-level windows keep things pleasantly cool, even without air conditioning.

Close by on the same floor you'll find a **horse stall** in which the imam was wont to stable his favourite steed. Continuing down the stairs from here you'll pass a **women's jail** (a standard feature of Omani forts) – not especially inviting, although it's at least a bit less claustrophobic than the men's jail a few steps below.

The southern wing

Continue to the bottom of the steps and you'll find yourself back next to the central courtyard. Turn right at the bottom of the stairs to enter the fort's southern wing, home to the finest sequence of interiors of any fort in Oman.

The ground and first floors

Once again, rooms on the **ground floor** have a practical emphasis, including soldiers' quarters, an armoury and yet another jail (entered via a tiny hole in the wall). Climb the stairs around the back of the soldiers' quarters to reach the **first floor**, home to a further superb pair of *majlis* (signed "public reception rooms") embellished with richly painted ceilings – the red, black and gold ceiling in the second room is particularly fine. A library stands on the opposite side of the stairs with two-tiered windows with rustic little wooden shutters.

The second floor

A further flight of stairs, framed with delicately moulded arches, leads up to the **second floor**, formerly the inner sanctum of the ruling imam and home to a suite of even more lavish rooms. These include the so-called "Sun and Moon" room, with yet another richly painted ceiling, the imam's beautiful private *majlis* and, finest of all, the imam's personal "suite" (as it's described), a pair of rooms with intricately carved, rather Indian-looking filigree stone arches and wooden shuttered windows, although only one small section of the original painted ceiling survives. Steps continue from here up to the top of the fort, emerging opposite the rooftop mosque.

Tomb of Bil'arab bin Sultan bin Saif

Return to the entrance into the central keep and head through the door on your right to reach the crypt-like grotto beneath the northern wing. Here you'll find the wonderfully atmospheric **tomb of Bil'arab bin Sultan bin Saif** (see page 235), who is said to have died by his own hand at Jabrin in 1692 at the end of his unhappy thirteen-year reign. The tomb is surrounded by arches carved with Qur'anic script and with the *falaj* flowing beneath. Yet another flight of stairs heads up next to the tomb, leading to the public reception rooms on the first floor.

ARRIVAL AND DEPARTURE	**JABRIN FORT**
By car From Bahla, take the main road south from the fort, following the signs for Highway 15, then pass straight through the roundabout, over the highway and straight	through the next roundabout – continue south for 2km and the castle will be signed off to your right.

ACCOMMODATION

Jibreen Hotel In the middle of Jabrin town, just south of the main road (about 200m west of the roundabout where the road heads south to the fort) ☎ 2536 3340. A rather uninviting place in a cheerless town-centre location.	Service is friendly and the rooms are large and reasonably comfortable, although you'll have to put up with some of Oman's ugliest furniture. Unless you're really stuck, you'd be better off pushing on to Bahla, Ibri or Nizwa. <u>25 OR</u>

Salut

About 30km south of Bahla and 2km north of the town of Bisya; look out for the signs to "Salut Castle and Archeological Site" • Free

About 20km south of Jabrin Fort is the ancient settlement of **Salut**, scattered widely across a flood plain at the convergence of two wadis. Its fort, Bronze Age towers and beehive tombs, similar to those found at Bat (see page 142), piqued the interest of researchers in 2004, and since then it's risen to become perhaps the busiest archeological site in all of Northern Oman. There's also restoration work afoot, and it's likely only a matter of time before official inclusion on the UNESCO World Heritage Site list.

Scholarly findings have suggested a place for Salut at the heart of Omani history, linking it to the first arrival of Arabian tribes, the first appearance of the Omani *falaj* system, and the birth of some of the country's oldest myths. According to legend, Solomon travelled here to find the old castle completely abandoned (aside from a sole, talkative eagle), subsequently ordering the local jinn to dig the first underground water channels in order to bring the place back to life. Indeed, Iron Age settlers flourished here in the first half of the first millennium BC, building on top of the older, largely forgotten settlements of many centuries prior and constructing an impressive irrigation system and a thick-walled **castle**, the scant remains of which reward visitors today.

Apart from a rebuilt section of the outer walls and a reconstructed Bronze Age tower, there isn't a terrible amount to see at Salut, though it's worth the short hike up through the castle ruins to take in the settlement's scale. You can also walk up the hill opposite the castle to the northeast – capped with a **beehive tomb** and an oddly reconstructed, columned **shrine** – for an impressive view back on the castle and its dusty surrounds. For a look at the site's archeological finds, including pottery, bronze tools and weapons, check out Salut's virtual museum at ☏ ancientoman.cfs.unipi.it.

Al Batinah and Al Dhahirah

ANCIENT TOMBS AT JEBEL MISHT

Al Batinah and Al Dhahirah

North of Muscat lies Al Batinah, a fertile region which stretches along the coast beyond the capital all the way up to the UAE border. Its name – meaning "the belly" – relates to the Western Hajar mountain range, the "backbone" of Oman immediately to the west. This was once the most vibrant and cosmopolitan region in Oman, thanks to its wealth of natural resources and proximity to the great civilizations of Mesopotamia and, subsequently, Persia, although the gradual emergence of Muscat as the country's principal city and port led to a steady decline in Al Batinah's economic fortunes, and things are a lot quieter now. Away from the main coastal highway, most of the region is pleasantly comatose, with a sand-fringed coastline, dotted with fishing boats and old forts and backed by endless date plantations.

3

At the southern end of the region lies the personable town of **Seeb**, within hailing distance of the capital and international airport, and sleepier **Barka**, home to a fine fort (though closed for renovations at the time of research), the absorbing old Bait Na'aman and occasional bull-butting contests. Both Seeb and Barka make good bases from which to explore the Batinah's main attraction, the so-called **Rustaq Loop**, a fine drive between the coast and the foot of the Hajar mountains, taking in the superb forts at **Nakhal**, **Rustaq** and **Al Hazm**, with numerous dramatic wadis shooting off into the hills en route, offering myriad off-road opportunities. Back on the coast, the **Sawadi and Daymaniyat Islands** offer some superb diving, although otherwise there's not much to detain you before you reach **Sohar**, Oman's former commercial capital and still the largest town in the north, although there are few physical reminders of its long and illustrious history.

Inland from Al Batinah, **Al Dhahirah** region is one of the least visited parts of the country and covers a wide and largely featureless expanse of gravel desert stretching from the UAE border down to the mountains around Bahla – the striking Jebel al Hawra and surrounding mountains, hemming in the sleepy town of **Yanqul**, are a welcome exception. Few tourists make it here, unless transiting between Oman and Al Ain in the UAE via Al Dhahirah's main town, **Buraimi**. Home to a pair of fine forts and with a lively mercantile atmosphere, Buraimi serves as a convenient entry or exit point if you're heading to or from Abu Dhabi or Dubai, although it's also well worth a visit in its own right. From Buraimi, a spectacular road runs over the mountains and down **Wadi Jizzi** to the coast at Sohar.

Alternatively, the fast and relatively traffic-free Highway 21 arrows south from Buraimi to the little-visited but surprisingly interesting town of **Ibri**, home to yet another old fort and souk, and the remarkable old mudbrick village of As Suleif. Beyond Ibri lie the villages of **Bat** and **Al Ayn**, home to a fascinating scatter of Bronze Age beehive tombs and other structures, some of Oman's most important archeological remains.

Highlights

① Seeb One of the region's most interesting towns, with colourful shops and souks, and a breezy seafront. See page 115

② Bait Na'aman, Barka Atmospheric old fortified house whose beautifully restored interiors offer a fascinating glimpse into the life of Oman's former rulers. See page 118

③ Nakhal Fairytale fort at the foot of the towering Jebel Akdhar. See page 122

④ Wekan Spectacular mountain village perched high above the Ghubrah Bowl. See page 123

⑤ Daymaniyat Islands These rocky little islands offer a wealth of wildlife, along with some of the country's finest diving and snorkelling. See page 128

⑥ As Suleif Absorbing ruins of one of Oman's finest old walled villages, with a labyrinthine tangle of mudbrick houses, mosques and watchtowers. See page 141

⑦ Al Ayn Intriguing collection of Bronze Age beehive tombs in a dramatic mountain location. See page 143

HIGHLIGHTS ARE MARKED ON THE MAP ON PAGE 114

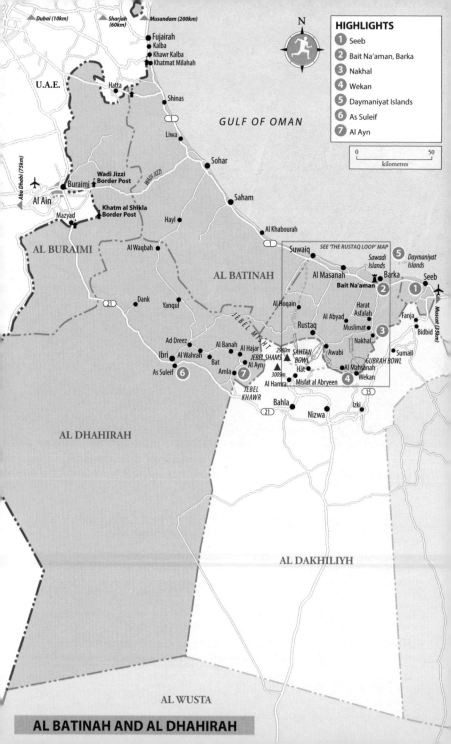

AL BATINAH AND AL DHAHIRAH

Seeb

A fifteen-minute drive west of the international airport, the engaging town of **SEEB** (or Al Seeb, as it's usually signposted, also As Seeb, As Sib, or just plain Sib) sees few tourists, but is well worth a couple of hours of your time or, even better, an overnight stay in order to experience a slice of quintessential contemporary Omani life. Despite now being in danger of being swallowed up by the suburban sprawl of Muscat, Seeb is easily the liveliest and most interesting of all the towns along the coast north of the capital, with a vibrant commercial atmosphere and a colourful main street.

Seeb's proximity to the airport makes it a convenient first or last stop on a tour of the country, while it's also a good base from which to tackle the Rustaq Loop.

Wadi al Bahais Street

A walk along Seeb's principal thoroughfare, **Wadi al Bahais Street**, is surprisingly absorbing; the architecture may be modern and functional, but the various merchandise on display offers a fascinating snapshot of Omani trade in miniature – pretty somnolent during the day, although lively (and brilliantly illuminated with neon shop signs) after dark.

The main road describes an extended loop (all one-way traffic) through the town centre, splitting just past the Oman Oil petrol station. Where the main road divides into two you'll see a number of furniture shops selling **mandoos**, modern versions of the traditional wooden chests with elaborate metalwork decoration which can be seen in forts all over the country, their design largely unchanged for hundreds of years.

Past here, the first section of the road is dedicated to a colourful array of **textile shops**, their windows filled with pouting mannequins dressed in eye-poppingly spangly

3

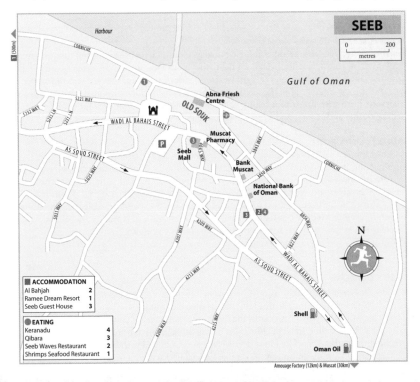

SEEB

0   200
metres

Harbour

CORNICHE

Gulf of Oman

S221 WAY

S232 WAY

S235 LN

S231 LN

WADI AL BAHAIS STREET

OLD SOUK

Abna Friesh Centre

Muscat Pharmacy

AS SOUQ STREET

S023 WAY

S011 WAY

Seeb Mall

Bank Muscat

National Bank of Oman

3843 WAY

3850 WAY

CORNICHE

4209 WAY

4207 WAY

4213 WAY

4208 WAY

3829 WAY

4125 WAY

AS SOUQ STREET

WADI AL BAHAIS STREET

3856 WAY

N

Shell

Oman Oil

ACCOMMODATION

Al Bahjah	2
Ramee Dream Resort	1
Seeb Guest House	3

EATING

Keranadu	4
Qibara	3
Seeb Waves Restaurant	2
Shrimps Seafood Restaurant	1

Amouage Factory (12km) & Muscat (30km)

3

THE CHANGING FACE OF SEEB

The area around Seeb is the focus of several ambitious government-funded **construction projects**, which no doubt have been planned with one eye on a not too distant future when the town has been swallowed up by Muscat's ever-expanding sprawl. The most comprehensive of these projects is Madinat al Irfan, a planned "city" to the west of the airport which will fill the gap between Seeb and Muscat proper.

The **Oman Botanic Garden**, currently under development near Wadi al Khoud to the south of Seeb, will be one of the largest of its kind in the world once it is finally complete – designs had only just been unveiled at the time of writing, so completion will take another few years at least. The vision is for a thousand-acre site combining futuristic biomes with a reconstruction of Oman's eight natural habitats, including wadis, mountains and deserts, as well as, rather impressively, every single plant species native to the Middle East.

On a similarly ambitious note, the **Oman Aquarium**, due to open in spring 2018 as part of the new Palm Mall, will be the largest of its kind in the Middle East, serving as a home for thirty thousand sea creatures.

---

dresses, alongside other places retailing more sober (but still richly embroidered) *abbayat*, the black robes which most Omani women wear in public over their house clothes. Many of the fabric shops offer **tailoring** services – a good place to get cheap clothes made up, or to pick up a cut-price copy of your favourite shirt or frock. There are also a large number of shops selling **gold jewellery** in traditional Omani designs. Past here (around *Al Bahjah* hotel) the mercantile angle changes, with shops specializing in Omani **caps** and **musar** (turbans) alongside others selling traditional **perfumes**, some with pretty window displays of chintzy glass perfume bottles.

The old souk

Mon–Thurs, Sat & Sun 8–11.30am & 5–9pm, Fri 5–9pm

Further along, the street becomes more workaday. Continue past the large but uninteresting Seeb Mall on your left. Ahead you'll see the town's main mosque. Before reaching this, head into the tangle of alleyways on the right (seafront) side of the road. This is Seeb's **old souk**, one of the most interesting in the north, small but surprisingly labyrinthine, with narrow alleyways lined with little shops selling *halwa*, nuts and honey, along with further places selling clothes and fabrics, and a line of vegetable stalls under tattered awnings.

Abna Friesh Centre

In the Friesh Sons Centre on the east side of the souk • Mon–Thurs, Sat & Sun 8am–1pm & 4–10pm, Fri 4–10pm

Specializing in traditional herbal treatments, the popular **Abna Friesh Centre** boasts one of Oman's most absorbing window displays, with shelves packed with all manner of exotic purgatives and restoratives ranging from soap nut, toothbrush tree and humble plant through to purging garlic, arsenic and bright yellow chunks of sulphur. The **Abna Friesh Ayurvedic Medical Centre** next door offers a selection of similarly traditional nostrums, including the treatment of cancer using hot irons and herbs, Qur'anic exorcism and "therapy of the haunted by demons and magic".

The corniche

On the far side of the souk you come out on Seeb's long seafront **corniche**, where you'll find the town's fish market along with a long swathe of rather muddy sand – usually busy with half-a-dozen football matches later in the day. Continuing west along the corniche you'll pass a few shops selling small pet birds and others specializing in fishing equipment before reaching the **harbour**, enclosed by a large breakwater and lined with boats and piles of large, hemispherical wire-mesh fish traps, a bit like skeletal igloos with funnel-shaped openings.

Amouage factory

On the main highway to Nizwa about 1km west of Rusayl roundabout (look out for the blue signs on your right), down the small road just before Al Dar Interiors • Mon–Thurs & Sun 8.30am–5.30pm • Free • ⓦ amouage.com

Given Oman's obsession with all things olfactory, it's no surprise that the country is home to one of the world's most expensive and unusual perfumes. The upmarket **Amouage** brand was founded in 1983 by a member of the royal family and now produces around ten different scents for men and women, with sales outlets in around forty countries worldwide. Amouage perfumes all feature traditional Omani ingredients such as silver frankincense, myrrh from Salalah and rock roses from Jebel Akhdar; scents are packaged in quaint bottles inspired by the shape of a *khanjar* (for men) and the dome of a miniature mosque (for women).

Visitors are welcome at Amouage's **factory** just outside Seeb, a surprisingly small and homely place where you can watch bottles being individually hand-filled and packaged, and learn more about the various scents. If you fancy buying some, a bottle of the premier scent, "Gold", will set you back around 120 OR for a 100ml bottle, although there are also less expensive products on offer including soaps, body lotion, travel sprays and candles.

ARRIVAL AND GETTING AROUND   SEEB

By taxi A pre-paid taxi from the airport to Seeb costs 8 OR, and there are plenty of taxis cruising the streets around the town itself.

ACCOMMODATION

Given its size, Seeb musters a reasonable choice of accommodation options, with the added bonus of a couple of decent hotel restaurants and other licensed venues thrown in for good measure.

Al Bahjah Wadi al Bahais St ☎ 2442 4404, ⓦ rameehotels. com; map p.115. Pleasingly old-fashioned and slightly chintzy hotel with spacious and very comfortably furnished rooms, which are well maintained if not exactly stylish – the avocado bathrooms are about forty years late, for example. They're generally very pleasant, though, even if the distant thumping of the various in-house entertainment venues occasionally intrudes. Facilities include free use of the pool at the *Ramee Dream Resort*, the decent *Keranadu* restaurant (see page 117), and the pan-Asian *Oriental Fusion*. The hotel is also home to a couple of bars in the form of the *Al Massarrat* sports bar and the 24/7 *Al Saadah Café*. **23 OR**

Ramee Dream Resort 1.5km west of the centre, just behind the corniche ☎ 2445 3399, ⓦ rameehotels.com; map p.115. There's an air of the vintage American motel about this resort, set low around a palm-fringed pool, but

there's nothing old hat about the rooms, which are stylishly modern and extremely comfortable. Bathrooms feature separate showers and huge bathtubs. The pool is the only one in Seeb (non-guests 3 OR/hr; *Al Bahjah* hotel guests can use it for free); other facilities include the licensed *Kalpaka* Indian restaurant, specialising in Keralan Malabar cuisine, and, somewhat incongruously, a billiards room and library. Breakfast is available for an extra 3 OR. **35 OR**

Seeb Guest House Main road, diagonally opposite Al Bahjah hotel ☎ 2442 3202, ⓔ seebguesthouse@ gmail.com; map p.115. Simple but comfortable no-frills guesthouse whose rooms are showing their age a little, but are a bargain nonetheless. No facilities to speak of, but the restaurant and bars of the *Al Bahjah* hotel are just over the road. Tends to get booked solid, so advance reservations are pretty much essential. **18 OR**

EATING

The only **licensed** venues in the town centre are the *Keranadu* restaurant at *Al Bahjah* hotel, or the *Al Massarrat* sport bar. The *Kalpaka* restaurant at *Ramee Dream Resort* (see above) is also licensed.

Keranadu Al Bahjah hotel, Wadi al Bahais St ☎ 2442 4404; map p.115. One of the few half-decent Indian restaurants in northern Oman, specializing in spicy Keralan cuisine, and with a good spread of North Indian favourites too – anything from *malai kofta* and butter chicken through to masala dosa and malabar fish curry (and with a good vegetarian selection too), plus a few Chinese and continental options. It's licensed, and serves food until 2am, making it

the place to come in Seeb for a midnight snack. Most mains around 1.5–3 OR. Sat–Thurs noon–3am, Fri noon–2am.

★**Qibara** Seeb Mall ☎ 2442 8000, ⓦ qibara.com; map p.115. This polished new restaurant is the name on everyone's lips in Seeb, and quite rightly. The menu is a wide-ranging affair, with Indian and Chinese classics sitting alongside burgers, pizzas and the odd traditional Omani dish. Don't let that put you off, though – everything is good,

3

and they don't overstretch themselves. The decor is a curious blend of the traditional (adobe-style walls and ornately carved Arabian doors) and the trendy (reclaimed furniture and light fittings made from repurposed fans), but it works, and the prices aren't unreasonable (mains 1–4 OR). Mon–Thurs & Sun 11am–midnight, Fri 1pm–midnight.

Seeb Waves Restaurant Corniche, just east of the souk ☎2442 5556; map p.115. This breezy seafront café is a good place to sit out and people-watch after dark. Food is average, with the usual Omani café fare including shwarmas plus chicken/mutton/prawn/fish/cuttlefish

biryanis, *qabooli* and *kebsa*, along with some Chinese options. Mains around 1–2 OR. Daily 9am–2am.

Shrimps Seafood Restaurant Dama St ☎9503 3490, ⓦfacebook.com/SeafoodOman; map p.115. This unassuming restaurant overlooking the beach has a limited menu, but when the food's this good, that isn't an issue. 1.6 OR gets you vast quantities of fresh squid, shrimp or fish, spiced and grilled and served with similarly generous portions of salad, garlic paste and bread – simply wrap up and feast. This is lunch as it should be. All dishes 1.6 OR. Daily 10am–12.30am.

Barka

A forty-minute drive west of the airport lies the low-key **BARKA**. As with many other places along the Batinah coast, the rather sleepy town you see today gives little sense of its former importance, when it was a major centre of local Gulf trade. The imposing **fort**, built during Ya'aruba times and subsequently expanded by the Al Bu Saids, is the major sight in the town itself (although closed for renovations at the time of research), while just outside lies the superb old **Bait Na'aman** fortified house. At the time of writing, a mixed-development project known as **Hayy al Sharq** was in the planning stages, set to incorporate a theme park, equestrian centre, and wildlife and water parks.

The fort

Turn right at the T-junction in the centre of town and head along the road past the shops for about 200m

At the time of research, **Barka Fort** was closed, with no re-opening date in sight, in order to undergo extensive renovations of the type which have spruced up the forts at Nakhal, Rustaq and Al Hazm. Entering the fort, steps lead up through the large gateway-cum-entrance hall to reach the raised central courtyard. Ahead, at the top of the steps, stands a simple little **mosque**. On your right, a second gateway leads into the residential section of the fort, housing the former apartments of the town's *wali* (local governor), spread over two floors. The two rooms on the upper floor are positioned so as to make the most of refreshing sea breezes (as well as enjoying a strong aroma of fish from the adjacent souk). As in many rooms in Omani forts, the windows here are set at floor level, making it possible for the one-time residents to loll on a rug while enjoying the sea winds. Steep wooden steps lead up from here to the rooftop terrace at the highest point of the fort – on a clear day you can see the Daymaniyat Islands, way out to sea, as well as the humped, rocky outline of the main Sawadi island closer to hand on your left.

The remainder of the structure has a more military emphasis, with high curtain walls punctuated with three towers, two round and one hexagonal. The latter, entered via a particularly impressive pair of spiked doors, is the biggest, and the strongpoint of the fort, with a spacious interior supported by a single enormous column and six large cannon pointing out over town.

On the far side of the fort, next to the ocean, lie Barka's **fish and vegetable souks**, busiest in the morning.

Bait Na'aman

Off Highway 1 • Mon–Thurs & Sun 8am–2pm • 500bz • Drive around 5km north of the roundabout by the Lulu hypermarket along the main coastal highway then turn right off, following the signs to A'Naaman and (just afterwards) the Barka Health Center, following the road as it twists back towards the coast; the house (not signed) is about 3km down the road on your left

THE BANQUET MASSACRE AT BARKA

Barka Fort's main claim to fame is as the site, in 1747, of one of the most important events in Omani history: the final expulsion of the Persians from the country and the foundation of the Al Bu Said dynasty (see page 236), whose descendants continue to rule Oman to this day.

The architect of the affair was **Ahmad bin Said**, the popular governor of Sohar and Barka, who had a few years previously signed a treaty with the Persians. Ahmad decided to affirm his friendship by inviting the entire Persian garrison at Muscat to a banquet at Barka Fort. The banquet was well under way when, it is said, there was a sudden beating of drums and the public crier announced: "Anyone who has a grudge against the Persians may now take his revenge!" According to one version of the story, all the Omanis present immediately fell upon their unarmed guests and did away with the lot of them, apart from two hundred soldiers who cried for mercy. These were put on a ship for Persia, although according to legend a mysterious fire swept through the ship, and all aboard, with the exception of Ahmad's sailors, were burned alive or drowned. An alternative version of the event states that Ahmad bin Said simply executed a few of the Persians, but allowed the rest to go free, or sent them back to Persia.

3

Barka's most interesting attraction is the beautiful old fortified house of **Bait Na'aman**. The unusually tall and narrow house, with alternating square and round towers, looks rather like someone has taken a perfect slice out of one of Oman's larger forts. It is thought to have been constructed around 1691–92 by imam Bil'arab bin Sultan, or possibly his brother, and successor as imam, Saif bin Sultan, and was used by both during their visits to the area. According to one tradition, this is also where Sultan Said bin Sultan murdered his unpopular predecessor Badr bin Saif in 1806 (see page 235) with a single blow from his *khanjar*. The entire building was beautifully restored in 1991 and has been renovated and well maintained since.

The ground floor

Unlike some of Oman's forts, the house has been fitted out with a lavish selection of traditional furnishings and fittings, giving the place an engagingly domestic

BULLFIGHTING À LA BATINAH

Barka is one of the various locations along the Batinah coast where you can catch the traditional Omani sport of **bull-butting** (which can also be seen in neighbouring Fujairah in the UAE). Unlike Spanish bullfighting, bull-butting is a bloodless contest between animals, rather than bull and matador. The sport is thought to have been introduced by the Portuguese, although its origins probably go back to antiquity, and it appears to have roots in both ancient Persia and classical Greece.

Contests are between large Brahma bulls, traditionally fed up on a diet of milk and honey. Animals are matched according to weight and led into the arena to do battle, at which point (all being well) they will lock horns – although some bulls just turn around and run away, frantically pursued by their owners. The winning bull is the one which either pushes the other to the ground or forces it to give up its ground. Most fights last less than five minutes, and ropes attached to the bull mean that they can be pulled apart (with difficulty – some of the bulls weigh around a ton) if things start turning ugly.

Meetings are held on Fridays during the winter months from around 4pm, lasting a couple of hours and attracting a good-natured, but exclusively male, audience. Contests alternate on a weekly basis between Sohar, Shinas, Barka and Seeb. Barka's other claim to sporting fame is that it holds the honour of having hosted the inaugural Tent Pegging World Cup back in 2014.

Barka's **bull-butting arena** is on the northern edge of town. To reach the arena, turn left at the T-junction in the town centre and follow this road for around 3km; the low-walled enclosure is down the side road signed to the Barka Health Center.

atmosphere and making it much easier to imagine what life was like for its former inhabitants than in many other Omani heritage buildings. **Downstairs** you'll find the original bathroom and stone toilet, both connected to an underground *falaj* that formerly brought water all the way from Nakhal. There's also a storage room, in which dates were pressed (the holes in the floor were used to siphon off the juice), as well as a pitch-black ladies' jail.

The upper floor

The main living areas are situated **upstairs**, with a sequence of rooms attractively furnished with traditional rugs, cushions, crockery and jewellery. These include the men's and ladies' *majlis*, plus a quaint bedroom with four-poster bed and a wooden hatch in the floor through which water could be drawn up from below. Nearby is the private *majlis* of the imam, equipped with a secret escape passage, and a watchtower with pit-like jails for miscreants.

The roof

Further stairs lead up to the **roof**. The main tower is supported by beautiful teak beams, with old pictures of ships scratched onto the walls. The tower originally housed six cannon, backed up by three more cannon in the house's second tower – an impressive array of firepower for what was essentially a private residence rather than a proper fort.

ARRIVAL AND DEPARTURE   BARKA

By car The original town sits on the coast, just north of the coastal highway – to get here, take the turning off the roundabout by the big Lulu Hypermarket and drive for 4km to reach the T-junction in the middle of the town.

ACCOMMODATION

Al Nahda Resort & Spa Take the road inland to Rustaq off the Lulu roundabout heading inland (on the left if approaching from Muscat) and drive for around 3km; the resort is signposted on the right ☎ 2688 3710, ⓦ alnahdaresort.com. This five-star resort is currently the only recognizable hotel near Barka town itself, occupying a huge swathe of lush grounds, with accommodation in beautiful Mediterranean-style suites and villas. Facilities include a big outdoor pool shaded by citrus and mango trees, floodlit tennis courts and two restaurants: the grand, colonnaded *Khalab*, and the al fresco *Nozha*, serving wood-fired pizzas and barbecue dishes. The resort is also home to one of the best spas north of Muscat. 25–30 percent discounts in summer. 55 OR

The Rustaq Loop

Easily the most rewarding attraction in Al Batinah is the so-called **Rustaq Loop**, a fine day's drive combining magnificent mountain scenery with three of Oman's finest castles – at **Nakhal**, **Rustaq** and **Al Hazm**. There are also a few other minor sights en route, while the surrounding mountains offer endless possibilities for off-road driving through spectacular wadis. Recent renovations of the castles at Rustaq and Al Hazm have restored them to their former glory, although at the time of research Rustaq Fort, while open to visitors, was largely empty – as opposed to the forts at Nakhal and Al Hazm, both brought to life by museum-style exhibits and interior decor allowing you to imagine what life would once have been like for their inhabitants.

The loop is strung out along single-carriageway **Highway 13**, a fast and usually fairly traffic-free (except between Barka and Nakhal) stretch of road. The only **accommodation** on the loop itself is a single, rather unappealing option at Rustaq and the beautiful, but expensive, *Dunes by Al Nahda*, although the trip can easily be done in a day from either Barka, Seeb or even Muscat. The following account describes the loop travelling in a **clockwise direction**, although there's no reason why you shouldn't tackle it in the opposite direction.

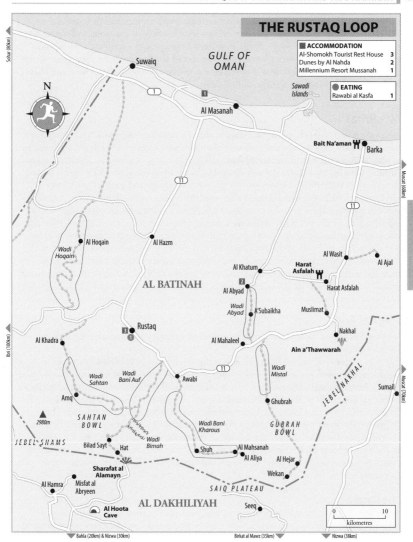

THE RUSTAQ LOOP

■ ACCOMMODATION	
Al-Shomokh Tourist Rest House	3
Dunes by Al Nahda	2
Millennium Resort Mussanah	1

● EATING	
Rawabi al Kasfa	1

GULF OF OMAN

Suwaiq

Al Masanah

Sawadi Islands

Bait Na'aman Barka

Al Wasit

Al Khatum

Harat Asfalah

Al Abyad

Harat Asfalah

A'Subaikha

Al Ajal

AL BATINAH

Al Hazm

Al Hoqain

Wadi Hoqain

Muslimat

Wadi Abyad

Rustaq

Al Mahaleel

Nakhal

Ain a'Thawwarah

Al Khadra

Wadi Sahtan

Wadi Bani Auf

Awabi

Wadi Mistal

JEBEL NAKHAL

Sumail

Amq

2980m

SAHTAN BOWL

Ghubrah

GUBRAH BOWL

Wadi Bani Kharous

JEBEL SHAMS

Bilad Sayt Hat

Wadi Bimah

Shuh

Al Mahsanah

Al Aliya

Al Hejar

Wekan

Sharafat al Alamayn

Al Hamra Misfat al Abryeen

SAIQ PLATEAU

AL DAKHILIYAH

Al Hoota Cave

Seeq

0   10
kilometres

Sohar (80km)

Muscat (60km)

Ibri (100km)

Muscat (70km)

Bahla (20km) & Nizwa (30km)   Birkat al Mawz (35km)   Nizwa (38km)

3

Harat Asfalah

About 2km off Highway 13 • Daily 24hr • Free • Follow the brown signs, turning right off Highway 13, then right and then left along increasingly narrow and twisting roads until you descend into a date plantation, at which point you'll see the castle on your right

Highway 13 heads off from the main coastal road at Barka. The opening section of the loop is fairly humdrum, with featureless scenery either side of the road until you approach Nakhal and the mountains begin to come increasingly into view.

Some 7km before Nakhal (and 22km from the coastal highway), brown signs point west off Highway 13 to the little-visited remains of the fort at **HARAT ASFALAH**. Compared to the other, much more grandiose forts around the Rustaq Loop, this is a decidedly homely affair, with a nicely restored section of crenellated wall bounded by a pair of towers (with a couple of old cannon) and a neat little gateway. Walk through the gateway to reach a small, windowless mosque (with an unusual little *mihrab* on the external wall) and a small kitchen, with a hole for fires in the floor and a neat little round chimney directly above. Steps lead from here up to the rooftop, offering fine views over the adjacent date plantations. The rest of the fort has now disappeared, the space it formerly occupied now covered by the modern village, dotted here and there with a few collapsing old mudbrick buildings.

Muslimat

The turn-off to Muslimat is signed on your right from Highway 13, around 750m before the turning to Nakhal; follow this road for around 1km until you reach the village; ignore the turning on your right, following the road as it veers left, through the small modern souk; the old village lies just past here, on the left-hand side of the road

Around 6km beyond Harat Asfalah down Highway 13 lies another of the loop's buried curiosities at **MUSLIMAT**. Drive through the modern village and park by the trio of old cannon which still stand guard by the roadside under a tree. Behind here, a neatly restored gateway leads into the remains of Muslimat's old mudbrick village. Steps to the right lead up to the usual mudbrick mosque on a high raised terrace. On the other side of the gateway lies a rubble of collapsed buildings plus a single intact round watchtower with a distinctive tapering upper section (designed to reduce the impact of cannonball fire). Next to this stands an unusually imposing two-storey battlemented mudbrick mansion with finely decorated windows, although the facade has been rather unpleasantly rebuilt with incongruous Italianate arches and lumpy concrete breezeblocks.

Nakhal Fort

About 1km off the main road, just right of the road through the village (and surprisingly easy to miss, despite its size) • Mon–Thurs, Sat & Sun 9am–4pm, Fri 8–11am • 500bz

The first major stop on the Rustaq Loop is the small town of **NAKHAL** (also spelled Nakhl, from *nakhl*, meaning "palm"). The town is home to one of Oman's most picture-perfect **forts**, dramatically situated atop a small natural rock outcrop and backdropped by the jagged peaks of the Jebel Nakhal, a spur of the main Western Hajar range. As with many Omani forts, the **history** of the castle is somewhat convoluted. The origins of the fort probably date back to pre-Islamic times, although the structure was continuously remodelled over the following centuries, including a substantial rebuilding in the mid-seventeenth century, while the present gateway and towers were apparently added in 1834 during the reign of imam Said bin Sultan. The entire structure was comprehensively restored in 1990 and has been continuously maintained since.

The Barzah

Enter through the main gate (where you buy your ticket), then walk up the steps and turn left through an impressively spiked pair of wooden doors and a second gateway to reach the interior of the fort. To your left is the finely carved stone archway which leads up to the fort's main residential quarters. Opposite this is the **Barzah**, a large two-storey building which sits atop the fort's outer walls above the main gateway. This was formerly home to the *wali's majlis* (or "sitting room", as it's translated); the room on the lower floor was used in winter, while in the hotter summer months the *wali* would move to the airier room on the upper floor, which makes the most of whatever sea breezes are blowing in from the coast.

The east tower

Continue past the Barzah, where you'll find a kitchen, followed by a small watchtower equipped with loopholes just big enough for a rifle barrel, plus wider openings through which (in traditional Omani fashion) boiling date juice or honey could be poured onto attackers below. Past here is the imposing **east tower**, reached by a narrow flight of stone steps and equipped with further rifle-sized apertures, plus wider embrasures for the fort's cannon, one of which survives *in situ*.

The Wali's living quarters

Retrace your steps to the Barzah and head through the archway opposite, from where further steps lead up past a date store and a large jail to reach the **wali's living quarters**. This was the castle's main residential section, with a series of rooms arranged around a small terrace at the highest point of the fort, including the *wali*'s own bedroom, along with a living room, guest room and rooms for boys, girls and women, all modestly furnished with old rugs, crockery and fine old wooden chests, plus a couple of antique (and very rickety) four-poster beds. The women's room, despite being the highest in the fort, is notably less breezy than the *wali*'s bedroom opposite, as it faces inland.

The middle and western towers

Exiting the women's room, turn left and follow the steps and walls around the rest of the complex and thence back to the entrance. En route you'll pass the fort's **middle** and **western towers**. The latter is equipped with a neat little wooden ladder built into the internal wall, while there are particularly fine views from the small watchtower immediately outside across the fort's impressive quantity of spade-shaped battlements and out over the sprawling date plantations and rugged mountains beyond.

Ain a'Thawwarah hot springs

Daily 24hr • Free • At the end of the main road through Nakhal – carry on past the fort and follow the pretty but narrow little road for around 2.5km as it twists between high-walled date plantations to reach the springs (there's parking space at the end of the road)

A short drive from Nakhal Fort lie the **Ain a'Thawwarah hot springs**, a popular picnic spot with locals – the whole place tends to get crammed at weekends, which can make it difficult to find a parking space. The water here is invitingly clean and clear, and full of tiny fish. Walk up past the small picnic area, at the end of which you'll find the spring itself, with surprisingly warm water gushing out of the rock. This is a nice spot to stop for lunch while you're exploring the Rustaq Loop; there are a few cafés and roaming coffee sellers, or you could do as the locals do and pack a picnic.

Wadi Mistal and the Ghubrah Bowl

About halfway between Nakhal and Awabi, a sign points south off Highway 13 towards **Wadi Mistal** (tarmac road for the first 6km, then good graded track for another 25km before the final ascent to Wekan village). The wadi begins by passing through a narrow gorge, its floor covered in a tumble of huge grey boulders, before opening out into the **Ghubrah Bowl**, a huge, flat gravel plain, ringed on the left by the cliffs bounding the southern edge of the Jebel Nakhl and, at the far end, by the peaks of the Jebel Akhdar.

Wekan

It's a swift if rather bumpy ride across the Ghubrah Bowl to reach the village of **Al Hejar** on the far side, from where a very steep, rough and slightly stomach-churning road (4WD essential) climbs up to **WEKAN** (also spelled Wakan, Wukan), one of the most spectacular mountain villages anywhere in Oman. There's parking in the village, while a restored watchtower provides an optimal viewing platform from which to admire the bowl and encircling mountains below. It's particularly popular each February, when its terraced gardens come alive with the blossom of hundreds of apricot trees.

WALKING IN WEKAN

Wekan is the starting point for the **hiking routes** W24b and W25 (see page 94). Even if you don't fancy tackling either walk in its entirety, it's well worth exploring the opening section of walk W25, which winds up through the picture-perfect terraced gardens to the rear of the village, running alongside a bucolic little *falaj* that tumbles down from the mountainside above – arguably the prettiest short walk in Oman. The walk is waymarked (albeit not very clearly) from the village centre and it takes around twenty minutes to reach the top of the village.

Wadi Abyad

About 3km beyond the turn-off to Wadi Mistal, a signed turn-off on the right points to the village of **A'Subaikha**, the starting point for trips into the pretty **Wadi Abyad** ("White Wadi"). This is quite different in character from the wadis on the southern side of Highway 13, set between low ophiolite hills and dotted with palm trees and rock pools. The water in some of the pools often turns a distinctive milky white due to the high concentrations of dissolved calcium it contains, and which sometimes crystallizes into a fine covering, like warm ice. The whole place is particularly lovely towards dusk, when the low light brings out the rich russet colouring of the surrounding hills and the whole valley seems almost to glow.

Driving the wadi is something of a challenge. There's no actual track here, it's simply a question of picking your way across the gravel-covered wadi bed, treacherously loose and deep in many places – speed is of the essence in order to avoid getting bogged-down. There's also usually a fair bit of water hereabouts, so expect to ford a few streams en route. You can get about 5km down the wadi before your way is blocked by rocks. Wadi Abyad is also a popular camping spot, particularly at weekends, meaning that if you do get stuck, you should be able to find someone to help pull you out.

Nakhal to Rustaq

The section of Highway 13 **between Nakhal and Rustaq** is easily the most scenic of the entire loop (and usually fairly traffic-free), with the high mountains of the Western Hajar towering above the road on your left, while to your right lies an unusual landscape of small, crumbling red-rock hills with jagged ridgetops and summits – a good example of Oman's characteristic ophiolite landscapes (see page 94).

Awabi Fort

Around 2km off Highway 13 on the far side of the modern town – follow the brown signs • Mon–Thurs & Sun 8am–2pm • Free

Some 35km on from Nakhal, the town of **AWABI** is home to yet another **fort**. The quaint, toy-like structure is built in a mixture of stone and mudbrick with a small mosque, looking like an oversized shoebox, standing in front of the gates. It's rather more angular than other forts in the area, which combined with the abundance of exposed stonework makes it resemble a crumbling European castle from certain angles. Inside, too, the roughly moulded walls, covered with coarsely finished *sarooj*, give the place a pleasantly rustic look – a lot more authentic than the polished surfaces of most other restored Omani forts. The main tower is an interesting study in traditional Omani living arrangements, boasting no fewer than three hole-in-the-floor toilets, all carefully designed so that waste products would fall outside the castle walls and into the village below.

A few kilometres west of Awabi you pass the end of the spectacular track which descends from the mountains via **Wadi Bani Auf** (see page 101).

Wadi Bani Kharous

Immediately behind Awabi fort, a narrow cleft in the mountains announces the start of **Wadi Bani Kharous**, one of the most spectacular along the Rustaq Loop, and now easily accessible thanks to the construction of a new black-top road stretching all the way to the end of the wadi at Al Aliya, some 25km from Awabi (although the last couple of kilometres are extremely narrow and twisty as they run through the wadi's final two villages).

The wadi is surprisingly developed, with a string of seven villages forming a ribbon of almost continuous settlement, although the scenery is beautiful throughout, hemmed in between high limestone cliffs, their summits sculpted into delicate rock pinnacles. The last few kilometres are especially pretty, as the wadi narrows and fills up with date palms and mango trees, with houses stacked up on rock ledges on the hillside above. The wadi is also one of the most important geological sites in Oman, exhibiting a range of rock formations spanning over 500 million years, from the Cretaceous period to the Late Proterozoic era, the latter being some of the oldest in the country.

Rustaq

3

Tucked up beneath the northern escarpment of the Hajar mountains, **RUSTAQ** is one of the most venerable settlements of the interior. Sadly few remains of the town's illustrious history survive, however; modern Rustaq is a sprawling and rather characterless place, and far less interesting than its old rival, Nizwa. Rustaq's huge **fort**, restored but largely empty, has potential which is as yet unrealized.

The town is effectively divided into two distinct sections: the "old" town and fort, which lies just south off Highway 13, and a "new" town, about 3km further north along Highway 13 on the way to Al Hazm, clustered around the turn-off to Ibri and the modern Rustaq Mosque, a vast white structure with a pair of soaring minarets.

Brief history

The town owes its place in Omani history to the redoubtable imam **Nasir bin Murshid bin Sultan al Yaruba** (see page 234), founder of the Ya'aruba dynasty, who was elected imam at Rustaq in 1624 and made the town his principal centre of operations during his subsequent 25-year reign. The town was also a favoured base for Ahmed bin Said (see page 236), founder of the later Al Bu Said dynasty.

Rustaq's importance was the result of its strategic position between the coast and the mountains, guarding the exit points of several nearby wadis through which goods would have been transported from the *jebel* above. The town developed into a major centre for local commerce, craftsmanship and other trades, home to some of the country's finest metalworkers and silversmiths, and also renowned as the source of some of Oman's best *halwa* and finest honey – bee-keeping remains a popular local occupation to this day.

Rustaq Fort

At the back of the old town • Mon–Thurs, Sat & Sun 9am–4pm, Fri 8–11am • 500bz

Tucked away at the back of the old town (and clearly signposted from Highway 13) is Rustaq's mighty **fort**, one of the biggest in the country, with a huge, soaring central keep surrounded by extensive walls. The fort, like the others of the Rustaq Loop, has undergone significant renovations in recent years and is in good condition, but it attracts fewer visitors than Nakhal and Al Hazm and is less well equipped to receive them. Unlike elsewhere, all the rooms have been left empty, meaning it's harder to imagine what life would once have been like here. It's also poorly lit, meaning you may well find yourself stumbling around in the dark, but it's quite a fun place to get lost in if you do find the lights are off.

The fort is one of the most ancient in Oman. The original structure is thought to have been built by the Julanda dynasty fifty years before the arrival of Islam, and was subsequently expanded in 670 AD and again in 1698, while further towers were added by Sultan Faisal bin Turki in 1906. The extensive compound is provided with its own *falaj* and surrounded by low exterior walls topped by a quartet of towers, the tallest rising to almost 20m. Inside sits the tall central keep, built over three levels, plus an armoury and a fine mosque.

Around the fort

The old **souk** in front of the fort has long been an important meeting place for traders from the *jebel* and the coast, and hosts a good range of stalls selling traditional handicrafts and souvenirs. Most of the rest of Rustaq is modern and largely forgettable, although it's worth strolling around the back of the fort, where a cluster of decaying mudbrick houses stands around a small blue-domed mosque. Close by, a diminutive, rather Indian-looking mudbrick mausoleum sits atop a small rise, offering a superb view of the fort and the vast swathe of date palms which envelop the old town.

Al Hazm Fort

From Rustaq, turn left at the roundabout in the centre of Al Hazm town – the fort is 1km along this road, clearly visible on your left • Mon–Thurs, Sat & Sun 9am–4pm, Fri 8–11am • 500bz

The last point of interest on the Rustaq Loop is the modest little town of **AL HAZM**, home to another oversized **fort**. This one has benefitted, perhaps the most of any forts in this area, from extensive government-led renovations, and its imposing chambers and corridors are brought to life by a brilliant audio guide. There are also fun, if slightly naff, exhibits – think plastic prisoners in the jails, and spooky lights and noises in the secret passageway. The gatekeeper is very helpful and keen to feed visitors with free coffee and dates. The fort was built by the Ya'aruba imam **Sultan bin Saif II** (see page 235), who briefly established Al Hazm as capital of Oman in preference to Rustaq, and who is buried inside. This is one of the biggest of all Oman's fortified structures: a huge stone box containing a disorienting labyrinth of corridors and rooms, complete with the usual living quarters, prisons, mosque and its own dedicated *falaj*, clustered around a diminutive central courtyard – although there's not much to see from the outside, which is disappointingly plain.

ACCOMMODATION

THE RUSTAQ LOOP

THE RUSTAQ LOOP

Dunes by Al Nahda Wadi al Abyad Sands; from Barka, turn off Highway 1 onto Abiyad Rd and continue for about 20km; turn right just before the green mosque and continue for 7km ☎ 9723 5700, ⊛ dunesbyalnahda. com; map p.121. Sitting slap-bang in the middle of the Rustaq Loop, equidistant from Rustaq, Nakhal and Barka, this ultra-luxe desert camp is incredibly beautiful – if eye-wateringly expensive – and makes for a convenient and more accessible alternative to Wahiba Sands for those based in Muscat who wish to spend a night in the desert. Accommodation takes the form of huge, lavish "tents" – actually solid-walled polygonal structures with billowy throws draped over the walls and ceilings – complete with studded wooden doors, sofas, TVs and fully equipped en-suite bathrooms. The food at the *Fleur* restaurant (the usual mix of Indian, Arabian and international dishes) is good,

and an extensive cocktail menu is among the offerings at the licensed *Dune Bar*. A programme of activities includes camel rides and sand surfing. Rates are on a half-board basis. **125 OR**

RUSTAQ

Al Shomokh Tourist Rest House In the new town about 500m down the Ibri road opposite the Makkah hypermarket (just past the Oman Oil petrol station on the right-hand side of road), about 4km from Rustaq fort ☎ 2687 7071, ⊖ alshomokh234@gmail.com; map p.121. This unassuming one-star is currently the only place to stay in Rustaq itself, though it's probably best avoided. The welcome is friendly, although it's exceedingly expensive for what you get, with simple and slightly dog-eared rooms with TV and fridge, plus squat toilets in the small attached bathrooms. Breakfast included. **50 OR**

EATING

Assuming you're exploring the loop in a single day, you'll probably find yourself in Rustaq around lunchtime, although unfortunately there's not much on offer when it comes to eating. For no-frills drinks and snacks, the most convenient option is *Rawabi al Kasfa*, or walk five minutes to the stretch of main road nearest the fort where you'll find a few basic

coffee shops and cafés serving up the usual Indian curries and biryanis. The new town to the north has much more choice, including some international chains, but nothing particularly inspiring. Alternatively, follow the locals' lead and have a picnic, or buy lunch, at the Ain A'Thawwarah hot springs (see page 123).

RUSTAQ

Rawabi al Kasfa Behind the fort on the western side (between the fort and the main road) ☎ 9645 3320; map p.121. This friendly restaurant is nothing spectacular, with the usual assortment of shwarmas and biryanis on offer in an uninspiring environment, served at little plastic tables and chairs. What marks it out from the other outlets on the main road is the somewhat surprising selection of health-orientated juices and smoothies (800bz–1.2 OR), which are just the thing after a couple of hours tramping around the fort. Mains 1–2 OR. Daily 9am–1am.

The Sawadi and Daymaniyat Islands

Travelling north on the coastal highway from Barka, the main draw before you reach Sohar is the **Sawadi and Daymaniyat Islands**, one of the country's leading dive spots, but equally rewarding to visit for a snorkel or swim. The islands can be visited on trips with diving companies from Muscat (see page 62), but the best local base – indeed, the only hotel to speak of between Barka and Sohar – is the *Millennium Resort Mussanah* (see page 129), where the professional SeaOman run a diving operation.

Sawadi Islands

The rocky and windswept **Sawadi Islands** lie just offshore; the largest of the seven islands is almost within spitting distance of the beach, a large rocky hump topped by a string of watchtowers, while the other smaller islands lie further out to sea. It's possible to walk across the sand to the main island at low tide, though take care you don't get stranded when the tide comes back in; at other times **boat trips** can be arranged by bargaining with the local fishermen on the beach for around 5 OR. The **beach** here is littered with exotic-looking seashells, perfect for a stroll and a spot of beachcombing.

Daymaniyat Islands

Much further out to sea (30min–1hr by boat), off the coast midway between Barka and Seeb, the **Daymaniyat Islands** (also spelled Dimaniyat or Dimaaniyat) are one of Oman's premier dive spots. Virtually everyone who comes here does so to dive, or at least snorkel (see page 129). There are nine low, rocky little islets here, strung out in a line from east to west and clustered in three quite widely separated groups, surrounded by coral reefs (you'll probably fly directly above them when landing at Muscat International Airport). The islands have been protected as a **nature reserve** since 1996 and provide an important nesting site for hawksbill and green turtles, as well as a wide range of migratory birds including the increasingly rare sooty falcon (which can also be found in the Sawadi islands), one of the few migratory raptors which actually nests and breeds in the region. Given their protected status, access to the Daymaniyats is restricted, and you're not allowed to land on the islands from the beginning of May until the end of October; the rest of the year you'll require a **permit** (6 OR/day to visit and dive), which can be arranged by your tour operator. Flouting the regulations carries a 500 OR fine, which is doubled for repeated offences.

The coastal highway to Sohar

The long swathe of fertile coastline **between Barka and Sohar** shows the Batinah at its most untouched, with countless date plantations meandering along the coast, interspersed with sleepy villages, the occasional fort and endless swathes of beach littered with boats – if you're lucky you may spot examples of the traditional *shasha*, an antique style of reed-boat

DIVING THE DAYMANIYATS

Contrary to what is sometimes said, **diving** at the Daymaniyats is technically easy and suitable even for non-PADI-qualified divers. The waters around the islands boast excellent visibility, abundant soft and hard corals, descending in places to depths of 20m, and swarms of colourful little tropical fish and nudibranchs. The main attraction, though, is the islands' oversized **marine life**, including leopard sharks, barracuda, shoals of moray eels, rays, turtles and huge sea horses, while you're almost guaranteed the chance to spot a whale shark between July and September.

GETTING TO THE DAYMANIYAT ISLANDS

It's around a 1hr boat trip from *Millennium Resort Mussanah* to the Daymaniyats, depending on exactly which of the twenty-odd dive sites scattered around the islands you're going to. Diving and snorkelling trips to the Daymaniyat Islands can be conveniently arranged through SeaOman, while most dive operators in Muscat (see page 62) also arrange trips here, though obviously it's a much longer (and somewhat more expensive) trip.

SeaOman Millennium Resort Mussanah (see page 129) ☎ 2427 4201, ⓦ seaoman.com. Professional outfit offering a programme of two dives per day (45 OR for one day, progressively cheaper the more days you book), departing for the Daymaniyats at 8am and returning at 4pm. Diving equipment can be hired for 15 OR/day. Snorkelling is also on offer for 25 OR/day, including equipment hire. A full range of PADI courses are also available, from beginner to dive master. There is another SeaOman outlet at The Wave development near the airport in Muscat (see page 62).

made from bundles of dried palm fronds, which was once common throughout the Gulf. It's around 150km from Barka to Sohar, a ninety-minute drive along the busy coastal highway (which doesn't actually run within sight of the sea), although it's much more enjoyable to get off onto the small roads which run alongside the coast here and there.

Al Masanah

From Barka, it's a drive of around 30km north along Highway 1 to reach the turning for **AL MASANAH**, then a further 5km to reach the town itself, where you'll find the town's **fort**, a square high-walled structure next to the road by the seafront. The fort is unusual in being built almost entirely of stone, rather than mudbrick, with bands of roughly hewn rocks (including the occasional piece of coral) held together with layers of pebble-encrusted mud.

Wudan as Sahil

From Al Masanah you can follow signs along the coast (but out of sight of the sea) through the village of **Wudan as Sahil**, home to the *Millennium Resort Mussanah*. It's not a particularly scenic drive, although the road is fast and largely deserted, and at least gets you away from the mad traffic on the main coastal highway for a bit.

ACCOMMODATION   **WUDAN AS SAHIL**

Millennium Resort Mussanah ☎ 2687 1555, ⓦ millenniumhotels.com; map p.121. Wudan as Sahil provides the slightly unlikely setting for this sprawling resort complex sitting on a fine stretch of coast overlooking a small marina, with stylish modern rooms and a good spread of restaurants – it's rather a long way from anywhere else, but it's the only option in between Barka and Sohar, and is the logical choice for diving the Daymaniyat Islands (see page 129). 45 OR

Suwaiq

Follow the road north of Wudan as Sahil for just over 20km and you'll find yourself in **SUWAIQ**, a neat little town arranged around a large seafront **fort**, typical of the numerous similar structures which dot the Batinah coast, encircled by long crenellated walls with a tower (three round and one square) at each corner and a tall, narrow keep poking up inside. It's not open to the public, unfortunately, so you won't get any further than the impressively large wooden doors.

Al Khabourah and around

North of Suwaiq it's another 36km along the coastal highway until you reach the turn-off to **AL KHABOURAH**, 2km away on the coast and home to yet another of the sturdy little square forts that guard the Batinah coast. The **fort** here stands right on the seafront – a rather plain structure, its entrance guarded by a pair of very rusty cannon. At the time of research, the fort was closed to undergo extensive renovations, in part to counter the effects of salt and humidity levels brought on by centuries of battering from the coastal winds. By the time you read this, the fort should be open to visitors once more.

North of Al Khabourah, Highway 1 continues to Saham, although it's possible to follow a winding little back road which hugs the coast all the way up, twisting through an endless straggle of sand-coloured villages, occasionally running alongside the sea and little scraps of boat-covered beaches – a lovely glimpse of the backwaters of the Batinah that few tourists ever see. It's decidedly slower going than the main highway, however – don't expect to get from Al Khabourah to Saham in anything under an hour – and there are no signs so you'll have to follow your nose, keeping to the right whenever there's a choice of roads.

Saham

At the end of the road, **SAHAM** is a lively, slightly scruffy little place. The obligatory **fort** (with four chunky square towers) sits on the seafront. A long road runs north and south from here, lined with a few unusually grand (though now decidedly dilapidated) ocean-facing villas, an impressive number of mosques and a long strip of muddy beach with hundreds of boats pulled up on the sand and, towards dusk, dozens of football matches in progress.

Sohar and around

The major city in northern Oman, **SOHAR** boasts a long and eventful history, and a leading place among the nation's seafaring exploits – according to local tradition, no less a personage than Sindbad hailed from Sohar (see page 134), while for a number of centuries the town served as the capital of Oman, and was the centre of an extensive trading network stretching up and down the Gulf.

Sadly, despite its lustrous Arabian Nights heritage, modern Sohar is a somewhat anodyne place. Nothing remains of the old town, while its major attraction, the imposing **Sohar Fort**, was closed for renovations at the time of writing (and has been for the better part of a decade). The best reason to come here is to crash out for a few days on the **beach** at the attractive *Sohar Beach Hotel* or the *Radisson Blu*. Otherwise there's little cause to visit unless passing through en route to the UAE border crossings at Buraimi and Khatmat Milahah (a couple of further sights north of town, Liwa and Shinas, are other options for breaking up the journey), or as a jumping-off point for the scenic road up to Yanqul and Ibri in the Dhahirah.

Brief history

Sohar is one of the oldest towns in Oman, and was for many centuries the most important port and commercial centre in the country, until the rise of Muscat from around the sixteenth century onwards. The Sohar region has enjoyed continued prosperity for at least six millennia, probably forming part of the legendary country of **Magan** (see page 229), which once supplied Sumer with many of its raw materials. Copper was mined in the nearby **Wadi Jizzi** (see page 136) as far back as the fifth century BC, and Sohar developed as a prosperous centre for smelting and mining, as well as a major agricultural centre.

The arrival of Islam

By the time **Islam** arrived in Oman, Sohar had established itself as the capital of the region, and remained so until the beginning of the second imamate in 793 AD, when the seat of the imams was moved for security reasons to Nizwa, which was judged, correctly, to be less vulnerable to attack.

Sohar retained its pre-eminent commercial position, nonetheless – "The hallway to China, the storehouse of the East", as the eminent tenth-century historian Al Muqaddasi described it. Unfortunately, the city's wealth also attracted less welcome visitors, usually hailing from neighbouring Persia. In 971 and again in 1041 a Persian fleet overran and sacked the city, while around 1276 the city suffered at the hands of almost five thousand Mongol raiders from Shiraz, although it had at least partly revived by the time Marco Polo visited around 1293.

The Portuguese

Worse still was to follow the arrival of the **Portuguese**, who occupied Sohar in 1507 and controlled the city until 1643, when they were finally evicted by the Omani forces of Nasir bin Murshid (see page 234). The Persians returned to Sohar yet again in 1738 under the command of Nadir Shah, but were beaten off by **Ahmad bin Said**, the city's brilliant governor and future ruler of Oman (see page 236), who endured another nine-month-long Persian siege in 1742 before finally capitulating to the far larger forces of his attackers.

Sohar remained an important city following the establishment of the Al Bu Saidi dynasty, but was gradually eclipsed by Muscat as the country's major seaport and slipped increasingly into the sidelines of Omani history – apart from a brief moment of notoriety in 1866 when Sultan Thuwaini was murdered by his son Salim in the city's fort.

Modern Sohar

Sohar has enjoyed something of an **economic resurgence** over the last few decades – during the 1980s, the old copper mines of Wadi Jizzi were reopened by the Oman Mining Company for the first time in over a thousand years, with further large new deposits being discovered inland around Yanqul and Ibri. More recently, the vast new **Sohar Port**, opened in 2004, may yet restore the city to its maritime pre-eminence.

The city also leapt briefly into the international headlines in early 2011 when it became the focal point of nationwide protests (see page 245) against the government. Sohar's importance as a hub of industry is such that the Omani government are pinning high hopes on the city as part of their plans to diversify the economy away from the current reliance on oil – set to be Oman's biggest challenge in the years and decades to come.

The fort and around

Sohar's snowy-white **fort** sits proudly atop a small natural mound, next to the sea just south of the old town centre, an imposing structure with a tall keep rising within the enclosing walls. The fort is thought to date back to pre-Islamic times; Amr bin Al Aas, envoy of the Prophet Mohammed, is said to have been received here by the ruler of Sohar in the year 630 AD. Archeological surveys suggest that the present-day fort was rebuilt on the rubble of the original structure in around 750 AD, and probably modified at various times by later Omani rulers, as well as by the Portuguese. At the time of writing, the fort had been closed for a decade while undergoing intensive renovation by a French team; it appears to be almost complete, although it was supposed to be finished by 2011, so when it will actually re-open remains uncertain.

Almost next door to the fort stands the large **Sultan Qaboos Mosque**, with its eye-catching gold dome.

The handicrafts souk

Sohar St • Mon–Thurs, Sat & Sun 8am–noon & 5–9pm, Fri 5–9pm

A five-minute walk inland from the fort is the town's new **handicrafts souk** (signed "Omani Craftsman's House" on one side of the gate and "Al Qala'a Souq for Handcrafts Industries" on the other), occupying a neat little walled enclosure decorated with miniature watchtowers. There are sixteen shops here, although only eight were open at the time of research, including a silversmiths, a shop selling traditional medicines and a few other places flogging the usual *khanjars*, *mandoos*, guns (real and toy) and other souvenirs.

The Friday Market

As Souq St • Mon–Thurs, Sat & Sun 8am–noon & 5–9pm, Fri 5–9pm

Near the souk, the **Friday Market** (open daily, despite its name) occupies an open-air pavilion filled with stallholders selling fruit, vegetables and animal feed – worth a look if you're around in the morning, although things are usually pretty quiet after around 11am.

North of the fort

North of the fort lies **old Sohar**, the site of the original town, bounded by dried-up wadis to the north and south, though it's now old in name only: the eminently forgettable shops and villas here date back only to the 1990s, when the old souk was demolished.

More appealing is the parallel seafront **corniche**, with a breezy waterside walkway under interminable blue lampposts. Continuing along the corniche some 750m north of the old town centre brings you to the town's striking modern **fish market**, its elegantly curved roofline designed to echo that of a traditional Arabian dhow.

The best bits of **beach** are at the top end of town, in between the *Sohar Beach Hotel* and the *Radisson Blu*, with a wide, mud-coloured swathe of sand, scattered with seashells and with fine coastal views. Next to the beach lies an attractively shady **park** arranged around a large lake.

South of the fort

South of the fort, you can follow the road for about 5km through an attractive string of oases before turning inland to reach the coastal highway at Suwayhirah roundabout. This part of town is also where you'll find the local **bullfighting arena** (see page 119) in a large circular enclosure with sloping stone sides. The arena is two blocks east of the large stadium.

ARRIVAL AND GETTING AROUND   SOHAR

Even by Omani standards, Sohar is exceptionally spread out, sprawling along the coast for over 20km. Most activity is now focused around the main coastal highway and the big malls that flank it rather than the small and decidedly comatose "old" town.

By bus Mwasalat buses drop passengers off in the centre of the old town, opposite the taxi rank on Sohar St.

Destinations Buraimi (3 daily; 2hr); Burj al Sahwa (3 daily; 2hr 30min); Mabelah (3 daily; 2hr); Muscat (3 daily; 3hr).

3

THE DATE PALM: TREE OF LIFE

There are an estimated eight million date palms (*Phoenix dactylifera*; in Arabic, *nakhl*) in Oman, and travelling around the Batinah you'll rarely be out of sight of the endless plantations which blanket the coast. Dates have been a staple food in the Middle East for thousands of years; the wood of the date palm also provides an important source of building material, while leaves and fronds are used to make baskets, ropes and medicines – a remarkable variety of uses which has led to the date palm's popular description as the "tree of life".

The date palm is one of the oldest cultivated fruit trees in the world. They are believed to have been grown since ancient times from Mesopotamia to prehistoric Egypt, possibly as early as 6000 BC – one of the first human efforts at systematic agricultural cultivation. The date palm is mentioned in both the Bible and the Qur'an. Mohammed urged his followers to "cherish your father's sister, the palm tree", and Muslims still traditionally break their Ramadan fast each night by eating a date.

Dates also underpinned the traditional nomadic lifestyle of the Omani interior, providing a small, light, concentrated and long-lasting source of nutrition which was perfectly adapted for the Bedu's itinerant lifestyle. Dates are something of a self-contained nutritional super-fruit, and an excellent source of protein, vitamins and minerals. Their high sugar content (40–80 percent) also protects them against bacterial contamination and makes them extremely durable – dried dates can last for years. They can also be pressed for their juice, used to make wine, syrup and vinegar; in earlier times, boiling date syrup was used as an offensive weapon poured onto attackers below fort walls.

CULTIVATION

According to a traditional saying, the date palm "needs its feet in water and its head in fire", a combination provided in Oman by intensive **falaj** irrigation and the country's burning summer temperatures. Date palms grow rapidly, up to 40cm per year, reaching heights of up to around 30m. Trees can live for around 150 years, producing over 100kg of dates annually. Over forty varieties of date are grown in Oman, with over 150,000 tonnes of fruit produced annually – easily the largest crop in the country, and, until the discovery of oil, far and away the most economically important.

Dates take around seven months to mature. Unripe dates range in colour from green through to red or yellow, becoming darker and sweeter as they ripen. There are hundreds of different varieties, ranging widely in size and colour – the best are highly prized by local connoisseurs, much as fine wines are in France. There are three basic types: soft (such as the popular Medjool variety), semi-dry (such as Deglet Noor) and dry. Only the female date palm produces fruit, however. In the wild, trees are entirely wind-pollinated, and yield little fruit. Cultivated date palms are pollinated by hand, with flowers from male date palms being sold in local souks and then strategically placed in the branches of female trees (although wind machines to blow pollen onto the female flowers are also sometimes used). Most fruits are harvested between August and December. In many places, dates are still handpicked, although mechanical shakers may be used in larger plantations.

> ### SINDBAD AND SOHAR
>
> Sohar is often claimed to be the birthplace of the legendary **Sindbad** (or Sinbad), hero of the "Seven Voyages of Sindbad the Sailor", one of the most famous tales in the *One Thousand and One Nights*, subsequently recycled into countless films, cartoons and books. It's a nice story, given Oman's historic seafaring prowess, and one you'll probably see recycled a few times in local tourist literature, although sadly it has little basis in fact – attempts to claim the legendary sailor as a local Sohari appear to be simply an attempt to acquire prestige by association, rather as the English have adopted St George (who was actually a Roman soldier from Palestine).
>
> Sindbad himself is clearly a mythical figure, a composite hero whose legendary adventures derive from centuries of seafaring folklore and assorted travellers' tales derived from a wide variety of sources. According to the *One Thousand and One Nights*, Sindbad was a merchant from Baghdad, who set sail from Basra, although the stories of his seven voyages most likely derive from Persian sources, or perhaps from the famous collection of Sanskrit fables known as the *Panchatantra*. The name Sindbad itself is Persian rather than Arab, and may even be derived from Sindh (now a province in Pakistan), from which the names of both the Indus River and, ultimately, India, derive.

By plane The Sohar International Airport, out near the *Crowne Plaza* hotel, opened in 2017 and currently flies to Doha in Qatar (twice daily) and Sharjah in the UAE (8 weekly).

By taxi There are usually some taxis hanging around in the car park on the other side of the wadi from the bus station in the centre of the old town.

ACCOMMODATION

Atlas Hotel Apartments Around 1km north of the Globe roundabout behind the Diwan Silk building ☎ 2685 3009, ✉ atlashotel27@gmail.com; map p.131. Functional modern block with alarmingly pink-hued rooms and ageing bathrooms. The comfortable apartments sleep one to four; the larger ones come with kitchen and sitting rooms. Uninspiring, but as cheap as anywhere in town. __20 OR__

Crowne Plaza Buraimi Highway ☎ 2685 0850, ⓦ crowneplaza.com; map p.131. Palatial five-star standing in monumental isolation across the Buraimi highway from the airport, the best part of 20km from the town centre – a slightly surreal slice of upmarket opulence more or less in the middle of nowhere. The whole place has plenty of smooth contemporary style, with suave (if smallish) modern rooms with dark-wood finishes and all mod-cons, a pair of stylish restaurants, plus the usual slightly sad sports bar. There's also a large and attractive pool and poolside terrace lined with sunloungers, though unfortunately the view is of pylons, landing planes and distant factories. __34 OR__

Green Oasis Hotel 5km inland off the coastal highway along Muwelah St ☎ 2684 6442, ✉ greensohar@gmail.com; map p.131. One of the cheapest options in Sohar, though no bargain, in an uninspiring setting next to a main road about 5km from the coastal highway and 8km from the fort. Rooms are simple, functional and on the grubby side; so-called "executive" and "deluxe" rooms have a balcony or terrace, and little else extra. There's also a small pool and a restaurant, but no bar. The hotel is directly opposite the big Oman Medical College – a useful landmark, given the lack of signage. __21 OR__

Mercure Sohar Highway 1, opposite the Sohar Sports Complex ☎ 2235 4800, ⓦ mercure.com; map p.131. Extremely comfortable, if somewhat sterile, four-star on the Batinah highway on the southern fringes of town. The modern rooms are lent a touch of personality by line drawings on the walls depicting Sohar Fort, while decent international food – and a superb breakfast buffet – are on offer at the *Mosaic* restaurant. There's plenty of shaded seating, including comfortable sofas, around the outdoor pool. __29 OR__

★ **Radisson Blu** Al Zafaran Beach ☎ 2664 0000, ⓦ radissonblu.com/hotel-sohar; map p.131. Occupying a plum location on the beach just north of the Sohar Beach Hotel, this stylish, modern five-star is the best place to stay in Sohar. Rooms are supremely comfortable, if somewhat generic, with the majority overlooking the beach. For the best views, head up to Al Khaimah rooftop bar; there's another slick bar by the pool, and the choice of Arabic or Thai cuisine at the Al Zafaran and Amaranthai restaurants. The resort is also home to Sohar's finest spa. __36 OR__

Sohar Beach Hotel Off Sultan Qaboos Rd, on the coast 4km from Sallan roundabout ☎ 2684 1111, ⓦ soharbeach.com; map p.131. Sitting on the beach a few kilometres north of the town centre, this relaxing four-star is a pleasant, although curiously more expensive, alternative to the *Radisson Blu*. The main building is built to resemble a miniature white fort, with low-key Arabian touches and rooms spread in wings around the garden. Rooms are attractively plush, and there are also some family-sized chalets. There's a nice big pool in the attractive gardens, plus a strip of rather brown and pebbly beach. Facilities include a simple in-house spa, the pleasant *Al Jizzi* lounge bar, a beach bar and the attractive *Sallan* restaurant. The hotel is also home to a somewhat sleazy bar and disco, soundtracked by a live Filipino band, and the actually quite pleasant *Arabesque*, which hosts Arabian music and dance performances. **40 OR**

EATING AND DRINKING

Even by Omani standards there's a distinct lack of decent places to eat in Sohar, and you'll most likely end up eating where you're staying, although *Radisson Blu* and *Sohar Beach Hotel* both have some decent offerings.

Al Khaimah Radisson Blu, Al Zafaran Beach ☎ 2664 0000, ⓦ radissonblu.com/hotel-sohar; map p.131. The most sophisticated spot in Sohar to enjoy a nightcap, with a range of cocktails, beers and non-alcoholic drinks available. It's a popular spot for shisha, and Arabic meze dishes are also on offer. Mon–Thurs, Sat & Sun 6pm–3am, Fri 6pm–2am.

Sallan Sohar Beach Hotel, off Sultan Qaboos Rd ☎ 2684 1111, ⓦ soharbeach.com; map p.131. The best place to aim for if you fancy heading out to eat, dishing up a well-prepared selection of continental, Chinese, Indian and Arabian mains (around 5–8 OR) on its attractive outdoor candlelit terrace, or inside, if it's too hot. Daily 6am–11pm.

Liwa

Some 25km north of Sohar, the coastal settlement of **LIWA** is home to the inevitable **fort** (not open to the public), its extensive curtain wall and five round towers topped with unusually spiky sawtooth battlements, with a tall and narrow keep inside – a design somewhat reminiscent of that of Suwaiq Fort (see page 129) further down the coast. Unusually, the fort doesn't lie on the coast, but 1km or so inland. Continue along the road past the fort to reach the seafront.

South of here stretches the enormous new **Sohar Port** complex with its impressive tangle of cranes, cargo ships and containers; to the north, in complete contrast, a meandering sea inlet threads its way behind the beach, lined with mangrove thickets and with abundant birdlife – a fine place for a quiet picnic.

Shinas

A further 36km north of Liwa, the town of **SHINAS** is notable mainly for being the most northerly town in Oman (excepting Musandam, of course). As throughout the Batinah, fishing is the main industry here, with a busy harbour enclosed by two curling breakwaters; much of the local catch ends up on the restaurant tables of Dubai. There's also yet another identikit **fort** (more or less behind the harbour), while the neat little covered souk next door is also worth a quick look. Most foreign visitors will only come to Shinas on the way to Musandam as part of the new Mwasalat **ferry** service.

The UAE border

If you're in Shinas but not en route to Musandam, you're probably continuing on into the **UAE** through one of two border crossings in the area (for details of border formalities, see page 137). The first continues due north to reach the border at **Khatmat Milahah**. The second heads inland to reach the border at **Hatta**.

Yanqul

The recently opened highway between Sohar and **YANQUL** offers perhaps the easiest way of getting between the coast and the mountains. It's a drive of around 75 minutes along a fast and scenic highway, with hardly any traffic. The road is fairly tedious for the first 40km or so (excepting a sign to the jovial-sounding village of Beer Jam about 25km out of Sohar) but becomes increasingly dramatic as the mountains approach and the road begins to hairpin upwards, eventually breasting the crest of the ridge slightly over halfway to Yanqul, before descending into the village of Al Waqbah.

Yanqul itself is a remote and rather sleepy little place lying in the shadow of the huge triangular Jebel al Hawra and surrounded by eye-catching mountain formations – slender rock pinnacles, craggy ridgetops, table mountains – which make for enjoyable viewing during the drive from Sohar to Ibri.

Bait al Marah and old Yanqul

To reach Bait al Marah fort, turn right at the T-junction at the beginning of Yanqul (if approaching from Sohar) and turn right along the road to Dank; the fort is about 1km along, on the right

It's worth stopping at Yanqul to have a look at the town's attractive mudbrick fort, the **Bait al Marah** (not open to the public), built at the beginning of seventeenth century by the Nabhani dynasty. The **old village** behind is also interesting, with dozens of crumbling mudbrick houses in an advanced state of decay, plus more modern concrete homes with colourful (though faded) metal doors. Most of the houses are now abandoned, although the *falaj* still flows in places.

ARRIVAL AND DEPARTURE   YANQUL

By car The road to Yanqul runs off the Globe roundabout in Sohar (although it's not signed to Yanqul, only to Wadi Habib). Note that there are no petrol stations between Sohar and Yanqul, while there are also a couple of wadis about 30km out of Sohar which are prone to flooding.

Wadi Jizzi

The 100km trip from Sohar to Buraimi takes around an hour and a half along Highway 7, following the course of **Wadi Jizzi**, formerly one of the most important trading routes in Oman, linking the coast and hills, and also important since antiquity for its copper deposits, which were exported as far afield as Mesopotamia and Persia.

The stretch up to the **Wadi Jizzi border post** (see page 137) en route to Buraimi is dual carriageway, fast and normally pleasantly traffic free, with the added bonus of superb mountain scenery en route. The first section of the road is dominated by the outline of Jebel Sohar, the high and isolated peak away to your left. Later on, the highway winds up into the hills, past a long succession of magnificently craggy peaks – the Omani landscape at its barest and most dramatic.

Buraimi

Highway 7 from Sohar ends at the town of **BURAIMI**, pushed up right against the border next to the more or less contiguous UAE city of Al Ain. Evidence of human settlement here dates back for some five thousand years, and the Buraimi oasis was historically one of the most important inland settlements in this part of Arabia thanks to its position astride the major trade route between Sohar, Wadi Jizzi and the interior, with a string of villages growing up around the various oases which dot the area. These have now been divided by the modern Oman–UAE border, while Buraimi itself has been comprehensively overtaken by the neighbouring – and now much wealthier and busier – Al Ain. Because of the town's distance from pretty much everywhere else in Oman and the border hassles associated with visiting it (see page 137), Buraimi doesn't feature on many Omani itineraries – which is a shame, given the town's bustling mercantile atmosphere and pair of fine forts.

Modern Buraimi is an engagingly lively place, with a large Indian and Pakistani population and a distinct buzz – the main road through town just east of Al Hillah Fort is particularly colourful, with an incredible quantity of ladies' tailoring shops stuffed full of extravagantly embroidered clothes and adorned with brilliant neon signs. In many ways the town feels closer to Dubai and Abu Dhabi than Muscat, which of course geographically it is – every second or third car seems to be from the UAE, while you're likely to see as many white Emirati headrobes as Omani caps. There are several interesting things to see in Buraimi town – as well as a further slew of attractions over the border in Al Ain (see page 138).

Al Khandaq Fort

Just south of the Fruit and Vegetable Souk • Mon–Thurs & Sun 8.30am–2.30pm • 500bz

The main sight in Buraimi proper is the immaculately restored **Al Khandaq Fort**, thought to have been built during the rule of Sultan Said bin Sultan in around 1842 – as suggested by a brass cannon bearing this name and date which can be found inside.

The fort occupies a slightly elevated position above a dried-up wadi, its somewhat vulnerable location compensated for by the deep moat which surrounds it. The exterior design of the fort is quite unlike any other in Oman (although somewhat reminiscent of nearby Jahili Fort just over the border in Al Ain): modest in size but prettily decorated, with diminutive, slope-sided round towers adorned with zigzagging triangles and chevrons. The interior of the fort is relatively bare, consisting of a large gravel courtyard from where ramps and steps lead up to a walkway around the battlements, with a couple of small buildings clustered below.

The Fruit and Vegetable Souk and Wholesale Souk

Just north of Al Khandaq Fort • Mon–Thurs, Sat & Sun 8am–noon & 5–9pm, Fri 5–9pm

A couple of hundred metres north of Khandaq Fort lies Buraimi's interesting huddle of souks. The large **Fruit and Vegetable Souk** occupies a rather grand edifice resembling a kind of postmodern fort. Inside, Indian and Pakistani traders preside over vast piles of colourful edibles; a couple of shops at the front sell quaint traditional wooden furniture, with ingenious lattice effects made out of mangrove poles and palm branches

---

BORDER PRACTICALITIES

Visiting Buraimi is significantly complicated by the bizarre fact that you have to technically "leave" Oman in order to reach the town. **Approaching from Sohar**, there is a border post on the main Highway 7 at **Wadi Jizzi** about 40km before Buraimi. You will be stamped out of Oman here (and, if you are on a single-entry visa, have it cancelled), even though the road beyond the border post is still in Omani territory – you don't actually reach the UAE border until Al Ain, 40km distant. If you're visiting Buraimi only and then returning directly to Sohar it should be possible to not have your visa cancelled, but make this very clear when you present your passport to avoid having your visa cancelled.

As of 2018, **entering the UAE** from Buraimi town is no longer possible for foreigners. Instead, you'll have to pass through the **Khatm al Shikla**, accessible from Highway 7 about 25km east of Buraimi. Approaching from Ibri along Highway 21 the UAE border is at **Mazyad**, about 25km before Buraimi. Be aware that foreigners can no longer cross from Al Ain to Buraimi in the town centre, so if you cross into the UAE at Mazyad you'll either have to go back on yourself and use the same border or drive east to Khatm al Shikla if you want to re-enter Oman. When you leave the UAE, you'll be charged an exit fee of 35 AED. Officially, re-entering Oman at either Wadi Jizzi or Mazyad is subject to the new e-visa rules announced in 2018 (see page 25). This means, if you're planning on re-entering Oman on another single-entry visa, you will have to have applied for it in advance at Ⓦ evisa.rop.gov.om. To be on the safe side, it's best to have a multiple-entry visa if you're planning on crossing from Oman to the UAE and then back again. In practice it can take as little as ten minutes to clear border formalities, although half an hour is a more realistic rule of thumb.

AL AIN

Al Ain has a surprisingly rich collection of sights (for more on which, see the *Rough Guide to Dubai*). The **Al Ain National Museum** (Mon–Thurs, Sat & Sun 8.30am–7pm; Fri 3–7pm; 3 AED; ⓦvisitabudhabi.ae) boasts interesting exhibits on the city's history, while the picturesque **Sultan bin Zayed Fort** next door (same hours and ticket) is famous as the birthplace of Sheikh Zayed bin Sultan Al Nahyan (ruled 1966–2004), the much-loved ruler of Abu Dhabi and first president of the UAE. The nearby **Livestock Market** and **Al Ain Souk** are also worth a look, as is the idyllic **Al Ain Oasis** (daily 8am–5pm; free) immediately west of the museum, the largest of the seven oases scattered across the city.

Further sights lie spread out across the city. On the western side of Al Ain Oasis stands the sprawling but rather uninteresting **Al Ain Palace Museum** (Mon–Thurs, Sat & Sun 8.30am–7.30pm, Fri 3–7.30pm; free) and the much more rewarding **Jahili Fort** (Tues–Thurs, Sat & Sun 9am–5pm, Fri 3–5pm; free), also home to an excellent little exhibition detailing the life and extraordinary exploits of legendary explorer **Wilfred Thesiger** (1910–2003), who stayed at the fort in the late 1940s. About 8km north of the city, the **Hili Gardens and Archeological Park** (daily 4–11pm; free) is the site of one of the most important archeological finds in the UAE, and includes the Great Hili Tomb (though it may actually have been some kind of temple), dating from the third century BC.

ACCOMMODATION

Al Ain Rotana ⓣ03 754 5111, ⓦrotana.com; map p.139. The best of Al Ain's low-key five stars, conveniently close to the city centre, with modern, if unspacular, guest rooms. Facilities include an outpost of the French Polynesian restaurant *Trader Vic's*, the Lebanese *Min Zaman*, and the serene Zen Spa. **459 AED/48 OR**

Danat Al Ain Resort ⓣ03 704 6000, ⓦalain. danathotels.com; map p.139. In a very peaceful setting on the edge of town, this hotel has pleasant, modern guestrooms and a very stylish Indian restaurant, *Tanjore*, as well as Italian and international dining options. The Irish pub, *McGettigan's*, is a good bet for big-screen sport. **406AED/43 OR**

Hilton Al Ain ⓣ03 768 6666, ⓦhilton.com; map p.139. Rooms are rather dated, although set in attractive grounds. There are two pools – one a family pool with waterslides – and a choice of Italian, Arabian, Tex-Mex and Japanese restaurants. **407 AED/42 OR**

tied together with coconut string. The **wholesale souk** next door (in a similar building) is usually quieter, with merchandise including big piles of dried fish, sacks of dates and large bundles of wood.

The Old Souk

Just north of the Fruit and Vegetable Souk • Mon–Thurs, Sat & Sun 8am–noon & 5–9pm, Fri 5–9pm

Beyond the Fruit and Vegetable Souk, on the far side of the small car park, lies the **old souk**, the third and most interesting of the three souks, in a small white building with a fake watchtower at its centre. This is notably more traditional in flavour than its neighbours. The aisles to either side are full of little shops selling big stacks of spices, plus shoes, food, walking sticks and traditional toy rifles. There's also an unusual section at the back run by Bedu women selling spices alongside locally produced honey and rose-water, best appreciated while having a drink at the small café beneath the central tower.

Al Hillah Fort

Behind the Fruit and Vegetable Souk • Mon–Thurs & Sun 8am–2pm • Free

Flanking the other side of the car park between the fruit and vegetable and old souks lies the second of Buraimi's two forts, **Al Hillah Fort**, re-opened to the public in early 2018 after extensive renovations. A low-slung sandstone edifice, it's rather plain and box-like from the outside, but full of interest within. It's actually a walled residential complex rather than a proper fort – the walls come with the usual battlements and rifle slits, but there are no proper defensive towers or cannon on display.

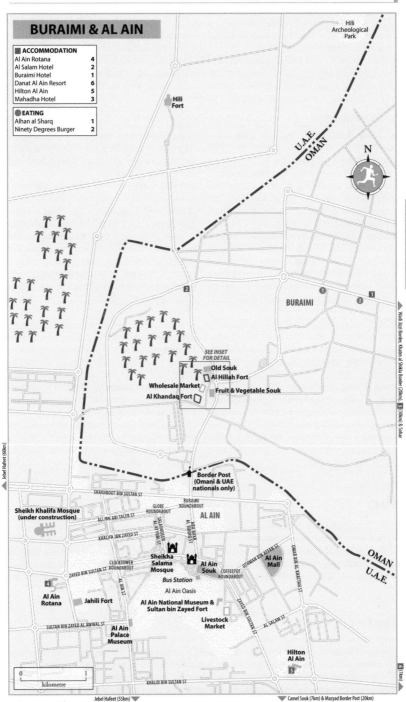

BURAIMI & AL AIN

ACCOMMODATION
Al Ain Rotana	4
Al Salam Hotel	2
Buraimi Hotel	1
Danat Al Ain Resort	6
Hilton Al Ain	5
Mahadha Hotel	3

EATING
Alhan al Sharq	1
Ninety Degrees Burger	2

Hili Archeological Park

U.A.E.
OMAN

N

3

Hili Fort

BURAIMI

SEE INSET FOR DETAIL

Old Souk
Al Hillah Fort
Wholesale Market
Al Khandaq Fort
Fruit & Vegetable Souk

Wadi Jizzi Border, Khatm al Shikla Border (20km) ▶ ③ (30km) & Sohar

Jebel Hafeet (60km) ◀

Border Post
(Omani & UAE nationals only)

SHAKHBOOT BIN SULTAN ST

Sheikh Khalifa Mosque
(under construction)

GLOBE
ROUNDABOUT

BURAIMI
ROUNDABOUT

ALI IBN ABI TALEB ST

AL AIN

KHALIFA IBN ZAYED ST

SALAHUDDEEN
AL AYYUBI ST

ABU BAKR
AL SIDDIQ ST

CLOCKTOWER
ROUNDABOUT

Sheikha
Salama Mosque

ZAYED BIN SULTAN ST

AL AIN ST

Al Ain
Souk

COFFEEPOT
ROUNDABOUT

OTHMAN BIN AFFAN ST

Al Ain
Mall

OMAN
U.A.E.

④
Al Ain
Rotana

Jahili Fort

Bus Station

Al Ain Oasis

Al Ain National Museum &
Sultan bin Zayed Fort

OMAR BIN AL KHATTAB ST

ZAYED BIN SULTAN ST

AL SALAM ST

SULTAN BIN ZAYED AL AWWAL ST

Al Ain
Palace
Museum

Livestock
Market

Hilton
Al Ain

⑤

KHALID BIN SULTAN ST

⑥ (1km)

0	1
kilometre	

Jebel Hafeet (55km) ▼

Camel Souk (7km) & Mazyad Border Post (20km) ▼

The entrance gateway leads into a large gravel courtyard, empty save for a small mosque with external *mihrab* and quaint little freestanding gateway with wooden doors. Go right from here to reach the complex's **second courtyard**, where you'll find one of Oman's finest clusters of traditional residential buildings, with three impressive two-storey buildings, embellished with superb wooden doors and carved details including unusual windows formed out of interlocking triangles; climb to the roofs of any of the three for fine views over the complex.

ACCOMMODATION   BURAIMI

Al Salam Hotel On the road to Sohar, about 2km north of Al Khandaq Fort ☎2565 5789, ⓦalsalamhotelburaimi.com; map p.139. Well-run three-star – not as nice as the *Buraimi Hotel*, but a fair bit cheaper. Rooms are comfortable but some of the decor is truly hideous, with gold curtains, gaudy chairs and crushed velvet sofas. There's a coffee shop and (unlicensed) restaurant downstairs. **15 OR**

Buraimi Hotel On the road to Sohar, about 2km east of the centre ☎2564 2010, ⓔalburaimihotel@hotmail. com; map p.139. Pleasant, slightly old-fashioned three-star that welcomes guests with a somewhat bizarre miniature faux fort marking the entrance. Rooms are large and very comfortably furnished, while facilities include

a decent-sized, if rather murky, pool in the scruffy little walled garden at the back and a passable restaurant (licensed) serving a wide range of international food (mains around 3 OR). **20 OR**

Mahadha Hotel Highway 7, just before the turning to Khatm al Shikla border crossing ☎2565 9126, ⓦmahadhahotel.com; map p.139. This new, slightly eccentric property is a little out of town but convenient for the border crossing at Khatm al Shikla, and nicer than the options in Buraimi itself. Rooms are spacious and comfortable, with a quirky design blending traditional features, like wall arches, with a ubiquitous textured stone cladding. Passable international food is on offer at the *Al Nafoora* restaurant. **29 OR**

EATING

There are the usual cafés scattered around town, including a particularly lively line of coffee shops and restaurants directly opposite the *Buraimi Hotel* serving up good shwarmas, grilled chicken, curries, samosas and juices. The only licensed venue in town is the restaurant at the *Buraimi Hotel*.

Alhan al Sharq Opposite Buraimi Hotel ☎2565 2226; map p.139. It doesn't face much competition for the title of Buraimi's finest Turkish restaurant, but there's certainly nothing wrong with the food at *Alhan al Sharq*, which encompasses vast *pide* (Turkish flatbread pizza), juicy kebabs, and the house signature dish, grilled quail. Mains 2–7 OR. Daily 8am–11pm.

Ninety Degrees Burger Main Rd, next to the Shell station before the mosque ☎9250 5539; map p.139. This ever-popular burger joint may not be the place to come to sample traditional Omani cuisine, but it does a surprisingly good line in burgers, fries, chicken and shakes, and makes for a more interesting alternative to *McDonald's* next door. Mains 2–4 OR. Daily 9am–1am.

Ibri

Strung out along Buraimi-Nizwa highway (Highway 21), more or less in the middle of nowhere, **IBRI** sees few foreign visitors, although it boasts a surprisingly absorbing cluster of traditional sights including a fine fort, interesting souk and one of the region's most memorable walled mudbrick villages at nearby **As Suleif**. The town was formerly a stronghold of Ibadhi conservatism, though modern Ibri derives its importance from its proximity to Fahud, where Oman's first oil was discovered in 1964.

The fort

Directly to the east of the old souk • Mon–Thurs, Sat & Sun 9am–3pm, Fri 8–11am • Free

The main sight in town is the large and carefully restored **fort**. Inside, the spacious gravel courtyard is surrounded by an interesting jumble of buildings and towers. To the right of the entrance stands the main defensive tower, an impressive three-storey structure; to the left, the remains of a mudbrick mosque with a deep well built into the platform alongside; and, on the far side of the courtyard, a residential building. Head left across the courtyard, through a second gateway, to reach a subsidiary courtyard, where steps lead up to a sizeable **mosque**, one of the largest in any Omani fort and still in use today, although kitted out with eyesore modern glass windows and metal pillars. This is actually only half the fort; the rest, beyond the mosque, remains closed to the public.

Around the fort

The area **around the fort** is significantly less manicured, but ultimately much more memorable, with dozens of imposing **mudbrick houses** (and a particularly fine ruined mosque opposite the fort) in various states of ruin, dotted here and there with little patches of dead oasis with decapitated palm trees. It's a perfect picture of the physical passing of old Oman – intensely atmospheric, and rather sad. Pressed up hard against the west wall of the fort is the town's attractive old **souk**, including some neat little arcaded sections.

As Suleif

The resident guardian will meet you at the entrance and show you around • No admission price, although a small donation would be appreciated

On the southern edge of town lies Ibri's most absorbing attraction, the remarkable walled village of **As Suleif**, a huge clump of collapsing mudbrick buildings which crown a small hill next to the main Nizwa highway. Like so many settlements in Oman, the old mudbrick village was abandoned a few decades ago in favour of the modern concrete villa development that now stands beside it, and the original settlement is now

3

A NASTY AFFAIR AT THE BURAIMI OASIS

A sleepy backwater for much of its history, Buraimi briefly captured the world's attention in the early 1950s as a result of the so-called **Buraimi Dispute** – one of the defining events in Oman's twentieth-century history, and one which neatly encapsulates the Wild West atmosphere of the early days of oil prospecting in the Gulf. The **origin** of the dispute was the result of Saudi Arabia's claim in 1949 to sovereignty over large parts of what was traditionally considered territory belonging to Abu Dhabi and Oman, including the Buraimi Oasis. The Saudis (supported by the US Aramco oil company) backed up their claim by referring to previous periods of Saudi occupation dating back to the early nineteenth century, although their real interest in Buraimi stemmed from the belief that large amounts of oil lay buried in the region.

In 1952 a small group of Saudi Arabian soldiers occupied **Hamasa**, one of three Omani villages in the oasis, claiming it for Saudi Arabia and embarking on a campaign of bribery in an attempt to obtain professions of loyalty from local villagers. They also tried to bribe **Sheikh Zayed al Nahyan**, governor of Al Ain, tempting him with the huge sum of US$42 million – an offer which Sheikh Zayed pointedly refused. The affair was debated in both the British Parliament and at the United Nations, although attempts at international arbitration finally broke down in 1955. Shortly afterwards the Saudis were driven out of Hamasa by the Trucial Oman Levies, a British-backed force based in Sharjah; for an eyewitness account of this action, read Edward Henderson's *Arabian Destiny* (see page 253). The dispute wasn't finally resolved until 1974, when an agreement was reached between King Faisal of Saudi Arabia and Sheikh Zayed (who had subsequently become ruler of Abu Dhabi and first president of the newly independent UAE). Ironically, after all the fuss, the area proved singularly lacking in oil.

The dispute gave Buraimi its proverbial fifteen minutes of fame, even inspiring an episode of *The Goon Show* entitled "The Nasty Affair at the Buraimi Oasis". More importantly, it put a final end to centuries of Saudi incursions into Oman, as well as establishing the legendary reputation of Sheikh Zayed, one of the modern Gulf's most charismatic statesmen, who succeeded in repulsing the oil-rich Saudis and their American cronies long before Abu Dhabi had found its own huge oil reserves. As one foreign observer put it, "He [Zayed] was very proud that, when he had nothing, he told them to get stuffed."

slowly crumbling into picturesque ruin – it's very atmospheric, and looks more like the ruin of hundreds, rather than tens, of years.

The entire village is impressively fortified, with high walls at the front and sides, and a string of watchtowers stuck like candles into the massive rock outcrop at the back. Inside is an incredibly labyrinthine, kasbah-like tangle of old roofless houses and other structures including a mosque, jail, various wells, *majlis*, food stores, a room for pressing dates and a "hanging tower" at the summit of the rock where unfortunates were taken to be executed. The remains of various inscriptions moulded onto arches or inscribed on rocks can also be seen.

ARRIVAL AND DEPARTURE   IBRI

By car To reach the fort and old town, take the turning signed "Ibri Souk and Town Centre" from the middle of Ibri (on the right-hand side if approaching from Bahla), then take the unsigned left-hand turn about 100m beyond, heading up past the Makkah Hypermarket on your left then following the road for about 1km as it curves round to the right, bringing you to a small roundabout. Head straight across this and follow the narrow road through the souk to reach the fort (there's a large car park in front of it).

ACCOMMODATION

★ **Ibri Oasis Hotel** 9km from the town-centre roundabout along the Buraimi highway, just past the Ibri Sports Complex stadium ☎ 2569 6172, ✉ iohotel@ omantel.net.om. The only place to stay in town, this is a surprisingly nice hotel given the scarcity of tourists, although the complete lack of competition means they are resting on their laurels a bit, and the interior could do with a revamp. That said, the service is very friendly, the rooms spacious and very comfortably furnished, and there's a decent (licensed) restaurant and bar with live Arabian music. __39 OR__

Bat and Al Ayn

East of Ibri, Highway 21 roars purposefully east towards Bahla, just under 100km distant. The area is home to two of Oman's most celebrated prehistoric sites: the **beehive tombs** at **Bat** and **Al Ayn**. The former is more likely to appeal to dedicated archeologists or students of ancient history than casual visitors, though the latter, with a string of tombs lined up dramatically atop a rocky ridge, is well worth the detour from the main highway.

Bat

Around 30km east of Ibri, the small village of **BAT** is home to a remarkable array of **Bronze Age tombs**, towers and other remains, listed as a UNESCO World Heritage Site since 1988 (along with those at nearby Al Ayn). The site dates back to between 2000 and 3000 BC, forming, according to UNESCO, "the most complete collection of settlements and necropolises from the 3rd millennium BC in the world". To the untrained eye, it's difficult to make much sense of the remains you see on the ground, although the sheer scale of the ruins is impressive and the whole place is particularly beautiful towards dusk, when the light turns the surrounding hills a rich russet, their ridges dotted with the enigmatic remains of one of Oman's most ancient civilizations.

There are some four hundred tombs scattered around the hills of the archeological site, although many have collapsed and now look essentially like large mounds of rubble.

The white tower

From the car park, it's a 5–10 minute walk up to the remains of the circular **white tower** you probably saw on the drive in, halfway up the hill overlooking the wadi. This is one of a number of such structures dotted around the site, now standing about 1m high after restoration (although they may originally have been up to 10m tall), with a distinctive triangular door, walls formed from beautifully carved and carefully fitted pieces of stone and an interior divided into two "rooms" by a single wall down the middle. The exact function of this and other similar towers around Bat – or, indeed, what they originally looked like – remains unknown.

Outlying towers and tombs

Two further **towers** stand next to one another in the wadi below; one has been restored using white stones, and the other using ochre, which makes for a nice photo, although the underlying archeological reasoning behind two-tone restoration remains unclear. Continue walking up the wadi for another ten minutes to reach an enclosure protected by a green wire-mesh fence (padlocked at the time of research). Inside are three neatly restored beehive **tombs** (very similar to the towers, though a little smaller), one constructed out of white stones, the other two out of ochre, along with half-a-dozen other tombs in various stages of collapse. The remains of further partially intact beehive tombs can be seen along the ridgetop beyond.

ARRIVAL AND INFORMATION   BAT

By car Getting to Bat is the first challenge, and you'll need a 4WD (unlike for Al Ayn). From Ibri, follow the road to Yanqul for about 15km then take the signed turn-off on the right to Bat and follow the road as it loops through the small village of Ad Dreez. Follow the road for about 14km until a signed turn-off to the tombs on the left just after a Shell station. You'll come to the tombs after about a kilometre. From Yanqul, follow Highway 8 towards Ibri until it becomes Highway 9, shortly after which turn left into Ad Dreez and follow the instructions above.

Information More information and photographs of the tombs at Bat and Al Ayn can be found at ⓦwhc.unesco.org/en/list/434.

Al Ayn

It's a 10min walk from the road up to the tombs, although there's no obvious path; cross the wadi bed and scramble up a track roughly opposite the big mosque at the entrance to the village

Some 37km east of Bat, the small village of **AL AYN** is home to another superb collection of Bronze Age necropolises. The appeal of the tombs here is their spectacular setting, strung out along a narrow ridgetop and dramatically backdropped by the craggy outline of **Jebel Misht** (literally "Comb Mountain", named on account of its distinctively serrated ridgetop), one of the largest of the various geological "exotics" which dot this part of Oman. There are 21 tombs in total, most of them well preserved, and late afternoon is a particularly magical time to see them.

ARRIVAL AND DEPARTURE   AL AYN

By car To reach Al Ayn from Bat, follow the directions outlined under Bat above but keep following the road until you reach a T-junction just before Al Ayn village. Turn left here and you'll see the tombs up on your left on top of the ridge as you drive into the village, around 500m past the T-junction. Al Ayn is also accessible via two side-roads from the Ibri–Nizwa highway, without a 4x4. Approaching from Ibri, take the turn-off at the village of Kubarah signed to Amla. Approaching from Nizwa, take the turning about 13km further down the road by the Al Maha petrol station, also signed to Amla.

Musandam

CRUISING THE FJORDS NEAR KHASAB IN A
TRADITIONAL DHOW BOAT

Musandam

At the far northeastern tip of the Arabian peninsula (and separated from the rest of Oman by a wide swathe of UAE territory), the dramatic Musandam peninsula is perhaps the most scenically spectacular area in the entire Gulf. Often described as "The Norway of Arabia", the peninsula boasts a magical combination of mountain and maritime landscapes, as the towering red-rock Hajar mountains fall precipitously into the blue waters of the Arabian Gulf, creating a labyrinthine system of steep-sided fjords (*khors*), cliffs and islands, most of them inaccessible except by boat. Musandam remains one of Oman's great wildernesses, with a largely untouched natural environment ranging from the pristine waters of the coast, where you can see frolicking dolphins, basking sharks and the occasional whale, through to the wild uplands of the jebel, dotted with fossils and petroglyphs.

The main town in Musandam proper is lively little **Khasab**, at the top of the peninsula and connected to the outside world by the spectacular **coastal road** which runs down via Bukha to the UAE border at Tibat. Khasab offers the perfect base for boat (or diving) trips out on the marvellous **Khor ash Sham** while, further afield, the remote town of **Kumzar** is the endpoint of the perhaps even more spectacular sea trip out along the coast and into the Straits of Hormuz; Khasab is also the starting point for mountain safaris up the mighty **Jebel Harim** and beyond. Unless you're driving from the UAE – which is possible, but no picnic (see page 152) – getting a plane or boat to Khasab (see below) is the only way to get to Musandam.

Khasab

Musandam's major town, **KHASAB**, sits at the far northern end of the peninsula in a narrow plain squeezed in between the mountains – one of the few sizeable areas of flat coastal real estate in the entire peninsula. It's a small but lively place, and one which feels a long way from the rest of Oman, the slightly Wild West atmosphere stoked up by hordes of locals charging around in pick-up trucks, bands of Iranian traders loading up goods in the Old Souk and the occasional roar of an Omani airforce jet or the daily flight from Muscat coming in to land.

Khasab is the obvious place to base yourself while exploring the peninsula. The town divides into two parts: the modern **New Souk**, and the more ramshackle **Old Souk** down near the port, which is where you'll also find the interesting fort. The town is also home to virtually all Musandam's accommodation, while its location and the number of tour agents in town makes it a good base for dhow rides out into the *khors*, diving trips and 4WD excursions into the mountains. Many visitors to Khasab

KHASAB COASTAL ROAD

Highlights

❶ **Khasab Fort** Engaging Portuguese fort, with old wooden dhows lined up in the courtyard and award-winning museum displays on traditional life in Musandam. See page 149

❷ **Khor ash Sham** Musandam's largest and most beautiful *khor*, the perfect place to spend a day on the water, swimming, snorkelling and dolphin-spotting. See page 155

❸ **Sea trip to Kumzar** Marvellous sea journey to the famously isolated town of Kumzar, at the northernmost tip of Musandam. See page 158

❹ **Jebel Harim** Take a "mountain safari" up Musandam's highest peak, rising amid dramatic rocky landscapes at the heart of the peninsula.

See page 160

❺ **The coastal road from Khasab to Bukha** Explore Musandam's stunning coastal road as it hugs the cliff-lined coast south of Khasab. See page 163

❻ **Diving the coasts and the khors** Enjoy some of the best diving in the Middle East and discover an unspoiled underwater world of coral reefs and sea caves, teeming with macro life, sharks and rays. See page 157

❼ **Prehistoric petroglyphs** Marvel at millennia-old rock carvings, depicting people and wildlife, at sites including Wadi Tawi. See page 164

HIGHLIGHTS ARE MARKED ON THE MAP ON PAGE 148

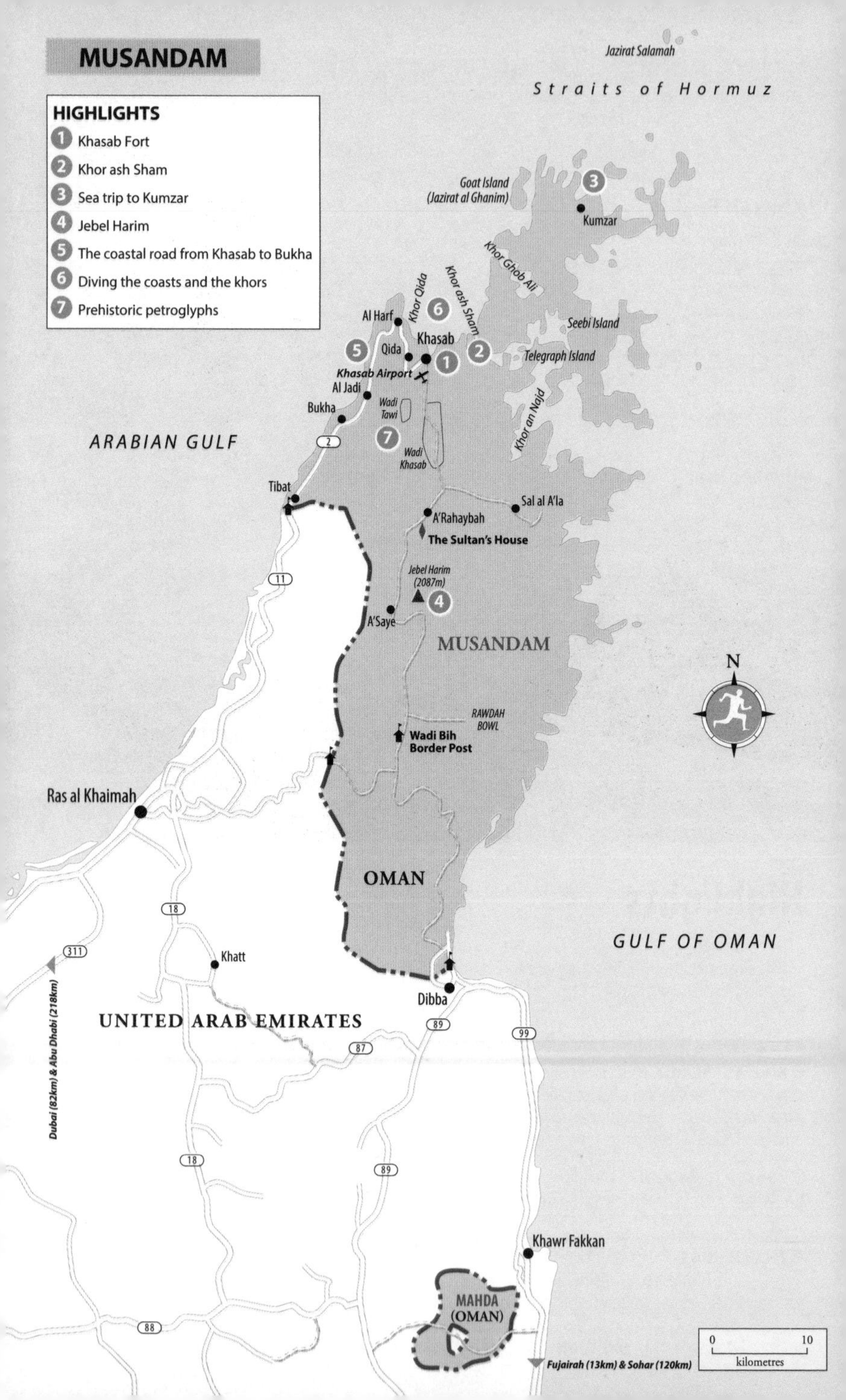

MUSANDAM
HIGHLIGHTS
1 Khasab Fort
2 Khor ash Sham
3 Sea trip to Kumzar
4 Jebel Harim
5 The coastal road from Khasab to Bukha
6 Diving the coasts and the khors
7 Prehistoric petroglyphs
Jazirat Salamah
Straits of Hormuz
Goat Island (Jazirat al Ghanim)
Kumzar
Khor Ghob Ali
Khor ash Sham
Khor Qida
Seebi Island
Telegraph Island
Al Harf
Khasab
Qida
Khasab Airport
Al Jadi
Bukha
Wadi Tawi
Wadi Khasab
Khor an Najd
ARABIAN GULF
2
Tibat
Sal al A'la
A'Rahaybah
The Sultan's House
11
Jebel Harim (2087m)
A'Saye
MUSANDAM
N
RAWDAH BOWL
Wadi Bih Border Post
Ras al Khaimah
OMAN
18
GULF OF OMAN
311
Khatt
Dibba
UNITED ARAB EMIRATES
Dubai (82km) & Abu Dhabi (218km)
89
99
87
18
89
Khawr Fakkan
MAHDA (OMAN)
88
Fujairah (13km) & Sohar (120km)
0
10
kilometres

are here on day-trips from Dubai and elsewhere in the UAE. You'll see surprisingly few visitors in town after around 4pm in the afternoon – which is all the more reason to stay the night.

Khasab Fort

The corniche, opposite the harbour • Mon–Thurs, Sat & Sun 9am–4pm, Fri 8–11am • 500bz

Down near the Old Souk, the town's pretty stone **fort** was built by the Portuguese in the seventeenth century as part of their efforts to control passing maritime trade. The fort was originally on the seafront, though the waters have since receded a considerable distance, leaving the structure high and dry. It's not the biggest or grandest in Oman, but Khasab Fort has won an international Museums and Heritage award for its exhibits, which make it the best attraction of its kind in the country.

A couple of large wooden **dhows** stand outside, while three smaller boats sit in the courtyard within – a *battil*, *mashuwwah* and *zaruqah*. The *battil* (the one closest to the entrance) is particularly attractive, sporting the pretty cowrie-shell decorations around the prow and rudder which are typical of Musandam. The boat's bow and stern also display a rare extant example of the traditional "stitched" method of boat building (see page 178), with planks literally sewn together using coconut thread. Close by stand modern replicas of a traditional *bait al qufl* ("house of the lock") and a *barasti* (palm thatch) summer house, ingeniously constructed using stone pillars with permeable walls fashioned out of palm branches.

The circular tower

In the centre of the courtyard stands the fort's most unusual feature: a large and completely detached **circular tower**, intended to provide an additional refuge in case the outer walls were breached. Entrance is via a ramp on one side and steps on the other, with a hearth built into the exterior wall below. The interior is filled with wide-ranging and informative exhibits covering various aspects of Musandam's geology, culture and history – a welcome and unusual feature among Oman's forts, even those which have been recently redeveloped.

Around the walls

From the entrance, steps lead up to the **walls** and a **walkway** on which you can make a circuit of the fort and its various towers – a couple of which still have their mangrove-pole ladders set into the interior walls.

The second tower around houses various colourful but rather unedifying displays on traditional Musandam culture, featuring colourful rugs, crockery and some droll mannequins. There's also an interesting re-creation of a traditional apothecary's shop and a display of fine traditional silver jewellery including enormously chunky elbow rings, necklaces featuring characteristic pouches ("Qur'an boxes") used to store texts from the holy book (worn as magic charms to ward off evil). A couple of these also incorporate the large silver Maria Theresa *thaler* coins which were widely used throughout the Gulf and East Africa during the eighteenth and nineteenth centuries and which were often incorporated into traditional Omani jewellery (and are still widely available in souvenir shops around the country to this day).

The Wali's Wing

The tower on the breezy sea-facing side of the fort houses the **Wali's Wing**, erstwhile residence of the *wali*, or governor, of Khasab. This is decorated with the usual old rugs and coffeepots alongside more unusual *wali*-related bric-a-brac, including antique sewing and writing boxes, expired tins of boot polish and bottles of ink, and an old Philips radio.

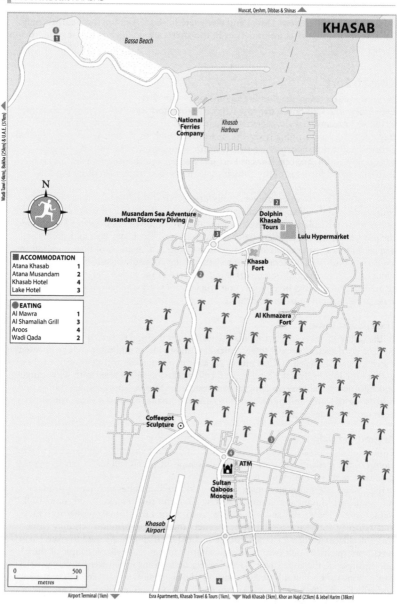

Muscat, Qeshm, Dibbas & Shinas ▲▲

KHASAB

Bassa Beach

National Ferries Company

Khasab Harbour

N

Musandam Sea Adventure
Musandam Discovery Diving

Dolphin Khasab Tours

Lulu Hypermarket

Khasab Fort

Al Khmazera Fort

■ **ACCOMMODATION**
Atana Khasab	1
Atana Musandam	2
Khasab Hotel	4
Lake Hotel	3

● **EATING**
Al Mawra	1
Al Shamaliah Grill	3
Aroos	4
Wadi Qada	2

Coffeepot Sculpture

ATM

Sultan Qaboos Mosque

Khasab Airport

0 ———— 500
metres

Wadi Tawi (4km), Bukha (25km) & U.A.E. (37km) ▲

Airport Terminal (1km) ▼   Esra Apartments, Khasab Travel & Tours (1km), ▼ Wadi Khasab (3km), Khor an Najd (23km) & Jebel Harim (38km)

The Old Souk

West of the fort lies Khasab's **Old Souk**, a huddle of shops, cafés and travel agents which was formerly the epicentre of the town's vibrant contraband industry (see page 153). Many of the businesses here still advertise themselves as specializing in "Import & Export" – a polite way of saying smuggling – and even now the souk still sees regular boatloads of Iranian traders pitching up during the day to take delivery of assorted household goods which they load into boats and cart off for resale back home.

Al Khmazera Fort

Halfway between the old and new souks • Mon–Wed, Sat & Sun 9am–2pm • Free • The fort is signed from the New Souk; follow the road through the oasis and you'll see it on your left in front of a prominent blue-domed mosque

Sprawling away behind the fort lies Khasab's extensive **oasis**. Tucked away in the middle of this lies **Al Khmazera Fort**, a rather plain structure with two round towers at opposite corners and a sequence of rooms inside arranged around a little courtyard. En route to the fort, look out for the particularly eye-catching villa (on the left) with an enormous model dhow poised precariously above the gateway.

Bassa Beach

Heading out along the coastal road, about 1km past the harbour (and just before the *Atana Khasab* hotel) lies **Bassa Beach**. Despite its name, Bassa isn't so much a beach as an enormous car park, although there are majestic views of the coast, and the tiny ribbon of muddy sand is piled high with a treasure-trove of washed-up seashells (along with less appealing domestic rubbish) – perfect for an hour's idle beachcombing.

THE SHEHI

4

Musandam is inhabited by three main tribes; the Dahoori, Kumzari (see page 158) and, by far the largest of the three, the **Shehi** (often anglicized to "Shihuh"). The Shehi formerly had a rather mysterious and fearsome reputation, said to speak a language unintelligible to anyone but themselves and living a reclusive life up in the mountains, eking a frugal and difficult existence out of one of Arabia's most inhospitable environments. Notably different from the Bedu and townspeople of the plains, many of the Shehi formerly lived in mountain **caves** or natural rock shelters, which were converted into simple little dwellings with the addition of a couple of stone walls and wooden doors. They also carried a small axe on a long handle (known as a *jirz*), rather than the *khanjar* found elsewhere in Oman, which could serve both as a weapon and a climbing stick. The Shehi remain the dominant clan in modern Khasab – you'll see the name Al Shehi on shop signs all around town, especially in the Old Souk – although many have now moved out to exploit the greater economic opportunities in neighbouring Ras al Khaimah (RAK), and RAK-registered cars are a common sight around town.

The **origins** of the Shehi remain unclear. One theory is that they were the original inhabitants of Oman who were gradually driven north into the mountains by waves of Yemeni and Nizari Arabs arriving from the south. Another, more colourful, tradition claims that they are descended from the survivors of shipwrecks marooned on Musandam's rocks over thousands of years – anecdotes record the occasional birth of Shehi children with fair hair and blue eyes. Their language, too, had a similarly cosmopolitan flavour, although, unlike Kumzari, it remains a dialect of Arabic, rather than an original language. As Ronald Codrai, writing of a visit to the peninsula in the 1950s in his entertaining *Travels to Oman: 1948–1955*, put it: "That they spoke a different dialect was soon obvious, but it was Arabic, although sometimes spoken more gutturally through closed teeth and, once or twice, I thought I detected a Somerset accent."

The Shehi (along with other Musandam tribes) formerly migrated on a **seasonal** basis, spending the winters farming in the mountains or fishing in the *khors* before heading down to Khasab to harvest dates during the summer. Not surprisingly, given Oman's rising prosperity, the Shehi and other tribes of Musandam, the younger generations particularly, are steadily abandoning the hard traditional life of their ancestors, meaning that many of Musandam's villages are being steadily **depopulated** as their inhabitants depart in search of a more comfortable existence in Khasab or elsewhere, leaving nothing behind but locked houses and wandering goats.

ARRIVAL AND GETTING AROUND   KHASAB

Getting to the peninsula has become increasingly easy in the past few years thanks to the introduction of daily flights; there is also a bus-and-ferry service from Muscat via Shinas (see below). Even so, it's still much easier to reach Khasab from Dubai (a drive of around 3–4hr) than from the Omani capital; for information on driving to Musandam from the rest of Oman, see the box below. If you're staying in Dibba (see page 165), there's another ferry which travels there from Shinas (see below).

BY PLANE

The easiest way of getting to Musandam is to fly. Oman Air operate daily flights from Muscat to Khasab (and back again) in small twin-prop planes. The flight takes 1hr 10min, with fares in the region of 30 OR each way. Convenience aside, the flight also offers spectacular views of the mountains: the last ten minutes before landing in Khasab must be one of the world's most

---

DRIVING TO MUSANDAM

The road trip up to Musandam **from the rest of Oman** may look like an interesting adventure on paper, but is actually a bit of a slog, involving four sets of border formalities and many kilometres of largely featureless driving. This is especially the case if you take the tedious western route via Dubai, although the route up the east coast of the UAE is significantly more pleasant, and offers the chance to have a look at the relatively little-visited eastern and northern edges of the UAE en route.

Travelling from Oman, the trip can also work out to be surprisingly expensive. If you don't have a multiple-entry visa, you'll have to buy two new **Omani visas**, each at a cost of 20 OR – one for entering Musandam and one for re-entering the rest of Oman. However, under the new e-visa rules announced in 2018 (see page 25), each new Omani visa must be applied for in advance at ⓦ evisa.rop.gov.om. Therefore, it's much easier, not to mention cheaper, to have a multiple-entry visa (50 OR) if you're planning on driving to Musandam from the rest of Oman. On top of this cost, you'll also pay 35 dirhams (around $10/£7) each time you exit the UAE. If driving yourself you'll need to get additional **car insurance** from your car-rental operator covering you to drive in the UAE – expect to pay around 20 OR, which will cover you for a week. By the time you've paid for visas and insurance, you might well be looking at a total cost of around $170/£120 – which works out about the same as the average plane fare.

BORDER CROSSINGS FROM THE UAE

There's only one surfaced road into Musandam: this enters the west side of the peninsula at **Tibat** from Ras al Khaimah emirate, then runs up the coast to Khasab. The border post at Tibat is open 24hr. Count on around thirty minutes to clear Omani and UAE border formalities, although it can take significantly longer at weekends and on public holidays. There's a second entry point to Musandam on the eastern side of the peninsula at **Dibba**, but this is not open to independent travellers except those from GCC countries. If, however, you are staying at *Golden Tulip Dibba* or *Six Senses Zighy Bay*, they can arrange a border pass for you in advance. Bookings must be made at least seven days in advance and you have to provide the hotel with scans of your passport and visa so they can arrange a border pass for you. Under this system, you won't need to get a new Omani visa when you enter Musandam.

THE ROUTES

There are **two main routes** from the rest of Oman up to the Musandam border post at Tibat, taking roughly 4–5 hours from Sohar or Buraimi, or around eight hours from Muscat. The first starts at **Buraimi** and then follows Route E66 from Al Ain down to the edge of Dubai, and then the Emirates Road (Route 311) up to Ras al Khaimah, a boring and often stressful drive along two of the UAE's busiest highways (maps show some quieter cross-country roads, but these are surprisingly difficult to find without local knowledge). A slower but more pleasant option is the drive exiting Oman **north of Sohar** at Khatmat Milahah then heading up the attractive east coast of the UAE along Highway 99 through Fujairah and Khawr Fakkan to Dibba, before looping back round to Ras al Khaimah via highways 87 and 18.

Unfortunately, whichever route you take there's no way of avoiding **Ras al Khaimah**, a major bottleneck, exacerbated by the hopeless lack of signage – if in doubt, try to keep driving in the general direction of the mountains.

MARLBORO TIME: SMUGGLING IN KHASAB

Khasab was formerly infamous as the epicentre of the Oman–Iran **contraband trade**, thanks to its strategic location at the tip of the Arabian peninsula, just 45km from Iran across the Straits of Hormuz – a mere 45 minutes by speedboat. Up until 2001, taxes on US goods in Iran encouraged a flourishing trade in smuggling, with as many as five thousand Iranian boats visiting Khasab daily, arriving laden with boatloads of goats destined for the slaughterhouses of RAK and returning across the Straits of Hormuz weighed down with consignments of tea, electronics and, especially, cigarettes. Locals describe the golden age of smuggling as **"Marlboro Time"**, and the sight of thousands of Iranian speedboats loading up with piles of duty-free cigarettes was formerly a tourist attraction in its own right. The smuggling trade also provided a major source of income for locals in Khasab, who provided transport and other logistical services – accounting for the extraordinary number of pick-up trucks around town, formerly used to shift vast quantities of contraband tobacco and other goods down to the waiting boats.

Since 2001, successive changes in **customs regulations** in Iran and the UAE have led to the virtual demise of smuggling in Khasab. Cigarettes are now exported legally from Jebel Ali Free Port in Dubai, while the goats with which the Iranians formerly made themselves welcome are delivered directly to Ras al Khaimah in the UAE. The town still sees a fair number of Iranian traders even so – perhaps two or three hundred boats a day – although the lifting of international sanctions on Iran in 2016 has put the kibosh on a recent mini-renaissance in illegal smuggling. These days, the legitimate boats are granted a 12-hour pass, although they aren't allowed further into town than the Old Souk (where you'll often see them loading up trucks with old washing machines, fridges and suchlike) and must leave by sunset – a rather tame legacy of the town's former customs-busting bravado.

4

spectacular plane journeys, and is worth the ticket price alone.

BY FERRY

It used to be possible to take a ferry directly from Muscat to Khasab, a very pleasant way of making the journey. In 2017, however, a new "land and sea" service was launched courtesy of state transport agency Mwasalat. Under the new system, a bus carries passengers between Muscat and Shinas, a coastal town near Oman's northern border with the UAE, from where a ferry departs for Khasab. This has made an already long trip rather less appealing, although it takes no longer overall than before, and the ferry trip is still very scenic – although still not a patch on the view through the plane windows.

Times For the latest timetables and price details, head to ⓦnfc.om. At the time of writing, buses depart Muscat for Shinas every Sunday and Thursday at 10am, arriving at 1.30pm; the ferry then departs Shinas at 3pm the same day, arriving in Khasab at 7pm on Sundays and 6pm on Thursdays. Going the other way, ferries depart from Khasab on Tuesdays and Saturdays at 1pm, arriving in Shinas at 5pm (Tuesdays) or 4pm (Saturdays). The ferry from Shinas to Dibba takes 2hr 30min and departs on Sundays (12.30pm), Wednesdays (2pm), Thursdays (1pm) and Saturdays (noon).

Fares The fare is 18 OR one-way/35 OR return in "economy class", 29 OR one-way/57 OR return in "business class" (which offers better views from the front of the boat), and 41 OR one-way/81 OR return in "VIP class", where you share a cabin with just seven other passengers. Children aged 4–12 travel for half price, and under-4s go free. It costs 40 OR to take a rental car on the ferry, which, annoyingly, is roughly four times what it costs to take a privately owned car registered in Oman. Motorbikes can be taken for 3 OR, and bicycles for 1 OR.

Ticket agents There are two options for buying tickets in Muscat. The first, and easiest, is to book your ticket through a local travel agent (tour operators in all the city's upmarket hotels should be able to organize this for you). Alternatively, reserve by phone on ⓣ 2449 5453 or by email via ⓔ reservation@nfc.om. You can buy tickets in Khasab at the National Ferries Company office (ⓣ 2673 1802) down by the port, or, more conveniently, through *Khasab Travel & Tours* or *Musandam Sea Adventure* (see page 154).

BY TAXI

Khasab is very spread out, and, maddeningly, there are no conventional taxis. If you're arriving by ferry or plane, you'll need to arrange for your hotel to pick you up or you'll be facing a long, hot and dusty walk with your luggage.

BY CAR

All tour operators (see page 154) should be able to arrange car rental (either 2WD or 4WD), although it's a good idea to book this in advance as vehicles may not always be readily available and there's no other way of travelling independently in Musandam.

INFORMATION AND TOURS

There's a surprisingly large number of **tour operators** in town, many with offices in the Old Souk. Most of these places are only erratically open, and some appear to be on permanent siesta, but there is a growing number of reliable, professional outfits to choose from, with a few listed below. The stock in trade of all local operators is **khor cruises** and **mountain safaris** (see page 163), and tour operators are also the best source of local **information**.

Dolphin Khasab Tours Lulu Hypermarket, opposite Khasab Fort ☎ 2673 0813, ⓦ dolphinkhasabtours.com. Since 2007 this friendly, professional outfit has been one of the most popular tour operators in town, offering a more extensive programme of activities than some of their competitors. The staples are still dhow trips and mountain safaris in Jebel Harim, but other options include disembarking from the dhow to kayak through the *khors*, fishing, and camping in a secluded cove at Seeb al Gareeb. Daily 8.30am–8.30pm.

Khasab Travel & Tours Around the back of the airport, south of the New Souk, opposite the Esra Apartments ☎ 2673 0464, ⓦ khasabtours.com. The leading operator in town is this extremely professional and well-run outfit which has more or less single-handedly pioneered tourism in the peninsula since opening for business in 1992, with an excellent roster of guides, many of whom are veritable treasure-troves of local information. They also operate handy city tours, including of Khasab itself and the petroglyphs at nearby Wadi Tawi. There's another office at the *Atana Khasab* hotel; boats depart from Khasab Harbour. Daily 9am–1.30pm & 5–8pm.

Musandam Sea Adventure Khasab Rd, next to Diwan Al Amir hotel, Old Souk ☎ 2673 0424, ⓦ msaoman.com. A smaller outfit based down in the Old Souk, and another reliable option. Alongside the usual dhow and mountain trips, they offer mountain biking in the *jebel* and day trips to Dibba, including a dhow trip, banana boat ride and fishing – a good way to explore another corner of Musandam if you don't have your own transport. They also offer multi-day trips taking in Kumzar (see page 156) and beach camping. Daily 8am–8pm.

ACCOMMODATION

Khasab has a passable range of accommodation given its modest size, although rates everywhere are comparatively high for what you get. Budget accommodation is limited to the *Lake Hotel*, which is still no snip and is probably best avoided if at all possible.

Atana Khasab About 3km from Khasab on the main road to Bukha ☎ 2673 0777, ⓦ atanahotels.com; map p.150. A few kilometres out of town, this attractive four-star is, along with its sister property *Atana Musandam*, the most upmarket option in Khasab. Occupying a dramatic, if rather windy, hillside overlooking the coast, the hotel has an attractive pool and terrace with views over the sea. Now in the hands of the government-funded OMRAN group, the hotel has been recently renovated, and rooms are comfortable, if a little bland; some have balconies, and all promise either sea or mountain views. Facilities include the (licensed) Omani *Al Mawra* restaurant, a hilltop shisha bar and a terrace café. 82 OR

★ **Atana Musandam** Khasab Harbour ☎ 2673 0888, ⓦ atanahotels.com; map p.150. This lovely hotel combines a great location with luxurious accommodation, housed in a collection of square-roofed Arabian-style buildings cresting the tip of Khasab Harbour. Rooms are similarly traditional but luxurious, with lovely dark wood furniture, woven wooden ceilings and adobe-style walls; each room also has a balcony. There's a spa and a decent restaurant, although it is unlicensed unlike that of the *Atana Khasab*. 94 OR

Khasab Hotel On the main road, 750m south of the New Souk ☎ 2673 0267, ⓦ khasabhotel.net; map p.150. Welcoming visitors with a naff plastic mini-fort facade, this somewhat quirky hotel is one of Khasab's cheaper options, although like everywhere else here, it's overpriced. Good value tours are on offer, though, and the spacious, comfortable rooms and slightly old-fashioned decor are not without their charms; other facilities include a children's play area, outdoor pool, and decent restaurant. Cash only. 32 OR

Lake Hotel On the main road just north of the turning to the fort, Old Souk ☎ 2673 1664; map p.150. There's not a lake in sight, but this simple budget hotel does at least have a convenient location on the edge of the Old Souk, near the fort. It's also the cheapest option in town, but sadly has little else going for it – rooms are small, televisions may not work, mattresses are hard and you may find yourself playing host to the occasional small but inquisitive cockroach. 20 OR

EATING

You won't actually starve in Khasab, but don't expect any culinary surprises. There are a number of places to eat in the New Souk plus a further string of low-key cafés in the Old Souk, though nothing to get very excited about, with the possible exception of *Aroos* (see below). A number of places in the Old Souk also double as **shisha cafés**, with huddles of pipe-smoking locals sitting out on the pavement after dark amid clouds of fragrant tobacco.

Al Mawra Atana Khasab, 3km from Khasab on the main road to Bukha ☎ 2673 0777; map p.150. The only licensed venue in town along with the *Atana Khasab*'s bar, this restaurant is named after a traditional stove found in Omani homes, and serves a range of good Omani dishes alongside the usual selection of curries and biryanis. As ever in Khasab, the catch of the day is probably a good bet. Mains 2–6 OR. Daily noon–1am.

Al Shamaliah Grill Bani Mohamed Obaid St, New Souk ☎ 2673 0477; map p.150. One of the best places to eat in town, this bright, clean restaurant offers up a wide-ranging menu which runs the gamut from takeaway-style burgers and fried chicken to more substantial Indian, Chinese and Arabian grilled dishes. There's also nice outdoor seating on the square in front. Mains 1–4 OR. Daily 9am–midnight.

★ **Aroos** On the main road north of the Mosque roundabout, New Souk ☎ 9362 5949; map p.150.

This smart outfit in the New Souk is a cut above other Musandam dining options in terms of atmosphere and quality of food, with a menu encompassing a wide range of traditional Arabian dishes, Indian curries and superb spicy seafood grills. It's a beautiful space, too, with latticed wooden screens and Arabian wall arches lit with lanterns. Mains 1.5–6 OR. Daily noon–11.30pm.

Wadi Qada Near the main road 300m south of the turning to the fort ☎ 9983 4205; map p.150. Something of a local favourite, this Iranian restaurant's faux-rustic exterior is a little odd, but the food and the service are both great. Seating is either at tables or on low-slung sofas, and the menu includes juicy kebabs, aromatic biryanis and some delicious non-alcoholic drinks – try the pomegranate juice or fragrant tea. Most mains 1.5–3 OR. Daily 11am–midnight.

The khors

Looked at on the map (or from the window of a plane), the northernmost tip of Musandam resembles a strange Rorschach blob: a mad tangle of mountains and water, dotted with dozens of *khors*, bays, islands and headlands, and ringed about with sheer cliffs and craggy red-rock mountains. The peninsula's remarkable landscape is the result of unusual geological processes: the *khors* themselves are actually flooded valleys, formed as a result of Musandam's progressive subduction beneath the Eurasian continental plate, which is causing the entire peninsula to tilt down into the sea at the dramatic rate of 5mm a year.

The chance to get out on the water and see something of the magnificent *khors* and coastline around Khasab is the unquestioned highlight of any trip to Musandam. The easiest and most popular trip is out along the marvellous **Khor ash Sham** – the largest of all the *khors*.

Khor ash Sham

The longest and most dramatic of all the Musandam *khors*, **Khor ash Sham** stretches for some 16km in total, hemmed in between two high lines of mountains, the bareness of the craggy surrounding rocks offering a surreal contrast with the invitingly blue waters of the *khor* itself. A string of remote **hamlets** dots the shoreline, accessible only by boat; each is home to just ten or so families. All water has to be shipped in by boat, while children must commute to school in Khasab. Not surprisingly, the *khor*-side

---

DOLPHIN-SPOTTING IN THE KHORS

The *khors* boast a healthy population of **dolphins**, and you've got probably an eighty percent chance of seeing at least one pod during a full-day dhow cruise. Dolphins are attracted by the sound of boats' engines and the water churned up in their wake – they'll often swim alongside passing dhows, dipping playfully in and out of the water, reaching remarkable speeds and keeping up quite easily with even the fastest dhows.

GOING ROUND THE BEND IN MUSANDAM

Despite its rather unprepossessing appearance today, **Telegraph Island** was once a crucial hub in the nineteenth-century information superhighway, and a vital link in the chain of communication between Britain and her Indian empire. At a time when mail between London and Bombay took at least a month to arrive, messages could be sent between the two cities in as little as two hours via submarine telegraph cables – or the "Victorian internet", as it has been neatly described.

In 1864, the governments of India, Turkey and Persia agreed to join up their existing land telegraphs using a submarine cable through the Gulf and on to Karachi. Almost 2400km of cable was manufactured and laid out, passing through Musandam en route. In 1865, a small telegraph repeater station was constructed on the island formerly known as Jazirat al Maqlab, but ever since as Telegraph Island, a site chosen since it offered greater security than the mainland against potentially hostile local tribes. The station played a crucial role in the success of the cable. Telegraphic signals relayed over copper cable inevitably fade with distance, and the function of the station was to receive and relay, or "repeat", signals received from either London or Bombay.

Unfortunately, the location was one of the remotest in the empire. The mental and physical privations suffered by officials marooned on Telegraph Island quickly became the stuff of colonial legend, so much so that relief crews sailing eastwards around the tip of the Musandam peninsula coined the expression "**going round the bend**" to describe their mercy missions – an expression which has since become Oman's lasting contribution to the English vernacular and a fitting tribute to the sufferings of Telegraph Island's Victorian castaways.

The station lasted just three years and in 1868 the cable was diverted away from Musandam and rerouted via the Iranian island of Hengham.

---

settlements are becoming steadily depopulated as the younger generation of villagers tire of the rather monotonous life of their ancestors and move off to Khasab or beyond. Those who remain live in the villages for just six months a year, earning a living through fishing, before decamping to harvest dates in Khasab during the summer months, when the water in the *khor* becomes too hot for fish.

Telegraph Island

About halfway down Khor ash Sham lies lonely **Telegraph Island** (or Jazirat Telegraph), an extremely modest lump of rock named after the British telegraph station that formerly stood here. The extensive foundations of the old British buildings survive, along with a flight of stone steps leading up from the water. The island is a popular stopping point on dhow cruises, which often halt here for lunch. Boats can moor next to the island at high tide; at low tide you'll have to swim across. It's a popular fishing spot, and a great place to snorkel, with a kaleidoscopic array of critters including angel fish, parrot fish, and clown fish easy to spot through the crystal clear water.

Kumzar

One of the most inaccessible settlements in Oman, the famously remote town of **KUMZAR** sits perched in solitary splendour at the northernmost edge of Musandam, hemmed in by sheer mountains and accessible only by boat. While Kumzaris are very welcoming, they have occasionally had a difficult relationship with visitors in the past – for a time, foreigners were not even allowed to disembark and enter the town, but that rule has been lifted. Nevertheless, strictly speaking, the few visitors that make it here require a permit, which tour operators will arrange as part of a trip; this wasn't being enforced at the time of research, however.

Kumzar's main curiosity is its **language** (see page 158), which has developed unique characteristics after centuries of isolation. Otherwise the town tends to remain far from the headlines, with the odd notable exception: impressively, Kumzar Football Club

DHOW TRIPS AND DIVING IN KUMZAR AND THE KHORS

The half- or full-day **boat trip** down Khor ash Sham is the most popular tour from Khasab, while the waters around the northern Musandam peninsula boast some of the finest **diving** in the Middle East.

BOAT TRIPS

Trips are on traditional wooden **dhows**, sitting on deck under an awning; expect to share your boat with around ten to twenty other people. **Half-day** *khor* cruises (usually 9.30am–1.30pm or 1.30–5pm) cost around 15 OR per person including drinks, but no lunch. These trips go as far as Telegraph Island and include one stop for swimming and snorkelling. **Full-day** cruises (usually 10am–4pm) cost around 20 OR per person, including lunch and drinks, and will get you to Seebi Island at the far end of Khor ash Sham, with a couple of swimming/snorkelling stops en route. Note that prices are often quoted in AED, such is the volume of visitors from the UAE.

Most operators can also set up **overnight** dhow trips, normally either sleeping on board or camping on the beach. These range from simple combinations of beach camping and full-day dhow cruise (around 35 OR/person) to multi-day trips taking in tours of Khasab, dhow cruises, mountain safaris and hotel accommodation (around 200 OR/person with Khasab Travel & Tours; prices vary according to how many people book).

Khasab Travel & Tours Around the back of the airport, south of the New Souk, opposite the Esra Apartments ☎ 2673 0464, ⊛ khasabtours.com. All operators offer essentially the same packages at the same prices, although *Khasab Travel & Tours* (see page 154) tend to provide the most experienced and informative guides. Daily 9am–1.30pm & 5–8pm.

DIVING

The waters around the northern Musandam peninsula are home to a superb range of marine life including magnificent manta and eagle rays, hammerhead, zebra, leopard and whale sharks, minke whales and turtles, as well as myriad smaller tropical fish. Underwater habitats include beautiful coral gardens, sponge-covered rocks, dramatic submarine walls and a couple of wrecks. Despite what's often said, **diving** around Musandam isn't only for experienced divers with many hours in their log books – even unqualified divers can take the plunge. The best **dive sites** are around Kumzar (see page 156), a 45min–1hr journey by speedboat from Khasab (although trips are often cancelled in bad weather), while there are a couple of further sites in the more sheltered waters of Khor ash Sham and elsewhere.

Musandam Discovery Diving Off Khasab Rd, behind Musandam Sea Adventure, Old Souk, Khasab ☎ 9968 2932, ⊛ musandam-discovery-diving.com. Currently the only specialist dive centre in Khasab, this professional company runs a variety of courses and dive trips in the *khors*, as well as guided fishing trips. Two dives cost 45 OR with equipment or 35 OR without, while a single night dive costs 35 OR. Non-divers and snorkellers can come along for the ride for 10 OR. You can also learn to dive here, with an introductory Discover Scuba Diving course costing 55 OR; multi-day courses go up in price to 220 OR. Daily 8.30am–noon & 3.30–7.30pm.

KAYAKING

Khasab Travel & Tours and *Musandam Sea Adventure* (see page 154) both have **kayaks** for rent, which can be carried on board dhows going into the fjords, although no guides are available, so you'll have to have a reasonable understanding of what you're doing before venturing onto the water.

overcame teams of far greater resources, both human and financial, to win Oman's regional cup in 2016.

There's not much to see here, and certainly nothing in the way of tourist facilities, although it's still worth making the trip out here for the magnificent coastal scenery en route, as well as for the opportunity to experience Oman at its most remote and reclusive. Many of Musandam's best **diving** spots are also located in the waters around Kumzar (see page 157).

KUMZARI

Geographically, Kumzar is a paradox. By land, this is one of the most remote and inaccessible settlements in Oman. By sea, however, the town overlooks the Straits of Hormuz, one of the world's busiest shipping lanes, a fact reflected in the unique language spoken by its inhabitants. **Kumzari** is still very much a living language, despite the fact that it is spoken only in Kumzar town itself and on Larek Island in Iran, just across the Straits of Hormuz. Until quite recently older generations remained determinedly monoglot, speaking nothing but Kumzari – and according to local reports there's at least one old man in the village who remains resolutely unfamiliar with any other tongue. However, a little sadly, if inevitably, Arabic is beginning to dominate in every corner of life; local children speak it not only at school, but increasingly at home. TV is all in Arabic, and many families feel that their children learning English and Arabic is more of a priority than teaching them Kumzari.

The basis of Kumzari is **Farsi** (the language of Iran, which Kumzari most obviously resembles), mixed up with a hearty dose of **Arabic** and **Hindi** (the result of long-standing trade with India), plus a significant number of loan words from assorted **European** languages including English, Portuguese, French, Italian and Spanish – a remarkable linguistic melting pot. The numbers for one to five – *yek, do, so, char, panch* – for example, are almost identical to their Hindi equivalents, while the Kumzari word for bread, *naan*, will also be familiar to anyone who has ever eaten at an Indian restaurant. Many **European** loan words have also entered the language, including (to name just a few) *upset, door, light, starg* (stars), *cherie* (child), *toilette* (meaning, in Kumzari, a haircut) and *bandera* (from Spanish, meaning "flag"). Things have occasionally got slightly lost in translation, however: the word *kayak*, for instance, means a speedboat rather than a canoe, while the words *open doro* can serve as an instruction not only to open the door, but to close it too.

4

Kumzar's inhabitants live largely by fishing for nine months of the year, netting barracuda, tuna, kingfish and hammour (much of which ends up in the restaurants of Dubai), before retreating to Khasab for the hot summer months: if you're planning a visit, it's worth bearing in mind that Kumzar becomes a ghost town in the summer.

Brief history

The settlement is said to be around seven hundred years old, its inhabitants including a hotchpotch of ethnic groups ranging from Yemeni to Zanzibari – the colourful theory that sailors shipwrecked off the nearby coast were also integrated into the population is backed up by the remarkable number of European and Hindi loan words found in Kumzari. The town's population currently stands at around four thousand, with its own school, hospital, power station and desalination plant.

The boat trip to Kumzar

The **trip** out to Kumzar by speedboat takes around 45min–1hr from Khasab, or around 2hr 30min by dhow. The ride takes you out past the magnificent sea cliffs enclosing the entrance to Khasab harbour, past the entrance to the fine Khor Ghob Ali, and then **Goat Island** (Jazirat al Ghanim), ringed with fluted limestone cliffs. In the past, local Kumzaris would often bring their sheep and goats across to the island by boat to graze, given the lack of suitable pastureland around Kumzar itself – hence the name. Throughout the trip, there is remarkably little sign of human habitation, saving a few military buildings on Goat Island.

Beyond Goat Island you enter the **Straits of Hormuz**, with magnificent seascapes, craggy headlands and a considerable number of oil tankers; the three rocky islands way out to sea are collectively known as the **Jazirat Salamah**, the most northerly piece of Omani territory. Ten minutes or so later you round a final headland, getting your first sight of Kumzar, with its colourful huddle of buildings backed up against the sheer

VIEW FROM JEBEL HARIM

wall of the mountains behind. Space is very much at a premium here; it's said that the village cemetery was filled hundreds of years ago, and that locals are now obliged to bury their relatives in the grounds of their own houses.

ARRIVAL AND DEPARTURE KUMZAR

By boat tour The spectacular sea journey to Kumzar is slightly more tricky and potentially a lot more expensive than a boat tour of Khor ash Sham. It's possible to arrange a dhow through *Khasab Travel & Tours* and *Musandam Sea Adventures* (see page 154) for around 45 OR/person with four people, or 90 OR/person with two; pre-booking is advised. The return trip takes around five hours.

By water taxi Water taxis charge the inflated price of 120 OR to ferry tourists to Kumzar, but there is no reason to pay for this given the price of the boat tour.

Jebel Harim and the Musandam mountains

Although the *khors* are the principal attraction of Musandam, the peninsula's **mountainous interior** runs them a close second. Here you'll find some of the wildest and most spectacular landscapes in Oman, comprising a string of great limestone peaks and massifs known by locals as the Ru'us al Jebel, or "Peaks of the Mountains". Mightiest of these peaks is **Jebel Harim**, Musandam's highest mountain.

The mountains are usually explored from Khasab on either a half-day or full-day mountain safari with a local driver aboard a 4WD. **Half-day safaris** usually take in Wadi Khasab, Khor an Najd, Sal al A'la, A'Saye and Jebel Harim. **Full-day trips** continue beyond Jebel Harim as far as the Rawdah Bowl. It's worth doing the full-day safari if possible – the Rawdah Bowl itself isn't especially memorable, but the mountain scenery beyond Jebel Harim and the ridgetop drive above Wadi Rawdah are simply magnificent.

Wadi Khasab

Safaris begin by following the new tarmac road which runs from the southern end of Khasab, behind the airport and down through the broad **Wadi Khasab**. The wadi has provided mixed blessings. Rich alluvial soil, washed down the valley from the mountains, has long underpinned Khasab's agricultural prosperity (the name Khasab, in Arabic, means "fertility"), although the wadi has also been the source of devastating flash floods; a large dam, built in 1986 across the wadi just south of Khasab, now protects the town.

Sal al Asfal and Khor an Najd

After about 7km you'll see the unsurfaced road up into the mountains and Jebel Harim (signposted to Dibba) heading off on the right. Beyond here you enter the area known as **Sal al Asfal** ("Lower Plain"), a dead-flat plain which was formerly sea bed. Some 5km past the turn-off for Dibba you'll reach an unsigned dirt road off on the left leading to **Khor an Najd**. It's a stiff climb – 4WD is essential – up past a military firing range to the crest of the ridge, from where there are bird's-eye views of the *khor* far below, and of the road hairpinning precipitously to a small scrap of rather unattractive beach. It's also possible to **camp** here: it's a popular spot at weekends with Dubaians. Drinking water is available, but there are no other facilities.

Sal al A'la

From Khor an Najd tours return to the main road, where your driver may show you a **bait al qufl** (see page 161), which can be found here and in most other parts of Musandam. The next stop is usually the end of the tarmac at **Sal al A'la** ("Higher

Plain"), about 20km from Khasab, also known as Khalidiya after the local Birkat al Khalidiya, meaning "Spring of Eternity" – somewhat ironic, since it has now dried up.

The area is one of the most fertile in the peninsula, thanks to its location in a bowl at the foot of the mountains in which rainwater naturally collects, both at the surface and underground. The plain is dotted with pretty stands of acacia trees and, following periods of rainfall, lush green grass, looking a bit like an unlikely patch of African savannah in the middle of the Gulf. Dozens of goats wander the area, feasting on acacia leaves, which explains why the lower branches on all the trees have been stripped bare up to a certain height – in summer hungry goats may even climb up into the branches of the more accessible trees in search of fodder.

A'Rahaybah and around

Tours return along the main road back towards Khasab then take the left turn onto the dirt road to Dibba which you passed earlier. The track is well maintained and graded, but steep in places; 4WD is essential.

From Wadi Khasab the track climbs doggedly upwards, offering increasingly wide-ranging views over the surrounding mountains. Most of these are an enormous mass of stratified, greyish limestone, interrupted in places by pockmarked extrusions of igneous rock created by volcanic explosions under the sea bed – a distinctively gloopy-looking substance, like a kind of geological cheese fondue. The porous rock is riddled with caves, many of which were formerly occupied by the reclusive Shehi.

The first village en route is **A'RAHAYBAH** (pronounced "A'Raheebah"), where you'll see patches of dried-up agricultural terracing – a result of the mountains' increasing aridity due to the falling water table. There's also a fine collection of *bait al qufl* on the mountainside above.

4

The Sultan's House

Above A'Rahaybah, your guide may point out a series of distinctive **rock formations**. One (popularly referred to as the "Titanic") on the top of the ridge above bears an

---

BAIT AL QUFL: THE HOUSE OF THE LOCK

Almost every village in the mountains of Musandam is home to at least one **bait al qufl** ("house of the lock"), a distinctive type of local building – looking more like an antique bomb-shelter than a traditional house – which is unique to the peninsula. The *bait al qufl* developed as a result of the migratory lifestyle of the local Shehi, who would leave their mountain homes during the summer months to go and work on the coast. Valuable possessions which they could not carry with them were left behind in the village, locked up in these miniature vaults. Although designed primarily for storage, *bait al qufl* were also used as living quarters, particularly in the depths of winter.

The *bait al qufl* was designed with the emphasis firmly on strength and security. Walls often reach thicknesses of 1m or more, fashioned out of enormous slabs of stone; the thickness of the walls had the additional benefit of keeping the interior cool in summer and warm in winter, as well as protecting its contents (and anyone inside) from the ever-present threat of rockfalls. *Bait al qufl* are usually around 6–7m high, although they look smaller from the outside since the floor is dug out 1m or so below ground level for additional strength and security; the buildings are also often surrounded with a raised platform to help drain rainwater and provide something to sit on. Huge earthenware jars were placed inside to store provisions such as water, dates and grains – the jars were often bigger than the actual door to prevent them being carried off, and had to be put in place before the walls were built up around them. Access is usually via a single tiny door, formerly secured with one or two chunky wooden padlocks, although most are now left open.

uncanny similarity to a steamship with a pair of funnels; nearby stands a distinctive rock pinnacle claimed to resemble the outline of a praying man. Halfway up the cliff-face between the two formations lies the **Sultan's House** (occupied until as recently as the early 2000s), a tiny cluster of primitive stone buildings perched on the narrowest of rock ledges. It's apparently accessible on foot or by donkey, although to the uninitiated it looks like only an accomplished rock climber could reach it. Assorted abandoned cave houses can be spotted slightly further up the track, tucked away beneath rock overhangs in similarly rocky and inaccessible locations.

A'Saye

About 45 minutes from the turn-off to Sal al A'la you'll arrive at the village of **A'SAYE** (also spelled "Sayh"; pronounced "See"), clustered around a neat little plateau set in a bowl in the mountains at 1105m. As at Sal al A'la, the bowl serves as a natural collection point for rainwater and fertile silt washed down off the mountains, offering an unlikely little patch of agricultural prosperity amid the arid surrounding mountains. The plateau is dotted with a patchwork of square fields in which the five hundred-odd villagers grow wheat, dates, figs and vegetables, with donkeys and goats rambling here and there.

Jebel Harim

From A'Saye, it's another 20 minutes or so to the highest point of the road, below the summit of **Jebel Harim**, literally "Mountain of Women" and at 2087m the highest peak in Musandam. The mountain takes its name from the days when local women would retreat to caves up here in order to avoid being carried off by pirates or rival tribes while their menfolk were away on extended fishing or trading expeditions. The actual summit is home to a radar station monitoring shipping way below in the Straits of Hormuz and is out of bounds, although there are superb all-round views from the road, with breathtaking views back to Khasab and onwards towards Dibba. Many of the rocks up here are also studded with superbly preserved **fossils**, offering the remarkable sight of ancient submarine creatures – molluscs, fish, clams and numerous trilobites – now incongruously stranded near the summit of one of Arabia's highest mountains.

Petroglyphs

The highest point of road (at around 1600m) sweeps through a large rock cutting next to an air-traffic control radar installation. Just below here, a track leads off to a fine collection of **petroglyphs** carved into mountaintop boulders: rudimentary but evocative weathered images chipped out of the stone, including matchstick human figures alongside animals such as gazelle, oryx, Arabian leopards and even what is thought to be a man on an elephant. Further fossils can be seen in the surrounding rocks.

The fossil wall

Past the summit, there are sensational views of the road ahead, as it runs along a narrow ridge before descending towards the Rawdah Bowl, plus stomach-churning views into the deep gorge below. En route you'll pass a remarkable **fossil wall**, formed out of what was originally a chunk of sea-bed rock and covered in a dense layer of fossilized impressions among which the outlines of crabs, starfish and shells can clearly be made out.

The Rawdah Bowl

The road south from Jebel Harim runs along the ridgetop then, after about 45 minutes, descends sharply into the wide bed of **Wadi Rawdah**, flanked by huge limestone cliffs. From here, a turning on the left runs down a side wadi into the expansive **Rawdah Bowl** (signed as "A'Rowdhah"), a neat little plateau a few kilometres across, enclosed by

---

TO DIBBA AND THE BORDER

It's around 50km (45min–1hr) from Rawdah to **Dibba** (see page 165) and the **UAE border**. The actual border post is at **Wadi Bih**, just a few kilometres south of the turn-off to Rawdah Bowl, but this is closed to all foreigners apart from citizens of the UAE. If you want to explore Dibba and the southern part of the peninsula you'll have to exit Musandam at Tibat and make your way cross-country via the UAE to reach Dibba itself.

---

mountains – it all feels a long way from anywhere, and pleasantly sheltered compared to the exposed landscapes en route. Despite its name (Rawdah means "garden", or a nursery of flowers), the plateau is rather bare, with large expanses of sand and gravel, dotted with acacia trees, telephone poles and a scatter of modern houses, with the occasional wild camel wandering around – a strange sight this high up in the mountains.

The plateau is also home to a handful of more venerable remains including abandoned old stone buildings, several *bait al qufl* and a couple of **cemeteries**, both Islamic and pre-Islamic, with neat lines of headstones formed out of roughly hewn pieces of stone; the bowl was formerly used as a local tribal battleground, which presumably accounts for the large number of people buried here.

TOURS   **JEBEL HARIM AND THE MUSANDAM MOUNTAINS**

Most operators (see page 154) offer a largely identikit range of **mountain safari tours.** These last either a **half day** (around 25 OR with a minimum of two people), which will get you as far as Jebel Harim, or a **full day** (around 45–50 OR, minimum 2 people), which will get you all the way to Rawdah Bowl (see page 162). You may be able to save a few rials off the price by shopping around, although discounted prices will probably mean you may get a dud guide as a result. While solo travellers will have more of a headache organizing mountain safaris, most tour operators will attempt to accommodate you by allowing you to join a larger group, in which case you will be charged half the prices listed above; however, this may mean spending a lot of time hanging around aimlessly while you wait to be assigned to a group.

Khasab Travel & Tours Around the back of the airport, south of the New Souk, opposite the Esra Apartments ☎ 2673 0464, ⓦ khasabtours.com. The guides provided by *Khasab Travel and Tours* (see page 154) are particularly informative. Daily 9am–1.30pm & 5–8pm.

ACCOMMODATION

There's nowhere to stay up in the mountains, although **camping** is possible in a number of places, including the beach at Khor an Najd, among the acacia trees at Sal al A'la, or in the remote Rawdah Bowl.

The coast road: Khasab to Bukha

The **coast road** (Highway 2) between Khasab and the UAE border at Tibat is still the only reliable land connection between Musandam and the outside world (at least if you discount the very rough road over the mountains from Khasab to Dibba described above). The 35km highway (around a 45min drive) is one of the most dramatic in the country, a fine feat of modern engineering with jaw-dropping sea views. If you fancy stopping for a picnic there are numerous little patches of beach with palm-thatch sunshades dotted along the road – the best is just before the village of Al Jadi, about 3km north of Bukha.

Wadi Tawi and the rock carvings

To reach the carvings, take the signed left turn from Khasab to the village of Qida, 4km away, then follow the road through the village for around 750m until the tarmac runs out – it's another 750m from the end of the tarmac along a dirt track, driveable, with care, in a 2WD, although it's a lot more pleasant to walk

The first 10km of the highway immediately south of Khasab's *Atana Khasab* hotel are perhaps the most dramatic of them all, as the road twists around **Khor Qida**, perched on

---

PETROGLYPHS

Musandam boasts an unusually rich collection of **petroglyphs** (from the Greek *petros*, meaning stone, and *glyphe*, meaning carving): simple rock art images which have been chipped out of boulders, cave walls or other convenient pieces of stone using sharp bronze, iron or stone tools and highlighted using a white pigment made from coral. Ancient petroglyphs can be found throughout the peninsula, often in the remotest places, and depict a wide range of subjects including people, animals (particularly horses and camels), as well as abstract symbols and geometrical patterns whose meaning has been lost. Dating the images is difficult, although the fact that most of them depict human or animal figures suggests that they may well pre-date the arrival of Islam (which prohibits the making of images of living creatures). Of Musandam's many petroglyphs, the most easily accessible are those at the top of **Jebel Harim** and those in **Wadi Tawi**.

---

the narrowest of ledges blasted out between the towering cliffs on one side and the sea on the other.

On the far side of the bay, some 4km south of Khasab, **Wadi Tawi** sports some fine prehistoric **petroglyphs**, showing boats, houses and soldiers on horseback. Drive carefully, if bringing your own vehicle, following the directions above and keeping a wary eye out for goats – of which there are many – en route (running one over could prove not only distressing but also surprisingly expensive). After about 500m you'll reach a cluster of ramshackle houses. Shortly afterwards, the track curves to the right in front of a brownish-white house, just past a well surrounded by three small trees. On your left you'll see a terrific mass of fallen boulders, a couple of which have been walled in to create tiny cave houses beneath the rocks (although they're no longer inhabited – or only by goats).

These boulders are where you'll find the **rock carvings**. Easiest to spot is the boulder with five separate carvings, including a trio of camels. A boulder to the right has a stylized figure on horseback, while you'll find another virtually identical horseman on the rock next to the door of one of the miniature boulder houses. It's fun to hunt around for other pictures, although in many places it's nigh-on impossible to tell whether the white dots are the remains of carvings or simply a natural mineral effect. Even if you don't find the carvings, it's a lovely valley walk between high limestone cliffs, pockmarked with caves, and with goats everywhere, often in the most unlikely places.

Al Harf

Past Khor Qida, the road climbs sharply upwards from the water to the ridgetop above, cresting the summit through a deep rock cutting before reaching the village of **AL HARF**, roughly halfway between Khasab and Bukha. This is the highest point of the road, with fabulous views – it's said that on a clear day you can see the coast of Iran. Unfortunately it's difficult to find anywhere to stop to enjoy the views along the narrow highway itself. The best option is to take the unsigned side-turning off the main road on the right about 500m past the summit rock cutting, then turn right again. This brings you to a peaceful vantage point with bird's-eye views out to sea, over Khor Qida and to the mountains inland.

Bukha

Around 25km twisting kilometres south of Khasab lies the modest little town of **BUKHA**. The principal attraction here is the fine old fort, which sits right next to the coastal highway backdropped by huge mountain cliffs (ignore the blue signs pointing inland to Bukha village).

The fort
Highway 2, just before the mosque on the left-hand side if you're driving from Khasab • Mon–Thurs & Sun 9am–2.30pm • Free

Built in the early sixteenth century, the **fort** originally stood right on the shore (which has since receded somewhat) and is surrounded on three sides by a now-dry moat in which, legend has it, unfortunate prisoners were formerly chained up and left to drown by the rising tide. Boxy rectangular towers sit on opposite corners of the fort, separated by the circular southeastern tower, which is distinctively pear-shaped; its curving upper storeys were apparently designed to reduce the impact of cannonballs. The whole thing is very neat and aesthetically pleasing, particularly as seen from inland, with the little fort sitting high on its pedestal against the rich sea green of the Persian Gulf.

There's not much to see **inside**, apart from a couple of unfurnished rooms set around a small courtyard with the *wali*'s apartment in the centre and a large pit covered by an iron grille – possibly some kind of prison. The rooms are largely undecorated, save for the usual evocative assortment of lanterns, wooden ladders and miscellaneous torture paraphernalia, such as old wooden stocks.

Sultan Qaboos Mosque
Just behind Bukha Fort

The town's gleaming new **Sultan Qaboos Mosque** was opened in 2016 as part of an ongoing wave of grand, government-funded places of worship. The style is the usual contemporary Islamic, with two minarets framing an ornately ornamented dome; it's very impressive, although non-Muslims are not allowed inside. More interesting is the **old mosque**, remnants of which still remain on the site – it actually looks much more like a house than a place of worship, with its humble stature and rough stone walls, and lacks both dome and minaret.

4

Dibba and around

At the southern end of Musandam, sprawling across the border with the UAE, lies the small city of **DIBBA** – a pleasant enough place, although not really worth a visit unless you can afford to stay at the idyllic *Six Senses Zighy Bay* resort (see page 167) further down the coast, or have a particular yen to explore the southern portion of the Musandam peninsula. Foreigners are only allowed to travel as far as the border post at Wadi Bih, however, which somewhat limits the area available for exploration.

Modern Dibba has something of a split personality, being divided into three parts: **Dibba Bayah** on the Omani side, **Dibba Muhallab**, part of the UAE's Emirate of Fujairah, and **Dibba al Hisn**, part of the UAE's Emirate of Sharjah. There's a **police checkpoint** at the **UAE–Oman border** where you'll have to show your passport when entering Oman, but no visa formalities. You will, however (unless you're a GCC citizen) require a **border pass**, which will be arranged by your hotel in Dibba – this effectively makes it impossible for non-GCC residents to turn up in Dibba without a hotel reservation. It's also important to note that the hotel must be booked at least seven days in advance, and you have to provide the hotel with a scan of your passport and visa so they can arrange your border pass.

Brief history
Sleepy though it may now be, Dibba was the site of one of the most important **battles** of early Islamic history. In 632 AD, shortly after the Prophet Mohammed's death, the forces of his successor, the caliph Abu Bakr, defeated those of a local ruler who had renounced Islam. A large cemetery on the plains behind the town (on the UAE side of the border) is traditionally believed to house the remains of the ten thousand rebels killed in the battle.

MADHA

South of Musandam, about halfway between Dibba and the Omani border at Khatmat Milalah, lies the curious Omani exclave of **Madha** – a tiny dot of Omani territory (comprising just 75 square kilometres) completely surrounded by the UAE. The area is reached via a single surfaced road off the main coastal highway between Khawr Fakkan and Fujairah city near the district of Qurayya.

The enclave is notable mainly for one geopolitical oddity: the village of **Nahwa** (a few kilometres further along the road past Madha town, at the end of the tarmac). Bizarrely, this village actually belongs to the UAE emirate of Sharjah, creating a Russian-doll effect whereby the UAE territory of Nahwa is enclosed within the Omani district of Madha, which is enclosed by the UAE emirates of Fujairah and Sharjah – which are themselves bookended by Omani territory on either side.

Dibba Muhallab and Dibba al Hisn

Fujairah's **Dibba Muhallab** is easily the largest and most developed of the three areas, and one of the UAE's more pleasant towns, built on a pleasingly human scale, with neat apartment blocks, tree-lined streets and a sweeping seafront corniche giving the whole place a pleasantly Mediterranean air. Sharjah's **Dibba al Hisn** is smaller, with a rather toy-town main street lined with identikit faux-Arabian villas and office blocks.

Dibba Bayah

Things are even quieter and significantly less built-up over on the Omani side of the border in **Dibba Bayah**. The pleasant seafront is fringed with a fine arc of golden sand, plus the occasional fishing boat, while just inland stands the obligatory **fort**, which isn't open to the public. To get to the fort, follow the brown signs inland to "Daba Castle", left of the main road through town about 750m north of the border checkpoint.

Wadi Bih

From the police checkpoint it's possible to travel north along the rough, graded track into the mountains as far as the official border post at **Wadi Bih** some 35km further on, though the border is closed to all but Omani and UAE nationals, so you can't go any further than this.

TOURS AND ACTIVITIES   **DIBBA AND AROUND**

Both the *Golden Tulip* and *Six Senses Zighy Bay* (see page 167) can organize **dhow cruises**, **mountain safaris** (although you can only get as far as the border post at Wadi Bih) and **diving trips**.

Extra Divers Zighy Bay Six Senses Zighy Bay ☎ 2673 5888, ⊕ extradivers-worldwide.com. The most reputable operator in this part of Musandam, offering dive trips suitable for all levels, and taking in hard and soft coral reef environments home to barracuda, nudibranchs, moray eels and leopard sharks. Prices range from 45 OR for one dive to 325 OR for ten dives over five days.

Nomad Ocean Adventures Corniche St ☎ 2683 6069, ⊕ discovernomad.com. This local operator offers diving trips off the coast of Dibba, as well as an extensive menu of dive courses ranging from entry level to advanced. A standard two-dive trip with equipment costs around 26 OR; courses begin at around 15 OR for pool-based Discover Scuba sessions and range up to 260 OR for advanced tech diving courses.

ACCOMMODATION

Dibba has the only **accommodation** in Musandam outside Khasab, and makes an interesting alternative base from which to explore the southern end of the peninsula. You can reach both places listed below from the UAE without having to buy an Omani visa, although you will need to make a reservation at least seven days in advance so that your hotel can arrange a **border pass** for you (see page 25).

Golden Tulip 2km north of the border on the coast ☎ 2683 6654, ⓦ goldentulipdibba.com. The location of this old-fashioned four-star gives it a pleasantly end-of-the-world feel, although the hotel itself is nothing to write home about considering the price. Rooms are comfortable but bland, arranged around attractive but rather tired-looking gardens and a smallish pool. Food at the *Khasab* restaurant is average, with a menu which spreads itself rather too thin across Arabian, Indian and European dishes, while there's also a café and the rather alarming, black-and-white striped *Zebra Bar*. The nice swathe of beach at least partly compensates. **99 OR**

Six Senses Zighy Bay ☎ 2673 5888, ⓦ sixsenses.com. This very exclusive resort is hidden away on the coast, a 15min speedboat ride or 23km drive north of Dibba (4WD required); 4WD limousine transport can also be arranged. Guests approaching by road also have the option of making the last part of the journey by tandem paraglide (70 OR/person) – either the maddest publicity stunt in Arabia or a wonderfully exhilarating way of arriving at reception. Gimmicks apart, the setting is blissful, tucked away beneath the mountains, with a fine swathe of beach and accommodation in attractive rustic villas sporting rough-hewn stone walls, lovely wooden ceilings and lots of palm thatch. All come with their own small pools and every imaginable convenience, and there's also a top-notch spa, although with rates from around US$1350 per night it's a very expensive treat. **520 OR**

4

Sharqiya

THE FISHING VILLAGE OF AYJAH, NEAR SUR

5 Sharqiya

Southeast of Muscat stretches Sharqiya ("The East"), a generous swathe of sea, sand and mountain, spread across the southeasternmost tip of the Arabian Peninsula. Officially divided into two governorates of roughly equal size, North and South, it's perhaps the most diverse part of the country, offering a beguiling snapshot of Oman in miniature, from the sand-fringed coastline, through the rugged Eastern Hajar mountains to the rolling dunes of the Sharqiya Sands. Culturally, too, the region retains a distinct appeal. It's Oman at its most traditional, with a long and proud history of tribal independence – and occasional insurrection against the authority of the sultan in Muscat. The interior of Sharqiya is also one of the few places in Oman where you'll still see evidence of the country's traditional Bedu lifestyle, with temporary encampments dotted amid the rolling sands – although the camels of yesteryear have all but been replaced by Toyota pick-up trucks and 4WDs.

In practical terms, Sharqiya divides into three main parts. The first is **the coast**, with a string of attractions including the historic towns of Quriyat, Qalhat and Sur, and the turtle beach at Ras al Jinz. Running parallel to the coast, the craggy heights of the **Eastern Hajar** mountains (Al Hajar Ash Sharqi) provide numerous spectacular hiking and off-road-driving possibilities, including the celebrated ravines of Wadi Shab and Wadi Tiwi. On the far side of the Eastern Hajar, the Sharqiya **interior** boasts a further swathe of rewarding destinations, including the magnificent dunes of the Sharqiya Sands, the slot canyons of Wadi Bani Khalid and a string of interesting towns, notably the personable market centre of Ibra and the staunchly traditional Jalan Bani Bu Ali.

It's possible to make a satisfying **loop** through Sharqiya by heading down the coastal highway to Sur and Ras al Jinz (see page 182), and then returning along the inland route via Ibra (see page 184) – or vice versa – passing the bulk of the region's major attractions en route.

Brief history

Something of a backwater nowadays, Sharqiya's rather sleepy present-day atmosphere belies its illustrious past, when its boat-builders, merchants and mariners made the region one of the most commercially vibrant and cosmopolitan in the country. Sharqiya's prosperity was founded on the sea, with a string of bustling ports and entrepots, most notably **Qalhat**, whose fame attracted visits by both Ibn Battuta and Marco Polo, as well as **Quriyat** up the coast. The pivotal moment in Sharqiya's history was the arrival in 1508 of the **Portuguese**, who sacked both Qalhat and Quriyat – an event from which neither town ever completely recovered. The demise of Qalhat, however, spurred the growth of nearby **Sur**, which subsequently became the capital of

DESCENDING FROM THE SALMA PLATEAU

Highlights

❶ Wadi Shab and Wadi Tiwi Two of Oman's most picture-perfect wadis, with palm-fringed ravines running between sheer sandstone cliffs down to the sea. See pages 175 and 176

❷ Jaylah and the Salma Plateau Superb off-road drive across the top of the Eastern Hajar mountains, passing the spectacularly located Bronze Age tombs and towers of Jaylah en route. See page 176

❸ Sur Southern Oman's most appealing town, with a pretty harbour fringed with watchtowers and the country's only surviving dhow-building yard. See page 178

❹ Ras al Jinz Arabia's premier turtle-watching destination. See page 182

❺ Ibra One of the region's liveliest and most personable towns, with a colourful souk and a pair of fine old traditional mudbrick villages. See page 184

❻ Sharqiya Sands Iconic desert landscape, with towering dunes, roving camels and superb sunsets. See page 190

❼ Masirah island Extreme remoteness is only half the charm of this desert island of windswept beaches off Sharqiya's far southern coast. See page 195

HIGHLIGHTS ARE MARKED ON THE MAP ON PAGE 172

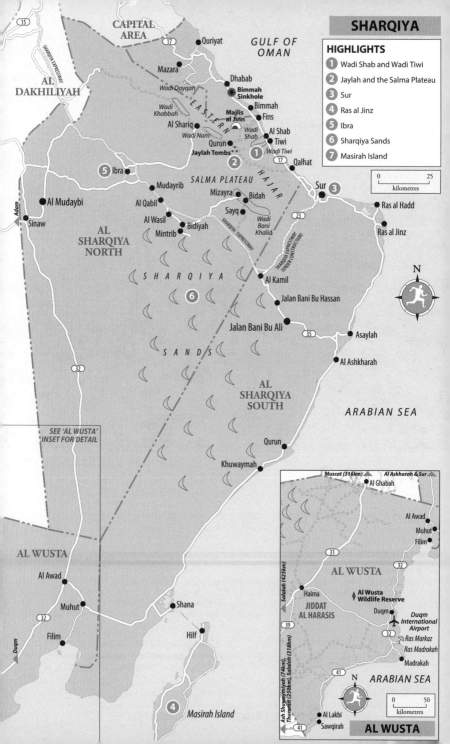

South Sharqiya, growing wealthy thanks to its dhow-building yards and lucrative trade in arms and slaves. Inland, **Ibra** – now the capital of North Sharqiya – also became rich for a time thanks to passing trade. Increasing **British** restrictions on slaving and arms smuggling during the nineteenth century led to a gradual eclipse in the region's fortunes, however, and during the early twentieth century Sharqiya became a major crucible of rebellion against the sultan in Muscat (see page 240), usually spearheaded by leaders of the powerful **Al Harthy** tribe, based in Ibra.

As with many of the country's other leading ports, Sur's fortunes have been revived since the accession of Sultan Qaboos by the construction of a massive new industrial complex, while the opening of the new dual-carriageway **coastal highway** in 2008 has further reinvigorated the region's economy – albeit at the cost of some of the area's former sleepy, slow-motion charm. Though lagging a few years behind, the interior appears on a similar track, provided a recent boost in the advent of yet another dual-carriageway – the newly-dubbed **Sharqiya Expressway**, expected to link Ibra to Sur by the end of 2018.

The Muscat–Sur coastal road

The most popular route into Sharqiya follows the smooth **Sharqiya coastal highway** from Ruwi in Muscat south to Quriyat and Sur, with the Arabian Gulf on one side and the rugged summits of the Eastern Hajar on the other. Although it's taken a toll on the various natural attractions en route, the highway has provided an undeniable boon to regional development and brought many of the area's attractions within easy reach. These comprise an interesting blend of the historical and the natural, including the old fort of **Quriyat**, the ruined city of **Qalhat**, the scenic dam at **Wadi Dayqah**, the off-road drive over the Eastern Hajar to Ibra – via the Bronze Age tombs of **Jaylah** – and, last but certainly not least, two of Oman's most spectacular wadis: **Wadi Shab** and **Wadi Tiwi**.

Quriyat

The first town of any significance south of Muscat, **QURIYAT** lies some 80km from the capital, a 45-minute drive from Ruwi along a fast and relatively empty new stretch of dual carriageway which weaves between the craggy foothills of the Eastern Hajar. Situated about 7km north of the highway as it swings west to the coast and onwards to Sur, the modest town is huddled around a low-key souk and an old **fort**, about half a kilometre from the seafront.

Quriyat had the dubious honour of being one of the first towns in Oman to experience the destructive attentions of the **Portuguese** fleet under Afonso de Albuquerque (see page 233). Albuquerque's soldiers attacked the town in August 1508, setting it ablaze and massacring its inhabitants – captives, it is said, had their noses and ears cut off, a popular Portuguese way of discouraging further resistance to their rapacious rule.

Quriyat Fort

Mon–Thurs & Sun 8.30am–2.30pm • Free

Quriyat's principal attraction is its two-hundred-year-old **fort**, which sits right in the middle of town, just beyond the souk on your left as you drive in. Following several years of much-needed renovations, it was re-opened to the public in 2013, allowing you to climb to its rooftop for views across to the harbour. It's not the most memorable of forts, though it's worth checking out the fine old wooden door at the entrance, flanked by a pair of rusty cannon. Shuttered ground-floor windows ring the building on three sides, suggesting that domesticity, rather than defence, was formerly the principal concern.

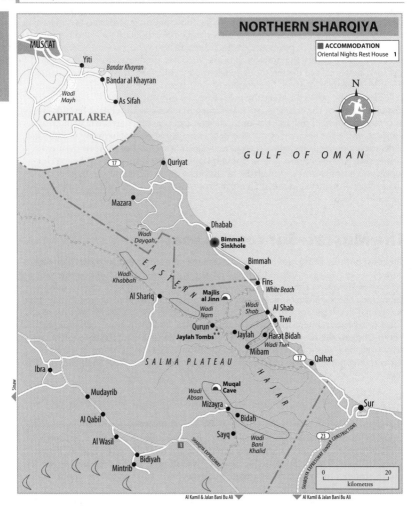

The seafront

Continue along the road past the fort and a large mangrove swamp to reach the town's pretty **seafront** corniche, at the end of which is the **harbour**, with boats drawn up on surrounding sands overlooked by a round watchtower sitting proudly just off the headland above.

Wadi Dayqah

Signed 19km off the coastal highway to the south of Quriyat • Daily 8am–10pm • Free

After winding through the rugged, arid mountainscape that encompassed the road from Quriyat, the first glimpse of this vast, shimmering expanse of turquoise water is quite the welcome sight. The reservoir measures some eight kilometres from end to end, supported by Oman's largest dam – built with the intent of providing 100 million cubic metres of water to the growing populations of Quriyat and Muscat. There's plenty of parking and a simple café-cum-restaurant beside the large, manicured park that overlooks the water, making a pleasant picnic spot from which to admire the panoramic views and people-watch when the weekend crowds arrive.

5

The Bimmah Sinkhole

Daily 7.30am–10pm • The exit to the park is signed off the coastal highway 38km south of the Quriyat turn-off (5km south of Dhabab turn-off and 8km north of the Bimmah turn-off); follow the road under the highway and down to the sea, then turn left at the T-junction (signed towards Dhabab and Hawiyat Najm Park) and continue for 1.5km, then left again at the sign to the park

The **Bimmah Sinkhole** is now enclosed within (and signed as) the Hawiyat Najm Park. Sadly, the sinkhole itself – formerly one of the coast's most magical beauty spots – has now been utterly defaced in the name of tourism, with an ugly stone wall erected around its rim and concrete steps with bright blue handrails running down inside, which has succeeded in reducing the whole place to the level of suburban naff. If you can ignore all this, the interior of the sinkhole is still rather lovely, with a miniature lake at the bottom, its marvellously clear blue waters populated with shoals of tiny tadpole-like fish, and reflections from the water playing on the layered limestone above.

Fins

South from the Bimmah Sinkhole, it's possible to drive along the **old coastal road** (tarmacked hereabouts) which runs close to the sea through Bimmah village and on to the village of **FINS**, 18km further on, where the tarmac ends – a pleasant change of pace and scenery from the coastal highway. There's a turn-off back to the highway a couple kilometres past Bimmah (10km along the road), and another one at Fins. Fins itself is flanked by an attractive string of white-sand **beaches** including the popular "White Beach", 5km south of the village, although the whole place attracts a steady stream of visitors, particularly at weekends.

Wadi Shab

The closest access road to the wadi lies about 600m to the north, with exits off the highway serving both directions; alternatively, approaching from Wadi Tiwi you can continue 3km north along the coast road • Boats to the trailhead run from the car park every few minutes 7.30am–5pm daily • 1 OR return boat fare

South of the Bimmah Sinkhole lie the dramatic Wadi Shab and Wadi Tiwi, a pair of spectacularly narrow mountain ravines, hemmed in by vertiginous sandstone walls with a verdant ribbon of date plantations and banana palms threading the base of the cliffs. Driving south, **Wadi Shab** is the first of the two you'll encounter, and perhaps the most rewarding. There's no road into the wadi (unlike Wadi Tiwi) – which is a significant part of its charm – though there's plenty of parking beneath the concrete flyover carrying the coastal highway. Here you'll find toilets, a simple café and boats that ferry hikers to the trailhead just opposite the pond. Note that no camping or cooking is allowed in the wadi.

After the first kilometre or so of the hike, the gorge narrows and a small footpath runs along a rock ledge just above the wadi floor, choked with huge boulders. Another kilometre or so up the valley, past further plantations and the faint ruins of old villages, the valley bends back to the left, where you'll soon reach some inviting rock pools that make a refreshing spot for a swim. About a couple of hundred metres along the water is a narrow passage beneath the rock (when water levels are high you'll have to hold your breath for a few metres to pass through) that opens up to a dreamy little cavern. Doubling back to where the pools begin, you can follow the rough trail along the right side of the canyon to reach deeper into the wadi, though be sure to arrive back at the trailhead in time for the last boat back to the car park. Understandably, the wadi's popularity with local and foreign tourists means that you're highly unlikely to have the place to yourself.

Wadi Tiwi

Well-signed off the coastal highway about 1km south of Tiwi (with exits serving both directions); the road wraps around to pass beneath the flyover, and is just about doable in a 2WD, assuming it hasn't been raining

A couple of kilometres south of Wadi Shab lies the almost identical **Wadi Tiwi**, another deep and narrow gorge carved out of the mountains, running between towering cliffs right down to the sea. It's less unspoiled than Wadi Shab, thanks to the presence of a road through the ravine (although, as at Wadi Shab, the dramatic scenery at the entrance has been marred by the construction of a large flyover), although it compensates with its old traditional villages, surrounded by lush plantations of date, banana and mango, and criss-crossed with a network of gurgling *aflaj*.

The paved road into the wadi starts off by tracing the valley floor for about 3km until reaching the first village of note. Here, the track narrows dramatically, squeezing its way between old houses and high stone walls. The road continues to wind along another 7km between plantations and past the rock pools which collect between the huge boulders below, becoming increasingly rough and steep – though mostly paved – before finally coming to an end at the village of **Mibam**. It's a spectacular, if nerve-jangling, drive. From here, it's a ten-minute scramble down to the wadi along a steep path through the date farms to reach a waterfall and a stunning set of pools. Mibam is also the launching point for the popular two-day hike over the mountains to reach Wadi Bani Khalid.

Jaylah and around

At the turn-off for Fins, brown signs point inland to the ancient tombs of **Jaylah** (or Gaylah) and the village of Qurun. This is one of the most memorable drives in Sharqiya, a spectacular off-road traverse of the barren uplands at the top of the Eastern Hajar with a cluster of wonderfully atmospheric **Bronze Age beehive tombs** en route. The track also offers a convenient short cut from the coast to Ibra, although it's probably no quicker than taking the main road through Sur. The route comprises about 50km of generally good graded track, but there are some pretty rough, and sometimes extremely steep, sections here and there – 4WD is essential, as are strong nerves if you're driving yourself.

Salma Plateau and Qurun

The route begins by switchbacking vertiginously up the flanks of the Eastern Hajar, a breathless thirty-minute drive with increasingly spectacular views down to the coast below. At the top, you reach the sere **Salma Plateau** at the summit of the Eastern Hajar: a rolling expanse of gravel plain, dotted with only the sparsest of vegetation. There's virtually no sign of human habitation until you reach tiny **Qurun**, one of the loneliest villages in Oman – little more than a haphazard cluster of houses tucked away in the lee of cliff, and feeling an awfully long way from anywhere.

The tombs and towers

Past Qurun, keep left, navigating a boulder-strewn section of wadi bed for a few hundred metres, after which the track resumes, becoming increasingly rough. About 7km west of Qurun you reach an unsigned T-junction. Turn right here for Ibra, or left to reach the first of a marvellous collection of Bronze Age **tombs and towers** which dot the surrounding uplands.

The most notable structure here is a single large tower, restored to a height of around 10m (you'll already have seen it up above on your left as you approach the T-junction), while the remains of six beehive tombs, which have survived in varying stages of completion, sit in a line along the very edge of the precipitous ridge beyond. The tombs are perfect examples of their type, crafted from finely cut stones, each with a small opening at the base, although it's the marvellously wild and remote location

MAJLIS AL JINN

Hidden away in the depths of the Eastern Hajar around 8km north of Qurun village lies the celebrated **Majlis al Jinn** ("Meeting place of the Jinn"), one of Oman's most spectacular and challenging destinations for adventurous speleologists. The Majlis is one of the world's largest cave-chambers, some 120m high – larger than the great pyramid of Cheops. Entrance to the cave is via three vertical sinkholes, involving a free descent of between 118m and 158m and including the sinkhole popularly known as "Cheryl's Drop", after the daring lady who first tackled the descent. Unfortunately, the cave has been closed since 2008, when the government, inspired by the success of Al Hoota Cave (see page 101), announced plans to develop the cave as a major tourist attraction. A likely reopening date has yet to be announced.

which really captures the imagination – a perfect example of the ancient Omani predilection for constructing funerary monuments in the highest, wildest and most remote places.

Turning right at the T-junction and continuing towards Ibra you'll see more tombs scattered about the mountainside to the right of the road. After another 3km you reach a **second cluster** of monuments spread out on either side of the road, including ten or so beehive tombs and a trio of well-preserved towers – perhaps even finer than the first group, although the location is less spectacular.

Wadi Nam

A series of isolated and ramshackle villages dot the bewildering network of tracks which crisscross the plateau, tucked away in hollows among the mountains. A few kilometres beyond the second group of tombs you reach another unsigned T-junction. Turn right here for Ibra, descending steeply down a poorly maintained track to **Wadi Nam**, a dramatic little valley hemmed in by sheer black-earth walls. From here, it's a straightforward, if bumpy, ride down the wadi to the village of **Al Shariq**, where the tarmac resumes and leads to Ibra, some 50km further on.

Qalhat

The ancient city of **QALHAT** was, up until the sixteenth century, one of the most important on the Omani coast – "A sort of medieval Dubai" as travel writer Tim Mackintosh-Smith described it in his *Travels with a Tangerine* (see page 253). Qalhat's importance derived from its status as the second city of the Kingdom of Hormuz, serving as a major commercial hub in the Indian Ocean trade routes. The fame of the city attracted visitors including both Marco Polo and Ibn Battuta. Despite its prosperity, the city suffered from certain strategic weaknesses. A *falaj* system provided a reliable source of water, but there was almost no agricultural land available and all food had to be imported by land or sea. Qalhat's already tenuous foothold on the Omani coast was further undermined by a serious earthquake at the end of the fourteenth century, while just over a hundred years later, in 1508, the newly arrived **Portuguese** delivered the *coup de grace*, sacking the city, massacring its inhabitants and setting its buildings and large fleet of boats on fire, an event from which Qalhat never recovered.

The ruins

The site was officially closed at the time of writing, although there's nothing to stop you walking up for a look

The **ruins** of the city, originally triangular in plan, cover an area of over sixty acres, although it's difficult to make much sense of the confusing wreckage of assorted walls and towers scattered over a rocky headland and along the adjacent wadi. The only notable surviving structure is the **Mausoleum of Bibi Maryam**, a quaint little cuboid

5

building enshrining the remains of the saintly Bibi Maryam who, according to Ibn Battuta, had ruled the city until a few years before his visit in 1330. The colourful tiles which covered the walls right up until the nineteenth century have now vanished, and the dome has also collapsed, though the remains of the delicately moulded arches and doorways have somehow survived the years.

ARRIVAL AND DEPARTURE   **QALHAT**

By car Exit the coastal highway at the brown sign for "Ancient City of Qalhat" and then continue west until you reach the coast road; from here, head south (right) for around 2km, wrapping around to face the highway, about 300m before which you'll see a brown sign for "Madinat Qalhat", pointing across the wadi bed to the east: follow this dirt track (passable in a 2WD) as it passes through small palm grove, past which you'll see ruins up on a hillock to your left. Park along here and walk up to the mausoleum.

Sur and around

Far and away the most appealing town in Sharqiya, **SUR** enjoys one of the eastern coast's prettiest locations, with the old part of town sitting on what is almost a miniature island, surrounded by a tranquil lagoon and offering views of mingled water and land in every direction. Sur is also one of the most historic settlements in the south, formerly a bustling port and trading centre whose maritime traditions live on in the intriguing **dhow-building yard**, the only surviving one of its kind in Oman. Further reminders of Sur's illustrious past are provided by the trio of forts and string of watchtowers that encircle the town and harbour.

Sur's attractions are quite spread out. The small but lively town centre and **souk** – a colourful tangle of brightly illuminated shops and cafés – lies at the western end of the island, from where the breezy seafront corniche runs down the coast for 1km or so to reach the old **harbour**, home to Sur's dhow-building yard and a trio of watchtowers, beyond which lies the pretty village of **Ayjah**.

Brief history

The easternmost major settlement in Oman, Sur has always looked to the sea. Following the demise of Qalhat in 1508, the town developed as the region's most important port, shipping goods to and from India and East Africa, and also established itself as the country's most important ship-building centre, vestiges of which remain. A succession of reverses during the nineteenth century eroded the town's fortunes, including the arrival of European steam-ships in the Indian Ocean, the British prohibition of slavery, the split with Zanzibar and the rise of the port of Muscat. Recent years have seen a modest revival in the town's fortunes thanks to the opening of the massive OLNG natural gas plant just up the coast.

The harbour

The prettiest part of town – and the obvious place to start a visit – is around the **harbour** at the southern end of the seafront corniche opposite the contiguous village of Ayjah. Three watchtowers on successively higher rock outcrops sit above the harbour, overlooking the suspension bridge connecting Sur and Ayjah and the restored lighthouse nearby, backed by an attractive sprawl of low white houses – one of southern Oman's prettiest views.

The dhow-building yard

Just past the suspension bridge is Sur's **dhow-building yard**, all that remains of the town's once flourishing boat-building trade and the only surviving dhow yard in

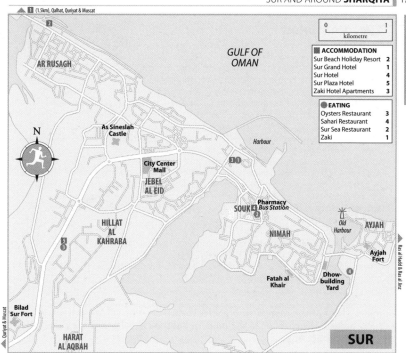

Oman. There are usually a couple of boats under construction here, while the carcasses of further old dhows can be seen further along the beach, awaiting restoration or recycling. Visitors are welcome to look around and watch the (now exclusively Indian) workforce chiselling, hammering, sawing and planing.

Fatah al Khair

Continuing south past the dhow yard, the road runs along the edge of the lagoon to where the old **Fatah al Khair** ("The Triumph of Good," roughly translated), an elegant ocean-going *ghanjah*, stands propped up next to the road on the waterfront as a monument to the city's maritime heritage. In 1993, when it was discovered to be the last-surviving vessel of its kind, the local government bought the vessel from its erstwhile Yemeni owner, bringing it to rest not far from the spot where its keel was laid in 1951. Plans to open a maritime museum in the adjacent building have yet to bear fruit.

Ayjah

Across the suspension bridge just east of Sur is the neat little village of **AYJAH** (also spelled Aygah), spread out along the headland bounding the western side of the harbour. Driving into the village, follow the brown sign pointing left towards the neat little **Al Ayjah Fort** (also known as Al Hamooda Fort; Mon–Thurs & Sun 8.30am–2.30pm; 500bz) – itself of little interest – and continue until you reach the picturesque waterfront. The village is one of the prettiest in Sharqiya: a low-lying huddle of simple old whitewashed waterside houses interspersed with more chintzy modern villas – many sport porticoes supported by the village's

5

THE OMANI DHOW

Oman was formerly famous for the excellence of its boats and the skills of its sailors, whose maritime expertise – backed up by a detailed understanding of the workings of the local monsoon (a word derived from the Arabic *mawsim*, meaning "season") – laid the basis for the country's far-reaching commercial network, and for its string of colonies in East Africa. Boats were formerly built at centres all along the coast, though only the one at Sur now survives – offering a fascinating glimpse into an almost vanished artisanal tradition.

The word **dhow** is generally used to describe all traditional wooden-hulled Arabian boats, although locals distinguish between a wide range of vessels of different sizes and styles. The traditional Arabian dhow – such as the large, ocean-going *boom* – was curved at both ends, while other types – such as the *sambuq* and *ghanjah* – boasted a high, square stern, apparently inspired by the design of Portuguese galleons. Traditional dhows were driven by enormous triangular **lateen sails** (a design which allowed them to sail much closer to the wind than European vessels), although these have now been replaced by conventional engines. Another peculiarity of the traditional dhow was its so-called **stitched construction** – planks, usually of teak, were literally sewn together using coconut rope, although nails were increasingly used after European ships began to visit the region.

For a fascinating insight into traditional Omani boat-building, seafaring and navigation, read Tim Severin's entertaining *The Sindbad Voyage* (see page 253); Severin's specially commissioned dhow – the *Sohar* – was built in Sur and now sits in the middle of a roundabout in Muscat (see page 61).

---

unique style of pillars topped with goblet-shaped capitals. It's worth tracing all the way around the harbour to the modern **lighthouse**, with fine sea views, plus a surprising number of goats.

As Sineslah Castle

3km west of town centre • Mon–Thurs, Sat & Sun 7.30am–6pm, Fri 8–11am • 500bz

The more worthwhile of Sur's restored forts lie towards the western side of town. **As Sineslah Castle** (also spelled Sunaysilah) sits in a commanding position on a hill just to the right (north) of the main road out of town – drive right up through the compound the gates to reach the car park. There's not much inside apart from a neat little mosque, a Qur'an school and a surprisingly civilized prison – unusually for an Omani dungeon, it even has windows. Steps climb up to the eastern and western towers, from where a walkway stretches around the parapet offering fine views over the white sprawl of Sur below, spiked with dozens of minarets and the occasional watchtower.

Bilad Sur Fort

6km west of town centre • Mon–Thurs & Sun 8.30am–2.30pm • 500bz

The over-restored **Bilad Sur Fort** stands 3km further down the road from As Sineslah Castle. It's almost twice the size, though much of it is taken up by the broad gravel courtyard. The most notable feature is the pair of unusually shaped, two-tier towers rising from the eastern walls.

ARRIVAL AND GETTING AROUND   SUR

By car Sur is about a 2hr drive from Muscat along Highway 17, and about the same from Ibra along Highway 23.

By bus/microbus Buses and microbuses depart from the bus station in the centre of the souk. Mwasalat (📞 25540019, 🌐 mwasalat.om) runs three daily buses to Azaiba in Muscat (3hr 50min–4hr 50min; departing 6am, 6.45am and 2.30pm) and two to Ibra (2hr 10min; departing 6am and 2.30pm).

By taxi A taxi to almost anywhere in Sur should cost no more than 300bz.

ACCOMMODATION

Sur Beach Holiday Resort 3km northwest of the town centre on the road to Qalhat ☎ 2554 2031, ✉ surbhtl@omantel.om; map p.179. This old-fashioned three-star resort looks like it's stuck in the 1970s, but compensates with a reasonable spread of facilities and a helpful and welcoming atmosphere. Accommodation is in a mix of cosy, old-fashioned rooms (some with sea views and balconies) or in two-storey villas (sleeping two), with living room and small kitchen, plus more modern and stylish furnishings. There's a stretch of slightly stony beach and a rather drab little pool, while facilities include an in-house international restaurant (7 OR for the dinner buffet), sports pub, Arabian live-music bar, gym and tennis court. Doubles 55 OR, villas 85 OR

Sur Grand Hotel About 4.5km northwest of the town centre on the road to Qalhat ☎ 2524 0000, ⓦ surgrandhotel.com; map p.179. Standing in isolation about a kilometre beyond the town's western edge, though just a few hundred metres from the beach, this airy new hotel offers wonderful views over the sea and towards the mountains from its well-appointed, modern rooms with balconies. There's also a wellness centre offering complimentary morning yoga and a good international restaurant downstairs (dinner buffet 7 OR), though perhaps the star attraction is the pleasant rooftop pool and terrace. 35 OR

Sur Hotel ☎ 2554 0090, ⓦ surhotel.net; map p.179. In a convenient location right in the middle of the souk – although inevitably not the quietest place in town – with simple but perfectly clean and comfortable rooms, helpful, knowledgeable staff and reasonable value at the price. 12 OR

Sur Plaza Hotel Around 4km inland from the centre ☎ 2554 3777, ⓦ omanhotels.com/surplaza; map p179. The town's most upmarket option, with pleasant public areas arranged around a central atrium, although rooms themselves are looking a little drab and tired. Facilities include *Oysters Restaurant* (see page 181). There's also a medium-sized pool with basic sun terrace and loungers, plus gym, business centre and a car rental office. 47 OR

Zaki Hotel Apartments 1km west of the centre ☎ 2554 5924, ⓦ zakihotelapartment.com; map p179. Spotless new hotel apartments recently opened by the same friendly and enterprising family that runs the restaurant of the same name next door. Each comes with a kitchen, and the most spacious apartments sleep four (45 OR). A breakfast buffet is served in the upstairs restaurant, while downstairs beside the reception is Sur's brightest little cafe (open 24hr). Unfortunately for light sleepers, there's a large mosque just across the street – best to avoid the apartments facing north. 35 OR

EATING

There's not much in the way of culinary diversion in Sur, and only a pair of licensed venues: *Oysters* at the *Sur Plaza Hotel* and *Cheers Bar*, a smoky sports bar attached to the *Sur Holiday Beach Resort*.

Oysters Restaurant Sur Plaza Hotel ☎ 2554 3777; map p.179. Facing the pool of Sur's top hotel, this is the most upmarket restaurant in town (and the only one that's licensed), with a wide-ranging international menu and nightly buffet (8 OR) that features Indian, Chinese and Italian cuisines. Daily 6am–11.30pm.

Sahari Restaurant Next to the Al Ayjah Plaza Hotel ☎ 2554 1423; map p.179. The restaurant and its spacious outdoor terrace boast a fine location overlooking the lagoon, offering a mishmash menu of seafood, Indian and Arabian cuisines (mains 1.5–7 OR), as well as greasy *fatayir* (from 1 OR), pizzas (from 2 OR) and desserts. Daily 8.30am–1am.

Sur Sea Restaurant Town centre, just west of Sur Hotel ☎ 9212 6096; map p.179. The best of the many

café-cum-restaurants scattered around the souk, serving up reasonable, well-priced food in a lively streetside seating – a great place for people-watching. The menu features the usual mix of quasi-Indian dishes and shwarmas (from 0.3 OR), plus some worthy seafood options (jumbo prawns 4 OR). Daily 7.30am–3am.

Zaki 1km west of the centre, just behind Zaki Hotel Apartments ☎ 2554 4249; map p.179. Popular, family-run place serving up some of Sur's top South Asian cuisine (chicken masala 1.2 OR) along with excellent seafood (grilled fish from 2.5 OR). The large, adjacent mosque ensures that it's particularly packed on Friday afternoons. Free delivery. Daily 6am–1am.

DIRECTORY   SUR

Banks and money There are numerous banks with ATMS along the main road and particularly within the souk.

Health There are several pharmacies along the main road into town and through the souk, including Ibn Sina (daily 8am–1pm & 4–10pm), 100m north of the *Sur Hotel*.

5

Ras al Hadd

The eastern coast of Sharqiya ends with a watery flourish at the little village of **RAS AL HADD**, sitting at the far southeastern corner of the country, overlooking the point where the waters of the Arabian Gulf merge with the Indian Ocean. The village's main attraction is as a convenient base from which to explore the turtle beach at Ras al Jinz (see page 182), although it's well worth a visit in its own right thanks to its pleasantly sleepy, somewhat end-of-world feeling, and impressive old fort, backed by a pair of extensive lagoons.

Ras al Hadd fort

Mon–Thurs & Sun 8.30am–2.30pm • Free

The main sight hereabouts is the sprawling **fort**, close to the sandy shore, looking (along with the rather grand mosque next door) incongruously oversized compared to the tiny buildings of the rustic village that surrounds it. Most of the interior consists of a huge empty courtyard, with a walkway stretching the length of the parapet and a large round tower at either end, each with a neat little toilet projecting from its topmost level.

ACCOMMODATION	RAS AL HADD

Turtle Beach Resort 3km east of town ☎9900 7709, ⊛tbroman.com. This old resort was recently given a new lease of life upon moving across the lagoon to a new location. Accommodation is in traditionally furnished chalets with tented roofs and patios shaded with palm fronds. All are en suite and equipped with a/c and flat-screen TVs. There's a licensed restaurant on- site, and perhaps best of all, it's set right beside a pretty cove. To reach the resort, head straight north through the roundabout at the entrance to the village, past the Al Maha petrol station, and follow this road to the end (about 5km), just beyond *Ras al Hadd Holiday Resort*. Half board costs an extra 2.5 OR per person. <u>**60 OR**</u>

Ras al Jinz and the southern coast

Some 17km onwards from Ras al Hadd – at the easternmost point of the Arabian peninsula – is **RAS AL JINZ**, home to Oman's most important **turtle-nesting beach**, visited by thousands of magnificent green turtles every year, hauling themselves up out of the sea to lay their eggs in the sand. This is perhaps the finest natural spectacle anywhere in Oman (even if, ironically, you can't actually see very much after dark) – a magical glimpse into a natural cycle which has been in existence for the best part of two hundred million years.

Visits begin at the smart, modern visitor centre, where you'll be assigned a group and wait for a guide to scan the beach. In the meantime, you can peruse the small but informative **museum** (daily 9am–9pm; 2 OR), documenting the life cycle of the turtles. Towards the end there's a tank sometimes containing tiny newborn turtles that were lost on their way to the sea that day. They are then taken back to the beach after sunset, when the cover of darkness allows them safer passage to sea.

When your guide gives the green light, you'll walk across the sands in the darkness to the edge of the waves, from where you'll see the ghostly silhouettes of perhaps a dozen or more green turtles emerging slowly from the surf and then heaving themselves

---

RAS AL JINZ: WHEN TO VISIT

The best time to see turtles laying their eggs is from **June to August**, when anything up to a hundred may arrive on the beach each night (although you're pretty much guaranteed to see at least one or two come to lay their eggs on any night of the year). Nesting turtles prefer **dark nights** rather than those when the moon is full.

5

laboriously up the beach – a Herculean trial of strength for these enormously heavy creatures. Half an hour later, having found a suitably sheltered location, the turtles begin digging themselves carefully into the beach, scooping out clouds of sand with their flippers to create a sizeable hole in which they then proceed to lay their eggs.

The whole scene is particularly magical at daybreak, as the sun rises, revealing the beautiful, cliff-fringed beach dotted with the great humped outlines of departing turtles, leaving great plough-tracks in their wake as they make their way slowly back down the beach before disappearing, exhausted, into the waves.

| **ARRIVAL AND TOURS** | **RAS AL JINZ** |

By car Ras al Jinz is 45km (a 40min drive) southeast of Sur, and about 80km (1hr 10min) north of Al Ashkharah.

By taxi Most hotels in Sur can arrange round-trip transport for around 20–25 OR per person.

Tours Tours to the 3km-long beach (part of a larger 45km protected zone) are strictly controlled, with a maximum of 200 visitors per evening and another 100 visitors per morning session. Unfortunately, demand for outstrips supply, and bookings either by phone or email are essential; three weeks or more in advance is recommended

since spaces usually get booked up early, even for early-morning tours and in the height of summer – you won't be charged if there are no turtles nesting at the time of your visit. Tours depart from the visitor centre (☎ 9655 0606, ⊛ rasaljinz-turtlereserve.com) at 9pm and 4am, last around 1hr–1hr 30min and cost 7 OR. No torches or photography (even without flash) are allowed on night tours, while photography is allowed on morning tours only after sunrise.

ACCOMMODATION

Al Naseem Camp 4km inland from the visitor centre, next to the road ☎ 9200 9427, ⊛ desertdiscovery.com/al-naseem-camp.html. A cheaper but less pleasant alternative to staying at the visitor centre, with accommodation in a compound of a/c palm-thatch huts and cabins, with no furniture apart from beds; all share rudimentary shower and toilet facilities. Rates include half board. Per person 25 OR

Ras al Jinz Turtle Reserve Visitor centre ☎ 9655 0606, ⊛ rasaljinz-turtlereserve.com. The most convenient way

to see the turtles is to say at the reserve itself. The visitor centre houses seventeen comfortable modern rooms, while a couple of minutes' walk down a cul-de-sac are twelve air-conditioned "eco-tents," by far the most luxurious option around. Rates include breakfast while the dinner buffet costs 8 OR, and your room key functions as your ticket to the museum and both evening and morning tours. Doubles 92 OR, tents 125 OR

Asaylah and around

South of Ras al Jinz it's a pleasant drive along the coast through a string of small, ramshackle villages. The landscape beyond **Asaylah** is particularly beautiful, with an unusual combination of mountain and desert, as the craggy limestone outcrops at the far southern end of the Eastern Hajar merge with the outlying dunes (some of them surprisingly large) of the Sharqiya Sands.

Al Ashkharah to Shana

A short drive beyond Asaylah and some 90km from Ras al Jinz, **AL ASHKHARAH** is the largest settlement along this stretch of coast, although not really much more than a tumbledown little fishing town with low ochre-coloured houses straggling along a wide stretch of beach.

There's a choice of routes from Al Ashkharah: either northwest along **Highway 35** to Jalan Bani Bu Ali and on to Ibra, or south along the scenic coastal road to **Shana**, the departure point for ferries to Masirah (see page 196), a journey of some 180km. The drive to Shana takes 1hr 30min–2hr along the fast single-carriageway road; there are several petrol stations along the way, but they don't always have fuel – best to fill up before leaving Al Ashkharah. It's a fine drive, with pleasant coastal scenery including a stretch of large rolling dunes beyond **Khuwaymah** (and with brief, distant

5

glimpses of the high dunes of the Sharqiya Sands rising further inland). The region is totally uninhabited apart from the ramshackle Bedu camps you'll see pitched alongside the road, from which children may occasionally emerge to chuck stones at passing traffic.

ACCOMMODATION	AL ASHKHARAH TO SHANA
Al Ashkhara Beach Resort 16km south of Al Ashkhara ☎ 9408 2424, ⊛ ashkhara.com. All alone facing a pretty stretch of white sand, with spacious, comfortable rooms and suites with private, trellis-roof terraces, some of which overlook the sea. It's a popular weekend getaway spot for families from Muscat, who take advantage of the pool, the playground and the activities on offer – jetskiing, fishing, horseback riding – while ensuring that the on-site restaurant stays open. At other times, however, it can be as quiet and lonely as its desolate surrounds. No wi-fi. **30 OR**	**Al Ashkhara Hotel** On the west side of the main road through Al Ashkhara, about 100m south of the Shell station. This run-down one-star has seen better days (probably in around 1950) but is tolerably clean and will do for a night if you get stuck. The central location means there are loads of (nearly identical) restaurants around – the *Golden Beach Restaurant and Coffee House* next door does good set dinners. **12 OR**

Ibra and around

The principal town of inland Sharqiya, **IBRA** grew rich thanks to its location on the major trade route between Muscat, Sur and Zanzibar. Evidence of the wealth accumulated by the town's former notables can be seen in the magnificent old mudbrick mansions of Al Munisifeh (see page 185), while the dozen or so **watchtowers** – standing guard on the jagged hilltops overlooking the approaches to town – remind of Ibra's one-time strategic importance. The town is also the home of the redoubtable **Al Harthy tribe**, whose repeated rebellions against the sultans of Muscat were such a feature of early twentieth-century Omani history (see page 240).

Modern Ibra has regained a good share of its historical importance. It's home to a technical college, a university, a large regional hospital and its very own Lulu Hypermarket, while the expansion of the new expressway promises to bring the rest of the country even closer.

Ayalat Ibra (Upper Ibra) – the modern town – is strung out along the main highway, a functional ribbon of banks, petrol stations and cafés. It's around 3km south of here to the older part of town, **Safalat Ibra** (Lower Ibra), which is where you'll find the lively **souk**, one of the largest in Sharqiya. Just west of here are the crumbling remains of **Al Munisifeh** and **Al Qanatar**, featuring some of the region's finest traditional mudbrick architecture. Ibra also makes a good base for explorations of the nearby Sharqiya Sands, as well as a possible starting point for the magnificent off-road drive to the coast via the tombs of Jaylah.

Ibra souk

600m west of the main highway in Safalat Ibra: take the turning signed Safalat Ibra directly south of the Shell station

The heart of Ibra's old **souk** is occupied by a large open-air pavilion mainly given over to the sale of fruit and vegetables. Look out for the small shop in the corner devoted to the (as the sign says) "Sale of Traditional Rifle Maintenance and Fire Arms", usually busy with a few old-timers bent over antiquated-looking weapons. There are also a few shops selling jewellery and *khanjars*, while the block immediately beyond the central pavilion is occupied by a string of carpentry shops turning out old-fashioned wooden doors and other traditional wooden items, although the workforce is now exclusively Indian.

The Women's Souk

Held close to the main souk on Wednesday mornings from around 7am to 11am

Ibra is also home to a celebrated **Women's Souk** (Souk al Hareem, or Souk al Arba'aa, meaning "Wednesday souk"). The souk is restricted to female traders and shoppers (in theory at least – the rule is not strictly enforced), with a wide selection of goods ranging from piles of cheap clothes and factory cloth through to traditional cosmetics and textiles; look for examples of the colourful and distinctive local Bedu embroidery which is sewn onto black abbayat or around the ankles of trousers.

Al Munisifeh

To reach the villages, continue south past the souk until the road veers to the left, then turn right, following the brown signs to Al Munisifeh Village, Al Qanatar Village and Al Qablateen Mosque

A couple of kilometres beyond Ibra souk lie the atmospheric old walled villages of Al Munisifeh and Al Qanatar, two of the finest in the region. Approaching by road, you come first to **AL MUNISIFEH**, surrounded by the remains of its original walls, with gateways at either side linked by a central street. The village comprises an assortment of modern houses interspersed with rather grand old buildings in a mix of mudbrick and stone – their size

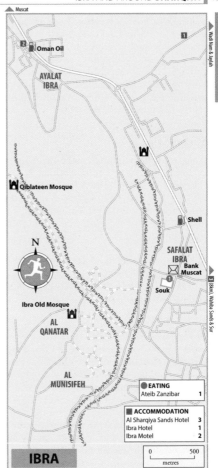

testifying to the wealth amassed by the village's merchants during Ibra's heyday athwart the trade route between Muscat and Zanzibar.

SIGN LANGUAGE, OMAN STYLE

One charmingly old-fashioned aspect of every souk in Oman is the lack of advertising. Visit any market in the country and you'll see lines of similar little shops all boasting exactly the same, resolutely factual, **signs** in Arabic, with their English translations below. "Coffee Shop" is probably the most common, closely followed by "Gents Tailoring" (with "Ladies Tailoring" not far behind), while other signs are similarly matter of fact – "Sale & Repairing of Dish & Television" for a TV shop, for instance, or "Sale of Fresh Mutton & Frozen". The accuracy of English translations is consistently high, and mistakes rare, although when things do go wrong they can do so spectacularly, such as the shop in Ibra souk advertising "Asle of Freah Ghigken" ("Sale of Fresh Chicken"). Occasionally bursts of unintentional linguistic whimsy also catch the eye, notably the local outlet advertising "Sale of Tobacco, Smoke & Derivatives" – a pleasantly fanciful way of saying they sell cigarettes.

5

The quality of the decorative work on many of the old houses is unusually high – look out for the remains of elaborate plasterwork, and finely carved wooden doorways and window frames. It's best to park before Munisifeh and follow the road through town, ducking off to explore the old buildings along the way. Virtually all are now uninhabited and partially derelict, although some have been discreetly restored, which has managed to preserve much of their original character while giving the comforting sense (unlike so many other abandoned Omani houses) that they aren't in danger of collapsing in the next heavy shower.

Al Qanatar

Emerging from Munisifeh along the main street, you'll wind through the fields for about 300 metres before reaching Al Qanatar, just beyond the remains of the old souk that lie off to the left of the road. Just beyond here, also on the left, a narrow street leads to Al Qanatar's restored old mudbrick **mosque**, raised on a platform above street level. As with similar very early mosques elsewhere in the country, such as the Masjid Mazari in Nizwa (see page 89), there's no minaret, just a tiny pepperpot dome on one corner. Non-Muslims aren't allowed to enter to see the fifteen stumpy columns massed inside, strikingly similar to those at the Al Hamooda Mosque in Jalan Bani Bu Ali (see page 194). Carry on along Al Qanatar's narrow main street, hemmed in between two-storey mud-brick houses, to find further hints of its former glory, with dozens of more beautifully carved, dilapidated doorways.

Al Qiblateen Mosque

Follow the wadi bed north past Al Qanatar to reach the venerable old **Al Qiblateen Mosque** ("Mosque of the Two Qiblas"), about ten minutes away on foot. Little more than a stone cube on the hillside, its importance lies in being perhaps the oldest mosques in the country, as evidenced by the small niche in the far left corner, an obvious afterthought in the structure's design. While this *mihrab* points roughly towards Mecca, the original one (on the far wall) was apparently built before Muhammad's injunction to stop praying towards Jerusalem. Dress conservatively when entering, and don't be fooled by the nearly identical structure about 200 metres south – you can count the niches to be sure.

ACCOMMODATION   **IBRA AND AROUND**

Ibra has a few decent **accommodation** options; there are also a couple of places further south along the main road to Sur (see page 178), or you can head to one of the many desert camps within the Sharqiya Sands (see page 190).

Al Sharqiya Sands Hotel 8km south of Ibra on the west side of Highway 23, just south of the turn-off to Sinaw and Al Mudaybi ☎ 2558 7099, ⓦ sharqiyasands.com; map p.185. A pleasant spot just outside of Ibra, with accommodation in clean though rather tired rooms set around a green courtyard with a decent-sized pool. There's a good licensed restaurant serving mostly Indian food, a cosy pub and a noisy cabaret hall with nightly dance and music performances next door. 42 OR

★ **Ibra Hotel** 500m east of the Wadi Nam roundabout ☎ 2557 1873, Eibrahotel@gmail.com; map p.185.

This centrally located hotel has clean, simply-furnished rooms lining a bright, open-air central hallway that leads to a big swimming pool out back, beside which is a decent restaurant. In the complex out front, there's a smoky bar with a pool table and a big, echoing music hall that hosts nightly performances. 30 OR

Ibra Motel 750m west of the Wadi Nam roundabout, behind the Oman Oil petrol station ☎ 2557 1666, Eibramtl@omantel.net.com; map p.185. One of the nicest budget hotels in southern Oman, with smart, spacious and very attractively furnished rooms at bargain prices. 22 OR

EATING

Outside of the main hotels, Ibra's restaurant scene is mostly limited to no-frills coffee shops. For picnic supplies, visit the deli at Lulu Hypermarket. *Al Sharqiya Sands Hotel* and *Ibra Hotel* have the city's only licensed venues.

Ateib Zanzibar Just north of Ibra souk ☎9212 6096; map p.185. Cheap and cheery little spot to fill up after wandering the souk, with hot, greasy South Asian-inspired snacks like vegetable, fish and chicken cutlets (100bz) and sambusa (50bz). The menu is in Arabic only, though it's easy enough to point out what you'd like through the glass partition. Daily 8am–1pm & 4.30–10pm.

Sinaw

Pressed against the far western edge of Northern Sharqiya, about 90km west of Ibra and 80km south of Izki, the town of **SINAW** makes a worthy diversion from the beaten path running from Ibra to the coast. Its remoteness is certainly part of the charm – other than being a stop on the long inland highway running the length of Sharqiya and on to Duqm and the Al Wusta coast, it's not quite on the way to anywhere, and thus sees very few foreign visitors. Its lively souk, however, remains one of the most interesting in the entire region.

Sinaw souk

The souk is in the centre of town; turn left at the big roundabout if approaching from Ibra via Al Mudaybi or from Izki centre

Sinaw is best known for its colourful **souk** – a rectangle of shops arranged around a large courtyard with an open-sided pavilion in the middle. The souk attracts large numbers of Bedu from the nearby Sharqiya Sands, including local women dressed in vibrantly coloured shawls, patchwork tunics and embroidered anklets, and others, less flamboyant, swathed in black abbayat and face masks. It's particularly lively on Thursday mornings during the weekly livestock market.

Old Sinaw

Tucked away in the extensive date plantations to the south of the souk lie the atmospheric remains of **old Sinaw**, comprising a pair of neat little villages nestled among the palms. The first is close behind the souk, while the second lies further into the plantations; both are crammed with fine two- and three-storey mudbrick buildings, some surprisingly well preserved.

Mudayrib

Some 18km south of Ibra, a sign points left off Highway 23 to **MUDAYRIB**. One of the prettiest villages in Sharqiya, Mudayrib is surrounded by an unusually fine cluster of six watchtowers on the encircling hills, which form a tight protective necklace around the small village below, all beautifully backdropped by the craggy peaks of the Eastern Hajar. The village boasts a number of imposing old **fortified houses** built, as at Ibra, by merchants who had grown wealthy on the back of trade with Africa. Some of them look almost like miniature forts, with battlemented rooftops, miniature towers and musket slits in the walls.

Al Wasil

About 16km south along the old highway from Mudayrib is the town of **AL WASIL**, its centre less than a couple of kilometres from the wall of dunes towering to the west – it's the access point for several camps in the Sharqiya Sands. Signs along the highway direct towards the old **castle** in the centre of town, partially restored in recent years though not the most interesting of the area's forts. A few openings in the walls allow you to walk in and explore the interior courtyard, sometimes used to host local events.

THE BEDU

Arabia's most iconic inhabitants, the **Bedu** (often Anglicized to "Bedouin") have long been seen – by Westerners at least – as the human face of the desert peninsula. For outsiders, the Bedu have come to personify a rather romanticized ideal of nomadic life amid the sands, with their distinctive lifestyle of ferocious independence, ceaseless tribal feuds and outbursts of legendary hospitality. Some of which is at least partly true.

Scattered across the interior of Oman and other countries around the peninsula, the nomadic Bedu tribes formerly eked out a marginal existence amid one of the world's most hostile natural environments, surviving in the depths of the desert by a combination of camel-raising, goat-herding and inter-tribal raiding – a lifestyle founded on a complex network of tribal allegiances, intimate knowledge of the local environment and extraordinary levels of physical resilience. Wilfred Thesiger's *Arabian Sands* remains essential reading for anyone with even a cursory interest in the region, offering a fascinating glimpse into the Bedu tribes' unique customs and traditions and a salutary corrective to some of the more flowery received notions of nomadic life.

Not surprisingly, virtually nothing survives of the harsh traditional Bedu existence described by Thesiger. Many Bedu in Oman have adopted settled, sedentary lifestyles, emigrating to the cities and merging with the population at large, while others have reinvented themselves as tour guides, offering modern visitors rewarding insights into the flora, fauna and traditional culture of the Sharqiya Sands. Traditional Bedu culture and customs do, however, linger on in many parts of southern Oman, particularly around the Sands themselves. Local Bedu here still follow a modified form of their traditional pursuits, raising livestock for part of the year before decamping to their plantations around Mintrib to harvest dates during the hot summer months. Bedu families can also often be seen frequenting the souks of Ibra and Sinaw, with the distinctive sight of local Bedu women in traditional face masks and elaborately embroidered shawls, trousers and tunics offering a colourful reminder of the interior's traditional, if now increasingly threatened, past.

Mintrib

Some 10km south of Al Wasil and about 2km west of the old highway is the little town of **MINTRIB** (also spelled Mintarib and Minitraib), home to a small, stout **castle**. The town is an important access point for the Sharqiya Sands, which rise immediately behind. Guides typically wait around in the car park outside the castle, offering tours of the sands (20/30 OR for half-hour/hour-long tours). There's a handy garage in the middle of town where you can have your tyre pressure reduced before venturing onto the sands.

Mintrib Castle

Main Street • Mon–Thurs & Sun 7.30am–2.30pm • 500bz

Built in in the early seventeenth century and expanded in the late eighteenth by Imam Azzan bin Qais, this newly renovated **fort** features unusual, slightly inward-sloping walls and a single, undernourished tower rising just a metre or so above the battlements. Centred on a well, the ground-floor **courtyard** has many of the standard features: a low-entry jail, small mosque, *majlis*, weapons cache and "murder hole" above the entrance (look up to see the narrow slit through which boiling date syrup was dropped on unwanted visitors). The **first floor** is more unique, with four thirty-metre vaulted corridors, impressive for having been built entirely without timber and lit in part by rifle slits notched into the outer walls. Climbing to the **rooftop** affords worthwhile views of the dunes rising behind the date palm oasis to the west.

5

The Sharqiya Sands

South of Ibra stretch the magnificent **Sharqiya Sands** (Ramlat al Sharqiya; also known as the Wahiba Sands) – "a perfect specimen of sand sea", as they have been described. This is the desert as you've always imagined it: a huge, virtually uninhabited swathe of sand, with towering dunes, reaching almost 100m in places, sculpted by the wind into delicately moulded crests and hollows. Tourist resorts apart, there are no permanent settlements in the sands, although some local **Bedu** still live here in somewhat ramshackle temporary encampments, particularly on the southern fringes of the sands around Al Ashkharah (see page 183). Otherwise, they remain hauntingly empty, although the endless tracks churned up by cavorting dune-bashers tearing around the sands in their souped-up 4WDs (and, along the main routes, obscene quantities of litter) mean that it's not quite as unspoiled as you'd expect. As a general rule of thumb, the further into the sands you penetrate, the more dramatic and untouched the landscape becomes.

The **dunes** themselves follow a surprisingly regular pattern, as a glance at Google Earth makes strikingly clear, running in long lines from north to south – an orderly sequence of so-called "linear" dunes formed by the conflicting winds blowing in from the eastern and southern coasts (and meaning that travelling across the sands from north to south is significantly easier than tackling them from east to west). They are also constantly on the move, shifting inland at an estimated rate of 10m per year.

For many visitors, overnighting amid the Sharqiya Sands at a **desert camp** is one of Oman's most memorable experiences – surrounded by the majestic outline of moonlit dunes, and with a twinkling tapestry of stars overhead.

GETTING AROUND THE SHARQIYA SANDS

By car The sands cover a considerable area: some 180km from north to south, and almost 80km from east to west. There are no roads in the Sharqiya Sands. A network of tracks (for which you'll need 4WD) crisscrosses the sands, although these are sometimes difficult to follow without local knowledge, being notional routes rather than physical tracks – meaning it's possible to get badly lost if you don't know what you're doing. Getting stuck in the desert is also a real possibility, and no laughing matter during the hot summer months; it's best to travel with at least one other vehicle if you're venturing away from established routes.

ACCOMMODATION

You don't get much for your money at any of the extensive string of **desert camps** dotting the dunes. Even the most basic camps come with a sizeable mark-up, while the nicer spots can cost as much as a plush Muscat five-star hotel. On the plus side, rates include breakfast and dinner, plus free coffee, tea and fruit. Most camps feature accommodation in some kind of pseudo-traditional tent or palm-thatch hut (which may be concrete inside). It's also worth bearing in mind that you can explore the sands without actually overnighting in them, either by staying in or around Ibra (see page 184) or along the highway further south at *Oriental Nights Rest House* (see page 192) or *Qawafel Al Mamoorh* (see page 193).

Getting to the desert camps You'll need a 4WD to reach all the desert camps apart from *Al Areesh* and *Al Reem* (see below), although all places can arrange to collect you from the main road, albeit often at a considerable price.

DESERT ECOLOGY IN THE SHARQIYA SANDS

Empty though they may look, the sands support a fascinating **desert ecology**. A celebrated expedition by the Royal Geographical Society in 1986 discovered 150 species of plant, including the hardy ghaf (*Proposis cinera*), which plays a major role in stabilizing the dunes, as well as providing firewood and shade. In addition, 200 mammal, bird and reptile species were discovered, ranging from side-winding vipers to desert hares and sand foxes. Most of these creatures are nocturnal, however, so you're unlikely to see much during the day apart from their tracks.

5

DESERT ACTIVITIES

The principal attraction of a visit here is simply the chance to be out among the dunes, and to spend a night in the desert. All the desert camps lay on various **desert activities**. Dune-bashing (see page 26) is a popular, if not particularly restful or environmentally friendly, way of exploring the sands; **camel or horse rides** (sometimes guided by local Bedu) offer a more peaceful alternative – expect to pay about 15 OR per hour. Other activities include **sandboarding**, **trekking** and **quad-biking**.

Desert Nights Camp, *Nomadic Desert Camp* and *Sama Al Wasil Tourism Village* are reached from Al Wasil village, 30km south of Ibra; *1000 Nights* and *Al Raha* are reached from Mintrib, 40km south of Ibra; *Al Reem* is much further south, near Jalan Bani Bu Hassan.

When to visit Many places can get noisy at weekends, when locals and expats descend on the region; if possible, visit during the week.

1000 Nights 20km further into the sands beyond Al Raha camp T9944 8158, ⍟1000nightscamp.com. Set deep in the sands, this camp's accommodation ranges from pleasantly authentic Bedu-style tents to unabashed glamping. The standard "Arabic" tents are relatively bare, little more than a couple of beds and a shared bathroom; at the next tier are the larger "Sheikh" tents, which come with nice open-air toilets and showers, while the much pricier glass-walled, a/c "Ameer" tents are even bigger, with attractive woven decorations, a couple of pieces of furniture and hot water; or there's more conventionally comfortable accommodation in the pair of two-storey, a/c "Sand Houses", built in traditional mudbrick style. Facilities include a small but pretty pool and mudbrick-style sun terrace, a quirky sit-out area in an old dhow, and a lovely (unlicensed) restaurant scattered with colourful cushions. Pick up from Mintrib is 40 OR return. Arabic tent $\overline{49\ OR}$, Sheikh tent $\overline{76\ OR}$, Ameer Tent $\overline{148\ OR}$, Sand House $\overline{172\ OR}$

Al Areesh Turn-off from Highway 23 around 27km south of Ibra (7km past Mudayrib turn-off), then 8km into the sands ☎9200 9427, ⍟desertdiscovery.com/al-areesh-desert-camp.html. Built in the lee of the dunes in a rather tame section of desert, this is one of the oldest and drabbest of the main camps, its main selling points being that it's relatively cheap and accessible by sealed road (apart from the last 750m or so, which should be fine in a 2WD), although this means the scenery is less majestic than at other places further into the dunes. Accommodation is in basic huts and Bedouin tents covered in withered palm fronds, all fitted with electric lighting and shared toilet facilities – alternatively, you can move your bed and sleep outside. Expensive for what you get. Per person $\overline{25\ OR}$

Al Raha 20km along the road past Mintrib Fort ☎9700 3222, ⍟facebook.com/pg/alrahacampoman. Set a considerable distance into the sands in a neat and

shady little garden surrounded by towering dunes, *Al Raha* offers perhaps the best value of the various camps. Accommodation is in rather unappealing concrete rooms (all en suite), some with a/c. There's a licensed restaurant and free tea and coffee served in the *majlis*. Round-trip transport for those without 4WD costs 30 OR. $\overline{20\ OR}$

★ **Al Reem** About 3km west of Highway 35, signed about 4km north of Jalan Bani Bu Hassan ☎9174 0009, ⍟alreem-desertcamp.com. In a wooded area on the edge of the desert near Jalan Bani Bu Hassan, this relatively new desert camp is one of the easiest to access from the road – only the last few minutes requires going off the pavement and over some scrub, which should present no problems for a 2WD. In addition to the basic, simply furnished tents there are options with all the mod cons, from standard rooms to a range of charmingly decorated tent and bungalow suites, including some for families of four (68 OR). Thoughtful, energetic staff provide a warm welcome, good food and occasional entertainment around a bonfire at night. Doubles $\overline{50\ OR}$, basic tents $\overline{42\ OR}$, tent suites $\overline{58\ OR}$

Desert Nights Camp Turn-off from Al Wasil, then 11km into the sands ☎9281 8388, ⍟omanhotels.com/desertnightscamp. Certainly among the most luxurious camps in the Sharqiya Sands, offering a real dash of Arabian style in the desert, although at a hefty price. Accommodation is in a string of individual "units" modelled after traditional Arabian tents, attractively furnished with traditional bric-a-brac and fabrics under a tent-style canvas roof, some of them large enough to sleep four (220 OR); standard rooms are cheaper but not nearly as nice. There's also an attractive licensed restaurant (with a live oud player nightly) and a nice bar, plus complimentary pick-up from the main road and a sunset ride through the dunes. Doubles $\overline{115\ OR}$, tent suites $\overline{130\ OR}$

Nomadic Desert Camp Turn-off at Al Wasil, then 20km into the sands ☎9933 6273, ⍟nomadicdesertcamp.com. A long-established camp deep in the sands, owned and operated by a local Bedu family and therefore offering a touch of authenticity other places lack. Accommodation is in simple but nicely furnished barasti huts, with shared bathroom only and no electricity, and there's an attractive *majlis*-cum-dining area. They also offer complimentary camel rides and round-trip transport from Al Wasil (10 OR per person). Per person $\overline{35\ OR}$

5

Sama Al Wasil Tourism Village Turn-off from Al Wasil, then 15km into the sands ☎ 2449 9309, ⓦ samavillages.com. Newish and well-equipped camp with accommodation in a neat circle of attractive sandstone chalets and tents (all en suite) in traditional Omani style, with pretty little rug-covered verandas. It lacks some of the atmosphere of more traditional tented camps, but compensates with above-average creature comforts, including proper beds, a/c, modern bathrooms, electricity and good food. Chalets 60 OR, tents 64 OR

Wadi Bani Khalid

Some 15km south of Mintrib along Highway 23, a side road heads northeast to wind up and over the mountains and then down into the dramatic **Wadi Bani Khalid**, perhaps the most attractive of the various wadis which dissect the western flanks of the Eastern Hajar. The wadi is also one of the greenest in Oman, dotted with a string of villages and plantations – the red-skinned banana is a local speciality, particularly in Bidah village.

Mizayra

It's 22km off the main highway to the little village of **Mizayra**. The road splits here: turn right for Bidah or head left into Wadi Absan (a subsidiary branch of the main Wadi Bani Khalid) and follow the tarmac through the plantations before reaching the end of the road and a small car park at tiny Muqal village. Several large **pools** dot the wadi hereabouts, a popular swimming and picnicking spot, especially at weekends, at which times latecomers often have to park well down the road from the car park.

Muqal Cave

Taking the path to the right of the pools and following the very rough, boulder-strewn track up the wadi for around fifteen minutes brings you to **Muqal Cave**. It's possible to enter the cave, although, depending on how tall you are, you'll have to crawl – or at least stoop painfully – through the narrow entrance in order to reach the main chamber. A torch is essential.

Bidah

About 3km south of Mizayra is the village of **Bidah**, framed by a beautiful series of waterfalls, the Shalalaat al Hawer, which run down above the village after rain. Bidah is also the starting point for a challenging hike through the canyon-like upper reaches of Wadi Bani Khalid, taking around 4–5hr to reach the village of Sayq on the far side.

ACCOMMODATION   **WADI BANI KHALID**

Oriental Nights Rest House 14km east of Bidiyah along Highway 23 (on the right-hand side of the road approaching from Ibra), just opposite the turnoff to Wadi Bani Khalid ☎ 9402 0668 or ☎ 9900 6215, ✉ zinalhajri1std@gmail.com; map p.174. Simple, ageing hotel in a walled gravel compound with worn but tidy rooms and a basic in-house restaurant where breakfast is served (an extra 1.5 OR). Staff organize tours both to hike the canyons of Wadi Bani Khalid and to the sands. 25 OR

Al Kamil and around

South of the Wadi Bani Khalid turn-off, the main road continues for a further 40km to the small town of **AL KAMIL**, where the road splits, with Highway 23 heading east to Sur (50km distant) and Highway 35 heading south to Jalan Bani Bu Hassan and beyond.

Al Kamil itself is home to a cluster of imposing **fortified houses** lined up in a row just off the main road: large and severely simple mudbrick boxes, almost completely unadorned save for their rooftop crenellations and turrets. The houses are on your left as you reach the roundabout on the southern side of town, identifiable by the large Muscat Pharmacy sign. A short walk to the east of here, within a quiet residential neighbourhood just beyond the open-air souk, stands the renovated fort housing the town's worthwhile **museum**.

Old Castle Museum

Well-signed about 200m east From the Al Kamil roundabout on Highway 35, 1km south from where it joins Highway 23 · 15 Oct–15 April daily 9am–5.30pm; no regular hours in summer months (call ahead) · 30min guided visit 2 OR · ☎ 9320 0166, ⓦ facebook.com/pg/oldcastlemuseum

Restored in 2003 on the order of the Sultan himself, Al Kamil's castle has since been returned to the descendants of the family that built it in the late eighteenth century. Owner Khalfan al Hashmi, great-great-grandson of the castle's founder, opened **Old Castle Museum** in 2013 after filling its rooms and courtyard with densely packed exhibits reflecting daily life in the Oman of yesteryear. Khalfan has been collecting since the age of fifteen, visiting hundreds of homes across the country in increasingly vain attempts to find and preserve traces of the past, single-handedly amassing and arranging some 14,000 antiques – palm works, pottery, coins, silverware, Henry Martin rifles, woven camel saddles, leather camel bags, and a marvellous 250-year-old carved doorway from Mombasa. The castle tour is certainly worth the stop in Al Kamil, and if Khalfan is around he may invite you for coffee and tales of an Oman that has all but disappeared.

ACCOMMODATION   **AL KAMIL AND AROUND**

Qawafel Al Mamoorh Hotel Apartments Southwest side of Highway 23, about 1km west of the junction with Highway 35 ☎ 2555 8777 or ☎ 9919 0819. Overlooking a dirt lot just north of Al Kamil, this friendly but sterile new hotel has spacious, clean rooms and better-value two-bedroom apartments with kitchenettes. There's no restaurant and therefore no breakfast offered, so you'll have to head into town. Doubles <u>35 OR</u>, apartments <u>40 OR</u>

Jalan Bani Bu Hassan

Some 16km south of Al Kamil, the modest town of **Jalan Bani Bu Hassan** is home to a sprucely restored **fort**, plus an interesting group of traditional **fortified houses**. In exploring this old neighbourhood, you may notice an unusually high concentration of mosques – indeed, like its neighbour to the south, Jalan Bani Bu Ali has a reputation as a bastion of religiosity. There's nowhere worth overnighting in the town itself, though there's an excellent desert camp nearby, *Al Reem* (see page 191).

The fort

Well-signed about 1km west of the highway near the centre of town · Mon–Thurs & Sun 7.30am–6pm · Free

Jalan Bani Bu Hassan's over-restored **fort**, built in the nineteenth century during the reign of Said bin Sultan on the ruins of a millennium-older structure, consists mostly of a large, empty courtyard inside. The most interesting part is the residential quarters at the far end, a disorienting complex of rooms arranged around a sloping terrace surrounded by an Escher-like tangle of steps, doors and battlements.

The fortified houses

About 700m north of the fort; to reach Awlad Murshid, take the right fork

Continuing along the road past the fort brings you to the oldest part of town, home to a fine cluster of traditional **fortified houses**, including one particularly impressive tower-house known locally as **Awlad Murshid** which you can glimpse over its crumbling

5

outer walls. It stands five storeys high, with distinctive layers of crumbling off-white *sarooj* (plaster) still clinging to its upper floors.

Jalan Bani Bu Ali

Some 10km south of Jalan Bani Bu Hassan, the town of **JALAN BANI BU ALI** is the most interesting in this part of Sharqiya: staunchly traditional, and with a certain reputation for religious conservatism and political independence. During the early nineteenth century, following repeated Saudi incursions into Oman, the local Bani Bu Ali tribe converted to the Wahhabi form of Islam practised in Saudi Arabia. It was the only tribe in the country ever to do so, and subsequently repudiated the rule of the sultan – who responded by dispatching a large armed force to crush the fledgling rebellion. Even now, the town retains a decidedly old-fashioned atmosphere, and visitors remain a source of (usually friendly) curiosity.

The old town

The modern part of town along the main highway is indistinguishable from any other in Oman. The **old town**, however, remains relatively untouched by the twenty-first century, with a sprawl of low, sand-coloured buildings and stands of dusty-looking palm trees sprawling around one of Oman's most marvellously atmospheric forts.

The fort

Head southwest off Highway 35 at the roundabout (opposite the Oriental Shopping centre), and drive straight into town for about 2km, where you'll come to a fork in the road divided by a trio of men's tailoring shops – head left to reach the fort (500m)

Jalan Bani Bu Ali's **fort** is probably the single largest unrestored mudbrick structure in the entire country: a huge, crumbling colossus which rises high and proud above the surrounding streets. Large parts of the structure have collapsed, though several soaring towers and the magnificent central keep survive – for the time being, at any rate.

Access to the **interior** is either via the various gaps in the partially collapsed walls – particularly along the southern side – or a single small door around the far (western) side. Inside there's a fascinating tangle of ruined buildings boasting the remains of fine arches and arcading. Look out for the quaint little mosque just south of the doorway along the western wall – topped by a pair of domes that are remarkably similar to those of the famous old fifteenth-century mosque at Bidiyah in the eastern UAE (the oldest in that country), suggesting a similar vintage for the building here.

Al Hamooda Mosque

Head 400m south from the fort along the road lining its western wall; the mosque's domes will be visible on your left-hand side

Near the fort stands the rustic **Al Hamooda Mosque**, a low, squat structure topped by 52 tiny domes and with a *falaj* running across its main facade. Unlike the fort, this has been carefully restored. Non-Muslims aren't allowed inside, though the main door is usually left open, allowing you a view of the unusual interior, filled with a dense cluster of stumpy columns – a very old style of mosque design that can also be seen at the Al Qiblateen Mosque in Ibra (see page 186).

ACCOMMODATION AND EATING	**JALAN BANI BU ALI**

Al Dhabi Tourist Motel 1km south of the main roundabout, next to the Shell station ☏2555 3307. The only place to stay in Jalan Bani Bu Ali is this simple but homely little one-star, jazzed up with fancy wooden doors and masses of plastic flowers. Eating options are limited, although there are a few low-key cafés scattered along the main road in the vicinity of the motel. **12 OR**

THE BARON INNERDALE

Tucked away in the military area at the northern end of the island (and therefore out of bounds, although pictures can be found online) stands a touching memorial to the unfortunate crew and passengers of the **Baron Innerdale** (or "Inverdale", as it's often incorrectly called, including on the monument itself). The *Innerdale* was travelling from Karachi to Liverpool in 1904 when she ran aground amid the Khuriya Muria islands. After three days, crew and passengers abandoned the ship in two lifeboats. One disappeared; the other (with 17 people aboard) made it to Masirah.

What happened next remains unclear. Probably a misunderstanding led to a fight, during which the stranded passengers were massacred – although there's no basis for the outlandish rumours that they were subsequently eaten by the islanders. Sultan Faisal responded by visiting the island, banishing the local ruling sheikh and having nine of the murderers executed. He also razed the village of Hilf and forbade the islanders to build permanent houses for 100 years – a ban that wasn't lifted until 1970.

Masirah island

Oman's largest island, remote **MASIRAH** remains largely off the tourist radar. Development here is muted, infrastructure basic and the whole place still sees more turtles than tourists, offering plenty of unspoiled coastline and beaches to explore for adventurous and well-equipped travellers with time (and a 4WD) on their hands. The major attraction of a visit here is the chance to go **turtle-watching** (see page 196), while the island's somewhat end-of-the-world ambience may also appeal to idle beachcombers and birdwatchers. If you've got camping gear and a 4WD, the island's pristine beaches offer numerous opportunities to sleep out under the stars.

Not that Masirah is entirely untouched. The northern tip of the island has already been swallowed up by industrial and military installations, while ambitious plans for the construction of a **causeway** linking Masirah with the mainland (currently being drawn up by an Omani-Korean team, though more details are yet to be announced) are likely to massively accelerate the pace of change, assuming it actually ever gets built. For the time being, however, Masirah remains a pleasantly sleepy sort of place, bordering on comatose.

Around the island

The ferry from the mainland deposits you at the small town of **Hilf** near the island's northern tip, home to a trio of petrol stations, a couple of ATMs and a pharmacy, plus a modest selection of shops in the town's small centre; there are no facilities elsewhere. Masirah is small enough to explore in a day but – at 64km long and 36km wide – big enough to get lost in, if that's what you want, with plenty of off-road tracks and coastal nooks and crannies in which to picnic or set up a tent. Much of the coastline is fringed with wide, sandy, windswept beaches, while inland rises a ribbon of low, rough-edged hills. A tarmac road circles the entire island, though to reach the island's most scenic beaches you'll need 4WD. Assuming you have your own tent and 4WD, there are superb, and still largely unexplored, **beach camping** possibilities all along the coast, particularly around the southern tip of the island.

Wild camping apart, Masirah's major attraction is its wildlife. In addition to the island's turtles, 328 species of **bird** have been recorded here, more than anywhere else in Oman, ranging from flamingos to plovers and parakeets. The island is also known for its remarkable **seashells** and other marine relics, including molluscs, gastropods, bivalves, cowries and sponges, a result of the cold currents which flow along the coast during the *khareef* (see page 202).

5

TURTLES OF MASIRAH

Masirah is best known for its **turtles**. Four of the five main species of marine turtle nest here (while the fifth species, the leatherback, can occasionally be seen feeding in the waters offshore). Masirah is believed to host the world's largest population of **loggerhead** turtles, while hundreds of green, hawksbill and olive ridley can also be found. Satellite tracking studies have shown that Masirah's loggerheads "commute" around the edge of the Arabian peninsula between the Red Sea and the Arabian Gulf, only rarely going further afield, nesting an average of four to five times a year, adding up to a staggering total of 15,000–30,000 egg-layings annually. Note that turtles nest only on the **east and far southwestern coasts** of the island; loggerheads favour the northeastern coast, while other species can be seen further south.

PRACTICALITIES

There are currently no official guided **turtle watches**, which means that you'll have to make your arrangements and ask locally about the best places to turtle-spot. Your best bet might be to head to the nesting site on the beach by the *Masirah Island Resort*, 10km from Hilf.

ARRIVAL AND DEPARTURE   MASIRAH ISLAND

To reach Masirah, you'll first have to make it to the harbour at **Shana** – a very modest scatter of official buildings with a long jetty leading out to the departure point for car-ferries to **Hilf**. If you get stuck on the mainland, there's extremely basic accommodation at the *Shana Port Hotel* (☎ 9136 4014; 12 OR), just opposite the petrol station 500m south of the jetty; and slightly better rooms at *Mahout Hotel Apartments* (☎ 9948 5485, ⓦ mahouthotels.com; 15 OR) in Muhut (also spelt Mahout or Muhoot), 60km from Shana back along the road to Muscat. Driving directly down to Masirah from Muscat is a bit of a slog – a good four or five hours, first along the dual carriageways of Highway 15 and the Sharqiya Expressway, then along the single carriageways of Highways 27 and 32. It's a lot nicer to approach from Sur (3hr 30min) along the coast road through Al Ashkharah. Unless you're well-prepared for long queues and general chaos at the ferry terminal, try to avoid travelling to Masirah on weekends and public holidays.

By slow ferry No booking is required for the slow ferries (1hr 30min–2hr; 10 OR per car; no charge for foot passengers), which leave when full – roughly every 1–2hr until about 6pm, although it's best to be at the jetty by 4pm, just in case. The service occasionally stops running in rough weather. The open-deck ferries are decidedly lacking in frills: there's limited seating on wooden benches around the bridge, but otherwise no facilities on board; it's more comfortable to do what the locals do and just sit in your car.

By catamaran You can book ahead for the much nicer catamarans (1hr; saloon car 8 OR; 4WD 10 OR; per person 3 OR) through the National Ferry Office in Muscat or in Shana (☎ 2521 6161, ⓦ nfc.om). Currently, these depart Sun at 9am, noon & 3pm from Shana and 9am, noon, 3pm & 5pm from Hilf; Mon noon & 5pm from Shana and 9am, 3pm & 5pm from Hilf; Tues 9am & 3pm from Shana and noon & 5pm from Hilf; Wed–Sat at 9am, noon, 3pm and 5pm from both Shana and Hilf. Check the website for the current schedule.

ACCOMMODATION

Danat al Khaleej ☎ 2550 4533, ⓦ danat-hotel.com. A pleasant place on the seafront road about 1km south of the harbour, with bright, medium-sized tiled rooms and villas, more of which are still in the works. There's an in-house multi-cuisine restaurant too – useful, since it's too far to walk into town. Doubles 30 OR, villas 50 OR

Masirah Beach Camp West coast of the island, 34km south of Hilf, signed about 1.5km along a sandy track off the road ☎ 9632 3524, ⓦ kiteboarding-oman. com. In a wonderfully remote corner of the island facing a pretty turquoise lagoon, this charming beach camp has basic, colourful huts by the water as well as a few a/c suites for a bit more comfort. Within easy reach of some of the island's best beaches, it functions as a base for kitesurfers, particularly during the *khareef* winds of

May–Sept. Breakfast costs an extra 3 OR. Huts 18 OR, suites 30 OR

Masirah Island Resort Well-signed on the east side of the island about 10km from Hilf ☎ 2550 4274, ⓦ masiraislandresort.com. This upmarket resort adds a welcome splash of luxury to Masirah's accommodation options. The building sits on the beach, which is wide but rather stony – considerable numbers of turtles nest right in front of the hotel from May to Sept (although there are no guided turtle watches). There are twenty-two rooms, all sea-facing with balcony, plus three attractive two-bedroom chalets with kitchen, sitting room and private entrance. Facilities include a big pool, gym and jacuzzi, plus licensed restaurant and bar, and staff can arrange diving, snorkelling, jet-skiing and fishing trips. Interesting displays

5

in the lobby cover the history and wildlife of the island. Doubles 65 OR, chalets 154 OR

Serabis Hotel On the seafront road about 1km south of the harbour and souk ☎ 9944 6680. Recently renovated hotel in a convenient location at the heart of Hilf, with a few dozen bland but well-kept doubles and triples as well as a few big family suites that sleep seven (65 OR). All are modern and spacious, albeit rather lacking in furniture, while most rooms have nice views up the corniche. There's a decent restaurant downstairs, and plenty of cafés within easy reach. 25 OR

EATING

The only upmarket (and licensed) restaurant in Masirah is at the *Masirah Island Resort*, which is also home to the only licensed bar on the island.

Turkish Restaurant One street back from the coast road, about 500m north of the ferry terminal ☎ 9219 8735. The best of the few simple cafés scattered around Hilf, this popular little spot has outdoor seating and serves up a well-prepared selection of grills, kebabs, shwarma and some meze (mains around 2 OR). Daily 8.30am–midnight.

Al Wusta

Beyond Sharqiya lies the province of **Al Wusta** (literally, "The Central Region"), a great expanse of gravel desert known as the **Jiddat al Harasis**, which stretches southwest all the way to Dhofar. The area is one of Oman's main oil-producing regions, but few tourists have made it here – unless tackling the long drive across the desert to Salalah – and even fewer stop. The recent extension of the scenic coastal highway in Dhofar has opened up an attractive alternative route, one that spans Al Wusta's seaward borders and carries on south all the way to Salalah. This option is best tackled over several days in combination with wild camping along its vast and lonely beaches – a classic slice of wild Oman at its most unspoiled.

Al Wusta Wildlife Reserve

Daily 7am–noon & 3–6pm • Morning or afternoon tours, led by members of the local Harasis tribe (who have guarded the reserve since its foundation) can be arranged on-site for about 20 OR • ☎ 9926 1893 • Coming from Muscat along Highway 31, the turn-off to the sanctuary is at Haima – it's about an hour's drive from here to the site; alternatively, it's about a 1hr 15min drive west from Duqm

The **Al Wusta Wildlife Reserve** (formerly known as the Arabian Oryx Reserve) is one of the most important wildlife conservation sites in Oman, though with a somewhat chequered past. The sanctuary was founded in 1982, becoming the first place in the Arabian peninsula to reintroduce free-ranging **oryx** herds into the wild following their virtual extinction during the 1970s (see page 250). The reserve's early years were an unquestioned success: by 1994 the resident oryx population had risen to 450 and the sanctuary was added to the UNESCO World Heritage Site list. Unfortunately, the increasing oryx population also attracted less welcome human attention. Over the following decade, the vast and vulnerable sanctuary was systematically decimated by local poachers and the resident oryx population fell to 65 – including just four breeding pairs. Faced with this disaster in 2007, the government announced its plans to reduce the size of the sanctuary by ninety percent in order to be able to guard it effectively. Shortly afterwards, it also acquired the dubious distinction of becoming the first place ever to be struck off the UNESCO World Heritage Site list.

Over the last decade or so the reserve has kept a low profile, consisting of little more than a fenced enclosure covering an area of just four square kilometres. Fortunately, conservation efforts of late have proven successful – as of December 2017 the oryx population had risen to 742, and, coincidental with sinking oil prices, plans were announced to re-open the reserve to large-scale tourism. The surrounding area is also home to the world's largest population of wild **Arabian gazelle** – which has more than

5

doubled over the last several years – as well as the only breeding sites in Arabia of the endangered houbara bustard. Other rare species such as the Nubian ibex, Arabian wolf, honey badger and caracal also live here, although they are very rarely seen.

Apart from **wild camping** outside the reserve, the nearest places to stay are in Haima or Duqm.

Duqm

An hour down the road past the Al Wusta Wildlife Reserve lies the port town of **DUQM** (also reachable via the road from Al Ashkharah which serves Masirah island). In 2007 it was earmarked for major development, with the aim of eventually transforming it into Oman's leading port and a major hub for exporting oil from the nearby inland fields. A decade later, although a certain amount of development has taken place, including a new airport opened in 2014, the ambitious plans for tourism development – as evidenced by a web of wide, paved roads with lonely signs announcing non-existent neighbourhoods – have yet to come to fruition. What can most aptly be called the town centre is the Shell station, around fifteen kilometres southwest of the port on Highway 32.

ARRIVAL AND DEPARTURE   DUQM

By car Duqm is a 5–6hr drive from Muscat along the single-carriage Highway 32, or a 6–7hr drive from Salalah, the faster but much duller route being via Haima along the inland Highway 31.

By bus Happy Line (happylineoman.com) operates one daily a/c bus between Muscat and Duqm, departing 6am from Duqm and 7am from Muscat (7hr 15min–8hr 15min).
By plane Duqm's domestic airport, about 20km south of the town centre, serves Oman Air flights to Muscat (6 weekly; 1hr 25min; ⊕ omanair.com).

ACCOMMODATION

City Hotel Duqm 500m east of the highway near the town centre ☎ 2521 4900, ⊕ cityhotelduqm.com. Centrally located but overpriced motel that nevertheless makes a comfortable rest stop on the long drive to or from Salalah, especially if you're not up for splurging on one of the beachside hotels. Rooms are sleek, modern, and more than adequate for a night or two, and there's a small gym and a good in-house restaurant. **48 OR**
Crowne Plaza 10km west of the town centre ☎ 2521 4444, ⊕ ihg.com/crowneplaza. As luxurious as it gets

in Duqm (just edging out the *Park Inn* that neighbours it to the south), this plush, well-managed resort offers a welcome splash of luxury, great for dusting off after desert camping along the coast. All 213 rooms overlook a gorgeous pool and the pristine beach just beyond. There are several licensed dining options, one of them doubling as a bar that features billiards, karaoke and occasional live music. **66 OR**

South of Duqm

The road **south of Duqm** has recently been tarmacked all the way south to Salalah, easily reached in one long day of driving. However, it's much more enjoyable to take two or three days meandering down the coast and camping on its remote beaches. Specific sights are thin on the ground, although the entire region remains largely untouched by the modern world, with traditional fishing villages, abundant birdlife and unspoiled coastal scenery: sandy beaches and salt flats with distinctive low cliffs of layered limestone, eroded by wind and sea into sinuous, wave-like shapes.

Ras Markaz beach

About 50km south of Duqm on the road to Ras Mas Madrakah, a sign points down a side-road to the left for **Ras Markaz**, one of the area's most picturesque beaches. It's about 14km to the water, most of the distance along paved road – all apart from a 4km stretch of dirt track that ends just before the smooth, blacktop descent to the beach.

5

Only a few dozen fishing boats are dotted along the northern end, each appearing helplessly tiny against the vast and beautiful backdrop that unfolds to the south – plenty of space for camping.

Ras Madrakah
A few kilometres south of the turn-off to Ras Markaz (about 60km from Duqm), another paved road leads east of the highway towards the peninsula of **Ras Madrakah**, its coastline marked with strangely shaped outcrops of blackish dolomite rock above a string of attractive white-sand beaches that offer more camping and beachcombing possibilities. At the small coastal settlement you'll arrive at a roundabout – turn right here to reach one of the area's longest beaches or head straight through (third exit from the roundabout) and then right onto the dirt track after two more kilometres in order to reach a set of rocky coves, many more of which can be explored further north of here.

Three Palm Tree Lagoon
Continuing down the coast, now along Highway 41, the track runs inland through barren desert, out of sight of the sea, skirting the northern edge of **Three Palm Tree Lagoon**, one of the various sea inlets which score the coast, attracting colourful flocks of pink flamingoes and other aquatic birdlife.

Sawqirah and beyond
There's virtually no sign of human habitation along this stretch of road until you reach the tiny village of **Al Lakbi**, some 250km from Duqm. Just south of town, the highway turns steeply up the escarpment to the right while another road continues south for a few more kilometres to the modest town of **SAWQIRAH**. Little more than a small cluster of houses and a toytown harbour facing a shallow lagoon dotted with fishing boats, Sawqirah will feel like Manhattan after what you've driven through. The coast immediately south of the village is particularly beautiful, with a high line of sea cliffs dropping sheer to the water below – although unfortunately you won't be able to see them unless you can hitch a ride on a local fishing boat. Another road heads up the valley to the east of Sawqirah before climbing the escarpment to join up with the main highway that marches on towards Ash Shuwaymiyah (see page 223) and Salalah – still another 420km away.

Dhofar

VAST DUNES OF THE RUB AL KHALI DESERT

Dhofar

Hugging the southern coast of the Arabian peninsula, the province of
Dhofar (in Arabic, Zufar) can seem a world away from the rest of Oman.
Separated from pretty much everywhere else in the country by a thousand
kilometres of stony desert, the region's history and identity have always been
largely separate from that of the rest of the Sultanate. Fabled in antiquity
as the source of the legendary frankincense trade, Dhofar boasted one of
Arabia's oldest and most cosmopolitan cultures – whose remains continues
to exercise historians and archeologists to this day. The region was only
brought under the control of the sultans of Muscat in the mid-nineteenth
century, while the Dhofaris continued to assert their independence until as
recently as the 1970s before finally being brought into the Omani fold.

Centrepiece of the region is the laidback city of **Salalah**, capital of Dhofar and by far
the biggest settlement for hundreds of kilometres in any direction. This is Oman with
a distinct, tropical twist: endless white-sand beaches line the coast, while coconut and
banana palms replace the ubiquitous date trees of the north and neat little pastel-painted
houses stand in for the fortified mudbrick mansions found elsewhere in the country.
The differences are especially striking during the annual **khareef** (June to August/early
September), when the rains of the southeast monsoon brush along the coast around
Salalah, turning the area to a fecund riot of misty green which has no equivalent
anywhere else in the Arabian peninsula. During this period Salalah is thronged with
visiting Omanis and other Gulf Arabs, who flock here to experience the unusual
pleasures of rain – an attraction that might well be considered overrated by most visitors
from outside the region – although the magical explosion of green, accompanied by the
bursting into life of seasonal waterfalls and streams, more than compensates.

Numerous attractions dot the hinterland of Salalah, enclosed by the arc of the scenic
Dhofar Mountains, dotted with wadis, gorges, sinkholes, blowholes and other geological
curiosities. Down at sea level, the **coast** is lined by huge, and largely deserted, strips of
pristine white-sand beach, picture-perfect **khors** and a string of quaint old fishing towns
as well as the ancient ruins of Sumahram and Zufar (now the Al Baleed Archeological
Park). The smooth new **coast road** takes in some of the region's most spectacular scenery,
winding west along the flanks of **Jebel al Qamar** to the Yemeni border and east beneath
the dramatic escarpment of Jebel Samhan. Deep in the region's **interior**, beyond the
mountains you enter the vast stony **desert** where you'll find the slight remains of the
legendary Ubar and, further on, the enormous dunes of the majestic Empty Quarter.

Brief history
The history of Dhofar is quite separate from that of the rest of the country, looking west
towards neighbouring Yemen rather than north towards the Omani heartlands. The region
as a whole rose to prominence, and economic prosperity, much earlier than most other parts

KHOR RORI

Highlights

❶ The khareef Arabia like you've never seen it: the countryside around Salalah turns a lush, misty green during the annual rains. See page 202

❷ Al Haffa Souk A magical traditional souk in old Salalah, piled high with frankincense and *bukhoor*. See page 207

❸ Wadi Darbat Scenic wadi, full of rock pools, roving camels and – during the khareef – a spectacular waterfall. See page 216

❹ Jebel Samhan Drive to the top of the Dhofar Mountains, with magnificent scenery, superlative views and a pair of vast sinkholes en route. See page 218

❺ Sumahram and Khor Rori Explore the ruins of ancient Sumahram, perched above the idyllic waters of Khor Rori. See pages 219 and 220

❻ The Hasik-Shuwaymiyah road Of the long, scenic coastal road linking the north with Salalah, this stretch – the last to be completed – is the most stunningly wild. See page 223

❼ The Mughsail to Fizayah road A dramatic highway that winds between frankincense-studded mountains and some gorgeously secluded beaches. See page 224

❽ Ubar and the Empty Quarter Take in the legendary "Atlantis of the Sands" before heading to the mighty dunes of the Empty Quarter. See page 227

HIGHLIGHTS ARE MARKED ON THE MAP ON PAGE 204

of Oman, thanks to the lucrative local **frankincense** trade. Frankincense was traded through the region from Neolithic times onwards, gradually developing into the so-called **Incense Route**, one of the ancient world's most extensive and important commercial networks. Frankincense was transported by sea from along the Dhofari coast and westwards up the Red Sea to Egypt, Africa and Europe, as well as eastwards across the Arabian Gulf and on to India. By land, caravans headed up via Shisr across the Empty Quarter to Bahrain and, westwards, into Yemen and then north to Medina, Petra and, ultimately, Egypt.

A string of **ports** developed along the coast of Dhofar to service the frankincense trade, including Sumahram (see page 219), followed by Mirbat, Sadah, Hasik and Zufar (the forerunner of modern Salalah, and the origin of the name "Dhofar"). The internal politics of the area remain obscure. The kingdom of Hadhramaut, in what is now southern Yemen, appears to have enjoyed some control over the region, while the influence of the Persian Parthians may also have been strong at various times. From around 300 AD onwards, the international frankincense trade went into a gradual decline, although Mirbat and Zufar, at least, continued as major commercial centres, exporting horses and spices in addition to frankincense and attracting many foreign visitors, including Marco Polo and Ibn Battuta.

The modern era

The region was only finally brought into the Omani fold in 1877, during the reign of **Sultan Turki bin Said** (ironically, just as his own capital in Muscat was coming under

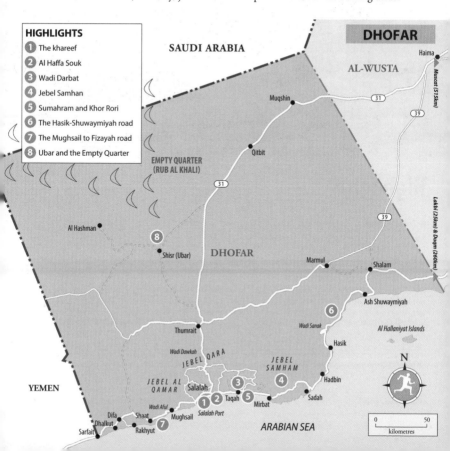

HIGHLIGHTS

1. The khareef
2. Al Haffa Souk
3. Wadi Darbat
4. Jebel Samhan
5. Sumahram and Khor Rori
6. The Hasik-Shuwaymiyah road
7. The Mughsail to Fizayah road
8. Ubar and the Empty Quarter

DHOFAR

SAUDI ARABIA

AL-WUSTA

Haima

Muscat (515km)

Muqshin

31

39

EMPTY QUARTER
(RUB AL KHALI)

Qitbit

31

39

Lakbi (25km) & Duqm (260km)

Al Hashman

8

Shisr (Ubar)

DHOFAR

Marmul

Shalam

Ash Shuwaymiyah

6

Thumrait

Wadi Sanak

Al Hallaniyat Islands

Wadi Dawkah

JEBEL QARA

Hasik

JEBEL AL QAMAR

JEBEL SAMHAM

N

YEMEN

Salalah

3

4

Hadbin

Wadi Aful

1 2

Taqah

5

Mirbat

Sadah

Difa

Shaat

Mughsail

Salalah Port

Dhalkut

7

Rakhyut

ARABIAN SEA

Sarfait

0   50
kilometres

increasing threat from the marauding Sharqiya tribes). Outside control was minimal to begin with, however, and in 1896 the local tribes rebelled, overran the sultan's fort in Salalah and murdered the garrison. Muscat eventually reasserted control, though its authority rarely ran much further than the immediate environs of Salalah itself, with the mountains remaining more or less autonomous under the patchwork of competing tribes.

Salalah played an increasingly important role in national affairs during the reign of **Sultan Said bin Taimur** (reigned 1932–70), who effectively moved the court from Muscat to Salalah, rarely leaving the city (or, indeed, his palace) during the final years of his rule. The province was wracked during the 1960s and early 1970s by the protracted **Dhofar Rebellion** (see page 242). In 1970, Sultan Said was overthrown in a bloodless coup in his Salalah palace and replaced by his son, Sultan Qaboos.

Despite having largely grown up in the region, Qaboos returned the court to Muscat. However, notwithstanding the loss of its resident sultan, Salalah shared the benefits of the Omani Renaissance (see page 244), while the comprehensive aid and infrastructure programmes which followed the end of the Dhofar Rebellion in 1976 also hastened economic development and helped quieten political unrest. Decades of swift growth followed, centred on the huge Raysut Industrial Area and Salalah Port, assisted by the opening of the local airport to international flights in 1975. Growth in tourism has lagged behind, though the airport's new and ultra-modern 300-million-rial terminal – finished in 2015 with the capacity to welcome up to two million passengers – hints of plenty more change afoot.

Salalah

Roughly midway along the Dhofar coast lies **SALALAH** ("The Shining One" in the local Jebali language), hemmed in between the spectacular crescent of the Dhofar Mountains on one side and the blue waters of the Arabian Sea on the other. Much of modern Salalah, Oman's second-largest city (although barely a quarter of the size of Muscat), is not much different from anywhere else in the country. Away from the functional city centre, however, it's still possible to sense something of old-time Salalah's alluringly languid, subtropical magic, with its lush banana plantations, lopsided coconut palms and superb white-sand beaches, more reminiscent of Zanzibar than Muscat – a feeling emphasized by the considerable quantities of African blood swilling around the local gene pool.

Salalah's exotic appeal is strongest around the old parts of town: in the aromatic alleyways of **Al Haffa Souk** and in the marvellous stretch of palm-fringed beach which spreads along the coast east from here to the remains of the ancient city of Zufar – now protected as the **Al Baleed Archeological Park** – and its adjacent **Museum of the Frankincense Land**. Inland, the modern city is less striking, but still boasts plenty of contemporary mercantile character, particularly along bustling **As Salam Street** and the more sedate **23 July Street**, just beyond which you'll find the engaging **Central Market**. Like Oman's other urban centres, it's all very spread out (plentiful taxis roam the streets, hooting for custom, should you become footsore), its suburbs continually fanning far to the west and northeast of the centre. Likewise, despite recent decades' influx of wealth, the city largely retains a muted, low-rise skyline – aside from the lavish coastal resorts, the flashiest part of town lies just west of the city centre, home to a Lulu Hypermarket and the giant new Salalah Gardens Mall.

From just about anywhere in Salalah you're well situated to explore the region as a whole, within a day-trip's reach of pretty much everywhere worth visiting.

The city centre

Bisecting the heart of modern Salalah, **As Salam Street** is the city's main shopping drag, and usually the liveliest place in town, especially after dark, with a long string of

6

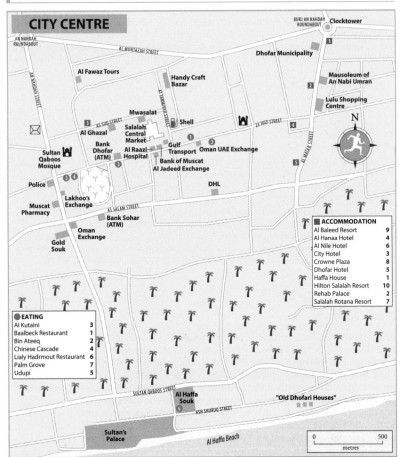

CITY CENTRE

Burj An Nahdah Roundabout

Clocktower `1`

An Nahdah Roundabout

AL MUNTAZAH STREET

Dhofar Municipality

Al Fawaz Tours

Mausoleum of An Nabi Umran `2`

Handy Craft Bazar

Lulu Shopping Centre

AN NAHDAH STREET

AL TAHRITAH STREET

Mwasalat

AS SUQ STREET `3`

Shell

N

Salalah Central Market

23 JULY STREET `4`

Al Ghazal

AL MAHA STREET

Bank Dhofar (ATM)

Al Raazi Hospital `3`

Gulf Transport `1`

Oman UAE Exchange `2`

`5`

Sultan Qaboos Mosque

Bank of Muscat

Al Jadeed Exchange

`9` `4`

Police

DHL

Lakhoo's Exchange

AS SALAM STREET

Muscat Pharmacy

Bank Sohar (ATM)

ACCOMMODATION

Al Baleed Resort	9
Al Hanaa Hotel	4
Al Nile Hotel	6
City Hotel	3
Crowne Plaza	8
Dhofar Hotel	5
Haffa House	1
Hilton Salalah Resort	10
Rehab Palace	2
Salalah Rotana Resort	7

Oman Exchange

Gold Souk

EATING

Al Kutaini	3
Baalbeck Restaurant	1
Bin Ateeq	2
Chinese Cascade	4
Lialy Hadrmout Restaurant	6
Palm Grove	7
Udupi	5

SULTAN QABOOS STREET

Al Haffa Souk

"Old Dhofari Houses"

`6`

ASH SHURUQ STREET

Sultan's Palace

Al Haffa Beach

0		500
	metres	

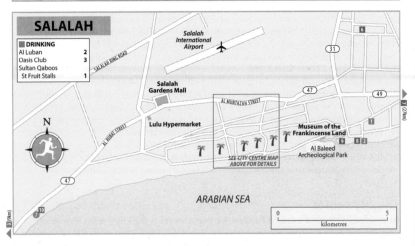

SALALAH

DRINKING

Al Luban	2
Oasis Club	3
Sultan Qaboos St Fruit Stalls	1

Salalah International Airport

SALALAH RING ROAD

`6`

31

47

49 → (27km)

Salalah Gardens Mall

AL MUNTAZAH STREET

Museum of the Frankincense Land

AL NIBAB STREET

Lulu Hypermarket

`1`

`9` `8` `2`

Al Baleed Archeological Park

SEE CITY CENTRE MAP ABOVE FOR DETAILS

N

ARABIAN SEA

47

3 (50m) `10` `7`

0		5
	kilometres	

closely packed shops selling anything and everything from gold and bespoke perfumes through to chintzy furniture and cheap shoes, dotted with dozens of low-rent cafés and a remarkable number of hairdressers (Salalah appears to boast more barbers per head of population than possibly any other city in the world).

The Gold Souk
An Nahdah St • Mon–Thurs & Sun 10am–1.30pm & 4.30–11pm

Just west of the junction with An Nahdah Street you'll find Salalah's modest **Gold Souk** (Souk al Dhahab), a single street of shops behind a small archway. There's actually probably more silver than gold on sale here – some shops stock interesting selections of chunky old Bedu antique silver jewellery, plus assorted *khanjars*, walking sticks and other touristy bric-a-brac.

23 July Street

The city centre's second main artery, **23 July Street** (commemorating the date of Sultan Qaboos's accession to the throne in 1970), is lined by large banks and many of the city's better restaurants, although relatively lacking in atmosphere compared to As Salam Street.

Sultan Qaboos Mosque
23 July St

23 July Street begins in style with the grandiose **Sultan Qaboos Mosque**, a huge, brownish-pink edifice that towers over the surrounding streets. The front elevation is particularly fine, with a pair of enormous minarets flanking the facade, and an unusual design with a small dome over the entrance framed by the much larger dome over the central prayer hall behind.

The Central Market and around
Tanmiyah St, 100m north of 23 July St • Daily 7am–9pm

A short walk east of the Sultan Qaboos Mosque, just north of the street, lies Salalah's appealing **Central Market**, a huddle of neat arcaded little buildings, dotted with cafés and shade trees and home to the city's main **meat, fish and fruit & vegetable markets** (unusually for Oman, these tend to stay open throughout the day and into the evening as well).

Mausoleum of An Nabi Umran
AL Matar St • Daily 6am–9pm • Free

Just north of the Lulu Shopping Centre on Al Matar Street is the **Mausoleum of An Nabi Umran**, home to the remains of a fourteenth-century Yemeni divine. Housed in a simple modern building, the tomb is remarkable chiefly for its extraordinary length, some 12m in total. The length of the tomb is perhaps explained by the fact that other members of An Nabi Umran's family were apparently buried in the same tomb, placed head to toe, rather than side by side.

Al Haffa Souk and around

Bounding the city centre to the south is a lush swathe of densely packed coconut and banana palm **plantations** – an incongruous touch of tropical abundance just beyond which the old town stretches along the coast. Just back from the broad white-sand beach lies Salalah's renowned old souk. Named after the old district in which it's situated, it's among the most interesting traditional markets in the entire country.

Al Haffa Souk
Sultan Qaboos St • Mon–Thurs & Sun 8am–noon & 4–8.30pm

Squeezed between the plantations and the beach is the marvellous **Al Haffa Souk** (also known as Al Husn Souk as it's set beside the palace), a pretty little area of small shops arranged around a neat grid of pedestrianized alleyways. The souk is particularly famous

6

FRANKINCENSE

Frankincense has been one of Oman's most famous and highly prized natural products since antiquity, and its heady aroma is never far away, wafting out of everything from homes, mosques and souks through to modern office blocks and hotel lobbies, providing the country with an instantly recognizable olfactory signature. The majority of the world's supply is now harvested in Somalia, while Yemen is also a major producer, although Omani frankincense – particularly that from Dhofar – is generally considered the finest.

Frankincense (in Arabic, *luban*) is a type of resin obtained from one of four trees of the Boswellia genus, particularly the **Boswellia sacra**, which thrives in the semi-arid mountainous regions around Salalah, often surviving in the most inhospitable conditions and sometimes appearing to grow straight out of solid rock. These distinctive trees are short and rugged, rarely exceeding 5m in height (and frequently shorter), often with a shrub-like cluster of branches rising straight from the ground, rather than a single trunk, and with a peeling, papery bark.

This treasured resin is a key element in traditional Omani life; a frankincense burner is traditionally passed from hand to hand after a meal in order to perfume clothes, hair and beards; it is also used as an ingredient in numerous perfumes, as well as in Omani *bukhoor*. Besides its aromatic properties, frankincense has many **practical uses**. Its smoke repels mosquitoes, while certain types of frankincense resin are also edible, and are widely used in traditional Arabian and Asian medicines to promote healthy digestion and skin. Even more cutting-edge medical uses are currently being investigated, including as a treatment for Crohn's disease, osteoarthritis and even cancer.

COLLECTION, GRADING AND BURNING

Frankincense is **collected** by making – or "tapping" – small incisions into the bark, causing the tree to secrete a resin, which is allowed to dry and harden into so-called "tears". Tapping and collection is a skilled but often arduous profession, now mostly done by expat Somalis. Trees start producing resin when they are around ten years old, after which they are tapped two or three times a year. Virtually all frankincense is taken from trees growing in the wild – the difficulty of cultivating the trees means that they're not generally farmed on a commercial scale, in the manner of, say, dates, adding to the resin's mystique.

There are many varieties of frankincense, sorted by hand and **graded** according to colour, purity and aroma. The whiter and purer the colour, the better the grade. More yellowish varieties are less highly valued, while at the bottom of the scale come the rather blackish Somali varieties. "Silver" (also known as Hojari) frankincense is generally considered the highest grade. Once graded, the resin is mixed with coals and burnt in a **frankincense burner**, ranging from simple clay pots to the colourfully painted examples favoured in Dhofar.

---

for its frankincense, *bukhoor* and *attar* (perfumes), of which various rare types can be found here: *shazri*, *sha'abi*, *najdi* and, perhaps finest of all, *hawjari* (or *hasiki*) – harvested from the wadis around Hasik. Many of the stalls selling aromatics are run by veiled female traders – you may find bargaining with someone when you can only see their eyes a little disconcerting.

The Sultan's Palace

Facing the beach at the southern end of Al Nahda Street stands the sprawling **Sultan's Palace** (Al Husn): a grandiose complex of marbled modern buildings protected by high walls – and a far cry from the old palace, in which Sultan Qaboos was kept by his father under virtual house arrest until the coup of 1970. The palace is now home to various government offices, and serves as the sultan's residence during his intermittent visits to the city.

Al Haffa beach and around

Stretching east from the souk is the old suburb for which it is named, bounded to the south by one of Salalah's prettiest stretches of **seafront**, a wide swathe of picture-perfect white-sand beach extending in either direction as far as the eye can see (although the strip flanking the Sultan's Palace is off limits). It's particularly lovely at dusk, as the sun dips into the ocean and locals come out to loll about or play football on the sand.

With the exception of a walled-off block of old homes just north of Ash Shuruq Street, beginning about 400 metres east of the souk, almost the entire old neighbourhood flanking the beach was razed in 2015 to make way for a new quasi-public space. For the time being, however, it remains a long, open patch of dirt, much appreciated by the footballers and cricketers that congregate here for early-evening pickup games. From the souk it's about a ten- to fifteen-minute stroll down the seafront promenade to reach its most alluring sight, a stand of windblown coconut palms sheltering some of the city's few remaining **old-style Dhofari houses**. Some are no more than minimalist cubist white boxes; others are more elaborate two-storey affairs with long arcaded balconies running the length of the upper storey.

Zufar

About 3km west of the souk lie the remains of the city of **Zufar** (alternatively spelt Zafar), the forerunner of the modern city of Salalah as well as the namesake of the modern province of Dhofar. Zufar was originally founded some three thousand years ago, but reached the height of its wealth and pomp from the twelfth to sixteenth centuries, when it served as a vital location in the trade routes linking Oman with the Gulf, East Africa, India and China, and whose fame attracted many visitors, including both Ibn Battuta and Marco Polo.

Al Baleed Archeological Site

Sultan Qaboos St, 4km east of Al Haffa Souk • Mon–Thurs & Sun 8am–7pm, Fri & Sat 4–7pm • Combined ticket for site and Museum of the Frankincense Land 2 OR; golf car tour of archeological site 500bz per person

The remains of Zufar are now protected as the **Al Baleed Archeological Site**. The ruins cover an impressively large area – a good kilometre from top to bottom – although most are extremely fragmentary, usually little more than the bases of walls and the occasional stump of pillar, and the greater part of the city still lies buried under the dunes, awaiting the trowels of future archeological expeditions. Helpful signboards dotted around the site offer interesting historical and archeological background.

The most rewarding area is at the **western end** of the site, where you'll find the considerable remains of the citadel, a great tumbling heap of masonry that was formerly the ruling sultan's palace, and the similarly impressive ruins of the Grand Mosque opposite, which once covered an area of over 1700 square metres, centred on a huge prayer hall supported by 144 columns – the largest of the fifty-odd places of worship that originally stood dotted around the city.

Museum of the Frankincense Land

Immediately east of the Al Baleed Archeological Site • Mon–Thurs & Sun 9am–9pm, Fri & Sat 4–9pm • Combined ticket with Al Baleed Archeological Site 2 OR

Right next to the entrance to the Al Baleed Archeological Site lies the somewhat mishmash **Museum of the Frankincense Land**, dedicated to the history of Salalah and Dhofar – although, despite the name, it offers only patchy coverage of the ancient frankincense trade itself. The first of the museum's two large rooms is the **Maritime Hall**, hosting interesting exhibits relating to Omani seafaring traditions and boat-building, including navigational instruments and beautifully crafted wooden models of various types of Omani boat – *boom, battil, ghanjah, sambuq* and so on.

Though somewhat randomly arranged, the adjacent **History Hall** is also worth a look, mostly for its muddle of prehistoric artefacts – pottery and metalwork finds from the local sites of Al Baleed next door, Sumaharam down the road and Shisr to the north. There's also a decent collection of medieval Arabic texts, a few of them replicas, while other exhibits – such as the spread on "Modern Oman" (complete with scale model of a motorway flyover and assorted suburban housing developments) – are little better than low-grade nationalistic propaganda.

ARRIVAL AND DEPARTURE   SALALAH

BY PLANE

There are 8–9 flights daily between Salalah and Muscat (1hr 40min), operated by Oman Air (7 daily; return fare 63 OR at the time of writing; ⓦomanair.com) and low-cost SalamAir (1–2 daily; return fare 42 OR; ⓦsalamair.com). Oman Air also runs daily flights to Dubai (1hr 45min). Book well in advance for flights during the *khareef*. Salalah's airport (☎2336 7461) is very central, just 1km north of the city centre along a sweeping avenue lined with coconut palms – a dramatically stage-managed entrance for your first sight of Dhofar. There are a number of car-rental agencies, plus money exchange and ATMs. There's also a pre-paid taxi kiosk (turn left as you exit the building).

BY CAR

There's a choice of routes to Salalah (see page 211). Car rental is most easily arranged at the airport, where you'll find branches of Europcar, Avis, Budget, Thrifty, Sixt and Mark; there's also a Budget office at the *Crowne Plaza* hotel and a Dollar office at the *Hilton*. A number of local firms have offices along 23 July St and around the bus station, usually undercutting rates offered by the international agencies, although vehicles may be older and less reliable. It's a good idea to book ahead during the *khareef*.

BY BUS

The bus terminal for Mwasalat and other firms is right in the middle of the city, near the Central Market. Departure schedules are often bulked up during the *khareef*.

To Muscat The bus journey from Muscat to Salalah takes around 12hr. Buses are adequate but not exactly luxurious, and it's a fair old slog, although still significantly cheaper than the plane. Mwasalat (☎2329 2773, ⓦmwasalat.om), set at the northwest corner of the Central Market, runs 3 daily buses to Azaiba in Muscat (7am, 10am & 7pm; 7.5 OR). The Gulf Transport Company (GTC; ☎2329 3303) operates from just southeast of the Central Market, with 7–8 daily departures for Muscat (7am, 10am, 1pm, 5pm, 6pm, 7pm, 8pm & 9pm; no bus at 1pm on Fridays; 7 OR). Al Ghazal Transport (☎2329 1314), about 400m west of the Central Market along As Suq St, runs four daily buses to Muscat (6 OR). You may be able to hop on a Muscat–Salalah bus in Nizwa, though you'll need to ring the relevant operator to reserve a seat and guarantee pick-up in advance.

To Nizwa To reach Nizwa from Salalah, you should be able to arrange to catch a Muscat bus and be set down at Firq, about 5km south of Nizwa's old centre, where you'll find plenty of taxis and micros to take you into town – although you'll probably still have to pay the full fare to Muscat.

To Dubai The Gulf Transport Company (GTC; ☎2329 3303) operates one daily bus for Dubai (3pm; 15h; 10 OR).

GETTING AROUND

Like most cities in Oman, Salalah's sprawled layout and scarcity of public transport – relying on which will almost certainly incur lost hours of walking and waiting – makes hiring your own vehicle the best option by many miles.

By car By far the best way of getting around Salalah and its surrounds. Smooth, wide, surfaced roads link almost everything of interest, though outside of the city you'll

need to stay alert for wandering camels. There are plenty of places to rent a car in town (see page 210).

DIVING IN DHOFAR

There's some rewarding – and still relatively little-known – **diving in Dhofar**. The main attraction here is the splendid sea life, including huge rays, moray eels, parrotfish, turtles and even the occasional humpback whale, all attracted by the nutrient-rich waters close to the shore. There's also some good coral – Dhofar is one of the few places in the world where you find corals and kelp growing together due to the cold waters produced during the *khareef*.

The **dive season** runs from late September or early October through to the end of May, interrupted by the arrival of the *khareef*, during which the water becomes too rough for diving. It's possible to dive straight off the beach here – the best **dive sites** are around Mirbat – while there are also offshore sites around Mughsail and the Hallaniyat islands (see page 222).

The most trusted local **operators** are ABT Divers (☎9989 4031, ⓦabtdivers.com), based at the *Hilton* (see page 213), and Extra Divers (ⓦextradivers-worldwide.com), with one base at the *Crowne Plaza* (see page 213) and another up the coast at the *Marriott* (see page 221) in Mirbat. Both outfits charge about 40 OR for two dives, and also arrange **snorkelling** trips and **dolphin-watching** expeditions.

DRIVING TO SALALAH

You can drive to Salalah along one of Arabia's longest desert highways, or if you have two or three days to spare, you may consider the even longer but far more scenic drive along the newly opened coastal road, an attraction in its own right.

THE INLAND ROUTE

It's slightly over a thousand kilometres from Muscat to Salalah along the **inland** Highway 31, one of Arabia's epic road-trips, although notable more for its sheer length (and the stamina involved in driving it) than for any scenic appeal. This is Oman as its emptiest and bleakest, although the views are not of romantic dunes but of an endless expanse of largely flat and stony **desert**.

Driving nonstop at the 120km/h speed limit you could theoretically do the trip in under nine hours, though a minimum of twelve is more realistic, and unless you're going to be sharing the driving you'd be well advised to break the journey overnight somewhere en route. The challenges of the drive shouldn't be underestimated. The sheer monotony of the road provides a certain kind of mental water torture, and the endless unchanging kilometres can easily lull one into a sense of hypnotic boredom and inattention in which accidents can occur, compounded by the sense of ant-like slowness you'll feel when traversing the desert, even when travelling at velocities well in excess of 100km/h.

There are a few **places to stay** en route, spaced at strategic intervals along the highway; the following are listed in the order you reach them travelling towards Salalah. All provide simple lodgings with unlicensed in-house restaurants, but not a great deal else.

Bader Al Salam Resthouse Adam, 205km south of Muscat, 815 north of Salalah ☎ 2543 5007. **10 OR**

Al Ghaba Resthouse Al Ghabah, 330km south of Muscat, 690km north of Salalah ☎ 9935 8639. **15 OR**

Arabian Oryx Hotel Haima, 525km south of Muscat, 495km north of Salalah ☎ 2343 6379, ⊜ arabianoryxhotel@gmail.com. **20 OR**

Al Ghaftain Resthouse Al Ghaftain, 625km south of Muscat, 395km north of Salalah ☎ 9903 6836, ⊜ sukumaralghaftain@gmail.com. **20 OR**

Qitbit Resthouse Qitbit, 750km south of Muscat, 270km north of Salalah ☎ 9853 9424. **20 OR**

Thumrait Tourist Hotel 940km south of Muscat, 80km north of Salalah ☎ 2327 9373. See page 227. **15 OR**

THE COASTAL ROUTE

A destination in itself, the new **coastal route** offers an exciting alternative to the long inland slog, comprising a far more memorable way of getting from the rest of Oman to Dhofar. Though easily extended to include points further up the coast and around the headland at Ras al Hadd, a quicker route from Muscat hits the coast at Al Ashkharah via Highway 35. From here, it's about 1050km to Salalah, with scenery alternating from barren nothingness to mountainous dunes, endless beaches and colourful lagoons. Highlights along the route include visiting Masirah island (see page 195), camping along the beaches of Ras Markaz or Ras Madrakah (see page 199), and traversing the spectacular, newly-blasted road from Ash Shuwaymiyah to Hasik (see page 223) – winding up and over the rugged escarpment of Jebel Samhan and hugging both sheer cliffs and virgin beach.

The journey is easily doable and very much worthwhile in a saloon car, though a 4WD will allow you to reach and camp at the best of the beaches, lagoons and wadis – most notably Wadi Ash Shuwaymiyah, the route's most dramatic canyon.

Much of the route's appeal lies in its pristine **camping** possibilities. Still, as with the inland route, there are some **accommodation** options along the coast – with a long spell of absence between Duqm and Ash Shuwaymiyah. The following are in north to south order, travelling from Al Ashkharah to Salalah. Most offer little more than the basics, though there is a smattering of midrange and upscale options in Duqm (see page 198) and Masirah (see page 195).

Al Ashkhara Hotel Al Ashkharah, 1050km north of Salalah ☎ 2543 5007. See page 184. **12 OR**

Mahout Hotel Apartments Muhut, 200km south of Al Ashkharah, 850km north of Salalah ☎ 9948 5485. See page 196. **15 OR**

City Hotel Duqm Duqm, 385km south of Al Ashkharah, 665km north of Salalah ☎ 2521 4900. See page 198. **48 OR**

Al Thalia Home Ash Shuwaymiyah, 775km south of Al Ashkharah, 275km north of Salalah ☎ 9914 8630. See page 223. **25 OR**

6

Taxis and microbuses These congregate in front of the HSBC on As Salam Street. The short hop from the centre to Al Haffa Souk will cost around 500bz in a microbus and 5 OR in a taxi. Microbuses to outlying towns are cheap (1 OR to Taqah; 2 OR to Mirbat), but infrequent, and often entail a long walk to reach the centre.

TOURS

Most tour operators offer a fairly standard range of half-day city tours, plus half- or full-day tours either west or east of the city, as well as desert tours to Shisr (see page 227), with perhaps an overnight stay in the Empty Quarter beyond.

Al Fawaz Tours City centre; 400m north of Sultan Qaboos Mosque ☎ 2329 4324, ☻ alfawaztours.com. Extremely clued-up and helpful operator with the widest range of tours on offer and some of the most competitive rates: city tours (26 OR per person), trips to the spectacular beach at Fizayah (32 OR), dolphin watching (32 OR), and overnighting at their own desert camp near Al Hashman in the Empty Quarter, taking in Ubar along the way (57 OR).
Around the Ocean 23km east of centre at Al Juweira Boutique Hotel ☎ 9933 4207, ☻ aroundtheocean.om.

With its main hub in the Hawana Salalah Marina, offering private speedboat charters, dolphin tours and dhow cruises (45 OR per person). There's a smaller branch closer to the centre at *Al Baleed Resort*.
Sumahram Falcon Crowne Plaza and Hilton hotels ☎ 9973 6226, ☻ facebook.com/sumahramfalcontours. One of the largest and longest-established tour operators in town, which runs the usual range of city tours, plus watersports, fishing and dolphin watching (25 OR per person).

ACCOMMODATION

Salalah boasts a good selection of budget hotels, most of them handily located right in the city centre. Mid-range options are thinner on the ground, while at the top end of the scale there are plenty on offer, spread along the beach at opposite ends of town; there's also the smart *Marriott* (see page 221) at Mirbat. Note that prices at most places more or less double (or more) during the khareef (June–Aug), when the town gets overrun with visitors – advance booking is strongly recommended.

CITY CENTRE

Al Hanaa Hotel 23 July St ☎ 2329 0274, ☻ alhanaa@omantel.net.om; map p.206. One of the nicest of Salalah's cheapies, with cosy, good-value rooms in a central location. It's also superb value during the *khareef*, when the already cut-price room rates rise by just 5 OR – not surprisingly, advance booking during this period is more or less essential. Breakfast included. **17 OR**
City Hotel As Suq St ☎ 2329 5252, ☻ cityhotelsalalah. com; map p.206. In a central location across from the Sultan Qaboos Mosque, the Central Market, the bus station and many of the town's best restaurants. It doesn't have much character, but rooms are spacious, modern and well furnished. Excellent value at the price. **15 OR**
Dhofar Hotel Al Matar St ☎ 2329 2300 or ☎ 2329 4358; map p.206. Old-fashioned Arabian-style one-star, with a chintzy foyer and plenty of rather solemn-looking grey marble. Rooms are spacious and comfortable – albeit a tad dated – and those on the higher floors have nice views over town. **12 OR**
Haffa House Al Matar St ☎ 2329 5444, ☻ shanfarihotels.com; map p.206. Recently renovated, good-value four-star with fancy marbled corridors, pretty Moroccan-style tilework and a pool. Rooms all have nice Arabian touches and there are good views from higher floors and a pleasant coffee shop downstairs. **30 OR**
Rehab Palace Al Matar St ☎ 9393 3862; map p.206. A relatively new six-storey hotel in a convenient position just opposite the mausoleum of An Nabi Umran and the

Lulu Shopping Centre, with clean, furnished apartments – all complete with kitchens – and an affordable café and restaurant downstairs. During the *khareef*, however, rates rise astronomically. **16 OR**

CITY OUTSKIRTS

★**Al Baleed Resort** Around 4.5km east of the centre ☎ 2322 8222, ☻ salalah.anantara.com; map p.206. Opened in 2016, this is the newest and most luxurious addition to Salalah's row of beach resorts, cradled conveniently between the beach and the lagoon, just east of the ancient ruins of Al Baleed. Its bright, modern design is complemented with striking, traditional-style facades, from the carved wooden doors and gorgeous rope-work reception to the Bedouin-style cushions that line the villas' privately enclosed pools. With its pool bar, pool-side four-poster beds and trio of fine restaurants, the communal areas are just as lovely as the rooms. A free shuttle bus links guests to the Al Baleed site and Al Haffa Souk. Doubles **195 OR**, villas **260 OR**
Al Nile Hotel About 1km east of Highway 31; 7km northeast of the centre ☎ 2322 5804, ☻ alnilehotelsalalah@gmail.com; map p.206. Though the location isn't central, *Al Nile* offers better value than the similarly-priced cheapies downtown, with tired but clean and spacious rooms (with loud air-coolers rather than a/c) that all come with kitchenettes and are set above the busy Mashour Shopping Centre. Staff are friendly, there's plenty

of parking out front and there are lots of restaurants within a block of the hotel. **12 OR**

Crowne Plaza Around 5km east of the centre ☎ 2323 8000, ⓦ crowneplaza.com/salalah; map p.206. This rather old-fashioned five-star resort looks a bit frumpy and uninspiring but compensates with its beautiful setting and very civilized price tag. Rooms (sea view or land view) and villas have been nicely refurbished, and there are spacious gardens to crash out in, plenty of pool space and a wide swathe of idyllic white-sand beach. Facilities include the run-of-the-mill *Darbat* and the more attractive seafront restaurant, *Dolphin Beach*, as well as a pool bar, a pair of nightlife venues – the *Al Khalif Bar* and *Al Luban* nightclub (see page 214) – and a nine-hole golf course. Tours and watersports (parascending, sailing and kitesurfing) can be arranged through the in-house Sumahram Falcon (see page 212), while there's also a booking office for the Mirbat-based *Extra Divers* (see page 210). Reasonable value during the *khareef*. Doubles **100 OR**, villas **165 OR**

Hilton Salalah Resort On the coast 5km west of the city centre ☎ 2313 3333, ⓦ salalah.hilton.com; map p.206.

Slightly smarter and more expensive than the *Crowne Plaza*, this hotel has a similar resort-like ambience (and some equally uninspiring architecture). The grounds, pool and beach are also pleasant enough, though the view of the massed cranes over the bay at Salalah Port doesn't inspire. Rooms are attractive and extremely spacious, and the hotel also boasts Salalah's best collection of restaurants, plus a sports bar and nightclub with live music. In-house amenities include the ABT dive centre (see page 210), while tours can be arranged through Sumahram Falcon (see page 212). **85 OR**

Salalah Rotana Resort About 23km east of the centre ☎ 2327 5700, ⓦ rotana.com; map p.206. Set on an artificial island enclosed within the over-developed Hawana Salalah Marina, this is the best of the area's cluster of plush resorts, though it's often overrun by charter tours from Northern and Eastern Europe. Its several hundred rooms and suites are bright and modern with colourful arabesque accents, while on site are two excellent restaurants (in addition to the neighbouring resorts' dining options), a beach bar facing a fine stretch of white sand, and – at the time of research – a water park in the works. **110 OR**

EATING

Salalah musters a reasonable spread of places to eat, with most of the best places clustered along 23 July Street, although if you want to wine and dine in style you'll have to head out to one of the five-star resorts on the edge of the city.

CITY CENTRE

Al Kutaini 23 July St ☎ 2328 9229; map p.206. Busy, no-frills Pakistani restaurant featuring a simple menu of chicken and mutton curries and biryanis (1.30–1.70 OR), plus assorted Indianized Chinese offerings. It's good, simple, nourishing fare at rock-bottom prices. Daily 7.30am–1am.

★ **Baalbeck Restaurant** 23 July St ☎ 2329 8834; map p.206. Friendly staff, a convivial atmosphere and a well-prepared selection of meze, grills and shwarmas (sandwich/plate 0.4/1.8–2 OR) pull in a regular crowd of locals and tourists to this deservedly popular Lebanese-style restaurant. Arrive early if you want to grab one of the handful of coveted outside tables – although the pleasantly rustic interior is just as nice. Daily 8am–1am.

Bin Ateeq 23 July St ☎ 2329 2384; map p.206. Identikit branch of nationwide chain, with the usual Omani-style food served up in stuffy and windowless little private dining rooms, with seating on the floor. Mildly interesting if you haven't tried it before, although the food is nothing to get excited about. Most mains 1–2 OR. Daily noon–midnight.

Chinese Cascade 23 July St ☎ 2328 9844; map p.206. The best Chinese restaurant in town, turning out a reliable range of moderately priced favourites such as Szechuan chicken (1.8 OR) and beef Manchurian (1.7 OR), as well as a few Thai and Malay specialties. Daily 11.30am–3.30pm & 6.30pm–midnight.

Udupi 23 July St, opposite Sultan Qaboos Mosque ☎ 2329 4055; map p.206. Cheerful Indian vegetarian

restaurant drawing a steady subcontinental clientele, with plenty of *dosa* (masala dosa 0.5 OR) and paneer dishes in every conceivable style, as well as hearty and generously-portioned North Indian mains (1.5–1.8 OR). Free delivery. Daily 7am–3pm & 5–11.15pm.

AL HAFFA SOUK AND THE OUTSKIRTS

★ **Lialy Hadrmout Restaurant** Al Husn Souk; map p.206. Entertaining Yemeni-style outdoor restaurant in a lovely location bang in the heart of the souk. It's a positive feast for the senses, with clouds of fragrant smoke, the noise of bread being endlessly pummelled and slapped into shape, and a colourful local crowd sporting some of the city's most rakish turbans. There's no menu: take your pick from chicken rice or beef rice (2.5 OR) or beef or chicken kebabs (200bz/skewer), featuring pieces of chewy meat interspersed with lumps of charcoaled fat (much tastier than it might sound), served with hummus and huge round doughy breads. Daily 7am–1am.

Palm Grove Hilton Hotel, 5km west of the city centre ☎ 2321 1234; map p.206. Rustic open-air restaurant with a solid mix of Indian, Arabian and pan-Asian cuisine, though the house speciality is fresh seafood (catch of the day 7.5 OR). Considering the good service, the lengthy drinks menu and the lovely beach-side setting, it's almost reasonably priced. If you'd prefer a prime cut of beef, head to the same hotel's restaurant, *Sheba's Steakhouse* (daily 6.30–10.30pm). Daily noon–10.30pm.

DRINKING

Apart from *Oasis Club*, most of the licensed venues are within the upmarket hotels, among them *Whispers Bar* at the *Hilton Salalah* and *Al Mina Bar* at *Al Baleed Resort*. For an alfresco coffee, tea or juice local-style, the place to head is the Central Market, dotted with dozens of tiny cafés and busy at most times of the day or night with locals shooting the breeze.

Al Luban Inside the Crowne Plaza Hotel ☎ 2323 8037, ⓦ crowneplaza.com/salalah; map p.206. Fancy lounge club set around a big stage, featuring occasional live bands and belly dancers. Thursday is DJ night. Within the same hotel you'll also find the more laid-back *Al Khareef* sports pub (Sat–Thurs noon–3pm & 6pm–2.30am, Fri 2pm–2.30am), which enjoys a superb view of the sea. Mon–Thurs, Sat & Sun 9.30pm–3am, Fri 9.30pm–2am.
Oasis Club About 15km west of the city centre; map p.206. Very well-kept local secret tucked away inside Salalah Port, attracting a lively crowd of sailors and local expats thanks to its affordable beer, good international food (from biryanis to boerwors for around 4 OR) and ten-

pin bowling. Come during the day to make use of their nice pool (3 OR), overlooking a pretty white-sand beach (off-limits). Sat–Thurs 11am–3am, Fri noon–3am.
Sultan Qaboos St Fruit Stalls Sultan Qaboos St; map p.206. For a drink with a difference, head out to one of the eye-catching lines of palm-thatched roadside fruit stalls which flank Sultan Qaboos Street just east of the *Crowne Plaza* turn-off. Mounds of fresh coconuts from the city's palm plantations sit piled up along the roadside here (along with plenty of bananas and papaya too), offering an authentically tropical thirst-quencher for under half a rial. Daily 8am–noon & 4–9pm.

DIRECTORY

Banks and money There are ATMs all over town, particularly along 23 July St; here you can also find a handful of foreign currency exchange offices, while there are a few more along An Nahdah St, among them Lakhoo's Exchange (Mon–Thurs, Sat & Sun 8.30am–1pm & 4–8.30pm, Fri 9–11.30am & 4–8.30pm).

Health There's a cluster of pharmacies on An Nahdah St between 23 July and As Salam streets, including the Muscat Pharmacy (24hr).
Post and couriers The main post office (Mon–Thurs & Sun 8am–7pm) is on a side road west of An Nahdah St; service can be painfully slow. There's a DHL on As Salam St.

East of Salalah

Of the numerous attractions clustered in the countryside around Salalah, the majority are located to the **east of the city**. The construction of extensive new roads (plus generally helpful signs) has made many places – which formerly required 4WD and a large slice of local knowledge – independently accessible to anyone with a saloon rental car. Leading attractions include the remains of the ancient port of **Sumahram**, once

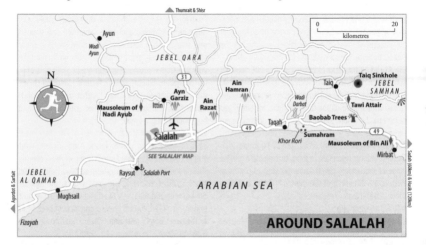

AROUND SALALAH

one of the key staging posts in the frankincense trade, overlooking the idyllic creek of **Khor Rori**. Close by lies **Wadi Darbat**, home to a spectacular waterfall during the *khareef*, and the even more dramatic uplands of the **Jebel Samhan**, whose sheer limestone walls tower above the coastal plain; the drive up to the top is easily combined with stops to see the cavernous sinkholes of **Tawi Attair** and **Taiq**. Further along lies the charming old town of **Mirbat**, while those with a sense of adventure and time to spare can follow the highway up the coast all the way to Duqm and beyond – particularly spectacular is the newly opened stretch of tarmac from **Hasik**, hugging the cliffs as it winds up and over the mountains to **Shuwaymiyah**, some 280km from Salalah.

All the main sights are fairly close to one another and can be visited in various permutations. A particularly rewarding **day-trip** can be made by combining the highlights of the area: Sumahram and Khor Rori with the road up Jebel Samhan via Wadi Darbat; or, alternatively, Sumahram and Khor Rori with Mirbat. With an early start you could just about squeeze all three into a longish day.

Ain Razat

23km from Salalah • Turn left off the coastal highway at the Al Mamurah roundabout and head north for 8km, then 1km down a signed side road on the right to reach a T-junction; turn left here and follow the road as it loops (one-way) around a small fenced-in ornamental garden (Thurs & Fri, or daily during the khareef)

Heading east out of Salalah, the coastal highway is fast dual carriageway as far as Mirbat, running through scrubby coastal deserts just out of sight of the sea. En route to Taqah you'll pass two of the dozens of freshwater **springs** (*ain* or *ayn*) strung out along the base of the Dhofar Mountains where they meet the coastal plains. Many have now been turned into local picnic spots, which tend to get crowded at weekends. The first you reach is **Ain Razat**. From the car park at the far end of the garden you can see a large cave in the hillside nearby, beneath which the waters of the spring collect in a small concrete pool. Turn right below the cave, from where there's a pleasant five- to ten-minute walk along a cobbled path beside the narrow watercourse. The waters here are crystal-clear and full of small fish, while the surrounding bushes play host to butterflies and small birds, including flocks of canary-yellow Rüppell's weavers, stripy-headed cinnamon-breasted buntings and distinctive white-spectacled bulbuls – which look as if they are wearing tiny black hoods with cut-out eyes.

Ain Hamran

6km along the coastal highway from Ain Razat, turn left at Al Hamran roundabout and follow the road for 5km as it descends into a wooded area, where you'll find a roundabout beside which you can park

In a fine setting at the foot of impressive black-stone cliffs, **Ain Hamran** is a peaceful spot, rather less developed than Ain Razat. The springs are in a small round walled-in pool from which a *falaj* emerges to feed the small coconut plantations below. From here, it's a pleasant stroll up towards the cliffs, through thickets of trees alive with the incessant twittering of tiny birds – green pigeons, laughing doves, bee-eaters, kingfishers and pipits – with larger birds of prey circling on the thermals overhead.

Taqah

Some 37km east of Salalah, a signed right-hand turn off the coastal highway leads to the sleepy coastal town of **TAQAH**, home to a small **fort**. Along the right-hand side of the road you'll pass the town's landscaped lagoon – a good place for spotting birdlife – and its strip of cultivated land, beyond which to the south stretches a fine wide-sand beach, dotted with boats and 4WDs.

Taqah Fort

Just off the main street; turn left at the fourth speed bump • Mon–Thurs, Sat & Sun 9am–4pm, Fri 8–11am • 500bz • ☎ 2325 8384

In the middle of town, Taqah's cute **fort** isn't especially impressive from the outside, but has been attractively restored within. The diminutive courtyard is centred on a fine old date palm, providing welcome shade, while a higgledy-piggledy jumble of stairs and terraces, equipped with old wooden handrails, leads off to the castle's various rooms. Those downstairs host some interesting exhibits on local life, while the *wali*'s suite upstairs has been prettily furnished with brightly coloured cushions, kitsch pictures and piles of Chinese bowls.

Around the fort

Opposite the entrance to the fort, note the impressive old **dhofari-style house** with finely carved wooden shutters – a style typical of the region. A couple of similar old houses can be found along the main street nearby. Immediately behind the fort, steps lead up to a second and much newer fortified structure, known simply as the **Burj**, or tower, sitting on a rock outcrop overlooking the town. Although the building is closed to the public, it's worth the climb up here for the fine views along the palm-fringed coast in front and the mountains behind.

Wadi Darbat

Some 7km beyond Taqah along the coastal highway you'll notice a dramatic cliff just to the left, which turns into a spectacular **waterfall** during the *khareef*, spouting cascades of water amid a tangle of lush greenery – one of Dhofar's most photographed attractions. This cliff marks the entrance to **Wadi Darbat** (also spelt Dhabat or Derbet), whose waters feed Khor Rori below. For the best view of the waterfall, take the small unsigned road on the left off the coastal highway about 100m before the signed turn-off to Tawi Attair. This leads after 1.5km to a parking space near the foot of the cliff-cum-waterfall, amid seasonal rock pools and with fine views of the tumbling waters above (or, in the dry season, of the pockmarked rocks of the cliff face – known as a "travertine curtain", a common geological formation in Dhofar – whose original sandstone has been dissolved by the force of the water into strange, wax-like shapes).

The top of the waterfall and beyond

A further 100m east along the coastal highway from the turn-off to the cliff, another turn-off on the left is marked by a cluster of signs pointing variously to Tawi Attair, Wadi Darbat and Taiq Cave; this is one of several roads that climb into the lofty uplands of the **Jebel Samhan**, as the section of the Dhofar Mountains east of Salalah is known.

The road begins by climbing steeply up into the hills, with sweeping views down to the coast and Khor Rori below. After 2.5km, head left at the turn-off signalled by a lone café, beyond which the road winds up the wadi for another 6km. After just 2.5km, you'll see a car park that marks the start of an enjoyable ten-minute walk off to the left to the **top of the waterfall**, through wonderful trees, alive with small birdlife, with probably a few wandering camels for company. Seasonal rock pools form up here during the *khareef*, although a sign warns of the dangers of bilharzia, should you be tempted to take a dip.

At the end of the road up the valley, past roaming herds of cows, camels and goats, is an even larger car park, with a café and restaurant on one side and the water's edge on the other, blocking further access up the valley. During the *khareef* the place is packed, with cars often parked well down the road, though there's water enough almost year-round for a boat ride deeper up the wadi (paddle boats 5 OR for 25min).

Tawi Attair

Signed about 19km north of the coastal highway just east of Taqah; after 17.5km you'll reach the town of Tawi Attair – turn left at the junction (after passing the Al Khareef Shopping Center on your right), following the sign to Jebel Samhan; the sinkhole is signed off to the right after about 1km

Most likely formed by the prehistoric collapse of the roof of an enormous subterranean cave, Tawi Attair is one of the world's deepest **sinkholes**, measuring some 210m from top to bottom – big enough to swallow a fifty-storey building. The name translates as "Well of Birds" on account of the many avian species which can usually be seen fluttering about in the sinkhole below, their calls magically echoed by the enclosing cliffs.

Steps lead down from the parking area to the litter-strewn viewing platform, although the view of the sinkhole is disappointingly limited. You'll get a much better (and cleaner) view if you head from the car park across the hillside to the right, aiming for the improvised tripod-cum-pylon structure that sits above the sinkhole, although even from here you still can't see the bottom of the chasm.

Taiq Sinkhole

About 12km north of Tawi Attair; after 3.5km along the Jebel Samhan road, turn left at the blue sign for Taiq Cave (also spelt Teyq or Teiq) and then follow this road for 8km before turning right at the blue-signed turn-off to the sinkhole (500km east)

Just beyond the thoroughly rustic settlement of **Taiq**, the plateau dramatically drops away into another vast **sinkhole** – most likely formed, as was nearby Tawi Attair, by the collapse of an enormous underground cave. According to estimates, this is the world's third-largest sinkhole, at around 1km long, 750m across and some 200m deep, with a total volume of ninety million cubic metres – a magnificent chasm in the mountains surrounded by sheer cliffs, riddled in places with holes like gruyère cheese, and also much easier to see than Tawi Attair due to the lack of surrounding vegetation.

Jebel Samhan

About 18km east of Tawi Attair along the Jebel Samhan road (15km past the turn-off for the Taiq Sinkhole)

It's worth following the **Jebel Samhan** road west to the top of the escarpment, the high, sheer cliffs of which tower over the coastal plains and the town of Mirbat far below. The scenery becomes increasingly barren near the top, as the last stands of

---

MAGNETIC POINT AND THE BAOBAB FOREST

Returning to the coast from the sinkholes of the plateau, it's worth considering the quieter, more easterly (though equally well-tarmacked) descent to the coast, which ends up near Mirbat. From the turn-off to the sinkholes in the town of Tawi Attair, head southeast for about 10km, where the road drops steeply towards the coast in a series of hairpin bends, hiding a pair of oddities along the way.

WADI HINNA

Just after the sixth hairpin bend, a dirt track leads off to the right of the road for a few hundred metres. Follow this to arrive at Wadi Hinna, home to a fine cluster of **baobab trees**, their enormous trunks scarred with age – an impressive botanical reminder of Dhofar's links with Africa.

MAGNETIC POINT

Another 2km down the road is one of Oman's weirdest curiosities, the baffling **Magnetic Point** (also known as Anti-Gravity Point). At one point along the track sloping down to the beach cars left in neutral will begin magically reversing themselves back up the hill. Local guides claim that this is the result of some mysterious magnetic phenomenon, although the more prosaic explanation is that it's probably just some kind of strange optical illusion – a local example of a so-called "Gravity Hill" (or "Magnetic Hill"), dozens of examples of which have been recorded worldwide.

JEBEL SAMHAN WILDLIFE

The Jebel Samhan uplands are one of the final strongholds of the Arabian **leopard** (*nimr*, a smaller subspecies of the African and Asian *pantherus pardus*). A few leopards still roam up here, caught on remote cameras in recent years and now collared and closely monitored by wildlife researchers. A number of other rare mammals also inhabit the area, including wolves, foxes, hyenas, gazelle and hyrax (a type of small rodent, like a fat, furry rat, which is – improbably enough – distantly related to the elephant), although these are similarly elusive without the services of an expert local guide.

stunted trees give way to bare uplands covered in rocks and hardy, ground-hugging vegetation until you reach the summit. There are a couple of parking places up here right next to the cliff-edge from which to enjoy the vertiginous views: the first near the large telecommunications station, and the second off on the left after a further 1.5km.

Sumahram

6km east of Taqah • Head south off the coastal highway about 500m east of the turn-off to Wadi Attair

Just east of Taqah are the absorbing remains of the old city of **Sumahram** (also spelt Sumhuram or Samahram), now protected as the **Sumahram Archeological Park**. Along with the nearby city of Zufar, this was formerly one of the major ports of Southern Arabia and an important conduit for the international frankincense trade network. Additionally, the recent discovery of pink and violet residue on amphorae shards found at the site suggest that the city also played an important role in the trade of purple pigment – another ancient luxury commodity. Founded as an outpost of the kingdom of Hadhramaut (in present-day Yemen), the city was first supposed to have been settled in first century AD, though further excavations have pushed the date as far back as the fourth century BC. The city prospered until the early fifth century before it was gradually abandoned, perhaps due to the formation of the sand bar across the mouth of Khor Rori, which closed the creek to shipping.

The site

Daily 8am–7pm • 2 OR

The **ruins of Sumahram** are far less extensive than those at Al Baleed, but have been much more thoroughly excavated and restored, while the lovely natural setting between coast and hills adds to the appeal. The ruins sit atop a small hill above the tranquil waters of Khor Rori: a neat rectangle of off-white buildings enclosed by impregnable **walls** made out of huge, roughly hewn slabs of limestone; the walls are more than 3m thick in places, and perhaps originally stood up to 10m high. Entrance to the city is via the remains of a small **gateway**, inside which you'll find two beautifully preserved **inscriptions** commemorating the foundation of the city, carved in the ancient South Arabic (or "Old Yemeni") *musnad* alphabet.

Inside, the town is divided into residential, commercial and religious areas, with the slight remains of a maze of small buildings packed densely together. These were originally at least two storeys tall (as the remains of stone stairways attest), although not much now survives of most beyond the bases of their ground-floor walls. The city's most impressive surviving structure is the **Temple of Sin** (the Mesopotamian moon god), built up against the northwest city wall – look out for the finely carved limestone basin in the ritual ablution room within. Nearby, the so-called **Monumental Building** is thought to have housed the city's main freshwater reservoir and well. At the rear of the complex stands the small **Sea Gate**, from which goods were transported down to boats on the water below.

By car Take the signed turning on the right off the main coastal highway 750m past the turning to Tawi Attair (and 5km beyond Taqah); follow this tarmac road for about 2km to reach the entrance to the site.

Information There are a couple of buildings devoted to providing information on the site. Just beside the car park is a sleek new information centre (daily 8am–6pm), with touch displays and a documentary running

on loop. There's a useful printed guide to Sumahram available here for 2 OR, while informative signs dotted around the site provide interesting historical and archeological background snippets. About 300m east of the car park is an archeological gallery (same hours), with a few glass-enclosed artefacts turned up at the site and a set of photos documenting the excavation process.

Khor Rori

2.5km past the Sumahram turn-off, take the graded track signposted off on the right

A couple of minutes' walk below the ruins of Sumahram lies the tranquil **Khor Rori**, the most attractive of the various *khors* that line the coastline around Salalah. A neat pair of symmetrical headlands flanks the mouth of the *khor*, which is separated from the sea by a low sand bank. As a result, the waters inside the creek (fed by Wadi Darbat) are freshwater, and full of fish, which in turn attract a fine selection of aquatic birds, while camels can usually be seen browsing the surrounding greenery. It's a wonderfully peaceful spot – so quiet that you can actually hear the splashes of fish in the water.

Mirbat

About 60km east of Salalah and 30km beyond the turn-off to Sumahram lies personable **MIRBAT**, one of Dhofar's most interesting smaller towns, and another in the chain of erstwhile frankincense ports that line the coast. Two miniature statues of prancing horses atop columns flank the entrance to the town – a whimsical memorial to its history as an important breeding centre for Arabian steeds. Just before the reaching the town the you'll pass one of the region's most important Islamic sites – the **Mausoleum of Bin Ali** – while on the northern outskirts stands Mirbat's small **fort**. South of here stretches the pretty **harbour** and the largely abandoned old quarter beyond.

Mausoleum of Bin Ali

Heading south towards Mirbat from the highway, turn right about 1km north of town and follow the road for 1km to reach the mausoleum

In the shelter of the scorched hills northwest of town stands the whitewashed **Mausoleum of Bin Ali**, topped by a pair of rustic onion domes. The pretty little structure is dedicated to Sheikh Mohammed Bin Ali al Alawi, a twelfth-century scholar and émigré from Hadhramaut (in Yemen). Inside, the saint's tomb lies under a green cloth in a darkened room heavy with incense. Though it's allowed to take a look inside, be aware that it remains a functional site of worship – before entering, women should don headscarves and shoes should be removed.

An extensive **cemetery** stretches away on the landward side of the mausoleum, dotted with thousands of headstones; male graves are marked with three headstones, female graves with two. Some of the gravestones are elaborately carved, with ornate Arabic inscriptions and other decorative flourishes; others are little more than simple, roughly hewn pieces of undecorated stone wedged upright in the ground. The oldest and finest headstones are clustered around the shrine itself, becoming progressively more modern the further down the road you go.

Mirbat Fort

Signed off to the right of the road into town • Mon–Thurs & Sun 9am–4pm & Fri 8–11am • 500bz

Mirbat's small, restored **fort** stands proudly above the waves on the northwestern outskirts of town. There's not much to see inside beyond a few rooms sparsely decorated with pots,

THE BATTLE OF MIRBAT

Mirbat Fort was the scene of perhaps the most important single conflict of the entire Dhofar Rebellion (see page 242), and what is also frequently claimed to be the finest moment in the history of the British SAS. The **Battle of Mirbat** began early in the morning of July 19, 1972, when around 300 heavily armed fighters of the Popular Front for the Liberation of Oman (PFLOAG) attacked the town's small garrison, based in the fort and surrounding buildings, guarded by just nine SAS soldiers and thirty-odd Omani troops, all under the command of Captain Mike Kealy, aged just 23.

The aim of the rebels was simple: to disrupt Sultan Qaboos's new policy of rapprochement; to demonstrate the weakness of the government's control even over towns close to Salalah itself; and to execute as many local government supporters as they could find in Mirbat itself once they had overwhelmed the garrison. The fact that this major political setback, and the potential murder of innocent civilians, was averted is mainly down to the skill and courage of the soldiers defending the garrison. The bravery of Fijian sergeant **Talaiasi Labalaba** in particular – who somehow succeeded in holding large numbers of PFLOAG fighters at bay by running across open ground under heavy enemy fire to single-handedly man an old World War II 25-pound artillery piece (a job normally requiring three men) despite severe injuries – has become the stuff of military legend. After hours of bitter fighting, but with the loss of just three men (including Labalaba), air support and SAS reinforcements arrived from Salalah, after which the rebel forces were driven back into the hills.

The battle was a major setback for the rebels, who lost perhaps as many as 200 fighters. Their failure to seize Mirbat, even with vastly superior forces, also boosted the morale and standing of government forces, and the peace effort in general. Sadly, the UK government's anxiety to keep the fact that British fighters were involved in Dhofar secret meant that the battle received little attention overseas, and those involved largely failed to receive the recognition many people feel they deserve. In 2009, a statue of Labalaba was unveiled at SAS headquarters in Hereford, though campaigns to have Sergeant Labalaba awarded a posthumous Victoria Cross have so far come to nothing.

baskets and rifles, though there are fine views past the crenellated walls of the parapet over the coast, the beach and mountains beyond. From the outside you can admire the fort's neat shuttered windows in square stone frames, its unusual hexagonal tower rising from the southeast corner, and the trio of old cannon facing the sea just opposite the road from the entrance.

The harbour and old town

Immediately below the fort lies the **old harbour**, a picture-perfect little sandy cove, dotted with boats and enclosed by a low rocky headland at the far end. You can walk across the sand to Mirbat's **old town**, with perhaps the region's best remaining collections of old Dhofari-style houses. Most are simple one- or two-storey cubist boxes – painted in faded oranges, blues and whites, their minimalist outlines enlivened with distinctive wooden-shuttered windows – and unfortunately it appears many are empty and fast falling into disrepair. There's a grand trio of large three-storey structures (one ruined) next to the main road, with diminutive towers and battlemented roofs, like miniature forts, strikingly similar to the domestic architecture of nearby Yemen. The one right next to the main road is particularly fine, with a couple of intricately carved wooden shutters, spiky battlements and a picture of a dhow etched into the plasterwork at the top of the small corner turret at the rear.

Beyond here lies Mirbat's prettier-than-average **main street**, with shops painted in cheery pastel pinks and oranges, with big green shutters.

ACCOMMODATION

MIRBAT

Salalah Marriott Resort On the coast around 7km east of Mirbat off the coastal highway en route to Sadah ☎2327 5500, ✆marriottsalalahresort.com. Set in solitary splendour on the coast east of Mirbat, this sprawling five-star resort looks like it's just crash-landed from another planet. Rooms are either in the main hotel building or in a costlier detached area of two-storey chalets. There's a large pool and pleasant gardens with a rather rocky stretch of beach at the end. Facilities include a couple of restaurants and bars, a spa, a car rental office, while the hotel is also home to the well-run Extra Divers (see page 210). Doubles <u>55 OR</u>, chalets <u>92 OR</u>

Sadah

It's 60km from Mirbat on to the next major settlement along the coast, the small fishing town of **SADAH** (also spelt Sadh), the road twisting and turning through rocky coastal hinterland, out of sight of the sea, with the towering escarpment of Jebel Samhan rising proudly on the left. Sadah itself is a small but surprisingly pretty little one-street town of balconied houses and a small harbour enclosed by rocky headlands. Formerly one of the leading frankincense ports along the Dhofar coast, it has now reinvented itself as a major centre for the collection of abalone, a type of sea snail, gathered by local divers, and highly prized in Chinese and Japanese cuisine, which is where most of the Omani produce ends up. There's also a small **fort** here (Mon–Thurs & Sun 8.30am–2.30pm; free).

Hasik

It's another 65km from Sadah (and about 190km from Salalah) to the remote outpost of Hasik. The largely barren landscape along the way is dotted with occasional frankincense trees – some of the region's finest frankincense, known as *hawjari* or *hasiki*, is cultivated in the wadis hereabouts. It's a long and rather lonely drive, although the second half of the journey, from the village of **Hadbin** to Hasik, provides some of Dhofar's finest **coastal scenery**, as the mountains of the Jebel Samhan cascade dramatically into the sea, with soaring sea-cliffs, rock pools and outlandish geological formations aplenty. Outside of the *khareef*, dolphins are easily spotted in the mornings along this stretch of coast. If you're heading further up the coast, it's best to fill up at Hasik's Al Maha station before setting off – the next opportunity is more than 90km away in Ash Shuwaymiyah.

THE HALLANIYAT ISLANDS

About 40km off the coast of Dhofar, due east of Hasik, lie the **Hallaniyat islands** (formerly known as the Khuriya Muriya islands): a miniature archipelago consisting of four small islands clustered around the main island, **Hallaniyah**, which is also the location of the islands' only permanent settlement.

The Hallaniyat have a rather curious **history**. In 1854, Sultan Said (see page 239) ceded the islands to the British after they had proposed a scheme for harvesting guano from them (the foreign secretary, Lord Clarendon, it is said, reciprocated the sultan's largesse by sending him a snuffbox in return). Guano was extracted for only a few years, however, and the islands were subsequently attached to the Aden Settlement, in what is now Yemen. They remained a British possession until 1967, when they were returned to Oman – despite Yemeni claims that, as part of the former Aden administration, they properly belonged to them.

The islands boast a string of unspoilt beaches, plentiful birdlife and turtle-nesting grounds, as well as some fine **dive sites**, including the wreck of the British ship, *The City of Winchester*, sunk by German forces in World War I. Though plans have been mooted over the years to launch regular ferry services from Hasik and Shuwaymiyah, the islands remain blissfully isolated. A few organized dive trips are currently offered on the *Saman Explorer*, a live-aboard operated by *Extra Divers* (see page 210), as well as fishing trips run by No Boundaries (☎9595 1810, ⊛noboundariesoman.com) and GT-Fishing Oman (☎9908 7178, ⊛gt-fishing-oman.com). Outside of all-inclusive tours such as these, the only way to reach the islands – for now – is to arrange a ride with a fishing vessel in Hasik, Sadah or Mirbat.

6

East to Ash Shuwaymiyah

The newly tarmacked highway north of Hasik presents some of Dhofar's most spectacular scenic highlights. Shortly after leaving town you'll pass through a police checkpoint, beyond which the road is squeezed between the white sand beach and a wall of towering **limestone cliffs**, the whole swathe sculpted smooth by millennia of wind and rain. A smattering of seasonal waterfalls here have formed drooping stalactites that hang from the cliffs in a few spots, some of the most impressive of which lie just above a large car park with toilet facilities to the left of the road.

North of here, the road heads inland, climbing high above the water with several further car parks affording fantastic views before descending again about 20km north of Hasik. Here, the barren landscape is suddenly interrupted by the sight of **Wadi Sanaq**, an oasis of green wrapped around a turquoise lagoon and flanked with rugged, yellow cliffs. A dirt road (passable for a 2WD in dry weather) heads off into the date palms, where there are some excellent, shady spots to camp and no services whatsoever.

From the wadi, the highway ascends steeply to the east and then north – even higher this time, to the very top of the plateau. The sweeping views from up here are Grand Canyon-like.

The highway finally descends the eastern edge of the Dhofar Mountains to emerge at a 30km stretch of wild beach, towards the eastern end of which is the tiny settlement of **Ash Shuwaymiyah**. Primarily a fishing village, it has an Al Maha station, a couple of accommodation options and a handful of basic restaurants. It's also the launching point for the broad, dramatic canyon that opens up to the northwest of the town, Wadi Ash Shuwaymiyah. Continuing north from here, the highway heads inland through the desert for the 150km drive to Sawqirah (see page 199) – the last filling station is in Shalim, 37km north of Ash Shuwaymiyah.

Wadi Ash Shuwaymiyah

From the main highway, turn left (north) just before reaching the town roundabout and keep straight beyond the town's main drag – the dirt track continues beyond here for about 25km

Lined with towering white limestone cliffs and dotted with rock pools and palm groves, **Wadi Ash Shuwaymiyah** is one of Oman's remotest and most memorable sights, offering dazzling vistas, plenty of lonely spots for camping and a chance of spotting the hyena, gazelle and ibex that roam here.

ACCOMMODATION — ASH SHUWAYMIYAH

Al Thalia Home Just north of the main highway, immediately behind the Al Maha station T 9914 8630, E jumabakhit17@gmail.com. Functional a/c rooms facing the petrol station, equipped with fridges and TVs, and sufficient for a night. Breakfast not included, though there are several café-restaurants on the town's main street, 300m to the west. **25 OR**

No Boundaries Lodge 500m north of the main highway T 9595 1810, W noboundariesoman.com. By far the most comfortable digs in town, with nine clean, a/c rooms that serve as regional home-base for No Boundaries, a fishing outfit that runs trips from here to the Hallaniyat islands. Book far ahead, especially during fishing season (Oct–April). Full board per person **60 OR**

Jebel al Qamar

West of Salalah lies **Jebel al Qamar**, one of the most dramatic sections of the Dhofar Mountains, which rear up out of the sea at the village of **Mughsail**, home to an impressive trio of blowholes. Marching westward along the coast in a sequence of steep, rugged crags and sea cliffs, the mountains tower above some remote stretches of coast, the most picturesque being the beach of **Fizayah** (also Al Fizayah). Beyond here the road rides the top of the plateau to the Yemeni border at Sarfait.

6

> ## MUGHSAIL'S BLOWHOLES
>
> Mughsail's **blowholes** comprise three small holes in the rock through which jets of seawater shoot into the air. They're particularly impressive during the *khareef*, when they spout plumes of water up to 30m high, regularly drenching unwary hordes of screeching tourists. Outside the monsoon they are less memorable, and during the driest parts of the year they cease to blow altogether, although the subterranean groaning of wind and water, eerily amplified by the blowholes themselves, is still strangely impressive.

Mughsail

The road heading west from Salalah meets the sea just a few kilometres east of the tiny village of **MUGHSAIL**, little more than a clump of houses on the hillside above the road. From the long white-sand beach that stretches up the coast from here are superlative views of the dramatic limestone mass of Jebel al Qamar plunging sheer into the sea to the west – reminiscent of the fjords of Musandam, at the opposite end of the country.

To reach Mughsail's **blowholes** (see page 224), turn left opposite the Al Maha petrol station down the road signed Al Marneef Cave and continue 1km to the car park. A short trail from here links the blowholes and offers further vistas of the soaring cliffs. **Al Marneef Cave** itself is not actually a cave, but a kind of open-sided rock shelter at the base of the weathered limestone outcrop that towers up to the rear of the blowholes.

Wadi Aful

Past Mughsail the road begins to hairpin steeply up into Jebel al Qamar, the "Mountains of the Moon" – as singularly wild and lunar as their name suggests, and utterly devoid of human settlement. Some 6km beyond Mughsail the road traverses the cavernous **Wadi Aful** via a spectacular set of hairpin bends which slalom downhill and then up for eight solid kilometres, the most dramatic feat of highway engineering in Oman (outdoing even the more celebrated road from Khasab to Tibat in Musandam), twisting and turning through deep rock cuttings chiselled laboriously out of the huge limestone cliffs.

Fizayah

Some 14km beyond Mughsail you reach the crest of the ridge with breathtaking views along the coast and down to the sea far below. On your left, a graded track (4WD recommended, though you might just get down it with care in a 2WD in the dry season) winds down to **Fizayah** beach, one of Dhofar's most memorable: an idyllic cove of sand hemmed in by spectacular sea-cliffs and wind-sculpted limestone formations.

Shaat and around

Past the Fizayah turn-off the road has a few more vistas in store as it continues along the top of the ridge, with brief glimpses down the coast and into some of the wild wadis that score the mountains inland. About 8km along is a police checkpoint (where you'll need to show some kind of ID and vehicle documentation if driving yourself), and after about 16km is the left-hand tarmacked turn-off for the tiny village of **Shaat**. Head south along this road for about 5km to reach a magnificent viewpoint overlooking a stretch of kilometre-high cliffs, towering over the sea just to the east, the sheer face of which is tinged with green almost year-round.

Further west along the main road, the scenery becomes relatively humdrum. However, if you do persevere you'll reach the pair of small port towns off the main road to Sarfait, each with their own swathe of white-sand beach. From Shaat, it's another 38km along to the turn-off to Rakhyut and another 60km for Dhalkut.

Jebel Qara

The section of the Dhofar Mountains north of Salalah – the **Jebel Qara** – is less spectacular than the ranges to the east and west, although it boasts a couple of worthwhile attractions, including the peaceful mausoleum of An **Nadi Ayub** (popularly known as Job's Tomb) and the **pools at Ayun**.

Ayn Garziz

From the An Nahdah roundabout in Salalah, head 3km west, then right (north) up the Ittin road and continue for 7.5km, after which you'll turn right down the signposted road to the springs, another 3km along

Heading northwest out of Salalah towards the Jebel Qara, the first attraction you reach is the local beauty spot of **Ayn Garziz** (also spelled Jarziz), one of the various springs dotting the base of the mountains that ring Salalah. The springs (which may dry up late in the season) nestle in a quaint natural cul-de-sac hemmed in by low limestone cliffs, dissolved into strange, wax-like shapes by the *khareef* rains and draped with fronds of hanging greenery. It's an attractive spot, kitted out with little gazebos for picnicking.

Mausoleum of An Nabi Ayub

Daily 6am–9pm • Free • 14km northwest past the turn-off for Ayn Garziz, turn left (signposted) and continue 1.5km down a steep, twisting side-road

Beyond Ayn Garziz, it's a fine climb up into hills to reach the **Mausoleum of An Nabi Ayub**, also known as **Job's Tomb**, after the long-suffering biblical patriarch. Job/Ayub is an important figure in Islamic, Jewish and Christian theology, appearing in the Qur'an as a prophet who suffered a series of divine tribulations. Quite how or why his supposed mortal remains ended up in the hills above Salalah remains unclear, although it's worth bearing in mind that there's also a rival Druze tomb of Job in the Al Chouf

---

TRIBES AND LANGUAGES OF DHOFAR

Ethnically and linguistically, the original inhabitants of Dhofar – an intricate patchwork of mountain and desert **tribes** of which the Qara, Mahra and Bait Kathir are perhaps the most notable – have far more in common with the people of neighbouring Yemen to the west than with their fellow Omanis to the north. Jan Morris, writing during the mid-1950s in *Sultan in Oman* (see page 253), described "tribes of strange non-Arab peoples, often living in caves, almost naked, speaking languages of their own and maintaining their own obscure manners and customs." Other distinctive cultural traditions persisted until recent decades. The Qara, for instance, refused to eat chickens or any kind of egg, while their women were forbidden from touching the udders of the tribe's cows (the cow being considered generally superior to a mere female, whose touch might offend it). Their religious beliefs also appeared somewhat unusual. As Morris described it, "They were nominally Moslems … but their theological principles seemed to be a trifle hazy: whenever I saw any of them praying during my stay in Dhufar, they were turned not towards Mecca, but towards the sun."

Modernization and rising prosperity mean that physical reminders of traditional Dhofari life are now increasingly rare (and virtually extinct in Salalah itself), although up in the hills you may spot occasional examples of the region's traditional round stone huts with straw roofs, or come across elderly Dhofaris wearing the distinctive indigo-dyed robes

The original Dhofari tribes are also interesting from a linguistic point of view, speaking a range of South Arabian Semitic **languages** closer to Amharic (one of the languages of modern Ethiopia and Eritrea) than Arabic, and offering a living link with the region's pre-Islamic history. The most important of these are Shehri (also known as Jebali – literally, "mountain"), spoken by the Qara, with around 25,000 native speakers; and Mehri (or Mahri), spoken by the Mahra, with an estimated 70,000 native speakers in Oman. All Shehri and Mehri speakers are also fluent in Arabic.

region of Lebanon, and that the towns of Magdala in present-day Israel and Urfa in southern Turkey both claim to have been the site of Job's various trials and misfortunes.

Whatever the tomb's historical credentials, it's an attractive site, and well worth the visit. The **mausoleum** itself is a small, domed concrete cube that sits inside the gardens of a weather-worn mosque. It's an enjoyably cool and peaceful spot, full of flowering shrubs and small birds, and with fine views over the *jebel* and down to Salalah way below. **Inside** the mausoleum (don't forget to remove your shoes when entering) lies the prophet's long tomb, covered in green cloth; the size of the tomb is explained either by the theory that more than one person is buried in it, or by the more entertaining belief that human beings in the days of Job were of far greater size than ourselves, and that people are, contrary to all scientific thinking, not increasing in size, but shrinking. Charts stuck to the walls of the tomb show the genealogies of various prophets including Abraham, Moses, Job, Jesus and Mohammed; outside lie the remains of a much older building, along with a very roughly formed rock imprint in a concrete box in front of the tomb which is popularly claimed to be Job's own footprint, although it's difficult to be convinced.

Jebel Qara viewpoints

West of the Nabi Ayub's mausoleum, the main road climbs towards the escarpment of the Jebel Qara. Two of the best **viewpoints** over the valley below are marked along the way by large car parks with concrete gazebos that make popular picnic spots, roughly 1km apart. After 9.5km you reach a T-junction. Turn right here and follow the road for an exhilarating drive up to the top of the plateau, becoming increasingly rocky and barren as you gain height, with further views down into steep-sided gorges and wandering camels strolling unconcernedly across the road..

Wadi Ayun

Some 17km north of the T-junction is a turn-off on the left signed to "Ayoon". Go down this road for about 400 metres then bear left along the rough track (4WD only) for a further 4km to reach the secluded **Wadi Ayun**, a small, rocky declivity dotted with a picturesque series of reed-fringed rock pools. According to tradition, the pools are the source of the freshwater spring at distant Shisr (a comb dropped into the pools at Ayun is said to have reappeared at Shisr).

Wadi Dawkah

About 40km north of Salalah along Highway 31, a sign points west towards the shallow, sandy **Wadi Dawkah**. This is one of the cluster of places related to the ancient frankincense trade which were given World Heritage Site status by UNESCO in 2000 under the moniker "The Land of Frankincense" (also including the ruins of Sumahram, Shisr and Al Baleed). From the car park just off the highway, steps lead down to a viewing platform where you can take in the broad wadi, its arid bed dotted with frankincense trees. Many of them, especially those closer to the path, have been damaged by amateurish incisions made by passing visitors. Part of the wadi is fenced in and planted with new trees – the nearest thing to a frankincense plantation you'll find in Oman – although the general effect is decidedly mundane.

The interior

North of Salalah, the most alluring attractions lie over the Jebel Qara in the desolate expanses beyond. Here you'll find the fragmentary remains of the legendary city of

Ubar at the village of Shisr and, further inland still, in the great sand dunes at the edge of the **Empty Quarter**, one of the world's greatest and most inhospitable deserts.

Thumrait

The small Bedouin town of **THUMRAIT** lies some 32km north of Wadi Dawkah and 75km north of Salalah. The town is basically a glorified service station, with dozens of no-frills coffee shops catering to passing truck drivers, who pull up here in droves. If you're heading north, note that Thumrait is the last source of petrol before Shisr.

6

ACCOMMODATION   THUMRAIT

Thumrait Tourist Hotel At the end of the side road about 300m south of the Shell station ☎ 2327 9371. A simple one-star, although there's no real incentive to stay, given how close you are to Salalah – unless you've been travelling south and really can't face spending any more time on the road. **15 OR**

Shisr

Way out in the desert north of Thumrait lie the celebrated remains of the town of **SHISR**, popularly believed to be the site of the mythical ancient city of **Ubar** (alternatively, Wubar or Awbar). The ruins inspired one of the most famous archeological treasure-hunts of recent times (see page 30), although unless you have a particular interest in Arabian archeology, the site scarcely justifies the long journey.

The **remains** themselves are decidedly modest: the bases of a few walls, eight towers and the outlines of some buildings next to the rocky sinkhole into which the town suddenly disappeared some time between 300 and 500 AD. It will make a lot more sense if you've read Clapp's *The Road to Ubar*.

ARRIVAL AND INFORMATION   SHISR

By car Head along the main highway for 41km north of the Thumrait roundabout, where a turn-off points to Shisr, some 50km further on into the desert along a surfaced road. Head straight through the roundabout in Shisr and then turn right at the T-junction; the entrance to the site is about 50m ahead, to the right of a tiny coffee shop.

Information A new visitor centre, set just beyond the entrance gate, soon to be opened at the time of writing, plans to display artefacts turned up during the site's excavation.

The Empty Quarter

The legendary **Empty Quarter** (Rub al Khali) is one of the world's largest and most famous deserts, its pristine sands stretching into Yemen, Saudi Arabia and the UAE. The scale of the desert is jaw-dropping: a thousand kilometres long and five hundred wide – bigger than France, Belgium and the Netherlands combined. Most of it consists of huge swathes of dunes reaching heights of up to 300m, interspersed with gravel plains and occasional salt flats, such as the notorious "quicksands" of **Umm al Samim** – first described by Thesiger – into which even local Bedu venture only rarely and with extreme caution. Indeed, expeditions into the sands should only be attempted with a proper guide and full equipment, though you'll certainly be rewarded for the effort.

ARRIVAL AND TOURS   THE EMPTY QUARTER

By car With a 4WD you can reach the very edge of the Empty Quarter at the small settlement of Al Hashman, about 75km northwest of Shisr along a rough track: the sealed road gives way 3.5km beyond Shisr, at which point you'll find a small service station where you can release your tyre pressure. To travel beyond here, it is absolutely necessary to travel in convoy, preferably with the help of an experienced tour operator from Salalah.

Tours The best way to enjoy the desert is by signing up for an overnight trip from Salalah, such as those offered by Al Fawaz Tours (see page 212).

ARABIC SCRIPT CARVED ON THE DOOR OF BAHLA FORT

Contexts

History

Oman's history is a paradox. Much of the country's past remains blanketed in the sort of mystery that one would expect given its inhospitable terrain and remote location at the nethermost ends of the Arabian peninsula. And yet the country also boasts a recorded history stretching back well over five thousand years, and a wealth of archeological remains which are only now beginning to be slowly deciphered. Copper and other commodities were shipped from here to ancient Sumer, while the ancient frankincense trade in Dhofar has left tantalizing glimpses of ancient life in South Arabia. The armies of Persia's Cyrus the Great colonized parts of the region, while the early Islamic dynasties of Damascus and Baghdad also left their mark, as did later colonial powers including Portugal and Britain.

Put simply, the history of Oman is the story of two quite separate regions, each with its own distinct identity. The first is the inward-looking and staunchly conservative tribal **interior**, or "Oman proper" as it's sometimes described, an inhospitable and sparsely populated region, little visited by outsiders, and even less written about. The interior's barren geography, harsh climate and historically low population levels have all tended to work against the establishment of centralized authority, encouraging the patchwork development of independent regions under the control of competing tribes which endured right up until the second half of the twentieth century. The history of the interior is thus not so much that of a coherent nation as a vague confederation of clans, loosely joined by their shared Ibadhi beliefs (see page 232) and suspicion of outsiders – although as often as not at war with one another, when not confronting outside threats.

The second is the far more cosmopolitan history of **the coast**, shaped by its location on the Arabian Gulf and long-standing trading and cultural links with surrounding regions, from ancient Mesopotamia and Persia through to its wide-ranging connections with colonial European powers including Portugal, France and Britain. Omani settlements overseas in East Africa and Baluchistan (in what is now Pakistan) have also played a major role both in the country's economic past and present-day cultural make-up.

The history of **Dhofar** is largely separate from that of the rest of Oman (see page 202).

Magan (2300–1300 BC)

Evidence of human settlement in Oman goes back to at least 6000 BC, roughly around the time when rising sea levels stabilized at their current levels, establishing the outlines of the Arabian Gulf and Gulf of Oman. Early settlements

c. 2300 BC	1300–500 BC	530 BC
Sumerian cuneiform texts begin to reference the land of Magan (or Majan).	Construction of the hilltop fort of Salut; the region becomes integral to the regional frankincense and spice trade.	Persians conquer Oman under the leadership of Cyrus the Great, remaining a dominant presence until the arrival of Islam.

were generally coastal – huge piles of shells have been excavated at various places along the seaboard, representing the remains of innumerable prehistoric shellfish suppers.

The first recorded references to Oman date back to the Bronze Age. From around 2300 BC the region, under the name of **Magan** (or Majan), begins to crop up in cuneiform texts written in nearby Sumeria, in what is now southern Iraq. According to these, Magan (which probably also covered parts of what is now the UAE) was an important source of copper and other materials, some of which doubtless came from the rich mines in Wadi Jizzi, inland from Sohar, along with other sites such as Wadi Samad near Nizwa. This period (roughly 2500–2000 BC) is often described as the **Umm an Nar** period, named after a small island near Abu Dhabi where remains from this era were first excavated. The Umm an Nar culture is best known for its distinctive style of circular and "beehive" tombs, of which fine examples survive at Bat, Al Ayn, Jaylah and Salut, as well as in the UAE at Hili, just over the border from Buraimi.

The Umm an Nar period was followed by the so-called **Wadi Suq period** (c.2000–1300 BC), after the wadi near Sohar in which remains from this period were first discovered – again characterized by large tombs, both round and rectangular. Oman's **Iron Age** (c.1300–500 BC) has left fewer notable archeological remains, though there is evidence of a network of mudbrick villages and fortified hilltop settlements. Copper production also reached a peak during this period.

Persians and Arabs (530 BC–630 AD)

The first of the various large-scale invasions and migrations which would shape the history of Oman occurred sometime around 530 BC, when the Achaemenids of **Persia**, under Cyrus the Great, conquered "Mazun", as they called Oman – the beginning of an Iranian presence in Oman that was to last until the coming of Islam, well over a thousand years later. The Persians are believed to have introduced advanced irrigation techniques which subsequently developed into the Omani *falaj* (see page 83), leading to the development of widespread cultivation and a prosperous agricultural civilization.

How long – and how much of – Oman remained under Persian control is unknown, although it seems likely that their power ebbed and flowed over the next few centuries. Of more importance in the subsequent history of Oman are the large-scale **migrations of Arabs** which took place in the centuries following the arrival of the Persians. Most of Oman's current population can trace its ancestry to one of two different Arab migrations into Oman during the centuries before and after the birth of Christ. The first was of large numbers of southern Arabs, or Qahtani, from Yemen (and including the powerful Yaruba and Azd tribes, both of whom were to play a leading role in the subsequent history of Oman). Many of these appear to have come from the **Ma'rib** area, home to the legendary Queen of Sheba and of the huge Ma'rib dam, one of the engineering wonders of the ancient world. Successive failures of the dam, however, resulted in the gradual collapse in the region's prosperity, leading to the migration of large numbers of people into Oman between roughly the second century BC and the second century AD; even today those who claim Yemeni origins are known as **Yamani**.

2nd century BC–2nd century AD	4th century BC	630 AD
Large-scale Arab migrations from Yemen are spurred by repeated failures of the Ma'rib dam, followed by further migrations from Northern Arabia.	Sumahram established in present-day Dhofar, going on to flourish for almost a millennium.	'Amr ibn al 'As, envoy of the Prophet, brings Islam to Oman. The Persians are expelled.

The second major migration into Oman was of northern Arabs, or Adnani, also known as **Nizari**, from what is now the Nejd in central Saudi Arabia. Yamani–Nizari rivalries and quarrels would prove a lasting feature of Omani history, right through until recent decades.

The Yamani and Nizari gradually moved into Oman, slowly assimilating with the existing, Persianized population through a mixture of conquest and trade. The Arab immigrants tended to settle themselves in the Sharqiya and the Jebel Akdhar, while the Persians continued to dominate the northwest Batinah coast around Sohar – an early instance of the split between coast and interior which was to become a running theme in Omani history for the next two thousand years.

Islam, imams and Ibadhis (630–751 AD)

Oman was one of the first countries to embrace Islam, which was introduced to the country in **630 AD** by an envoy of the Prophet Mohammed, 'Amr ibn al 'As (who would subsequently earn a leading place in Islamic legend as the general in charge of the Muslim conquest of Egypt). 'Amr ibn al 'As decided to begin proselytizing in the town of Sohar, then the largest and most prosperous in the country, and home to a sizeable Persian population. In the event, however, it was the local Julandas, the rulers of the Arab tribes, who were converted to the new faith, rather than the city's Persian governor (the Persians were already followers of Zoroastrianism, one of the world's oldest monotheisms). The first act of the newly converted Julandas was to drive the Persians out of Oman.

The **death of the Prophet Mohammad** in 632 AD ushered in a period of instability, as various parts of the newly converted Islamic world revolted against the new caliph in Medina, Abu Bakr, leading to the so-called Wars of Apostasy (or Ridda Wars) – although despite the name these rebellions probably had more to do with politics than religion. One such uprising broke out at **Dibba**, led by the powerful Azd tribe under Laqit bin Malik. According to one version of events, Laqit was killed by an envoy of Abu Bakr in what was a relatively small struggle; other sources say that at least 10,000 rebels were killed in one of the biggest battles of the Wars of Apostasy.

Islam would henceforth remain unchallenged in Oman, although the exact form the religion would take in the country was still evolving. The turmoil which followed the Prophet Mohammed's death and subsequent fighting between his successors led to a dissident movement known as the **Khawarij** (meaning "Outsiders"; sometimes anglicized to "Kharijites"). Disillusioned with the conduct of their leaders, the Khawarij took an essentially democratic view of Islam, arguing that any suitable Muslim could be chosen as leader, and that any leader could be replaced if he failed to act in accordance with the teachings of Allah. Khariji attitudes travelled to Southern Arabia, where they became known as **Ibadhism** (see box below).

Conflicts with the Islamic centre continued during the reign of the fifth **Umayyad caliph**, Abd al Malik bin Marwan. Wishing to crush the "heretical" Omanis, in around 694 Abd al Malik dispatched a large punitive expedition which eventually succeeded in subduing the Omani rebels with terrible slaughter. The Umayyad dynasty

632 AD	694
The Prophet Muhammad dies, giving rise to the Ridda Wars (Wars of Apostasy). Opposition to Caliph Abu Bakr is crushed.	Khawarij ideas reach Oman, spawning the rise of Ibadhi Islam. Caliph Abd al Malik bin Marwan sends an army to quell the heretical Omanis.

IBADHISM AND THE IMAMATE

The school of Islam known as **Ibadhism** once flourished across Yemen, Oman and southern Saudi Arabia, but now survives almost exclusively in Oman, where it remains the most widely practised form of the religion, followed by around three-quarters of the population. Ibadhism began as a popular reaction against the perceived failings of the Caliphate, and its democratic character appealed to the independent-minded tribes of Oman and subsequently became an important marker of national identity.

Up until 1959, the nation's Ibadhi community was led by the **imam** – a kind of Omani pope. The imam – meaning "one who sets an example" – could come from any part of the community, so long as he (despite the sect's democratic credentials, the imam was always a man) possessed the necessary spiritual and personal qualities. The imam was traditionally elected by the *ulama*, a body of Muslims scholars; their choice then had to be ratified by the community at large. On occasion, an imam nominated by the *ulama* was rejected by the people, and a new one found. An imam could also be removed from power if he lost the support of the people, and if no suitable candidate was available the post could (and sometimes was) left vacant, often for considerable periods of time. At various times the offices of imam and sultan were held by the same person; at others, by two different figures – tensions between rival imams and sultans became a particular feature of Oman's troubled early to mid-twentieth-century history until the last imam fled the country in the wake of the Jebel War (see page 242), since when the office has lapsed, and shows no sign of being revived.

collapsed, however, just over fifty years later in 750, offering Oman a new measure of independence, during which its leaders took the opportunity to elect the country's first **imam** (see box, page 232), Julanda bin Mas'ud, in 751.

The era of invasions (751–1507)

The independence was short-lived, however. Just four years later Julanda bin Mas'ud was murdered by the invading forces of the new **Abbasid caliph**, Abu al Abbas (reigned 750–754), popularly known as As Saffa – "The Shedder of Blood". As Abbasid power waxed and waned, so Oman enjoyed greater or lesser degrees of autonomy, though they had to wait until the reign of the legendary caliph Harun al Rashid (786–809) to elect a **second imam**, Sheikh Mohammed bin Abi Affan. Sheikh Mohammed proved an unhappy choice, however, and was replaced just two years later by Imam Warith bin Kaab al Kharousi – an early example of Ibadhi democracy in action. Eventually, Harun al Rashid decided to send a punitive army, although his forces were destroyed in battle at Sohar.

This time Oman's independence lasted for around a century until 892 and the arrival of a new, 25,000-strong army, sent by the caliph and commanded by **Mohammed bin Nur**, governor of Bahrain, who led a murderous assault on the country, killing the imam and sending his head back to Baghdad. Next to arrive were the **Qaramita** (Carmathians), a radical Ismaili Shia sect from Bahrain, who had already caused widespread havoc across Syria and Iraq, and also sacked Mecca, killing 30,000 people and carrying off the Black Stone, one of Islam's most important relics, in the process. Not surprisingly, these constant attacks took a heavy toll on the

751	892	10th –12th centuries
Julanda bin Mas'ud becomes the first Ibadhi imam – ushering in an institution that would survive until 1959 – though he is killed four years later.	After a century of independence, the caliph's forces ravage Oman yet again, sending the imam's head back to Baghdad.	Oman is swept by further invasions and occupations – by the Carmathians from Bahrain and then by the Persian Buyids and Seljuks.

OMANIS IN EAST AFRICA

Despite the often chaotic situation at home, from early in its history Oman succeeded in extending its reach overseas, thanks to its expertise in shipbuilding and navigation. The Omanis are thought to have sent slaving expeditions to **East Africa** as far back as the seventh century, while the Julanda rulers defeated by the Umayyad caliph Abd al Malik bin Marwan in 694 (see page 231) are said to have fled to the "Land of Zanj", meaning East Africa. This Julanda arrival marked the beginning of a thousand years of continuous Omani presence, and often considerable power, on the East African coast, broken only briefly by a brutal Portuguese interregnum in the fifteenth and sixteenth centuries.

One of the oldest and largest of these settlements was the city-state of **Kilwa Kisiwani**, an island now belonging to Tanzania, founded as a trading centre in 957, becoming in its heydey the most important single entrepot along the East African coast; Ibn Battuta, visiting in 1332, described it as "amongst the most beautiful of cities, and elegantly built". Kilwa was just one of many such centres, and by the 1200s the Omanis had established a lasting presence at various locations along the African coast ranging from Mogadishu through to Mombasa and Zanzibar and down into Mozambique, trading in gold, iron, ivory, textiles, spices and, increasingly over time, slaves.

Despite the number of such settlements, and the riches passing through them, there was never such a thing as a formal Omani "empire" in Africa. These Omani settlements were largely independent from one another, and also from whoever happened to be ruling Oman, except during the rule of Said the Great, who actually transferred the entire Omani court to Zanzibar (see page 238).

region. Many of the country's *aflaj* were destroyed and large areas of agricultural land lost to the desert.

The gradual collapse of the Abbasid dynasty meant that the caliphs in Baghdad no longer interfered with Oman. New enemies rapidly appeared, however. In 971 and again in 1041 the **Buyids** arrived from Persia, sacking Sohar, and in 1064 the **Seljuks** followed, holding on to power for eighty years.

In the midst of such upheaval, a new dynasty entered Omani history in 1154, following the death of Imam Jaber Moussa bin Ali. This was the **Bani Nabhan** (Nabhani) dynasty, whose rulers constructed the vast fortress at Bahla and styled themselves as *malik* (king) rather than imam. Their dynasty continued until 1500, when the last Nabhani ruler, Sulayman bin Sulayman bin Mudhaffar, was removed and the imamate belatedly restored. Little is known of the period, though it appears that Nabhani power fluctuated over time, with their influence sometimes restricted to parts of the interior and sometimes reaching down to the coast; they also had to face various Persian invasions and tribal rivalries.

Further attackers arrived from Persia during the thirteenth century – although these were most likely **Mongol** soldiers (the Mongols then being in control of Persia) – while the whole Omani coastline appears to have subsequently fallen under the control of the island **kingdom of Hormuz**, just over the eponymous straits, in Persia.

The Portuguese (1507–1624)
Oman would soon come into contact with a new imperial power in the Indian Ocean: the **Portuguese**. Vasco da Gama himself is sometimes claimed (though with

1154	1507	1624
The Bani Nabhan dynasty is born, suspending the imamate for more than three centuries and erecting a massive fortress at Bahla.	A Portuguese fleet under Alfonso de Albuquerque bombards Muscat, initiating 150 years of Portuguese dominance along the coast.	Nasir bin Murshid bin Sultan al Yaruba is elected imam, initiating the Yaruba dynasty and gaining territory from the Portuguese.

no apparent evidence) to have stopped off in Oman during his historic first voyage to India in 1497–98, though the first sighting of the Portuguese in Oman had to wait another ten years until 1507, when a small fleet commanded by Admiral Afonso de Albuquerque appeared off Muscat. The Portuguese were offered safe passage by Muscat's governor and were in the process of taking on water on the beach when they were suddenly fired upon by soldiers sent by the king of Hormuz. The Portuguese responded by bombarding the city, overrunning and pillaging it and then reducing it to ruins – an unhappy start to a bleak 150 years of Portuguese rule over the coast of Oman.

The Portuguese gradually expanded their power along the coast east and west of Muscat, reaching as far as Sohar and Sur. Their conquests were accompanied with shocking levels of brutality and random cruelty: thousands of innocents were murdered, prisoners had their ears and noses chopped off and some coastal settlements, such as Qalhat, were so thoroughly destroyed that they never recovered.

The Portuguese thereafter remained in control of Muscat and the coast, largely unchallenged (bar an unsuccessful uprising in 1526) until 1550, when an **Ottoman fleet** set sail from Egypt to relieve Muscat, with thirty boats carrying 16,000 men. A month-long siege ensued in 1551, after which the victorious Ottomans sacked Muscat – proving no better than the Portuguese they had replaced. Ottoman control of the city lasted just two years, however, before the Portuguese retook it, subsequently fighting off another Ottoman attack in 1554, after which the Turks withdrew from the scene.

The Yaruba dynasty (1624–1742)

The next major turning point came in 1624, when **Nasir bin Murshid bin Sultan al Yaruba** was elected imam at Rustaq, initiating the **Yaruba dynasty**, one of the most important in Oman's history. The Yaruba (also spelled Ya'aruba or Ya'arubi) were possibly the oldest of all the Yamani tribes in Oman. They now provided the country with the charismatic leader it had craved for so long.

At the time of Nasir's election, the interior had splintered into at least five statelets, including Nizwa, Rustaq, Nakhal, Sumail and Ibra, with other forts and regions in the hands of independent tribal leaders and the Portuguese still ensconced in Muscat down on the coast. A strong leader for troubled times, Nasir set about reasserting the imamate's authority over the interior. The process took the remainder of his life, although he didn't live quite long enough to see its completion. By the time of his death in 1649, the last Portuguese were being driven from their strongholds in Muscat and it was left to his cousin and successor, Sultan bin Saif, to complete the work of recapturing the city, which was finally accomplished in 1650 (see page 53). In 1646 Nasir also signed a trade treaty with the British, the first of many such arrangements and the beginning of a relationship which was to last, on and off, for over three hundred years.

Like his cousin, **Sultan bin Saif** proved a strong and determined leader. Having seen off the Portuguese, he then launched a series of retaliatory missions, chasing them down to India and across to the east coast of Africa, gradually building up a stock of captured Portuguese ships until Oman had acquired the basis of a large and powerful navy. African-based Omani traders increasingly flourished, while considerable wealth

1650	17th and 18th centuries	1724–1742
Sultan bin Saif expels the Portuguese from Oman, eventually evicting them from Mombasa and Zanzibar in 1698.	Oman enjoys a prominent role in regional trade, the prosperity of its merchants significantly enriching the country.	Civil war, fought largely along Yamani–Nizari lines, cements tribal allegiances. The Persians take advantage of the chaos, seizing control by 1742.

began to pour into Oman for the first time in its history. The monies accumulated were used to fund a major overhaul of the country's *aflaj*, so crucial to its agricultural prosperity, and also to underwrite a countrywide building boom. Sultan bin Saif himself constructed the enormous round tower at Nizwa fort, while his successors added further major new castles at Nakhal, Al Hazm and Barka.

The later Yaruba rulers

Sultan bin Saif died in 1679 and was succeeded by his son, **Bil'arab bin Sultan bin Saif**, thus confirming the principal of hereditary succession – despite the fact that this was completely at odds with the democratic principles of the imamate and Ibadhi faith (during the 900-year history of the imamate, there had previously been only one instance of hereditary succession; now, suddenly, there had been three in a row). Excepting the construction of the beautiful fort at Jabrin (in which Bil'arab is buried), much of the rest of Bil'arab's unhappy reign was spent fighting with his brother, **Saif bin Sultan**, who acceded to the throne after Bil'arab's death at Jabrin in 1692.

Saif bin Sultan once again focused on trade and agriculture, investing further money in *aflaj* throughout the interior and planting thousands of date palms along the Batinah in an effort to encourage Arabs from the interior to settle along the Persianized coast. Saif bin Sultan also continued to harrass the Portuguese along the African coast, and increase his own wealth in the process; his forces captured Mombasa in 1698 (after a siege lasting almost three years), and soon afterwards drove the Portuguese out of Pemba, Kilwa and, most importantly, **Zanzibar**, leaving the Portuguese with no remaining East African possessions north of Mozambique. Zanzibar would subsequently play a crucial role in the later history of Oman, although development of the island didn't really take off until the reign of Said the Great, over a hundred years later. By the time of Saif bin Sultan's death in 1711 he is said to have owned seven hundred male slaves, twenty-eight ships and a third of all the date trees in Oman.

Yaruba turbulence and decline

Saif was succeeded by his son, **Sultan bin Saif II**, whose death in 1718 signalled a new era of turbulence. He was nominally succeeded by his twelve-year-old son, **Saif bin Sultan II**, the popular choice of the people at large, although realizing that Saif's youth made him unsuitable for such an important office, the *ulama* secretly elected his elder brother **Muhanna** to serve as imam. This was not a popular decision, however, and Muhanna was rapidly supplanted by his cousin, Yaarub bin Bil'arab, who was himself then forced to resign in favour of the young Saif bin Sultan II, who was assisted by his uncle, and leader of the Bani Hina tribe, Bil'arab bin Nasir. Unfortunately, Bil'arab bin Nasir succeeded in immediately upsetting Muhammed bin Nasir al Ghafiri, a prominent Nizari leader, who quickly organized his tribes in rebellion against the new Bani Hina ruler.

Civil war promptly erupted, with the rival factions divided broadly along Yamani–Nizari lines. The Yamani tribes were led initially by Khalf bin Mubarak of the Bani Hina tribe, and thus became known as **Hinawi** (from Hina), while the Nizari tribes under the command of Muhammed bin Nasir al Ghafiri became known as **Ghafiri**. (The names Hinawi and Ghafiri survive even today as a description of tribal allegiance,

1744	1798	1800
Ahmad bin Said Al Bu Said is elected imam, initiating the Al Bu Said dynasty. Three years later his forces rid Oman of the Persians.	A new treaty is signed with the British East India Company, ensuring British military aid.	Wahhabi forces from present-day Saudi Arabia occupy Buraimi – the first of numerous incursions.

being roughly synonymous with Yamani and Nizari respectively, although there has been much switching of allegiance since, including the Bani Ghafir themselves, who, ironically, are now counted among the Hinawi tribes.)

Mohammed bin Nasir al Ghafiri was initially victorious, taking both the young Saif bin Sultan II and his uncle Bil'arab prisoner. He was then elected imam (the third in as many years) and ruled the country for five years from Jabrin before being killed during a battle at Sohar in 1727, after which Saif bin Sultan II subsequently found himself elected imam for a second time.

Saif's position was far from safe, however. Confronted with further uprisings and popular disgust at his opulent and profligate lifestyle in Rustaq (including a particular weakness for Shiraz wine which would subsequently prove his undoing), he called upon the Persians for support. The Persians duly arrived in 1737 under the leadership of **Nadir Shah**, one of the most brilliant – and bloodthirsty – military commanders of his age, although it quickly became apparent that the Persians, having been unwisely invited in, were in no hurry to leave. Nadir's forces captured Muscat (excepting the forts of Jalali and Mirani, which remained in Omani hands) and then marched upon Sohar, where their initial attack against the city was repulsed by a certain Ahmad bin Said Al Bu Said, who was about to assume a pivotal position in Omani history.

By 1742 the Persians had seized control of large parts of the country. The nadir of this Persian incursion came when Saif bin Sultan II was invited to a banquet by the Persian commander **Taqi Khan**. Saif and the rest of his entourage were rendered insensible with large quantities of wine, after which Taqi Khan stole his signet ring and forged an order commanding the forts of Jalali and Mirani to admit the Persian forces, which they did. The unfortunate sultan awoke to one of the worst hangovers in history and the discovery that two of his key forts had fallen to the enemy, and soon afterwards sickened and died. His cousin and would-have-been successor, Murshid al Yaruba, had already died fighting the Persians in Sohar, meaning Saif's death heralded the end of the Yaruba dynasty, leaving the country leaderless.

The Al Bu Said dynasty begins (1742–1806)

A man for the moment was already at hand, however, in the shape of the redoubtable Hinawi leader, **Ahmad bin Said Al Bu Said**, the *wali* of Sohar – a man of brilliant abilities but humble origins who, it is said, started off by selling wood from the back of a camel. Ahmad had already fought off one Persian attack on Sohar and was busy resisting a second at the moment of Saif's death. After a stubborn nine-month siege Ahmad finally capitulated on honourable terms, and was subsequently confirmed by Taqi Khan as governor of Sohar and Barka – on condition he pay tribute to the Persian authorities in Muscat. He was then elected imam in 1744, ushering in the **Al Bu Said dynasty**, which endures to the present day.

Ahmad bin Said Al Bu Said immediately set about undermining the Persian garrison in Muscat by finding a plausible excuse to fail to make the required payments, meaning many of the garrison's troops received no wages, and deserted. In 1747, still professing his loyalty to the Persian governor, Ahmad invited the entire garrison to his fort in Barka for a **banquet**, where, having assembled his enemy, he did away with the lot of them (see page 119), thus freeing Oman once again from the Persian yoke.

1806	**1845**	**1857**
Said bin Sultan takes the throne, overseeing a prosperous half-century built largely on the trade of slaves and – subsequently – cloves from East Africa.	Said signs an agreement to outlaw the export of slaves from Omani-controlled East Africa.	Omani territories are divided between the sons of Said bin Sultan – one inherits Zanzibar, the other Oman.

Peace and prosperity returned during the 39-year reign of the new imam. Ahmad bin Said encouraged trade by sea and a programme of agricultural development at home. Muscat flourished and, from his seat at Rustaq, Ahmad attempted to strike a balance between coast and interior. He also raised a standing army and navy for the first time in Omani history. Tribal intriguing still threatened his position, however, initially by the remaining members of the Yaruba tribe (despite the fact that Ahmad had diplomatically married the daughter of one of the last Yaruba rulers), then by the Ghafiri, and finally, towards the end of his reign, by two of his own sons, Saif and Sultan (the latter was eventually forced to flee to Baluchistan, where he fortuitously inherited the province of Gwadur; see page 238).

Internal division and Wahhabi threats

Ahmad died in 1783, whereupon his second son, **Said bin Ahmad**, was elected imam (the last Omani leader to hold the post of both sultan and imam), in preference to the rebellious Saif and Sultan. Said appears to have been a reluctant ruler, however, and shortly afterwards his son **Hamad bin Said** wrested political control from his father and set up court in Muscat in 1784, where he took the title "Sayyid" (lord). His father remained as imam in Rustaq, a powerless religious figurehead, until his death in 1803. The union between coast and interior – and between religious and secular leadership – that Ahmad bin Said had carefully nurtured was once again split wide open.

Meanwhile, Muscat continued to flourish and the power of the city grew, even while the division between it and the interior widened. Sayyid Hamad died in 1792 of smallpox and was succeeded by his uncle, **Sultan bin Ahmad** (one of the two rebellious sons of Ahmad bin Said, who had subsequently found his way to Muscat from Baluchistan). Fearing challenges from his own family, Sultan came to an agreement at Barka in 1793 whereby he confirmed the position of his brother Said (who was still imam up in Rustaq) and handed over Sohar to another brother, Qais, effectively confirming the increasing importance of Oman's coastal areas, and the corresponding irrelevance of the office of imam.

In 1798, a new treaty was signed with the British East India Company, part of a system of military and diplomatic maneouvres by which the British hoped to ward off French designs on India, and by which Sultan hoped to benefit from the protection of the increasingly powerful British navy.

Not that all was peaceful at home. In 1800 Oman suffered the first of a string of invasions by the **Wahhabis**, from what is now Saudi Arabia, which were to plague it for the next century and a half. The Wahhabis besieged Qais bin Ahmad in Sohar and also occupied the Buraimi oasis, kicking off a long-running **territorial dispute** that would not finally be settled until 1974 (see page 141).

Sultan's death in 1804 was followed by the predictable bout of intriguing and infighting. Sultan's cousin, **Badr bin Saif** (deeply unpopular thanks to his Wahhabi sympathies) was notionally in charge for the next two years until being assassinated by Sultan's son, Said. At the same time, the Wahhabis returned and took advantage of the confusion to gain control of large parts of the interior.

1877	1932	1937
Sultan Turki bin Said expands Omani control to include Dhofar, though his rule is limited to the environs of Salalah.	Sultan Said bin Taimur takes the throne, charting an economically cautious course for Oman's development.	The Sultan grants a 75-year concession to the Iraq Petroleum Company to prospect for oil reserves.

GWADUR AND OMANI BALUCHISTAN

Sultan bin Ahmad's flight from Oman following his unsuccessful attempts to unseat his father Ahmad bin Said (see page 236) had one unexpected but important consequence. Sultan initially sought refuge abroad in **Gwadur** on the Makran coast of Baluchistan (in present-day Pakistan). The obliging local Baluchi ruler of Kalat granted Sultan possession of what was then an insignificant fishing village and the surrounding area, which Sultan retained following his return to Muscat and eventual accession to the throne, and which remained Omani territory until being finally sold back to Pakistan in 1958. Oman's long-standing links with Gwadur can still be seen in the large number of Omanis of Baluchi descent who migrated to the country over the years and who can now be found in towns and cities nationwide, in Muscat particularly.

Said the Great (1806–56)

The new ruler, **Said bin Sultan** (reigned 1806–56), sometimes referred to as "Said the Great", was just seventeen when he assumed power following the assassination of Badr bin Saif – the beginning of a half-century reign which, despite its murderous start, would see Oman reach the high point of its power and prosperity. He was also the first Omani ruler to take the title of "Sultan", which is still used by the country's supreme ruler today – thus becoming (rather confusingly) Sultan Said bin Sultan.

Not that all went smoothly to begin with, however; Wahhabi incursions continued until 1820, when Said was able to repulse them with help from the British and Persians. Said forged increasingly close links with Britain, whose government offered him protection in return for his assistance in quashing local Qawasim pirates (based in their stronghold at Ras al Khaimah in the present-day UAE) and in putting a stop – eventually – to the slave trade between Africa and Oman.

Said and Zanzibar

The latter part of Said's reign is inextricably linked with **Zanzibar**. The island had been in Omani hands since 1698, but remained something of a backwater until the sultan's first visit in 1828, when he passed laws obliging all landowners to establish **clove plantations**. Despite being met with initial resistance, the clove trade subsequently proved massively successful, underpinning the island's rapid development and increasing prosperity.

Said himself was increasingly drawn to East Africa, and in 1832 moved his official residence from Muscat to Zanzibar, attracted by the island's congenial surroundings and far more promising economic prospects – which was very much to Africa's gain, and Oman's loss. Established in Zanzibar, Said ruled over a string of Omani settlements stretching for almost 1600km along the East African coast, and for considerable distances inland – as well as continuing to exercise nominal sovereignty over Muscat and Oman, although his prolonged absences led to inevitable intriguing and skirmishes among rival pretenders to the throne.

From his new base in Zanzibar, Said also provided invaluable assistance to Victorian explorers including Richard Burton, David Livingstone, Henry Stanley and even early Christian missionaries intent on penetrating the interior of the continent; Burton

1955	1957–1959	1962
With British support, the Sultan's forces expel Saudi troops from Buraimi and proceed to occupy the whole of Oman.	Rebels are defeated in the 18-month Jebel War, resulting in Oman's last imam fleeing the country.	Oil is discovered in Yibal. The first exports are shipped five years later, fueling dramatic growth in the economy.

returned the favour by stating that Said was "as shrewd, liberal and enlightened a prince as Arabia ever produced." **Relations with Britain** remained warm: in 1834 Said gifted King William IV his largest ship, the seventy-four gun *Liverpool*, while in 1854 he presented an even grander offering in the shape of the Khuriya Muriya (Hallaniyat) islands (see page 222), off the coast of Dhofar.

Said, the British and the slave trade

Said's apparent willingness to assist British efforts in suppressing the huge **slave trade** between East Africa and Arabia was particularly notable – although whether such efforts were the result of political expediency or genuine humanitarian scruples is not entirely clear. An initial treaty was signed with the British in 1822, though this simply bound Said to forgo trading in slaves himself rather than take active steps to stamp out the Afro-Arabian slave trade between Omani settlements in East Africa and Oman – and the slave market in Muscat itself continued to flourish. The 1822 treaty was reinforced with a new agreement in 1839 before Said signed a third treaty in 1845 that finally outlawed the export of slaves from areas of Africa under Omani control. Nevertheless, the keeping of slaves remained legal in Zanzibar until 1897.

Whatever the reasons, Said's anti-slavery policy struck at the economic root of both Oman and its East African colonies. In Zanzibar, for example, no less than three-quarters of the estimated population of 200,000 were slaves, while a wealthy Zanzibari might have owned anything up to a thousand slaves – indeed Said himself is thought to have lost a quarter of his annual income as a result of the new prohibitions following the 1822 agreement.

Economic decline and tribal unrest (1856–1912)

Said's death in 1856 left the predictable power vacuum, with unhappy results for the country. Omani territories were divided between his two sons, **Thuwaini** and **Majid**, with the former taking Oman and the latter Zanzibar – a rather uneven arrangement, given that Zanzibar was then far richer than Oman. Thuwaini attempted to reclaim Zanzibar by force, but was beaten back, at which point the British Government of India intervened. Oman and Zanzibar would henceforth remain two separate states – with considerable economic costs to the former. Recognizing the financial implications of the loss of its former colony, Lord Canning, the Governor-General of India, ruled in 1861 that Zanzibar should henceforth pay the government of Oman an annual sum of 40,000 Maria Theresa Thalers, a settlement known as the **Canning Award**. Perhaps not surprisingly, Zanzibar almost immediately defaulted on its payments and the British authorities (having brokered the arrangement) were forced to make good the difference from 1871 until 1956. Zanzibar, meanwhile, remained under Al Bu Said rule until 1964, when it became part of Tanzania.

Thuwaini enjoyed his half of the inheritance for only ten years before being killed in 1866 by his son **Salim**, who then declared himself sultan. The unpopular Salim lasted just two years before being driven into exile by his cousin, the energetic but fanatical **Azzan bin Qais**. Azzan did slightly better than Salim, holding onto the throne for three years before being killed by **Turki bin Said** (another son of Said bin Sultan). Meanwhile, in 1869 the troublesome Wahhabis returned yet again, taking advantage

1962	1967	1970
The Dhofar Liberation Front mounts a campaign of sabotage against the Sultan's forces.	The People's Republic of Yemen is born, adding fuel to the Dhofari insurgency across the border.	Sultan Said is deposed in a bloodless coup by his 30-year-old son, Qaboos, who prioritizes an overhaul of Oman's infrastructure.

of the confusion to occupy the Buraimi oasis for the fifth time before being once again repulsed.

Following his defeat of Azzan, Turki bin Said was proclaimed sultan in 1871 with the support of the British government in London – with whom he immediately signed a further treaty aimed at repressing the slave trade and curbing the trade in arms. The increasingly impoverished tribesmen of the interior, however, regarded their new sultan as little more than a British puppet and soon rose up in arms. A series of attacks against Muscat ensued, spearheaded by the powerful **Al Harthy** tribe from Sharqiya under **Salih bin Ali al Harthy**. Salih bin Ali led successive raids against Muscat in 1874 and 1877, capturing Muttrah and threatening Muscat itself until being bought off by the sultan. A third attack followed in 1883, this time repulsed, again with British naval assistance.

Meanwhile, in the far southwest of the country, the independent province of **Dhofar**, previously a somewhat anarchic patchwork of competing tribal areas, was slowly being brought into the Omani fold. Said the Great had already dispatched a force to the region in 1829, although it wasn't fully integrated into Oman until 1877, when Sultan Turki bin Said sent soldiers to take control of Salalah and garrison the town. Even then, the sultan's authority rarely ran much further than the immediate environs of Salalah itself – a situation that persisted right up until the final suppression of the Dhofar rebellion (see page 242) almost exactly a century later.

Turki died in 1883 and was succeeded by his son **Faisal bin Turki**, though events continued largely as before. Despite constant Hinawi–Ghafiri conflicts in the interior, the two rival groups joined forces in 1895 for yet another march on Muscat, now led by **Abdullah bin Salih** (son of Salih bin Ali). This time the rebels succeeded in finally capturing Muscat itself, watched by the British, who studiously kept their distance, refusing to assist either side.

The rebels were, once again, eventually bought off by the increasingly indebted Sultan Faisal, who now found that his writ ran only from Muscat to Muttrah, along the Batinah coast and in Sur and a few places in the interior, including Izki, Nizwa and the strategic Sumail Gap. Inland, the tribes lapsed into poverty, and were driven to inter-tribal raids or even mass emigration.

The arrival of the French

One by-product of the British failure to intervene on his behalf during the 1895 insurrection was that (despite two sizeable loans from the British Government of India) the infuriated Sultan Faisal turned increasingly to the **French** – who also had the advantage of being altogether more pliable when it came to matters relating to the slave trade and arms smuggling. When Faisal granted the French coaling facilities at Bandar Jissah the British sent a warship to Muscat harbour to put the sultan in his place, after which he was forced to give up his flirtation with the French. Relations subsequently improved, and in 1903 the Viceroy of India, Lord Curzon, visited Muscat and wrote off the sultan's debts to the British Government of India.

Insurrection in the interior (1912–32)

The inhabitants of the interior, however, were not greatly impressed by such instances of imperial largesse. The last straw, so far as the Omani tribes were

1972	1982	1992
SAS and Omani forces repel rebel forces in Mirbat, a significant victory for Qaboos in Dhofar.	After becoming extinct in the wild a decade earlier, Oman's oryx are granted a second lease of life with the opening of the Arabian Oryx Sanctuary.	The remains of Shisr – believed to be synonymous with ancient Ubar – are discovered at the edge of the Empty Quarter.

concerned, came in 1912, when the sultan, under British pressure, established an arms warehouse in Muscat, effectively strangling the lucrative trade in trans-Arabian arms smuggling which provided one source of income in the increasingly poverty-stricken country. Unfortunately for the Omanis, many of these weapons were subsequently used against British soldiers in northwest India – hence the British desire to wipe out the trade.

In 1913, a meeting of Ghafiri tribal sheikhs arranged for the election, at Tanuf, of a **new imam**, the first since the death of Said bin Ahmad 110 years earlier. The revival of the office of imam was intended as a direct challenge to the authority of the sultan in Muscat (although the chosen candidate, one Salim bin Rashid al Kharusi, would remain a largely ceremonial figurehead in the conflicts to come). Civil war once again ensued. Shortly afterwards the rebels captured Nizwa and then Izki, after which the Hinawi tribes joined the uprising.

Then, in October 1913, Sultan Faisal died, and was succeeded by his son **Sultan Taimur bin Faisal**. Taimur thus inherited his father's parlous finances and a full-blown rebellion in the interior. Attempts at negotiation proved fruitless, and in 1915 the British Government of India was forced to send a battalion of Indian troops to Muscat to beat off a rebel attack led by Isa bin Salih (another son of the rebellious Salih bin Ali), culminating in a fierce battle at Muscat's Bait al Falaj (see p.00). The attack was repulsed, although the rebellion dragged on for five more years. Finally, in 1920, the **Treaty of Seeb** was signed between the two warring factions, whereby the sultan effectively handed over control of the interior to its tribal leaders, confirming the final division of the Sultanate of Muscat and Oman into two more or less autonomous states. The luckless new imam, Salim bin Rashid, meanwhile was assassinated in 1920 and suceeded as imam by Mohammad bin Abdullah al Khalili, a nominee of Isa bin Salih.

Sultan Said bin Taimur and the search for oil (1932–55)

The new sultan, Taimur, proved a reluctant ruler. In 1920, finding himself the virtually powerless ruler of a bankrupt state, hamstrung (as he saw it) by British interference, he sailed to Bombay and attempted to abdicate. The Government of Britain refused to accept his abdication, however, and the sultan himself refused to return to Muscat. He spent the next eleven years in India, during which power effectively passed to a council of ministers led by his young son, Said.

Taimur returned to Oman in 1931. In 1932, he was finally able to relinquish the throne and hand over power to his son, who became **Sultan Said bin Taimur**. Sultan Said enjoys a rather ambiguous position in the history of Oman. His early rule was marked by a commendable level of fiscal and diplomatic prudence, as he succeeded in liquidating his inherited debts and maintaining peaceful relations with the imam in the interior for two decades – although Oman as a whole lapsed into a state of almost medieval torpor, with most of the country's population leading lives of unremitting hardship and poverty.

The possibility of Oman finally achieving the means to break out of its endless cycle of isolation and poverty came thanks to **oil**, which was by the 1930s already transforming the economies of many other countries in the Middle East. By the 1940s, oil exploration was proceeding apace in Oman, although efforts at prospecting were

1996	2011	2012
Qaboos creates a council composed of an elected Consultative Council (Majlis Ash Shura) and an appointed State Council (Majlis ad Dawla).	As the Arab Spring sweeps the region, peaceful protests are held in Oman, leading to modest government reforms.	The new port of Duqm opens as part of Oman's ambitious diversification strategy.

significantly hindered by the fact that the interior (where the oil was presumed to be) was effectively an independent state, not to mention the difficulties presented by the country's inhospitable and largely unmapped terrain.

The situation was also complicated by further military and political skirmishes with the Saudis, who returned yet again to re-occupy the **Buraimi oasis**, largely in the hope that oil would eventually be found there (see box, p.136). Despite this setback, in October 1954 the sultan's forces captured Ibri, close to the site of the most important oil exploration in Fahud (see box, p.230), finally securing a base for oil exploration in the interior; for a first-hand account of this, read *Arabian Destiny* by Edward Henderson, who played a leading role in the affair (see page 253).

Following the loss of Ibri, and with the encouragement of the Saudis, the newly elected imam, **Sheikh Ghalib bin Ali al Hina'i**, launched attempts to have the Imamate accepted as a member of the Arab League – an effort to have the interior, or "Oman proper", recognized as an independent, sovereign state.

Tribal Resistance and the Jebel War (1955–59)

Faced with the occupying Saudis in Buraimi and Imam Ghalib's attempts at secession, Sultan Said and the British finally took action. In 1955, the Saudi forces were expelled from Buraimi with the help of the Trucial Oman Scouts (a small, Sharjah-based force consisting of a batallion of Arab troops under British command), after which the sultan's forces, with continued British support, went on to occupy the whole country, taking Rustaq and Nizwa en route. Shortly afterwards, Sultan Said travelled from Salalah to Muscat through his newly reconquered dominions, a journey memorably described in Jan Morris's *Sultan in Oman* (see page 253).

Resistance to the rule of Muscat was far from over, however – although it had more to do with the self-interested ambitions of local tribal leaders (and their Saudi backers) rather than the tribal population at large. The three leaders most responsible were **Suleyman bin Himyar al Nabhani**, the self-styled "King of the Jebel Akhdar", Imam Ghalib and his brother Talib. Insurrection flared up again in 1957, the beginning of an eighteen-month rebellion subsequently known as the **Jebel War**. At the beginning of the conflict, the nervous *wali* of Nizwa abandoned the city and its fort to the rebels, while the towns of Bahla and Izki capitulated immediately afterwards.

Sultan Said turned for help to the British, who provided both air and land forces, retaking Nizwa after one and a half days' fighting and routing the rebels. Suleyman, Talib and Ghalib fled into the heights of the Jebel Akhdar, where they clung on until January 1959, until being ousted in a final assault by combined Omani and British forces, after which they fled abroad.

Dhofari Insurgency and oil (1959–69)

The end of the Jebel War might have appeared to mark the final reunification of the country, but just as most of Oman was beginning to enjoy a new-found sense of peace and security (if not yet prosperity) the tribesmen of the Dhofar interior launched a new rebellion. The movement's figurehead was a dissatisfied tribal leader, Mussalim bin Nafl. In 1962, bin Nafl formed the **Dhofar Liberation Front** (DLF), obtaining arms

2014	2014–2015	2018
Oil prices decline sharply, putting immense strain on state funds and underlining the need for non-oil revenue.	Sultan Qaboos spends eight months in Germany for medical treatment, stoking debates over succession.	A massive new passenger terminal is unveiled at Muscat International Airport, capable of welcoming 12 million passengers per year.

and equipment from ever antagonistic Saudi Arabia, as well as support from the exiled imam Ghalib Bin Ali. From late 1962 onwards, bin Nafl and his troops began a series of sabotage attacks against oil vehicles, government posts and the British air base at Salalah.

Sultan Said's response to the insurrection was to assemble the so-called **Dhofar Force** (DF), a locally recruited irregular unit of just sixty men. The move backfired spectacularly when, in April 1966, members of the DF turned on their employer and attempted to assassinate the sultan. Sultan Said was so shaken by this that he subsequently rarely left the safety of his palace in Salalah – fuelling rumours that the British were running Oman through a phantom ruler. In fact, the sultan was still very much involved, launching a full-scale military offensive against the DF despite the advice of his British advisors, including heavy-handed punitive missions against villages thought to be harbouring rebels.

The rebellion assumed even more serious proportions in **1967**, thanks to two events. The first was the Six Day War and the crushing Israeli victory over the combined forces of Egypt, Syria and Jordan – a military disaster which radicalized opinion throughout the Arab world. Even more important was the British withdrawal from Aden and the establishment of the neo-Marxist People's Democratic Republic of Yemen (**PDRY**), also known as South Yemen. The new Yemeni government became a reliable source of arms, supplies and training facilities just over the border from Dhofar, and fresh recruits from among Yemeni groups, meaning that the rebels were increasingly well armed and organized.

Yemeni and other outside influences led to the rebellion becoming increasingly radicalized. In 1968 the movement renamed itself the Popular Front for the Liberation of the Occupied Arabian Gulf (**PFLOAG**), adopting an increasingly Marxist–Leninist stance that resulted in increased backing from South Yemen, China and Russia. The situation had all the makings of an Arabian Vietnam, with an absolutist monarch backed by the old imperial power of Britain on one hand, and a highly trained and motivated proto-Communist force on the other.

The insurgents were by now excellently equipped with automatic rifles, heavy machine guns, mortars and rockets. The Sultan's Armed Forces, by contrast, were chronically under-resourced and badly trained, with no more than a thousand fighters, many of them equipped with World War II-era bolt-action rifles. In addition, no Omani held a rank above that of lieutenant (a result of the Sultan's fears of opposition to his rule among the armed forces). The Sultan's Armed Forces were generally restricted to Salalah and its immediate environs, while the British RAF and Royal Artillery had to be deployed to protect the airfield at Salalah. By **1969** PFLOAG fighters had overrun much of the Jebel Dhofar, and cut the only road across it, from Salalah to Thumrait, effectively paralyzing the region, and persuading many observers, including the sultan's British advisors, that only a new ruler could save Oman from its gradual slide into anarchy.

The discovery of oil

Ironically, just as the Dhofar rebellion was threatening to tip the entire country into chaos, the key to its future prosperity was being uncovered, with the **discovery of oil** in 1962 at Yabil, and later at Natih and Fahud (see box above). Exports began in 1967, and although the reserves were modest compared to those in nearby Saudi Arabia, Abu Dhabi and elsewhere around the Gulf, they were at least sufficient to finally release the Omani population from the grinding poverty in which they had been previously trapped.

Unfortunately, Sultan Said's response to his new-found largesse was disappointingly half-hearted. Despite the new oil money pouring into the country, the sultan appeared struck immobile by a lifetime's habit of financial caution. These frugal habits had served him well in the past when the country was virtually bankrupt, but were no longer suited to massively changed circumstances. Instead of investing the money in much-needed development, Said simply consigned the new revenues of state to a chest under his bed – where they stayed.

OIL IN OMAN

The **search for oil** in Oman began in 1925 – although the very first geological survey of the country found no evidence of oil reserves. Despite this initial failure, hopes of oil remained, and in 1937 Sultan Said bin Taimur granted a 75-year concession to the Iraq Petroleum Company (IPC) to prospect for reserves.

Further prospecting was interrupted by World War II and serious exploration didn't begin until 1954, although oil company geologists were hindered by assorted tribal conflicts which blocked access to what was considered the most promising site, at **Fahud**, in the desert outside Ibri. Despite this, surveys of the Fahud region began later that year, although no oil was initially found. Further drillings followed, also without success. Continued logistical problems, allied to a surfeit of oil on the world market, led to most of the original stakeholders in the IPC withdrawing from the venture in 1960.

The perseverance of the two remaining companies, Shell and Partex, however, soon paid off. In 1962 oil was discovered at **Yibal**, in the Dhahirah desert south of Fahud, while in 1963 further reserves were discovered at nearby **Natih** and, finally, at **Fahud** (within a few hundred metres of the original IPC drillings). A 276km pipeline was laid, followed by the construction of a refinery at Mina al Fahal in Muscat, with the **first exports** being shipped in July 1967.

The effect of oil on Oman has been profound. Although the country has never enjoyed the fabulous oil revenues enjoyed by places such as Saudi Arabia, Abu Dhabi and Qatar, oil monies provided the funds with which to drag Oman out of poverty and give it a modern infrastructure. As of 2017, Oman was ranked the world's 19th largest oil producer and its 16th largest exporter (1.9 percent of the global total) while claiming the world's 22nd largest proven reserves. Even so, steadily dwindling reserves and steadily low oil prices – particularly since 2014 – have forced the country's leaders to take more active steps to diversify the national economy (see page 245), with the aim of reducing oil's contribution to GDP (about 34 percent in 2018) to under twenty percent by 2020.

The Omani Renaissance (1970–2000)

The end of Sultan Said's old-fashioned and autocratic rule finally came on July 23, 1970, when he was deposed in an almost entirely peaceful **coup** (organized with tacit British assistance and approval). His 30-year-old son, **Qaboos**, who had been kept under virtual house arrest by his father in the palace in Salalah, was installed in his place, while the deposed sultan was packed off into exile in England, where he spent the last two years of his life living in state at London's *Dorchester Hotel*.

The young sultan was faced with widespread dissatisfaction among his new subjects, endemic poverty and a nation which had totally lost touch with the modern world. His most pressing problem, however, was the continuing insurrection in **Dhofar**. To this he responded with characteristic decisiveness. His first act was to offer a general amnesty to all rebels, even offering cash incentives to surrendering insurgents. Allied to this was a comprehensive "hearts and minds" campaign, under the moniker "The Hand of God Destroys Communism" – an attempt to appeal to traditional Islamic values in opposition to the rebels' secular ethos. Rebels who surrendered were subsequently reformed into irregular units who were sent back out into the *jebel* as part of the propaganda war – and where, as locals, they had far more success than fighters from other parts of Oman. In addition, twenty British Royal Engineers were sent out to construct schools, health centres and to drill wells, an RAF medical team began operating out of Salalah hospital and money was provided for a Dhofar Development Programme. These peaceable efforts were also backed by strong military measures. The Sultan's Armed Forces were enlarged and re-equipped, while the Omani Air Force was also expanded.

As a result of these combined measures, the rebels were soon deprived both of local support and supplies from the PDRY. The decisive confrontation came at the **Battle of Mirbat** (see page 221), when 300 rebels attacked the Sultan's Armed Forces, which were under the command of nine SAS soldiers, only to be driven back with heavy losses. From this point on, the rebels were forced steadily backwards, their demise hastened by diminishing levels of support from the Soviet Union and China. The final defeat of the rebellion was announced in January 1976, although isolated incidents took place as late as 1979.

Modernization and reform

Meanwhile, Sultan Qaboos launched a far-ranging programme of modernization and reform – or the **Omani Renaissance**, as it is now popularly known. One of his first acts was to change the name of the country from the "Sultanate of Muscat and Oman" to "The Sultanate of Oman", thereby symbolically erasing the historical divide between coast and interior which had plagued the country for so long. Qaboos also made a concerted effort to have Oman recognized as a fully sovereign independent state, and by the end of 1971 the country had joined the United Nations, the Arab League and the International Monetary Fund.

At home, rapid development began. Qaboos had inherited a country with no newspapers, radio or television, no civil service and just one hospital, two graded roads and three schools. The average life expectancy was 47 (it has since risen to 77). Large numbers of new schools and hospitals were swiftly constructed and a civil service established. Efforts were also made to lure back home disaffected Omanis who had emigrated, while many Zanzibaris and Kenyans of Omani origin were welcomed to the country.

Political progress also followed. In 1996 Qaboos announced the formation of a bicameral "legislative" body known as the Oman Council, composed of an elected **Consultative Council** (Majlis Ash Shura) – first created in 1991 – and an appointed **State Council** (Majlis ad Dawla). The council holds very little legislative power, however, and all final decisions remain within the hands of the sultan and his advisors. Leading the way among Gulf countries, Oman granted women the right to stand for elections to the Consultative Council in 1994, the same year they were given the right to vote.

Oman in the twenty-first century

Twenty-first-century Oman is an increasingly modern and prosperous place – and virtually unrecognizable from the country of just four decades ago. A study in late 2010 by the United Nations Development Programme rated Oman – out of the 135 countries surveyed – as the "most improved" country over the previous forty years.

One measure of the country's stability was provided by events during the so-called Arab Spring of early 2011. What began as a political earthquake in Tunisia, Egypt, Bahrain and neighbouring Yemen, however, produced only a fairly modest ripple in Oman itself. Small-scale protests occurred in various parts of the country, centred on Majlis ash Shura in Muscat and the Globe roundabout in Sohar, although notably these were aimed more at perceived government corruption and cronyism, along with practical concerns such as unemployment and the cost of living, rather than with making any attempt to upset the basic political status quo; without exception even the most vehement demonstrators were adamant in professing their loyalty to Sultan Qaboos. Only in **Sohar** did events turn serious when a handful of protesters were killed while attacking a police station, although even there the situation was rapidly returned to normal. In response to the raised concerns, the sultan promptly announced a modest package of reforms, including financial aid to the unemployed and the creation of elected municipal councils.

Future challenges

Approaching a decade since the Arab Spring, significant challenges continue to face the country. Perhaps most pressing are the steadily dwindling oil reserves which have underpinned the country's transformation (and still translate to nearly eighty percent of state revenue). In recent years consistently low oil prices have placed immense strain on the state's available funds. Fortunately, the country's leaders have taken major steps to **diversify the economy** with the aim of reducing oil's contribution to GDP from the current thirty-four percent to less than twenty percent by 2020. The major growth area is industry and manufacturing, while the state has also made significant investments in education and technology. Another focus, though on a somewhat smaller scale, has been tourism, primarily of the luxury variety. Steady growth in this sector is currently on track to contribute as much as three percent to the GDP by 2020, and it is hoped that this number will rise to six percent by 2040.

Meanwhile, the country's burgeoning birth rate and youthful population (with a median age of just 25 years) has created a potential **demographic time bomb**, given the shortage of jobs for the large numbers of educated young Omanis entering the workplace. There is also an increasing resentment against the country's reliance on **expatriate labour**, and the perception that foreigners are taking what should, by rights, be Omani jobs (even if, in fact, at least some of these jobs are ones which Omanis themselves are unwilling or unqualified to perform).

The **role of women** in Omani society is also evolving. The first women members of Majlis ad Dawla were appointed in 2000, with women finally being given the vote in 2003. There are now more women than men in higher education, while they also make up well over a third of the country's civil service. Women can also stand for election to Majlis ash Shura, although there is currently only one elected female councillor out of a total of 85 (next elections in 2019). Women are slightly better-represented within Majlis ad Dawla, numbering six out of 83 members, all of which are directly appointed by the sultan.

One of the most important challenges ahead will fall on the shoulders of Sultan Qaboos' successor. Touting "Omani exceptionalism", the widely respected Sultan has been able to steer the country clear of the sectarian, Saudi-Iranian drama that has engulfed much of the rest of the region – staying aloof from the ongoing miliary campaign in neighbouring Yemen since 2015 and circumventing the blockade of Qatar that began in 2017. Omanis have good reason to hope that whoever is next in line will be able to maintain the country's steadfast independence in matters of foreign policy.

The succession question

Indeed, the question of who will eventually **succeed Sultan Qaboos** (aged 77 at the time of writing) is another concern, given that he remains childless (his only marriage, in 1976, having ended soon afterwards in divorce). Qaboos has failed to name his choice of successor, although the names of his two favoured candidates are said to be sealed within hidden letters kept in Muscat and Salalah, intended to provide guidance after his death in the event that the royal family cannot agree on a successor. The three sons (all now in their sixties) of Qaboos's uncle and former prime minister Tarik bin Taimur al Said have long been considered likely successors, particularly Sayyid Asaad bin Tariq Al Said – a graduate of Britain's Royal Military Academy Sandhurst, long-time army commander and special representative of the Sultan, who was appointed deputy prime minister for international cooperation in 2017. As the brothers have aged, the pool of candidates has extended to include family members of the next generation, the most highly considered among these being Sayyid Taimur bin Asad bin Tariq Al Said, the son of Sayyid Asaad.

The question of succession has become particularly pressing in recent years as rumours of the sultan's health issues have circulated. From 2014 to 2015, Qaboos was absent for eight months while receiving medical treatment in Germany, reportedly for colon cancer. At present, however, the beloved septuagenarian appears to be back on his feet – in "complete health" according to state media – and the nation whose spectacular transformation he has overseen can face the future with genuine, if cautious, optimism.

Fortified Oman

Oman is one of the world's most extensively fortified nations, a reflection of the unsettled nature of life in the peninsula in times past. There are more than five hundred forts in the country – indeed there's hardly a town in Oman which doesn't boast at least one, and often several – while numerous other examples of fortified architecture can be found, ranging from (fortified houses) and walled villages through to the innumerable watchtowers which dot the summits of ridges and hilltops across the land.

Omani forts

Forts played a vital role in the life of traditional Oman. Their principal function was, of course, military, providing a home to local militia and also serving as a refuge for the entire population of the village or town in case of attack. Forts also usually housed the residence of the local *wali* (governor) and his *majlis*, used to receive visitors and as a forum in which the *wali* and other local leaders would meet to discuss matters of importance. Not surprisingly, therefore, possession of the local fort offered whoever held it de facto control over the entire surrounding region.

Fort design

No two forts in Oman are exactly alike. Those built on flat ground along the coast tend to be square, typically – but not always – with a tower at each corner. Those in the mountains are usually built above the surrounding countryside on easily defensible rock outcrops, being moulded to the contours of the stone on which they sit, and thus more irregularly shaped. A few forts, notably those at Buraimi and Bukha, also have moats, although these are relatively rare. All forts have at least one tower (although most usually have several), which offered a good vantage point over the surrounding countryside and a raised position from which to fire in the event of hostilities.

Designs also changed over time. The introduction of the **cannon** into the Arabian military arsenal, in particular, had far-reaching effects on the design of Omani forts. Walls were thickened massively, while rounded towers also became the norm – both features which helped absorb and reduce the impact of cannonfire. Inside the fort, reinforced towers and terraces were constructed to provide a stable platform from which to fire cannon on approaching attackers; the great round tower at Nizwa, providing support for twenty-plus cannon offering a 360-degree line of fire, is perhaps the most famous example.

The interior of most forts is typically divided into military and domestic areas; the word "fort" can be translated in Arabic as either *qala* or *hisn* (or *husn*), although the former more properly refers to the military portions of a fort, while *hisn* describes the residential sections. Most forts include a large **courtyard**, with the *wali*'s **residential quarters** usually grouped together in one corner. These lodgings typically consist of the *wali*'s own bedroom/apartment, along with other bedrooms, a *majlis* (and perhaps a women's *majlis* as well), a kitchen, stores for dates and arms, barracks for the resident soldiers and at least one jail.

Defensive features

Whatever the design, defensive considerations were always paramount. All Omani forts are surrounded by high **walls** topped by battlements, ranging from spiky, saw-tooth crenellations to more rounded designs. Inside the walls, loopholes provided safe cover from which to fire on enemies below, along with openings down which boiling date juice could be poured (or heavy objects dropped) onto the heads of attackers. Windows, where they existed, were reinforced with heavy iron grilles and thick wooden shutters which could be secured from inside.

Potential attackers, assuming they managed to survive the barrage of musket and cannon fire (not to mention the cascade of boiling date juice) from above, would then have to breach the **gateway**. All Omani forts, even the largest, were provided with just a single entrance to limit access and provide security. Gateways themselves were typically protected by massive hardwood doors (often elaborately carved), reinforced with iron spikes. Inset within each large door was a second, much smaller, door with an unusually high sill, limiting access to one person at a time and forcing anyone entering into an awkwardly bent posture.

Inside, many forts feature a disorienting labyrinth of narrow stairways, designed to confuse intruders and restrict access to one person at a time. Some stairways (at Nizwa fort, for example) also boast further defensive features such as "murder holes" – overhead openings down which boiling date juice and heavy objects could be poured or dropped onto the enemy, or down which water could be poured to extinguish fires – and "pitfalls", deep dark holes into which unsuspecting attackers could easily tumble.

Given the general impregnability of Omani forts, many attackers chose to **besiege** them rather than storm them, although this too brought no particular guarantee of success; Nizwa Fort, for example, is said to have successfully resisted one siege lasting several years. All Omani forts boast their own well, while many also have dedicated *aflaj*, which guaranteed a reliable source of water; these were often designed to issue from the ground within the walls of a castle, avoiding the possibility of the water supply being poisoned by attackers outside. Some forts were also equipped with secret escape tunnels in the event that the trapped *wali* or other bigwigs decided to beat a hasty retreat.

Surs, watchtowers and walls

Slightly different from the traditional fort is the **sur**, or fortified house. Exactly where a fort ends and a *sur* begins is difficult to say, although *surs* tend generally to be smaller, taller and most domestic in character. Examples include the magnificent Bait Na'aman near Barka; the more modest but still solid and largely windowless mudbrick cubes which are such a feature of Sharqiya towns such as Ibra, Jalaan Bani Bu Hassan, Al Kamil and Mintrib; and the distinctive Yemeni-inspired examples found in Dhofar, Mirbat in particular.

Even more numerous than the country's forts are its **watchtowers** (*abraj*; singular: *burj*). In parts of the country (particularly driving up the Sumail gap, or around Ibra and other towns in Sharqiya) it seems that virtually every ridgetop and rock outcrop is dotted with at least one of these characteristic structures. Watchtowers were generally arranged in defensive chains surrounding an important town, mountain pass or oasis. The towers – usually circular, occasionally square – were designed to be impregnable, with earth or stone-filled bases, a single, difficult-to-reach doorway on an upper level (entrance would have been via a ladder, which was pulled up afterwards) and crenellated rooftops commanding 360-degree views of the surrounding area and offering elevated lines of fire over attackers below.

Walled towns and villages are also common throughout the country. The old walled quarter of Al Aqr in Nizwa, with its elaborate, crumbling gateways, is a particularly fine example, as is the nearby old town of Bahla, whose magnificent walls extend for some 12km. Walled villages include well-preserved Al Munisifeh and Al Qanatar in Ibra, and the remarkable fortified village of As Suleif in Ibri.

Building materials

The basic building material of all traditional Omani architecture is **mudbrick** (or adobe, from the Arabic *al tob*, meaning "mud"). Bricks were made from alluvial clay, containing a mixture of grit and silt – that from date plantations was generally considered to be the best for building. Chopped straw was added to the clay to reduce shrinkage and warping during the drying process and to improve resistance to erosion. The resulting mixture was then left to "cure" for four or five days before being moulded into bricks. **Stone**, readily available throughout the mountains, was relatively little used, perhaps because of the difficulty in transporting and cutting it, although it can often be seen in parts of larger structures, particularly in the foundations.

All structures, whether mudbrick or stone, were traditionally bound together with and then covered in **sarooj**, a type of mortar-cum-plaster. This was made from mudcakes which were fired together with limestone at extreme temperatures (in excess of 850°C) for as long as a week. The ashy residue was then pulverized and mixed with water and the resultant substance used to bind bricks and stone, and to provide a smooth lustrous finish.

Restoration

At the time of Sultan Qaboos's accession in 1970, most forts in Oman were in advanced states of dilapidation. Since then, the Omani government has made huge strides in the massive project of restoring the nation's traditional landmarks and making them safe for posterity – a massive undertaking covering hundreds of buildings. Many major forts have now been beautifully renovated and opened to the public, most notably the mighty Bahla fort (previously closed from 1987 until 2012), although work on others continues. Others, such as the mudbrick monster fort at Jalan Bani Bu Ali, remain entirely untouched despite their perilous condition, and with no sign of restoration in sight.

The fate of Oman's traditional **domestic architecture** remains even more parlous. Many of the country's old mudbrick fortified villages are steadily crumbling away, with large numbers now little more than roofless shells – undeniably picturesque at present, although in danger of vanishing completely in the next decade or so if urgent work is not begun to stabilize them.

Wildlife

Despite its largely arid and inhospitable environment, Oman supports a surprisingly wide range of animal life – although many creatures are rarely seen by casual visitors. The mountains are home to many of the country's most distinctive species, ranging from the shaggy tahr through to the legendary but famously elusive Arabian leopard. Inland, the desert plains of the interior are home to the iconic Arabian oryx and occasional herds of gazelle, while the coastal lagoons and salt-flats support large numbers of migratory bird species, including colourful flocks of pink flamingoes. The waters around Oman are rich in sea life, including an exceptional range of dolphins and whales, plus thousands of turtles which nest on shores around the country.

Mammals

Oman is home to around 75 species of **mammal**, although almost all are rare, and very seldom sighted in the wild. Perhaps the most famous is the **Arabian leopard** (*Panthera pardus nimr*) – the world's smallest, at under 1m long and half the weight of its African cousin. The government-run Arabian Leopard Project has recorded thirty-five leopards in Dhofar, and guesses that the actual number is probably around fifty, most of which inhabit the natural reserve of Jebel Samhan. Overall, it is estimated that there remain fewer than two hundred Arabian leopards in the wild, including some in Saudi Arabia and Yemen. Not surprisingly, the animal is listed as "critically endangered" – only one step up from "extinct" – on the International Union for Conservation of Nature and Natural Resources' "Red List".

Despite its modest size, the leopard is still the apex hunter in Arabia and has no natural predators (except humans), although leopard cubs are potentially at risk from foxes, hyenas and wolves. Male leopards have a territory of around 300 square kilometres and are opportunistic hunters, feeding on a range of smaller mammals and birds, plus human livestock – something which has brought them into conflict with humans in the past. This most notably took place in Musandam in the 1980s, when a systematic cull of local leopards was undertaken by tribesmen protecting their herds – none are believed to survive on the peninsula today. Fortunately, killing a leopard now entails a fine of 1000–5000 OR and up to five years in jail.

Antelopes and other mammals

The deserts of southern Oman are home to populations of various small- and medium-sized antelopes. Of these, the best known is the **Arabian oryx** (or white oryx; *Oryx leucoryx*; in Arabic, *al maha*). This has become one of the iconic animals of Oman – and, indeed, of other countries around the Gulf (particularly Qatar, where it's the national animal) – thanks to its distinctively long, sweeping horns. One theory holds that the oryx is a possible source for the myth of the unicorn, given that the two horns can easily merge into one when seen in side profile. Living in herds of around ten to fifteen animals, the remarkably strong and hardy oryx is perfectly adapted to desert life, and capable of going without water for months, surviving entirely off moisture contained in foliage. Despite being a favoured prey of Bedu hunters, the oryx's speed and well-developed reflexes meant that only relatively few were ever killed – at least until the advent of motorized vehicles and modern rifles in the twentieth century (see box opposite).

HUNTING AND CONSERVATION IN OMAN

Hunting has always played a crucial role in traditional Bedu life, as a combination of practical necessity (a large Arabian oryx could feed a family for a week) and sheer pleasure in the traditional thrill of the chase. In times past, this was a carefully matched contest between the hunter, on foot or camel-back, and his wary, fleet-flooted prey. The advent of modern motor vehicles and sophisticated rifles and other firearms in the mid-twentieth century destroyed this delicate balance, however, plunging many species into near extinction. In parts of Arabia the traditional Bedu hunt was replaced with posses of urban thrill-seekers in 4WD trucks literally machine-gunning their way across the desert, massacring as many as a hundred oryx and other creatures in a single afternoon. Not surprisingly, by 1972 the Arabian oryx had become extinct in the wild, with numerous other species, such as the region's gazelles and leopards, not far behind.

Oman's response to this ecological cataclysm was commendably swift, and under Sultan Qaboos the country has been in the vanguard of **conservation** efforts in the peninsula. The hunting of endangered species was made a criminal offence in 1979, and in 1982 the Arabian Oryx Sanctuary, now the Al Wusta Wildlife Reserve (see page 197) became the first of its kind in the Gulf. Important areas are now protected (in some form) across the country, including the Ras al Jinz turtle beach (see page 182), the Daymaniyat Islands (see page 128), and the Jebel Samhan nature reserve (see page 218), as well as various *khors* along the Salalah coast.

Other resident antelopes are the **Arabian gazelle** (or mountain gazelle; *Gazella gazella*) and the less common **reem gazelle** (or sand gazelle; *Gazella subgutturosa marica*). The unusual **Arabian tahr** (*Arabitragus jayakari*) is a mix of antelope and goat, with thick curved horns and a dense woolly fleece. It's now extremely rare in the wild, clinging to a few remote spots in the mountains. The **Nubian ibex** (*Capra ibex nubiana*) is another rare goat-antelope – males sport particularly impressive curved horns, reaching up to 1m in length.

Other rare mammals include canine species such as the Arabian wolf, striped hyena and Blanford's fox, small felines including the caracal, Gordon's wildcat (or sand cat), and the prettily named but famously ferocious honey badger. Rodents include the colourful Indian-crested porcupine and the small hyrax.

Birds

Oman's location between Europe, Asia and Africa makes its something of an ornithological crossroads, attracting a wide range of migrants, some of which also breed here – only about 90 of the 528 species of bird recorded in Oman are actually permanent residents.

Eye-catching common indigenous species which can be seen at any time of the year – even in Muscat – include Indian rollers, green bee-eaters, yellow-vented bulbuls and purple sunbirds. Large numbers of migratory **aquatic birds** frequent the coastal lagoons and creeks, including herons, sandpipers and plovers, which migrate here from their breeding grounds in northern Europe and Siberia. Even more seemingly incongruous are the colourful flocks of greater flamingo which frequent the south coast. Common **birds of prey** include the striking Egyptian vulture, often seen floating on the thermals over the Western Hajar, and the Steppe eagle.

Mountains, coast and desert all have their characteristic avian residents. **Dhofar** and southern Oman are particularly rich in birdlife thanks to the lush habitats produced by the annual *khareef* (monsoon), and the abundance of coastal lagoons. Some thirty species which aren't encountered elsewhere in the country can be found here, including Rüppel's weaver, Didric cuckoo and the African Scops owl.

For further information about the birds of Oman, get hold of one of the birdwatching guides (see page 254) or check out local experts Hanne and Jens Erikens' regularly updated website, ⓦ birdsoman.com.

Marine life

Oman's extensive coastline and relatively unspoilt marine environment plays host to an outstanding array of marine life. Larger marine creatures are particularly well represented – no less than twenty types of cetaceans can be found in the waters around Oman – although your only chance of seeing any of these is by going diving with a specialist operator (see pages 62, 129, 157 and 210).

Dolphins are a common sight in the *khors* of Musandam (especially the humpback variety) and along the coast near Muscat. The most common species around Muscat are spinner dolphins (named for their spinning leaps through the air), often in mixed groups with common dolphins, plus less frequently spotted bottlenose dolphins.

Oman's waters are also rich in **whales**, including blue, humpback, sperm and Bryde's, as well as false killer whales, killer whales and whale sharks. These are all much less frequently seen by casual tourists than dolphins, although they might occasionally be spotted on diving trips. The coast around Mirbat is probably the most likely area, thanks to the kilometre-deep submarine trenches, which run relatively close to shore. The southern coast is particularly interesting thanks to the effects of the annual *khareef*, which produces a stream of cold, nutrient-rich water in which sea kelp and other edibles flourish. A population of humpback whales inhabits the waters here – studies suggest it is one of the very few groups of humpback around the world which don't migrate, given that the seasonal variations in the local waters provide them with all they need.

Oman is also a superb **turtle-watching** destination. Four of the seven main species of marine turtle – the green, olive ridley, hawksbill and loggerhead – nest in Oman, while a fifth, the leatherback, can also occasionally be found in Omani waters. The major turtle-nesting sights are the green turtle beach at Ras al Jinz (see page 182), and the beaches of Masirah island (see page 195), which see visits from all four species. Turtles can also be seen nesting around Ras al Hadd (see page 182) and at Bandar al Jissah in Muscat (see page 62).

Books

There's a surprising amount written about Oman, largely by the various explorers, adventurers and soldiers who tramped through the country between the 1950s and 1990s in search of oil, insurgents and ancient ruins. Accounts of the modern nation are thinner on the ground, as are reliable accounts of the sultanate's earlier history. Books marked with the ★ symbol are particularly recommended.

HISTORY, EXPLORATION AND TRAVELOGUES

Ranulph Fiennes *Atlantis of the Sands*. Rambling account of Fiennes' twenty-year quest to discover the fabled city of Ubar (see page 227), starting during his service as an officer in the Sultan's Armed Forces in Salalah in the late 1960s through to the discovery of the ruins at Shisr in 1992. First-hand accounts of military action against Dhofari rebels and some interesting (if haphazard) forays into Arabian prehistory are the highlights, although the latter part of the book is marred by far too much autobiographical waffle, pointless name-dropping and random irrelevant accounts of assorted polar expeditions.

Ian Gardiner *In the Service of the Sultan: A First-Hand Account of the Dhofar Insurgency*. Written by a former Royal Marines officer, this crisply written account of the Dhofar rebellion offers a fascinating description of the conflict, while the early chapters of the book paint an absorbing picture of local life in Dhofar and elsewhere at the very beginning of the Omani Renaissance.

Hussein Ghubash *Oman: The Islamic Democratic Tradition*. This scholarly tome by a leading Gulf historian is the nearest thing currently available to a comprehensive history of the country. The book focuses on Oman's unique imamate and Ibadhi traditions, but also provides wide-ranging coverage of other events from the Bronze Age through to the 1960s, with particularly strong coverage of the colonial period.

Edward Henderson *Arabian Destiny*. An autobiographical account of Henderson's years in Oman and the UAE from 1948 to 1956 working for the Petroleum Development Trucial Coast, a position which gave him a privileged insight into the development of the modern Gulf. There are eyewitness accounts of the battle for Buraimi and of events preceding the outbreak of the Jebel War, and the book also features fascinating portraits of Muscat, Dubai, Abu Dhabi and Al Ain in the early 1950s. Unfortunately, it's difficult to get hold of outside the Gulf.

Tim Mackintosh-Smith *Travels with a Tangerine: A Journey in the Footsteps of Ibn Battutah*. Enjoyable account of the English Arabist and adventurer's journey in the footsteps of Ibn Battutah from Morocco to Istanbul, with visits to Sur, Salalah and the Hallaniyat islands en route.

Beautifully written, with a heady blend of often hilarious contemporary travelogue and recondite snippets of historical information.

★ **Jan Morris** *Sultan in Oman*. One of the best books ever written about the country. It provides a memorable first-hand account of Sultan Said bin Taimur's triumphal overland journey from Salalah to Muscat following the reassertion of his authority over the interior in 1955 (see page 241), offering an unusually sympathetic portrait of one of Oman's most misunderstood rulers. The almost medieval nation portrayed in the book has long since vanished, but still comes off the page with marvellous vividness, described in Morris's inimitably laconic and chiselled prose.

Marc Valeri *Oman: Politics and Society in the Qaboos State*. An authority on Omani politics, Valeri offers a scholarly yet accessible account of Sultan Qaboos' half-century reign. Based on extensive local research, the book assesses the monarch's legacy for the twenty-first century and lends a voice to the concerns of present-day Omanis.

Tim Severin *The Sindbad Voyage*. Entertaining account of Severin's attempts to build an Omani dhow according to traditional Arabian boat-building techniques, and then sail it from Oman to China. The first part of the book covers the incredibly complex and laborious process of constructing the boat, while the second records the voyage itself, during which Severin and his crew of eight Omani sailors and fifteen international passengers sailed for seven months and 10,000km from Muscat to Canton, braving monsoonal typhoons, international pirates and assorted maritime mishaps en route.

★ **Wilfred Thesiger** *Arabian Sands*. Arguably the finest book ever written about the Arabian peninsula, Thesiger's classic tome recounts his two epic crossings of the Empty Quarter and other remote wanderings around Oman, Saudi Arabia, Yemen and the UAE accompanied by a handful of trusted Bedu companions. The sheer difficulties, dangers and immense physical privations of Thesiger's various journeys make for a compelling read, while the detailed portrait of Bedu life among the sands offers unparalleled insights into the region's harsh, but also surprisingly intricate, tribal cultures, customs and beliefs – an elegiac memorial to a remarkable culture which was beginning to disappear even as Thesiger wrote about it.

Nicholas Clapp *The Road to Ubar: Finding the Atlantis of the Sands*. Entertaining account of the protracted hunt for Arabia's most famous lost city – far superior to Ranulph Fiennes' haphazard work (see page 253) on the same subject, and with a nice blend of ancient history and contemporary archeological adventure.

SPECIALIST GUIDES

Michael Hughes Clarke *Oman's Geological Heritage*. Beautiful coffee-table book bursting with wonderful photographs of Oman's weird and wonderful landscapes, plus interesting accompanying text.

Dave E. Sargeant, Hanne Eriksen, Jens Eriksen *Birdwatching Guide to Oman*. Detailed practical guide to birdwatching in the sultanate, including coverage of over sixty top birdwatching sites and lists of birds likely to be encountered, plus lots of maps and photos. The companion *Common Birds in Oman*, by Hanne and Jens Eriksen, provides comprehensive background (with 700 photos) on 310 species found in the country and the neighbouring UAE.

Explorer Publishing *Oman Trekking*. In-depth coverage (with basic maps) of twelve of Oman's finest trekking routes, mainly in the Western Hajar.

Explorer Publishing *Oman Off-Road*. Oman's off-road Bible, covering 38 of the best off-road drives countrywide, with routes plotted on large-scale satellite maps, plus detailed directions and GPS coordinates to help keep you on the right track.

Samir S. Hanna *Field Guide to the Geology of Oman*. Detailed coverage of Oman's unique geology, followed by seventeen field trips around the country (mostly in the Western Hajar). It's tricky to follow in places if you're not a trained geologist, but is full of absorbing insights into the formation of the country's remarkable landscapes.

Arabic

The national language of Oman is Arabic, spoken as a first language by almost all the country's native Omanis, and by many Asian expatriates as a second language; a few other indigenous languages still survive, including Shehri and Mehri (see page 225) in Dhofar and the remarkable Kumzari (see page 158) in Musandam. English is used widely in the business and tourism sectors – most people working in these areas will likely have at least a basic command of the language – and is also widely spoken and understood by the country's Indian and Pakistani community. Out in the sticks, however, knowledge of English can often be minimal, or even completely nonexistent. Various Asian languages are also widely spoken among the expat community, notably Hindu, Urdu and Bengali, while other languages like Swahili (spoken by Omanis of Zanzibari descent), Baluchi and Iranian may also occasionally be heard, particularly in Muscat.

Modern Gulf Arabic

Arabic (*al lugha al 'arabiya*), the world's fourth most widely spoken language, is the mother tongue of around 300 million people across the Middle East and North Africa. Variations in the language between different areas are considerable, both in vocabulary and pronunciation – the form of the language spoken in Oman and neighbouring countries, known as **Gulf Arabic** (*khaliji*), is particularly distinctive.

Arabic is not an easy language, for various reasons. It contains a range of **sounds** which are not generally encountered in European languages (such as the notorious *'ayn*, ع, whose production involves a kind of back-of-the-throat choking spasm which most westerners only experience immediately prior to being sick). These sounds are represented by a range of characters in Arabic which have no equivalent in the Roman alphabet, and although various ingenious systems have been developed to express the full range of Arabic sounds using Roman script, these require a certain amount of study. The transliterations given below are based on the simplest and most common-sense approach – although like all transliterations from Arabic they are, at best, somewhat approximate. The only way to properly write Arabic is to use the Arabic script, and the only way to learn correct pronunciations is to listen to locals.

Arabic **script** is another – albeit fascinating – challenge. There are no capital letters in Arabic, but many characters change (sometimes dramatically) depending on whether they appear at the beginning, middle or end of a word.

If you're interested in **studying Arabic**, this is a language where it really pays to get hold of a native speaker, if at all possible. Failing this, the rather expensive Rosetta Stone Arabic course is the next best thing. Of the standard book-plus-CD courses

---

GREETINGS

Perhaps the most notable feature of Gulf Arabic is its almost courtly array of **greetings** and other salutations (see below for the basics). Meetings between Omani friends are generally celebrated with a barrage of enquiries and responses concerning one's health, one's news, the health of one's wife, children, cousins, and so on which can go on for a considerable amount of time. Even total strangers can keep the pleasantries going for a surprisingly long time. Reference to a higher power is also a feature of the language, most commonly in two of Arabic's most characteristic phrases – *insh'allah* ("God willing") and *al hamdu'lillah* ("Praise be to god"), both of which you'll hear incessantly.

available, Palgrave Macmillan's *Mastering Arabic* by Jane Wightwick and Mahmoud Gaafar offers perhaps the best all-round introduction, while Routledge's *Colloquial Arabic of the Gulf and Saudi Arabia* by Clive Holes is the best of the very few courses specifically devoted to Gulf Arabic, although it has the major drawback of not covering Arabic script. For a more accessible and unusual introduction to the language, try the innovative *Earworms Arabic* (ⓦearwormslearning.com, also available from iTunes), which teaches the basics of the language by setting simple phrases to music.

ARABIC WORDS AND PHRASES

GREETINGS

Hello salaam 'aleikum (literally "Peace be upon you")

Hello (response) wa 'aleikum assalaam ("And peace upon you also")

Hello (informal) marhaba

Hello/welcome ahlan wa sahlan (response:ahlan beek/ya hala)

How are you? Shlonak? (to a woman:shlonek?)/ kaif al haal? (response: bi khair/zayn,meaning "good/well", or al hamdu lillah)

Goodbye ma'assalaama/fi aman illah

Good morning sabaah al khair

Good afternoon/evening masaa' al khair

Good night tisbah 'ala khair

How are you? kaif al haal? (response: al hamdu lillah)

Fine, thanks be-khair/al hamdu lillah/tamaam

God willing insha' allah

thanks be to god! al hamdu lillah

BASIC WORDS AND EXPRESSIONS

Yesaiwa/na'am

No la

Please min fadlak (to a woman: min fadlik)

Thank you shukran

Thank you very much shukran jazeelan

You're welcome 'afwan

OK tayib/zain/kwayyis

Not OK mish kwayyis

Come in/after you tafaddal (to a woman: tafaddali)

Excuse me 'afwan/lau samaht (to a woman: lau samahti)

Sorry 'afwan/muta'assif

Can I...? /It is possible? mumkin?

I don't know ma ba'raf

No problem ma fi mushkila

Perhaps mumkin

Not possible mish mumkin

What time is it? Kam as saa'a?

How much? Bikam?

How many? Kam?

What? Shu?

What is this? Shu hadha?

There is fi

There is not ma fi

Let's go/hurry up yalla

Slow down shwaya-shwaya

old qadeem

new jadeed

big kabeer

small saghir

little shwaya

much kiteer

beautiful zayn

hot haar

cold baarid

open maftuh

shut mughlaq

cheap rakhees

expensive ghali

too expensive kiteer ghali

very expensive ghali jidan

money fulus

I'm ill ana mareed

MEETING PEOPLE

My name is ... ismi ...

What's your name? shu ismak? (to a female: shu ismik?)

Where are you from?Inta min wayn? (to a female: inti min wayn?)

I'm ... ana ...

British Britani

Irish Irlandee

American Amerikanee

Canadian Canadee

Australian Ostralee

New Zealand Newzeelandee

I like ana bhib

I like this bhib hadha

I don't like ana ma bhib

I don't like this ma bhib hadha

I understand ana fahim/fahma

I don't understand ana ma fahim/fahma

Do you speak English? Tehki ingleezi?

I'm (not) married ana (mish) mitjawaz (fem: mitjawazah)

I don't speak Arabic ma atkallam 'arabi (or just la 'arabiya)

I have 1/2/3/children 'andi walad/waladain/thalathat awlaad

ARABIC NUMBERS

Numbers in Oman are usually written western style as 1, 2, 3 and so on, although you'll also often see the traditional Arabic numerals. One curiosity of Arabic numerals is that they're written right-to-left, like western characters, rather than left-to-right, like Arabic characters.

How do you say in Arabic … kaif teqool … bil 'arabi?
May I take a photo? Mumkin assawar?
Go away! Imshi!

GETTING AROUND AND DIRECTIONS
How far is it to …? Kam kiloometer ila …?
Where is the …? Wayn al …?
room ghurfah
toilet hammam/ghurfat mai
museum mat-haf
hotel funduq/otel
airport mataar
post office maktab al bareed
bank bank/masraf
police shurta/boulees
chemist saydaliyeh
doctor doktor
hospital mustashfa
to ila
from min
in fi
left yasaar
right yameen
north shimaal
south janub
east sharq
west gharb
straight 'ala tool/seeda
here/there hena/henak
near/far gareeb/ba'eed
town/city madina/madinat
street shari'
bus baas
car sayaara
taxi taksee
petrol benzeen
diesel maazout

TIME AND DAYS
today al yoom
tomorrow bokra
yesterday ams
early mobakkir/badri
late mit'akhir
day yoom
daytime nahaar
night layl
Monday yoom al ithnayn
Tuesday yoom ath thalatha
Wednesday yoom al arba'a
Thursday yoom al khamees
Friday yoom al jum'a
Saturday yoom as sabt
Sunday yoom al had
hour/hours saa'a/saa'aat
two hours saa'tayn
what time is it? is-saa'a kam?
day/days yoom/ayaam
two days yoomayn
week/weeks usboo'/asabee'
two weeks usboo'ayn
month/months shahir/shuhoor
two months shahrayn
always daayman
never abadan
sometimes ahyaanan

NUMBERS
0 ٠ sifr
1 ١ wahid
2 ٢ ithnayn
3 ٣ thalatha
4 ٤ arba'a
5 ٥ khamsa
6 ٦ sitta
7 ٧ saba'a
8 ٨ thamaniya
9 ٩ tis'a
10 ١٠ ashra
11 ١١ hida'ashir
12 ١٢ ithna'ashir
13 ١٣ thalatha'ashir
14 ١٤ arba'ta'ashir
15 ١٥ khamsata'ashir
16 ١٦ sita'ashir
17 ١٧ saba'ta'ashir
18 ١٨ thamanta'ashir
19 ١٩ tis'ata'ashir
20 ٢٠ 'ashreen
21 ٢١ wahid wa 'ashreen
22 ٢٢ ithnayn wa 'ashreen
30 ٣٠ thalatheen
40 ٤٠ arba'een
50 ٥٠ khamseen
60 ٦٠ sitteen
70 ٧٠ sab'een

80 ٨٠ thamaneen		**500** ٥٠٠ khamsamaya	
90 ٩٠ tis'een		**600** ٦٠٠ sittamaya	
100 ١٠٠ meya		**700** ٧٠٠ sabamaya	
150 ١٥٠ meya wa khamseen		**800** ٨٠٠ tamnamaya	
200 ٢٠٠ meyatayn		**900** ٩٠٠ tis'amaya	
300 ٣٠٠ thalathmaya		**1000** ١٠٠٠ alf	
400 ٤٠٠ rab'amaya			

FOOD AND DRINK

BASICS

mat'am restaurant
futour breakfast
ghadaa lunch
'ashaa dinner
ana ma bakul lahamI don't eat meat
ana nabaati (female: ana nabaatiya) I'm vegetarian
ladhidh delicious
bas, shukran enough, thanks
fatura/hisaab bill
salata salad
jubn cheese
zibda butter
bayd eggs
'asal honey
laban yoghurt
murabba jam
balah dates
zaytoon olives
sukkar sugar
bi/bidun sukkar with/without sugar
malh salt
filfil pepper
aruz (abyad) (white) rice
biryani biryani (see page 31)
marakh curry

DRINKS

mai water
mai ma'adaniya mineral water
haleeb milk
shay tea
'aseer juice
Nescafe/Nescoffee Western style coffee (not
    necessarily Nescafe)
qahwa coffee (usually Arabian style)
beera beer

MEAT

dajaj chicken
ghanam mutton
kabuli (or qabooli) Afghan-style biryani (see p.00)
laham meat (usually beef, although also possibly lamb
    or goat)

maqboos Saudi-style biryani (see p.00) (or machbus)
maqli fried
shuwa slow-roasted meat with rice

FISH

kenadh king fish
samak fish
samak al qersh shark
sharkha lobster

ARABIAN DISHES AND MEZE

baba ghanouj all-purpose dip made from grilled
    aubergine (eggplant) mixed with ingredients like
    tomato, onion, lemon juice and garlic
burghul cracked wheat, often used as an ingredient in
    Middle Eastern dishes such as tabouleh
fatayer miniature triangular pastries, usually filled with
    either cheese or spinach
fatteh dishes containing pieces of fried or roasted bread
fattoush salad made of tomatoes, cucumber, lettuce
    and mint mixed up with crispy little squares of deep-
    fried flatbread
halwa traditional dessert (see page 30)
jebne white cheese
kibbeh small ovals of deep-fried minced lamb mixed
    with cracked wheat and spices
khubzArabian-style flatbread
labneh thick, creamy Arabian yoghurt, often flavoured
    with garlic or mint
loubia salad of green beans with tomatoes and onion
saj Lebanese style of thin, round flatbread
saj manakish (or mana'eesh) pieces of saj spinkled with
    herbs and oil – a kind of Middle Eastern mini-pizza
sambousek miniature pastries, filled with meat or
    cheese and then fried
shwarma kebab (see page 29)
shish taouk basic chicken kebab, with small pieces of
    meat grilled on a skewer and often served with garlic
    sauce
tabouleh finely chopped mixture of tomato, mint and
    cracked wheat
tahini paste made from sesame seeds
waraq 'enab vine leaves stuffed with a mixture of rice
    and meat

Glossary

Abbasid third of the major Islamic caliphates (750–1258)

Adnani people from northern Arabia (see page 231)

aflaj plural of falaj (see page 83)

attar perfume

ayalat upper

ayn/ain spring

Azd Major Yamani (see page 259) tribe

barasti traditional palm-thatch hut

bait house

bait al qufl "House of the Lock" (see page 161)

balah dates (see page 133)

barzah see majlis

bilad village

bin "son of" (Sultan Qaboos bin Said, for example, means Sultan Qaboos, son of Said)

burj tower

bukhoor a kind of incense (see page 35)

caliph religious and political leader of the Islamic world

corniche seafront road, often with a pedestrian promenade as well

dallah traditional Arabian coffeepot

dishdasha the long robes (in Oman usually but not always white) worn by men throughout the Gulf; also known as thawb

falaj water channel (see page 83)

fanar lighthouse

ghafiri See page 235; often used interchangeably with Nizari (see page 259)

halwa traditional Omani sweet (see page 30)

higra The Prophet Mohammed's flight from Mecca to Medina, from which the beginning of the Muslim calendar begins, written "AH" (1 AH = 622 AD)

hinawi See page 235; often used interchangeably with "Yamani" (see page 259)

hisn/husn fort

Ibadhism The version of Islam professed by most Omanis (see page 232).

ibn son; variant of bin (see page 259)

imam religious rulers of the Omani interior

Imamate area of interior Oman ruled by the imams

jamal camel

janubiah northern

jawhara jewel

jazira/juzor island/islands

jebel mountain or hill

khanjar traditional Omani curved dagger

khor creek, inlet or (in Musandam) fjord

kummah Omani cap

luban Frankincense

Magan old name for Oman during Sumerian era

majan coral

majlis meeting/reception room in traditional Omani house

mandoos traditional Omani wooden chest with metalwork decoration

masjid Mosque

Mazoun Old Persian name for Oman

mihrab arch inside (or sometimes outside) a mosque indicating the direction of Mecca

misfat/misfah pool

mubrick traditional Omani building material, with bricks made out of mud mixed with pebbles and straw

muhafazah governorate; Oman is divided into eleven governorates (Al Batinah North, Al Batinah South, Al Buraimi, Ad Dakhiliya, Ad Dhahirah, Dhofar, Musandam, Muscat, Ash Sharqiya North, Ash Sharqiya South and Al Wusta)

musalla prayer hall in mosque

musar turban

nakheel/nakhl palm

Nizari Omani of Saudi or north Arabian descent

ophiolite type of red rock typical of Oman (see page 102)

qadi Judge

qal'at/qala fort

qahtani People of southern Arabia (see page 230)

qahwah/gahwah traditional Arabian coffee (see page 30)

qurum mangrove

ras headland

sarooj traditional plaster (see page 249)

sharqiya/sharqi eastern

shatti beach

safalat lower

sur fortified house (see page 248)

tawi well

thawb alternative name for dishdasha (see page 259)

travertine type of rock formation caused by evaporation of mineral-rich waters

Umayyad second of the major Islamic caliphates (661–750)

Umm an Nar Period of Arabian pre-history (see page 230)

wadi generic term for any kind of valley or riverbed, usually dry

wali local governor

wilayat administrative district; there are 61 spread within Oman's muhafazah

Yamani "Yemeni", signifying an Omani of Yemen descent

Small print and index

A ROUGH GUIDE TO ROUGH GUIDES

Published in 1982, the first Rough Guide – to Greece – was a student scheme that became a publishing phenomenon. Mark Ellingham, a recent graduate in English from Bristol University, had been travelling in Greece the previous summer and couldn't find the right guidebook. With a small group of friends he wrote his own guide, combining a contemporary, journalistic style with a thoroughly practical approach to travellers' needs.

The immediate success of the book spawned a series that rapidly covered dozens of destinations. And, in addition to impecunious backpackers, Rough Guides soon acquired a much broader readership that relished the guides' wit and inquisitiveness as much as their enthusiastic, critical approach and value-for-money ethos. These days, Rough Guides include recommendations from budget to luxury and cover more than 120 destinations around the globe, from Amsterdam to Zanzibar, all regularly updated by our team of roaming writers.

Browse all our latest guides, read inspirational features and book your trip at **roughguides.com**.

Rough Guide credits

Editor(s): Natasha Foges and Tom Fleming
Cartography: Ed Wright and Katie Bennett
Managing editor: Rachel Lawrence
Picture editor: Michelle Bhatia

Cover photo research: Sarah Stewart-Richardson
Senior DTP coordinator: Dan May
Head of DTP and Pre-Press: Rebeka Davies

Publishing information

Second edition 2018

Distribution
UK, Ireland and Europe
Apa Publications (UK) Ltd; sales@roughguides.com
United States and Canada
Ingram Publisher Services; ips@ingramcontent.com
Australia and New Zealand
Woodslane; info@woodslane.com.au
Southeast Asia
Apa Publications (SN) Pte; sales@roughguides.com
Worldwide
Apa Publications (UK) Ltd; sales@roughguides.com
Special Sales, Content Licensing and CoPublishing
Rough Guides can be purchased in bulk quantities
at discounted prices. We can create special editions,
personalised jackets and corporate imprints tailored to
your needs. sales@roughguides.com.

roughguides.com
Printed in China by CTPS
All rights reserved
© 2018 Apa Digital (CH) AG
License edition © Apa Publications Ltd UK
All rights reserved. No part of this publication may be
reproduced, stored in or introduced into a retrieval system,
or transmitted in any form, or by any means (electronic,
mechanical, photocopying, recording or otherwise) without
the prior written permission of the copyright owner.
A catalogue record for this book is available from the
British Library
The publishers and authors have done their best to
ensure the accuracy and currency of all the information
in **The Rough Guide to Oman**, however, they can accept
no responsibility for any loss, injury, or inconvenience
sustained by any traveller as a result of information or
advice contained in the guide.

Help us update

We've gone to a lot of effort to ensure that the second edition of **The Rough Guide to Oman** is accurate and up-to-date. However, things change – places get "discovered", opening hours are notoriously fickle, restaurants and rooms raise prices or lower standards. If you feel we've got it wrong or left something out, we'd like to know, and if you can remember the address, the price, the hours, the phone number, so much the better.

Please send your comments with the subject line "**Rough Guide Oman Update**" to mail@uk.roughguides. com. We'll credit all contributions and send a copy of the next edition (or any other Rough Guide if you prefer) for the very best emails.

Acknowledgements

Anthon Jackson: Thanks to Ibrahim and Humaid for making the research trip vastly more enjoyable, to Natasha for her superb editing and to Andy for bringing me onboard.
Daniel Stables: Big thanks go to everyone in Oman and at home who made working on this book so enjoyable. In particular, I'd like to thank Gavin Thomas for his invaluable advice and brilliant work on the first edition; my co-author

Anthon Jackson; Paris Goddard; Omar al Jabri and Austin Rebello; Farhan Mirza; Sudhesh Kumar; and my editors at Rough Guides, Andy Turner and Natasha Foges. Finally, thank you to my family, for their continuing help and support.

ABOUT THE AUTHORS

Anthon Jackson is a writer and photographer with a MA in Arab & Islamic Studies and a special love for the Middle East. Based in Aarhus, Denmark, he has contributed to more than half a dozen Rough Guides.

Daniel Stables is a travel writer and journalist, originally from Wiltshire and now based in Manchester. Specializing in Asia, Europe, North America and the Middle East, he has worked on several Rough Guides titles and writes for various websites and magazines. His work can be found at his website, ⓦdanielstables.co.uk.

Photo credits

(Key: t-top; c-centre; b-bottom; l-left; r-right)

Index

Main references are in **bold** type

Map symbols

The symbols below are used on maps throughout the book

International border	International airport	Sinkhole	Petrol station
State boundary	Domestic airport	Mosque	Hospital
Chapter boundary	Peak	Gate	Post office
Dual carriageway/expressway	Dune	Statue/monument	Parking
Major road & road number	Ruins/archeological site	Place of interest	Lighthouse
Minor road	Waterfall	Fortress	Building
Unpaved road	Spring	Border crossing	Stadium
4WD	Cave	Tower	Market
Ferry route	Palace	Castle	Cemetery
Wall	Baobab	Museum	Wadi area
Bridge	Oasis	Information office	Park/reserve
Cliff	Viewpoint	Internet access	Beach
Gorge	Port	Transport stop	

Listings key

- Accommodation
- Eating
- Drinking/nightlife
- Shopping